Oracle Siebel CRM 8 Developer's Handbook

A practical guide to co   automating, and
extending Siebel CRM   ons

Alexander Hansal

[PACKT] enterprise
PUBLISHING   professional expertise distilled

BIRMINGHAM - MUMBAI

Oracle Siebel CRM 8 Developer's Handbook

First published: April 2011

Production Reference: 1180411

Published by Packt Publishing Ltd.
32 Lincoln Road
Olton
Birmingham, B27 6PA, UK.

ISBN 978-1-849681-86-5

www.packtpub.com

Cover Image by David Guettirrez (bilbaorocker@yahoo.co.uk)

Credits

Author
Alexander Hansal

Reviewer
Iain 'Oli' Ollerenshaw

Acquisition Editor
Amey Kanse

Development Editor
Hyacintha D'Souza

Technical Editors
Merwine Machado

Indexer
Monica Ajmera Mehta

Editorial Team Leader
Vinodhan Nair

Project Team Leader
Lata Basantani

Project Coordinator
Leena Purkait

Graphics
Geetanjali Sawant

Production Coordinator
Shantanu Zagade

Cover Work
Shantanu Zagade

About the Author

Alexander Hansal has worked for various companies and governmental institutions as IT instructor and consultant. He started as a Siebel CRM instructor for Siebel Systems Germany in 2001. Since the acquisition of Siebel Systems by Oracle, Alexander has continued to support European customers as instructor and consultant for Siebel CRM and Oracle Business Intelligence.

Strongly believing in the power of information sharing, Alexander regularly discusses Siebel CRM and Oracle BI related topics on his weblog (http://siebel-essentials.blogspot.com).

About the Reviewer

Iain 'Oli' Ollerenshaw is one of Europe's most experienced independent Siebel professionals. He has spent over 10 years working with Siebel technology, beginning with a key role at Siebel Systems during the early stages of the Siebel product lifecycle. He has worked with several major Siebel clients in a number of sectors including Energy, Life Sciences, Finance, Defence, and Public Sector. He lives in Surrey, in the south-east of England, with his wife Debbie. They are expecting their first child in 2011.

www.PacktPub.com

Support files, eBooks, discount offers and more

You might want to visit www.PacktPub.com for support files and downloads related to your book.

Did you know that Packt offers eBook versions of every book published, with PDF and ePub files available? You can upgrade to the eBook version at www.PacktPub.com and, as a print book customer, you are entitled to a discount on the eBook copy. Get in touch with us at service@packtpub.com for more details.

At www.PacktPub.com, you can also read a collection of free technical articles, sign up for a range of free newsletters, and receive exclusive discounts and offers on Packt books and eBooks.

http://PacktLib.PacktPub.com

Do you need instant solutions to your IT questions? PacktLib is Packt's online digital book library. Here, you can access, read, and search across Packt's entire library of books.

Why subscribe?

- Fully searchable across every book published by Packt
- Copy and paste, print, and bookmark content
- On demand and accessible via web browser

Free access for Packt account holders

If you have an account with Packt at www.PacktPub.com, you can use this to access PacktLib today and view nine entirely free books. Simply use your login credentials for immediate access.

Instant updates on new Packt books

Get notified! Find out when new books are published by following @PacktEnterprise on Twitter, or the *Packt Enterprise* Facebook page.

For Jürgen

Table of Contents

Preface

Siebel CRM, Oracles' market-leading Customer Relationship Management software, can be tailored to customers needs. In this book, the ambitious developer will learn how to safely implement customer requirements in Siebel CRM using Siebel Tools, Siebel's own integrated development environment.

This book is a complete practical guide to Siebel Tools and how it can be used to implement custom requirements. The book teaches you to configure the Siebel CRM user interface objects as well as the underlying business layer objects by using real-life case study examples. In addition, you will learn to safely configure the Siebel data model.

Understanding and using the Siebel Event Framework for automation is also a key focus area of the book. You will gain a thorough and solid understanding of integration objects to support EAI interfaces. Chapters on Siebel Workflow, Task UI, and scripting prepare you for the most complex automation requirements.

This book uses a real-life case study to provide easy-to-follow examples for the majority of chapters. The examples are radically practical and can be easily adapted to similar situations in Siebel CRM implementation projects.

The book ensures that you know what you are doing and why you are doing it by providing useful insight along with detailed practice instructions. The book contains a multitude of explanatory tables, screenshots, and precise diagrams to illustrate the topics.

When you have finished the book, you will feel prepared to participate in Siebel CRM implementation projects. In addition you will be able to teach the **old dog** some new tricks.

What this book covers

Chapter 1, Siebel Tools and the Siebel Repository, introduces you to the user interface of Siebel Tools and the object definitions that form the Siebel Repository.

Chapter 2, Developer Tasks, lays the foundation for a solid understanding of common tasks in the development cycle.

Chapter 3, Case Study Introduction, provides an introduction to All Hardware, a fictitious company whose requirements serve as case study examples throughout the remaining chapters.

Chapter 4, Symbolic Strings, discusses the concept of symbolic strings, the central library of translatable texts that can be referenced from any object, that displays text in the user interface.

Chapter 5, Creating and Configuring Applets, teaches you how to create and modify form applets and list applets.

Chapter 6, Views and Screens, describes how to configure views and screens as well as how to register views in a responsibility.

Chapter 7, Business Components and Fields, introduces you to the important concepts of the Siebel business logic layer. You will learn how business components and their fields lay the foundation of the logical data model and how to configure them.

Chapter 8, The Data Layer, enables you to identify configuration options for objects that define the physical data model, such as tables, their columns and indexes.

Chapter 9, Business Objects and Links, completes the discussion of the business logic layer by introducing the concept of business objects and links. As in all chapters before, case study examples allow you to deepen your knowledge by providing a hands-on experience.

Chapter 10, Pick Lists, enables you to create static and dynamic pick lists on business component fields.

Chapter 11, Multi Value Fields, provides insight on how to configure multi value fields and their counterparts in the Siebel user interface.

Chapter 12, Configuring Access Control, shows how to configure business components to work within the Siebel Access Control framework in order to ensure data security.

Chapter 13, User Properties, introduces an important configuration option that allows developers to define specialized application logic while staying within safe declarative boundaries.

Chapter 14, Configuring Navigation, uses a case study example to explore the various possibilities of providing static and dynamic drilldowns as well as toggle applets.

Chapter 15, Customizing the Look and Feel of Siebel Applications, enables you to modify Siebel Web Templates and style sheets in a safe manner.

Chapter 16, Menus and Buttons, introduces the Siebel Event Framework and how to use it to configure user interface elements such as menu items, applet buttons, and toolbar buttons.

Chapter 17, Business Services, starts an exploration of the Siebel automation capabilities by introducing the concept of business services. You will learn about important preconfigured business services and how to invoke their methods.

Chapter 18, Supporting Integration Interfaces, brings information about integration objects and how to use them to support EAI interfaces. The chapter also introduces the EAI Siebel Adapter business service.

Chapter 19, Siebel Workflow, is the first of two chapters that explain the concepts and configuration options of Siebel Workflow processes. The chapter explains in detail how to create, simulate, and deploy workflow processes.

Chapter 20, Advanced Siebel Workflow Topics, explains how to use exception handling, subprocesses, loops, and other advanced techniques within Siebel Workflow processes.

Chapter 21, Siebel Task User Interface, introduces the Siebel Task UI and teaches you how to configure, test, and deploy task flows to allow better business process support for end users.

Chapter 22, Extending Siebel CRM Functionality with eScript, begins with an introduction to the Siebel scripting framework, discusses important aspects of the Siebel eScript language and shows you how to write a custom business service.

Chapter 23, Advanced Scripting Techniques, discusses topics such as browser scripting, translatable messages, and tracing while providing real-life examples.

Chapter 24, Deploying Configuration Changes between Environments, introduces the developer to techniques to migrate changes made to the Siebel Repository, administrative data, and files from the development environment to other environments.

Appendix A, Installing a Siebel CRM Self-Study Environment, guides you through the necessary steps to downloading and installing Siebel CRM software for a self-study environment.

Appendix B, Importing Code Files, provides brief step-by-step instructions on how to import the code files provided with this book.

Appendix C, More Information, gives you details of where to find more information on Oracle Siebel CRM.

What you need for this book

This book is for a technical audience. You will get most out of this book if you have a solid information technology (IT) background and familiarity with operating systems and relational databases. If you have experience with enterprise-class information systems, consider this an additional benefit.

It is strongly recommendable to use additional resources on your Siebel learning path. The course offerings of Oracle University (http://education.oracle.com) are a perfect start.

Who this book is for

The book is written with the role of a developer in mind who has to ramp up quickly on Siebel CRM, focusing on typical tasks such as implementing customer requirements by means of creating or modifying object definitions in the Siebel metadata repository using Siebel Tools.

Conventions

In this book, you will find a number of styles of text that distinguish between different kinds of information. Here are some examples of these styles, and an explanation of their meaning.

Code words in text are shown as follows: "A Siebel Tools archive file (AHA Customer Process Start View.sif) is available with this chapter's code files."

A block of code is set as follows:

```
function myTest(x : float ,y : float) : float
{
    return x*y;
}
```

Any command-line input or output is written as follows:

```
repimexp /A I /C "SEAW Local Db default instance"
```

New terms and **important words** are shown in bold. Words that you see on the screen, in menus or dialog boxes for example, appear in the text like this: "Click the **OK** button."

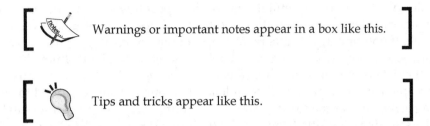

Warnings or important notes appear in a box like this.

Tips and tricks appear like this.

Reader feedback

Feedback from our readers is always welcome. Let us know what you think about this book—what you liked or may have disliked. Reader feedback is important for us to develop titles that you really get the most out of.

To send us general feedback, simply send an e-mail to feedback@packtpub.com, and mention the book title via the subject of your message.

If there is a book that you need and would like to see us publish, please send us a note in the **SUGGEST A TITLE** form on www.packtpub.com or e-mail suggest@packtpub.com.

If there is a topic that you have expertise in and you are interested in either writing or contributing to a book, see our author guide on www.packtpub.com/authors.

Customer support

Now that you are the proud owner of a Packt book, we have a number of things to help you to get the most from your purchase.

Downloading the example code for this book

You can download the example code files for all Packt books you have purchased from your account at http://www.PacktPub.com. If you purchased this book elsewhere, you can visit http://www.PacktPub.com/support and register to have the files e-mailed directly to you.

Errata

Although we have taken every care to ensure the accuracy of our content, mistakes do happen. If you find a mistake in one of our books—maybe a mistake in the text or the code—we would be grateful if you would report this to us. By doing so, you can save other readers from frustration and help us improve subsequent versions of this book. If you find any errata, please report them by visiting http://www.packtpub.com/support, selecting your book, clicking on the **let us know** link, and entering the details of your errata. Once your errata are verified, your submission will be accepted and the errata will be uploaded on our website, or added to any list of existing errata, under the Errata section of that title. Any existing errata can be viewed by selecting your title from http://www.packtpub.com/support.

Piracy

Piracy of copyright material on the internet is an ongoing problem across all media. At Packt, we take the protection of our copyright and licenses very seriously. If you come across any illegal copies of our works, in any form, on the internet, please provide us with the location address or website name immediately so that we can pursue a remedy.

Please contact us at copyright@packtpub.com with a link to the suspected pirated material.

We appreciate your help in protecting our authors, and our ability to bring you valuable content.

Questions

You can contact us at questions@packtpub.com if you are having a problem with any aspect of the book, and we will do our best to address it.

1
Siebel Tools and the Siebel Repository

One of the reasons why you decided to read this book might have been that you will contribute to an Oracle Siebel CRM project as a developer. You might have just started your new career or you are able to look back on years of professional experience. You may have had the privilege of receiving decent training or tried to master the steep learning path on your own. In either case, having a concise and complete guidebook at hand is very helpful.

In this book you will find comprehensive descriptions and real-life examples for configuration processes in Oracle's Siebel CRM. After a brief overview of the **integrated development environment (IDE)**, which goes by the name of **Siebel Tools**, and the typical developer tasks, we are ready to explore all aspects of configuration from the **user interface (UI)** to the Siebel business logic and physical layer, workflow processes, and scripting.

A case study scenario will provide meaningful examples for your exercises.

In this chapter, we will discuss the following topics:

- Siebel Tools User Interface
- Siebel Repository Metadata
    - Data Layer Object Types
    - Business Layer Object Types
    - User Interface Layer Object Types
    - Integration Layer Object Types
    - Automation Layer Object Types
    - Other Object Types

Siebel Tools user interface

Siebel Tools is a Microsoft Windows application that has been designed to view, visualize, and modify the **repository metadata** of Siebel CRM. It is an **integrated development environment** (IDE) that is used mainly by developers; however, at certain project phases, business analysts and technical architects benefit from access to the repository metadata as well.

We can launch Siebel Tools by clicking the respective item in the Windows start menu. The name and location of the start menu item varies with the version of Siebel CRM and the details entered during installation.

After providing username, password, and the data source in the login dialog box, Siebel Tools launches its GUI. In this section, we will describe the user interface elements of Siebel Tools.

The installation of Siebel Tools and other Siebel software products is documented in the book titled *Oracle Siebel CRM 8 Installation and Management* by the same author, and in the *Siebel Installation Guide for Microsoft Windows* of the official Oracle Siebel Applications Documentation Library (also known as **Siebel Bookshelf**). A quick guide for installing a self-study environment containing the Siebel Developer Web Client, the Siebel Sample Database, and Siebel Tools is also provided in the appendix section at the end of this book.

The Siebel Installation Guide for version 8.1 can be found at the following URL: http://download.oracle.com/docs/cd/E14004_01/ books/SiebInstWIN/booktitle.html.

If you have completed the installation of the self-study environment, you can follow the examples in this book.

To log in to Siebel Tools and the Sample Database, click the Siebel Tools shortcut in the Windows start menu, enter **SADMIN** as the username and password, and select **Sample** in the **Connect to** drop-down box. Click **OK** to log in.

The UI of Siebel Tools can be divided into the following elements:

- Title bar
- Menu bar
- Toolbar
- Docking windows
- Editors
- Status bar

The following screenshot is an example screen of Siebel Tools to help us locate these elements:

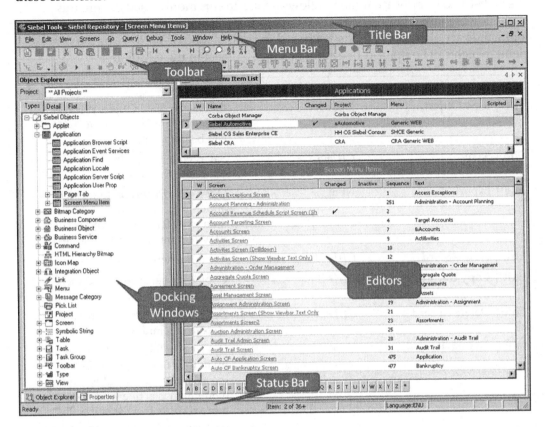

Title bar

The title bar displays the application name (**Siebel Tools**), followed by the name of the currently open repository (**Siebel Repository** in the preceding example) and the name of the currently open list view in the editors area in square brackets (**[Screen Menu Items]**).

Menu bar

The Siebel Tools application menu allows access to commonly used commands. The following table describes some of the most important menu items. Many of the commands are also available via keyboard shortcuts, toolbar buttons, or the context menu, which can be opened by right-clicking an object in the editor area:

Menu item	Keyboard shortcut	Description
**File	New Object...**	None	Opens the **New Object Wizards** dialog from where various wizards can be launched.
**File	Save**	*Ctrl+S*	Saves changes made in graphical editors to the database.
**File	Export...**	None	Opens the **Export** dialog which allows exporting the current list data to different file formats such as **CSV (comma separated values)**.
**Edit	New Record**	*Ctrl+N*	Creates a new record in list editors.
**Edit	Copy Record**	*Ctrl+B*	Copies the selected record including child records.
**Edit	Delete Record**	*Ctrl+D*	Deletes the selected record and associated child records.
**Edit	Change Records...**	None	Opens a dialog that allows setting up to four fields of the selected records to the same value. This menu item is active when two or more records in a list editor have been selected using Shift+*Click* or *Ctrl*+Click.
**View	Windows	...**	None	Allows opening various docking windows such as the **Properties** window.
**View	Toolbars	...**	None	Selection of toolbars to display.
**View	Options...**	None	Opens the **Options** dialog box, which allows setting various user-specific program options.
**Tools	Compile Projects...**	*F7*	Opens the **Object Compiler** dialog, which allows compiling entire projects.
**Tools	Check Out...**	*F10*	Opens the **Check Out** dialog.
**Tools	Check In...**	*Ctrl+F10*	Opens the **Check In** dialog.

Menu item	Keyboard shortcut	Description
Tools | Import from Archive...	None	Opens an archive (`.sif`) file and launches the **Import Wizard**.
Tools | Compare Objects...	None	Allows **visual comparison** of two object definitions in the same repository, in another repository, or in archive files.
Tools | Search Repository	None	Opens the **Search Repository** dialog, which allows full text search across the entire repository.
Tools | Utilities | Compare SRFs...	None	Allows comparison of two `.srf` files.
Help | Contents	None	Opens the Siebel Tools documentation.

Toolbar

Many of the most commonly used commands that have been described in the preceding table are available as toolbar buttons. Toolbars can be enabled or disabled by using the **View | Toolbars** sub menu. The following table describes the most important toolbars:

Toolbar	Description
Edit	Contains the **New**, **Save**, **Undo**, and other buttons.
List	Contains functions that are used in the list editor such as creating new records, navigating, querying, and sorting.
History	Contains the back and forward buttons and bookmark functionality.
Debug	Used during script debugging.
Simulator	Used during testing and simulating of workflow processes.
Format Toolbar	Contains buttons to control the format and layout of items in the form applet grid editor and flowchart editors such as the workflow process designer.
WF/Task Editor Toolbar	This toolbar allows accessing the functions to revise, publish, and activate workflow processes and tasks.
Configuration Context	Allows changing the browser and application context for applet editors. Note that this toolbar can be enabled only from the **View | Toolbars** menu.

Toolbars can be customized in a sense that a developer can choose which buttons should be available in the toolbar. To do so, we can click the **down arrow** icon at the right end of a toolbar and select **Add or Remove Buttons** as shown in the following screenshot:

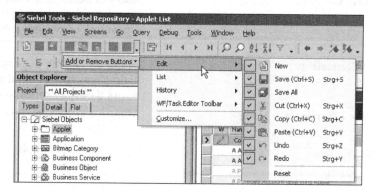

Docking windows

The various docking windows support the developer during tasks such as creating or modifying applets, views, and workflow processes. The docking windows can be opened via the **View | Windows** menu. The following table describes the most important docking windows:

Docking window	Description
Object Explorer	This is the main docking window, which displays the object types and their hierarchy in the Siebel Repository.
Properties	This window shows the properties of a selected item in alphabetical order or by category.
Controls/Columns	This window allows the developer to drag–and–drop available controls to the form applet editor or available list columns to the list applet editor.
Palettes	Depending on the main editor window, this docking window displays the available object types to drag-and-drop into the editor canvas. For example, when the workflow process editor is open, the window contains the available step types for workflow processes.
Applets	This docking window allows the developer to drag-and-drop different types of applets into the view editor.

Docking window	Description
Multi Value Property Window	Needed for the configuration of workflow processes, tasks, and entity relationship diagrams. Because of the "list" characteristic of this window, it appears along the bottom of the application by default.
Bookmarks	This window allows us to access bookmarks that can be created by the developer to navigate to commonly used object definitions more quickly.
Web Templates Window	Opens the **Web Template Explorer**, which allows displaying of the hierarchy of nested Siebel Web Templates and viewing of the content of the web template files (.swt).
Debug Windows	Available via the **View	Debug Windows** menu, these windows support the debugging processes of scripts and workflow processes.

The docking windows all share the characteristic of being arrangeable on the screen in free **floating** mode or **docked** mode. To create a free floating window, we have to right-click the **title bar** of a docked window and select **Floating**. The window can now be moved and resized across the available screen area.

To dock a floating window, we grab the window's **title bar** and drag the window to the desired dock location at the screen border. Once the mouse cursor reaches or crosses a dock location, a gray frame indicates the area and position that the window will occupy when the mouse button is released.

Dragging the title bar of one docked window exactly on top of the title bar of another docking window enables **stacked windows**. Tabs at the bottom of the window frame allow the selection of stacked windows. This mode is convenient when screen space is limited. The next screenshot shows an example of four stacked docking windows:

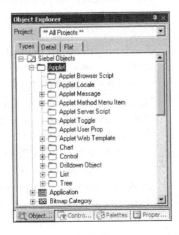

Using the **pin icon**, we can enable or disable the **auto-hide** functionality. In hidden mode, a docking window, or a stack of docked windows, is reduced to a tab bar at the border of the screen. Holding the mouse cursor over the tabs in this bar pulls out the window.

Editors

The editor area, or workspace, is a frame where the list editor and all other graphical editors and viewers appear. The following table describes the most important editors and viewers:

Editor/viewer	Description
Object List Editor	This is the main window that displays the list of object definitions for an object type selected in the Object Explorer window.
Web Applet Editor	Typically opened from the context menu on the Applet list via the **Edit Web Layout** command, this is the main graphical editor for form and list applets.
View Editor	The graphical editor for views is typically opened via the **Edit Web Layout** command of the View list's context menu.
Screen View Sequence Editor	The graphical editor, invoked from the screen list's context menu, allows developers to define the hierarchical structure of screens.
Menu Editor	Supports the graphical design of applet menus.
Script Editors	The script editors allow developers to write and debug scripts. The script editors are described in detail in a separate chapter.
Canvas/Flowchart Editors	Three different object types use the canvas editor for graphical design: Workflow Process, Task, and Entity Relationship Diagram.
View Web Hierarchy	Can be invoked on user interface objects such as applets, views, or screens, and displays the selected object in its hierarchical context.
View Details	This viewer can be invoked from business layer objects such as business components and business objects, and displays the selected object and its relationship to other objects.
View Relationships	Displays the relationships of the selected object (table or business component) to other objects of the same type.

The editor area supports arranging the windows in **full screen** mode as well as in **cascaded** or **tiled** window mode. The respective commands can be found in the **Windows** menu. In the full screen mode, easily set by double-clicking the title bar of an editor window, the developer can switch between the editor windows using a tab bar.

Status bar

The status bar at the bottom of the application window displays the following information:

- Record count for the list editor
- The current working language
- Status messages (for example, during compilation)

Navigating in Siebel Tools

The typical navigation scenario in Siebel Tools is to use the **Object Explorer** docking window to select the desired object type and then use the **Object List Editor** window to **query** for an existing object definition. The following example procedure shows how to select the **Contact Form Applet** and display a list of its controls:

1. In the **Object Explorer**, select the **Applet** type.
2. In the **Object List Editor**, press *Ctrl+Q* to initiate a new query.
3. In the **Name** column, enter **Contact Form Applet** (paying attention to case sensitivity).
4. Press the *Enter* key to execute the query.
5. In the **Object Explorer**, click the plus (**+**) sign to the left of the applet object type to expand the hierarchy and display the child object types of an applet.
6. Click the **Control** object type.
7. You can now use the **Object List Editor** to review the controls of the Contact Form Applet.

Siebel Repository metadata

The Siebel Repository is a key component of the Siebel architecture. The data stored in a repository is typically named **metadata** because it describes the architecture and logical behavior of a program in an abstract ("meta") manner. In the next section, we will discuss the content of the Siebel Repository in detail.

Developers and analysts use Siebel Tools to access and modify data in the repository tables of the Siebel database. Each modification must be made available to the Siebel executable by compiling a new version of the **Siebel Repository File (SRF)**. The following diagram depicts the relationships between Siebel Tools, the Siebel Repository File, and the Siebel executable:

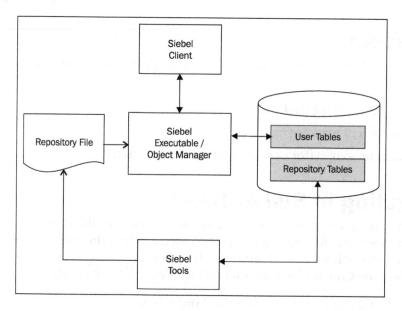

We observe that the Siebel executable, which is responsible for rendering the application to the end user in the browser, accesses a different set of tables than Siebel Tools.

Did you know?

There is no technical boundary between user tables and repository tables. There are circumstances where both applications (Siebel Tools and the application used by the end users) access the same tables. An example for this behavior can be found in the administration of **List of Values (LOV)** data for drop-down in pick lists. LOV data can be administered in Siebel Tools as well as the Siebel Web Client.

As indicated, the Siebel Repository can be described as metadata stored in a set of tables in a relational database. When modern programming patterns arose in the second half of the last century, developers and architects found that it is highly beneficial to separate the program logic into specialized layers.

The Siebel Repository metadata is organized in the following layers:

- Data layer
- Business layer
- Presentation layer
- Integration layer
- Automation layer

The data layer

The majority of enterprise software applications use **relational database management systems (RDBMS)** for data storage. Siebel CRM is no exception. The data layer of the Siebel Repository defines the physical storage of data used by all Siebel applications. The major object types in the data layer are:

- Tables and columns
- Interface tables
- Indexes

Tables and columns

The Siebel Repository holds the definitions of all tables that are present in the relational database. Tables and their columns are the fundamental building blocks of the physical data model or schema that is used by all Siebel applications.

The following list conveys some interesting facts about Siebel tables:

- The **Siebel Industry Applications (SIA)** schema contains more than 3000 tables.

- Each table has a set of system columns that hold data like the timestamp of the last update or the total number of modifications for each individual record.

- The ROW_ID system column is automatically populated with a unique identifier. This identifier is unique across the enterprise, which means that even if there are thousands of mobile users having their own local database, each record will have a ROW_ID value that will never be used for any other record.

- Even if the ROW_ID column is marked as the primary key in the repository, this information is not manifest in the RDBMS. The same is true for all foreign key definitions. The referential integrity of primary key-foreign key relationships is maintained by the Siebel application logic exclusively.

- The preconfigured tables cannot be modified by customers. Developers at customer projects are only allowed to add columns or tables to the repository.

Interface tables

In order to facilitate mass data exchange at the database level, interface tables are part of the Siebel database schema. When integration architects want to import data using the **Enterprise Integration Manager (EIM)** module, they have to populate the interface tables and then invoke the EIM server component.

Each interface table maps to one or more data tables. During import, EIM reads data from the interface tables and populates the data tables. When exporting data, EIM reads the data tables and writes to the interface tables. Other capabilities of EIM include updating, merging, and deleting operations against the data tables.

Did you know?

Direct manipulation of data in tables other than interface tables by means of SQL statements is not permitted because it can lead to severe data integrity problems and it can even render the Siebel application unavailable.

Indexes

For each table, the Siebel Repository defines a variety of indexes in order to improve query and sorting performance. Indexes are preconfigured to support various column and sorting combinations, and can be added or deactivated depending on the customer requirements.

Object type relationships in the Siebel data layer

Objects in the Siebel Repository reference each other. For example, an index definition references columns of the table it is defined for. Another example is an interface table that references one or more data tables. The following diagram depicts the object types in the data layer of the Siebel Repository and their relationships:

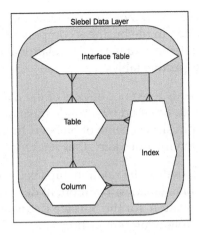

We can observe that a table is a set of columns. For each table, one or more indexes exist that reference one or more columns in the table. A table is mapped by one or more EIM interface tables, which themselves map to one or more tables.

In *Chapter 8, The Data Layer*, we will explore the object types and the customization options of the data layer in greater detail.

The business layer

The complexity of today's typical business requirements shapes the Siebel business layer. This layer serves as a level of abstraction from the data layer, by mapping real-world entities, their attributes, business logic, and relationships to reusable metadata object definitions.

The following is a list of the major building blocks of the Siebel business layer:

- Business components, joins, and fields
- Links
- Business objects

Business components, joins, and fields

Business components, their fields, and other child object types such as joins define the central application logic for all Siebel applications. We can imagine a business component as a technical implementation of a real life entity. For example, a service request or trouble ticket raised by a customer must be stored in Siebel CRM in a way that it can be easily assigned to internal employees to handle the request. In addition, the service request must be related to a customer account and to the product in question.

The **Service Request** business component implements this logic. The Siebel executable uses the information in the business component object definitions, in order to generate the SQL statements against the relational database to query and modify the records in the respective tables.

Therefore, business components reference objects of the data layer, namely tables and columns. Because the data accessed by a single business component is stored in more than one table (the physical schema of Siebel is highly normalized), the business component definition includes joins that reference other tables.

We can use Siebel Tools to visualize the relationships between business components and tables by right-clicking on a business component definition and selecting **View Details**. The resulting visualization, for the **Service Request** business component for example, is displayed in the following screenshot:

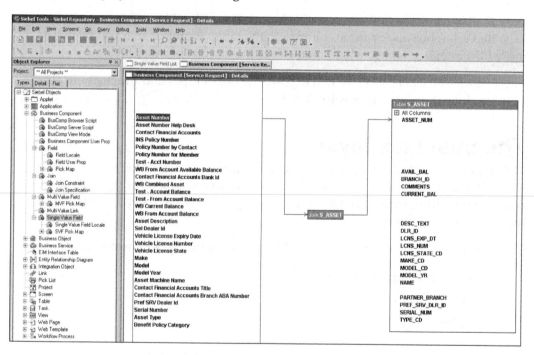

The **View Details** window in Siebel Tools allows inspecting the mapping from each field in a business component to a column in a table. The screenshot shows how the `Asset Number` field in the **Service Request** business component references the `ASSET_NUM` column in the joined table named `S_ASSET`. This relationship is graphically indicated by arrows that point from the field to the join and from the join to the column.

Links

In the real world, entities are related to each other. Business analysts use **entity relationship diagrams (ERDs)** to depict the relationships between entities. The following diagram represents an example of an ERD:

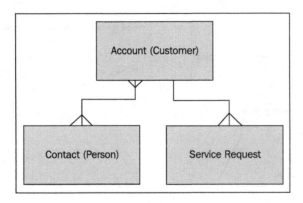

The example defines the relationships between a customer account, its related contact persons, and service requests. While the same contact person can be associated with many other accounts (a many-to-many or M:M relationship), only one account at a time can be associated with a service request (a one-to-many or 1:M relationship).

We have learned above that entities are implemented as business components in the Siebel Repository. The **relationship** between two business components is implemented as a **link**. Once business components are connected by a link, the application can easily retrieve a parent record and all associated child records from the database.

Business objects

A **business object** defines a collection of business components and the links that are used to relate the business components to each other. As a result, a parent—child hierarchy of business components is created. Siebel Tools allows visualizing the hierarchy of business components in a business object, by right-clicking on a business object and selecting **View Details**. An example result is depicted in the next screenshot:

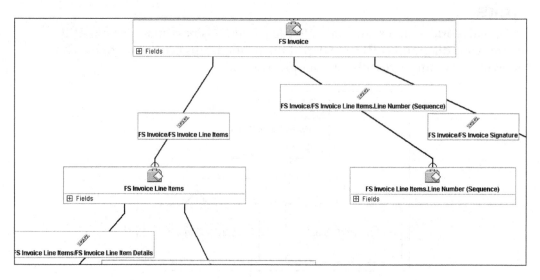

The example shows the parent—child relationships between the **FS Invoice** business component and its child business components. The link objects that connect the business components are visible in the screenshot as well.

Relationships of business layer and data layer objects

Business components, their fields and joins, as well as business objects and links have close relationships to other object types in the Siebel Repository metadata model. For example, business components and their fields reference tables and columns in the data layer. The following diagram depicts the major object types in the business layer and data layer along with their relationships:

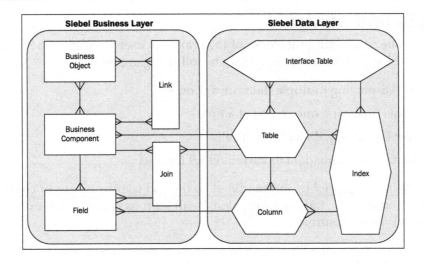

The relationships can be described as follows:

- A business component has multiple fields
- A business component references one base table
- Multiple joins can be associated with the business component and reference one table each
- Fields in a business component reference columns in the base or joined tables
- Links refer to one parent and one child business component
- Business objects are lists of business components and the links that are used to tie them together

We will learn how to modify and create object definitions in the business layer in various chapters across this book.

The presentation layer

Also named the *logical user interface*, the presentation layer defines how data is presented to the end user. We can describe the following major object types in the presentation layer:

- Applets and controls
- Views
- Screens
- Applications
- Menus and toolbars

Applets and controls

Applets are the major building blocks of the graphical user interface of a Siebel CRM application. Siebel CRM applications use the following applet types:

- **List**: Displaying multiple data rows at once
- **Form**: Displaying one record at a time
- **Tree**: Displaying data hierarchically
- **Chart**: Visualizing data in various chart formats

The data itself is displayed to and modified by the end user by means of **controls**. Text boxes, check boxes, radio groups, along with buttons and lists, are examples for different types of controls.

Developers use graphical editors to define the presentation layer objects. We can access the applet editor, for example, by right-clicking an applet definition in the Object List Editor and selecting **Edit Web Layout**.

Applets reference a single business component from which they receive data and to which they submit the method invocations when end users interact with the applet. For example, when a user clicks the **Delete** button on an applet, the respective method is invoked in the business component referenced by the applet. The application engine then generates the necessary SQL statement to delete the record from the database.

Following a strict programming pattern, applets themselves do not define any business logic. Applets and their controls only define which fields and methods of a business component are exposed to the end users.

Did you know?

In Siebel web applications, the look and feel — the font style, background colors, and so forth — is defined by cascading stylesheets that are situated outside of the repository. This is why the presentation layer is also called *logical* UI, whereas the files necessary to define the look and feel in the browser are part of the *physical* UI.

Views

We can describe a Siebel View as a web page that defines the arrangement of one or more applets on a layout template. The following screenshot shows the **Account Summary View** with one form applet on top and four list applets below in the Siebel web client:

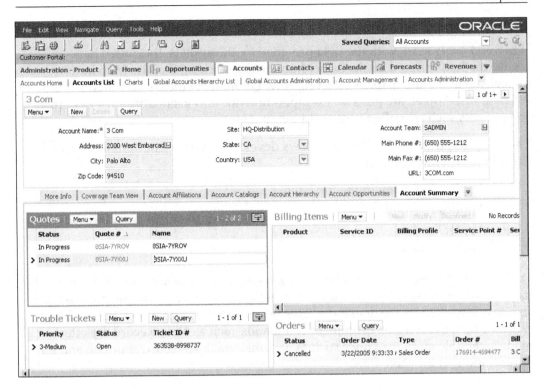

The list applets are arranged side by side for maximum visibility of the data that the end user needs for the business process. Each view references a single business object so that the application engine can use the link information to retrieve the correct child records for the selected parent record.

Screens

A screen is a collection of views that serve a similar purpose such as working with service request data or administering Siebel servers. In addition, a screen also defines the hierarchical order of the views and the labels that appear on clickable items such as tabs or links.

Applications

Following a rather simplistic but elegant design pattern, a Siebel application is not much more than a set of screens. In addition, an application object defines menus and web page templates to be used for rendering the user interface.

Menus and toolbars

When end users work with the data provided by the applets, they often have to invoke methods offered by the Siebel framework. Clicking the **Site Map** button to navigate to the site map, or selecting **New Quote** from the **context menu** of the Account List Applet, are just two examples how the end users utilize user interface components such as toolbar buttons or menu items.

The Siebel application architecture allows developers to place buttons and menu items in the following locations:

- Application menu in the top banner
- Application toolbar
- Applet headers
- Applet menus

Each of these buttons or menu items invokes a method or **command**, which is handled either by Siebel's out of the box functionality, or by workflow processes or script code written by the developer. This provides the automation functionality required by the end users. Prominent commands such as **New Record** are often made accessible more than once such as a menu item, a keyboard shortcut, and an applet button at the same time.

Relationships of presentation layer and business layer objects

Views, applets, and controls reference objects in the business layer. The references and the relationships of objects within the presentation layer can be visualized as follows:

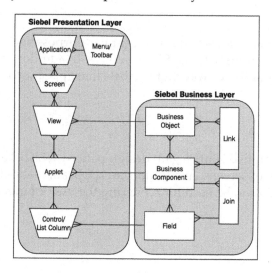

We can infer the following from the diagram:

- A Siebel application is a collection of screens
- An application defines the main menu and toolbars to be displayed
- Screens can be reused in other applications
- A screen is a collection of views
- A view is a set of reusable applets
- A view references one business object to establish the data context
- An applet defines a set of controls such as text boxes or buttons
- Each applet references a single business component
- There can be multiple applets referencing the same business component
- Each control in an applet references a field in the business component referred to by the applet

Chapter 5 and *Chapter 6* of this book will discuss how to modify and create presentation layer object definitions.

The integration layer

Modern enterprise applications are never installed and used standalone. On the contrary, they are very often part of complex IT infrastructures with multiple integration touch points. In order to provide a standardized interface definition to access Siebel data, the Siebel Repository provides the ability to define **Integration Objects**. In order to suit the different integration requirements such as mapping between Siebel and external schemas, integration objects can be defined as "internal" or "external".

Internal integration objects

We can start by imagining a scenario where an integration architect has to define a data interface between Siebel CRM and an external order management application. The architect's duties include determining the exact set of fields to be exchanged between the applications.

When the architect analyzes the definition of the **Order Entry - Orders** business component, which implements the entity of an order header, and the various child objects such as line items, he/she finds that there are hundreds of fields defined in Siebel CRM to store order data. The external system may either not be capable of storing all this information or simply not need all these fields.

This is why the Siebel Repository includes integration objects. Integration architects can create integration objects that reference business objects, their components and fields, and define a **subset** of the information made available by the business layer objects.

In other words, a Siebel integration object is a **schema definition** for data exchange via **enterprise application integration (EAI)** interfaces.

Did you know?

Whenever the Oracle Siebel CRM design team creates integration touch points with other applications such as Oracle BI Publisher for reporting, they choose integration objects as the mechanism to define the schema of data to be exchanged.

Internal integration objects define the interfaces for the Siebel business layer objects. They have a similar hierarchy as business objects, containing integration components and integration component fields. The following diagram depicts the object types of the integration layer and their relationship to the business layer's object types:

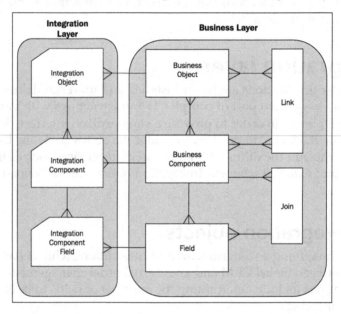

The following list summarizes the concept of internal integration objects:

- An internal integration object references a single business object
- The integration component definitions within an internal integration object reference business components within the business object
- Integration components define a list of integration component fields, each of which references a field in the business component referred to by its parent

External integration objects

The Siebel CRM integration architecture provides data mapping functionality in order to assist Siebel developers in creating rich interface definitions. A developer who wishes to map Siebel data to external data needs to import the external schema definition from a file (typically an XML schema definition file, or .xsd file) in Siebel Tools.

The import of an external schema produces so-called external integration objects, which are subsequently used by the Siebel data transformation engine to produce data sets that match the schema definition of the external systems.

In *Chapter 18, Supporting Integration Interfaces*, we will learn how to create integration object definitions to support EAI interfaces.

The automation layer

Enterprise software such as Siebel CRM must include features to automate business logic and provide business process guidance for end users. The automation layer of the Siebel Repository includes the following object types that allow developers to fulfill automation requirements:

- Business services
- Workflow processes
- Tasks
- Commands

Business services

Almost the entire business logic that can be found in a Siebel CRM application is the result of the work of business services. We can imagine a business service as encapsulated program code, which is designed to accomplish a certain task.

The Siebel Repository comes replete with hundreds of preconfigured business services. The following list gives an impression of business-service-based logic in Siebel CRM:

- Pricing logic in Siebel Order Management
- Customer self service and registration
- Asset and agreement management
- Import and export of XML data
- Importing external schema definitions in Siebel Tools
- Integration with queuing systems such as IBM Websphere MQ

Business services can be exposed as web services to provide the foundation for service-oriented architectures (SOA). They can be written in many programming languages, of which Siebel eScript is the most popular at customer projects. Developers at Oracle write C++ classes, which is another way to define functionality in Siebel business services. In addition, the Siebel application framework supports Java and Visual Basic as programming languages for business services.

Workflow processes

The Siebel Workflow module is known for its capability to orchestrate business services by defining the sequence of their invocation. Siebel Workflow is in fact 4GL—a fourth generation programming language that allows developers to implement complex business logic without the need to write program code.

Siebel Industry Applications (SIA) 8.1.1 are shipped with a repository that contains over 1300 workflow process definitions that drive the business logic of complex application modules such as order management, marketing, pricing, and user self registration. The following screenshot shows an example workflow process in the Workflow Process Designer in Siebel Tools:

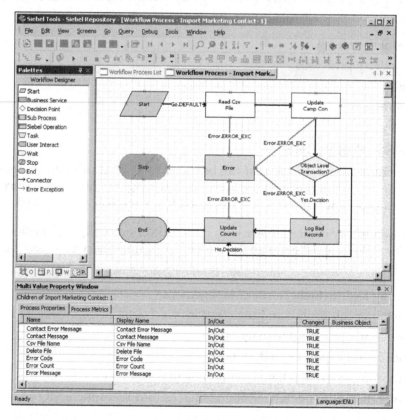

Siebel developers use the process designer to create and modify workflow processes. We can observe that a workflow is a series of steps, decision branches, and exception handlers — very similar to a written program.

We can access the Workflow Process Designer in Siebel Tools by right-clicking a workflow process object definition and selecting **Edit Workflow Process**.

Tasks

End users must be trained to perform various business processes and tasks in Siebel CRM. But some business processes are rather complex and also rarely executed, making it difficult to flawlessly perform a business process.

End users might require guidance for complex business processes in order to carry out all steps correctly and enter high quality data. The Siebel **Task UI** provides the technological foundation for creating task-based user interfaces and the technical flow behind them.

Similar to workflow processes, tasks define a sequence of steps with the main difference to workflow that user navigation is at the core of the task. So-called *task views* can be created to provide the input controls and data that a user needs at a certain step in the business process.

Developers use the **Task Editor** to create and modify task definitions. A task definition contains one or more *task view* steps, which implement the user interface for the given step of the business process.

Commands

Commands are reusable object definitions and act as invocation mechanisms for business services, workflows, or built-in methods of the Siebel application. They are typically referenced by menu items and toolbar buttons, and define the foundation for the invocation of Siebel functionality by the end user.

We will learn how to create business services, workflow processes, tasks, and commands in later chapters of this book.

The logical architecture of Siebel applications

We have now discussed the major object types of the Siebel Repository. Together with other object types and features, they form the logical application architecture. We can combine the information about the layers of the Siebel Repository in a logical architecture map as shown in the following diagram:

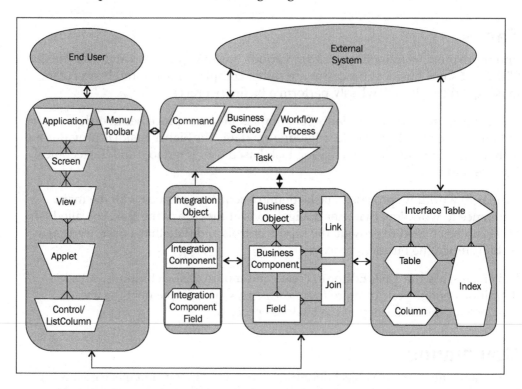

We can summarize the information in the diagram as follows:

- **The data layer** (hexagon shaped objects) of the Siebel Repository defines the physical storage of data such as tables, columns, and indexes

- **The business layer** objects (rectangle shaped objects), namely the business components, reference the data layer and serve as a level of abstraction to allow the modeling of real-world entities into metadata

- **The presentation layer** (trapezoid shaped boxes) includes all object types that are used to present data and functionality provided by the business layer to end users

- **The integration layer** (bookmark shaped objects) provides the foundation for data exchange with external systems

- **The automation layer** (rhombus shaped objects) and its business services enable the automation functionality of Siebel CRM
- **External systems** can be integrated with Siebel CRM by exposing objects of the automation layer or by using interface tables

Other object types

The following table serves as a quick reference, in alphabetical order, for other important object types in the Siebel Repository:

Object type	Description
Bitmap Category	Collections of bitmaps used for toolbar buttons or icons.
Content Object	Used in Siebel Content Management and Application Deployment Manager to represent data objects.
Entity Relationship Diagram	Allows drawing of entity relationship diagrams and links them to business layer object definitions such as business components, links, and fields.
Icon Map	Collections of bitmaps related to a specific value. Allows displaying of a graphic instead of text data in the user interface.
Message Category	Collection of messages to display to the end user.
Pick List	This object type defines the list of values (LOV) for drop-down lists and single value selection fields.
Project	A container for objects. Each object definition in the Siebel Repository must belong to one project.
Symbolic String	Represents a text string and its translations to multiple languages. Can be referenced from every object that displays static text in the user interface.
Type	Defines the object types and their attributes (properties) in the Siebel Repository.
Web Page	Relatively static user interface elements such as the login page.
Web Template	Pointer to physical .swt files in the WEBTEMPL folder of a Siebel application.
Workflow Policy and assignment-related object types	Used to define objects related to workflow policies and assignment manager.

Summary

Siebel Tools allows us to inspect, create, and modify various object types in the Siebel Repository. The logical Siebel architecture follows a strict principle of separated layers, thus providing the foundation for a stable yet extensible application framework.

The Siebel Repository metadata defines anything from the menu that an application displays to the tables and columns where the data is stored physically.

The business layer consisting of business objects, business components, and links (to mention the most important members) is the main abstraction layer and entry point for data access for end users and external systems alike.

In the next chapter, we will discuss the typical tasks for a Siebel developer.

2
Developer Tasks

In this chapter, we will describe the processes and tasks that a developer typically has to carry out during the configuration process. In addition, we will try to establish a thoughtful and well structured approach of customization **with the upgrade in mind**. The following topics will be discussed here:

- Initializing the local database
- Getting object definitions from the server database
- Projects and objects
- Siebel Tools options
- The development process
    - Checking out
    - Creating or modifying object definitions
    - Validating object definitions
    - Compiling object definitions
    - Testing and debugging
    - Checking in
- Local locking and prototyping
- Archiving object definitions
- Importing archived object definitions
- Comparing object definitions
- Searching the Siebel Repository
- Integrating external source control systems
- Automating developer tasks using command line options
- Keeping the upgrade in mind

This chapter's intention is to give a brief overview of the functionalities of Siebel Tools. Most of these features will be discussed in a real-life context later in this book.

Initializing the local database

The Siebel development environment is a separate installation of a Siebel Enterprise dedicated for the sole purpose of supporting development activities. Instead of making changes to the Siebel Repository in the server database, developers use **local databases** and local Siebel client installations on their workstations. This provides a secure environment for testing the changes before publishing them to the server environment and making them accessible for other developers.

The following diagram depicts the building blocks of a Siebel development environment:

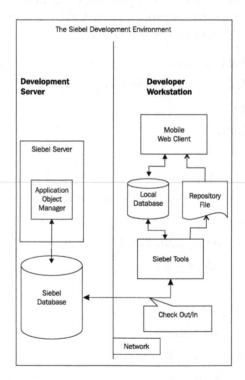

The following facts can be derived from the preceding diagram:

- **Siebel Tools**: installed on the developer workstation—connects to the local database
- **During the Check Out or Check In process**: described in more detail later in this chapter—Siebel Tools connects to the server database

- The developer uses the Siebel Tools compiler to create a new version of the **Siebel Repository File (SRF)**
- The Siebel Mobile Web Client is used to test the changes against the local database

 It is possible to use the local Siebel client installation to connect to a server database for testing purposes. The client is then named **Developer Web Client** because a network connection is necessary for this scenario.

The local database is a `Sybase.dbf` file, which is created using the `Siebel Remote` module which has been designed to support the mobile end user community. The process of registering developers as mobile clients and extracting the database schema and data for the local databases is described in detail in the book *Oracle Siebel CRM 8 Installation and Management* of the same author and in the *Siebel Remote and Replication Manager Administration Guide* in the Siebel bookshelf (`http://download.oracle.com/docs/cd/E14004_01/books/RRAdm/booktitle.html`).

We have to carry out the following steps in order to download and initialize the local database:

1. Establish network connectivity.
2. Verify settings in the client configuration files.
3. Download and initialize the local database.

Establishing network connectivity

For the initial download of the files that are needed to initialize the local database, the developer workstation must be able to establish a TCP/IP connection to the Siebel Remote server host machine.

Verifying settings in the client configuration files

The following parameters in the [Local] section of the `tools.cfg` file, found in the `bin` subdirectory of the Siebel Tools installation folder, must be set as described in the following table. The same settings must also be applied to all client configuration files (`.cfg`) such as the `uagent.cfg` file for Siebel Call Center—which will be used for testing with the Mobile Web Client.

Parameter	Description	Example Value
ConnectString	Defines the absolute path to the local Sybase database and includes parameters that are passed to the Sybase database engine.	D:\SIA81\TOOLS\local\ sse_data.dbf -q -m -x NONE -gp 4096 -c15p - ch25p
DockConnString	Defines the physical hostname or IP address of the Siebel Remote server.	devsrvr1
LocalDbODBCDataSource ([Siebel] section)	Name of the ODBC data source to access the local database.	SSD Local Db default instance

Downloading and initializing the local database

We can now launch Siebel Tools from the Windows start menu and log on to the local data source using the developer username and password provided by the administration team. The message that the local Siebel database was not found must be acknowledged with the **Yes** button.

The Siebel Remote Parameter dialog box is displayed next, prompting for the mobile client name, username, and the **future** password for the local database. Client name and username are usually the same. We should select a secure password (password policies may have been set by the administrator). Once we click the **Continue** button, the Siebel Remote software downloads the compressed schema and data files to the local workstation.

Once the files are downloaded, the **Siebel Upgrade Wizard** is invoked automatically. The wizard uses the downloaded files to create and populate the new local Sybase database in the location specified in the ConnectString parameter of the tools. cfg file. The following screenshot shows the Siebel Upgrade Wizard displaying its progress during the local database initialization:

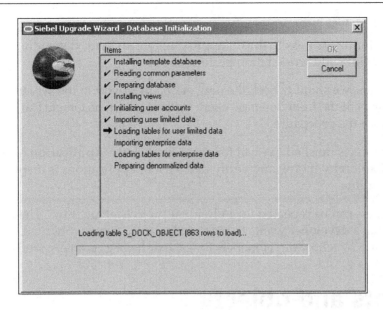

Once the Siebel Upgrade Wizard has completed all steps, Siebel Tools launches automatically.

Getting object definitions from the server database

Administrators can set the Extract all Repository Tables parameter to True before submitting the Database Extract job on the Siebel Server. When this is the case, the local database is already populated with repository data during the initialization process and developers can start working immediately.

If the parameter is not set to true, the repository tables in the local databases are empty and the developer has to use the Siebel Tools **Get** functionality to populate them.

To copy – or get – the full set of repository data from the server database to our local database, we execute the following steps:

1. If necessary, log on to Siebel Tools to the local database.

2. In the **Tools** menu, select **Check Out...**.

3. The **Check Out** dialog is displayed. If the repository tables in the local database are empty, all projects are selected by default.

4. Select the **All Projects** option to ensure that all projects are selected.

5. Click the **Get** button.

6. Wait for the process to finish (approximately an hour, depending on network bandwidth and workstation performance).

In case of errors, we should check the network connectivity to the server database and the settings of the local database client software, such as Oracle Database Client, before we retry the procedure.

Once the process is finished, we can for example click the **Application** object type in the **Object Explorer** window and verify that a list of applications is displayed in the **Object List Editor**.

The **Get** process can be repeated for individual projects at any time. The typical scenario is that a developer wants to pick up the latest changes checked in to the server database by fellow developers before she or he begins a new workday.

Projects and objects

Each object definition in the Siebel Repository must belong to exactly one project. A project can be considered a container for an arbitrary selection of object definitions. The Siebel CRM engineering team at Oracle defines the initial set of projects. Developers at customer sites can either choose to keep the order defined by Oracle or decide to change the project assignment for selected object definitions without affecting Siebel functionality.

In addition, we can create new projects if needed. The following procedure is an example of how to create a new project definition in the local developer database:

1. In the **Object Explorer** window, select the **Project** type.

2. In the **Object List Editor**, use *Ctrl+N* to create a new record.

3. Enter a meaningful name for the project, such as AHA Prototypes (see the following for an explanation of the prefix).

4. Check the flag in the **Locked** column to lock the project in the local database (making the project writeable).

5. Step off the record (using the *down arrow* key) to save it.

When creating new object definitions in the Siebel Repository, we should adhere to a consistent naming convention. Using a company-specific name prefix (AHA in the preceding example) is **mandatory** to avoid confusion with object definitions created by Oracle engineering.

As indicated previously, projects must have the **Locked** flag checked in the local database to be able to add object definitions and check them in later. Once the project is checked in to the server database, we can decide whether the project should allow **single object locking** (the default) or not.

Single object locking allows developers to check out and lock individual object definitions rather than an entire project thus reducing the amount of data to be copied between the developer workstation and the server database. In addition, the probability that a developer locks an object definition that other developers would like to work on decreases.

In the following sections, we will discuss the concepts of project and object locking in greater detail.

Siebel Tools Options

Before we start developing, we should take a look at the most important program options for Siebel Tools. We can launch the **Development Tools Options** dialog by selecting the **Options...** item in the **View** menu. The dialog has several tabs as depicted in the following screenshot:

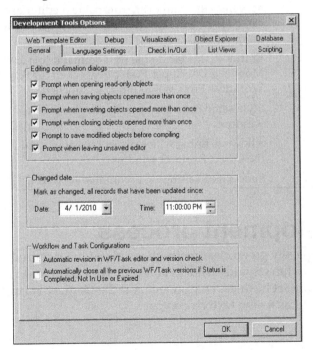

The following table describes the tabs in the Development Tools Options dialog and the settings that can be made.

Tab	Description
General	Allows enabling or disabling confirmation dialogs such as prompting to save before compiling. The date and time set in the **Changed date** section is used to mark all records with the **Changed** flag when they have been updated after this point in time. The **General** tab also includes options for the Workflow Process and Task editors.
Language Settings	The language set in this tab is used for string display, compilation and check in or check out.
Check In/Out	In this tab, integration with external source control systems can be enabled. In addition, the ODBC data sources for the local and server database can be set.
List Views	Controls the font size, spacing, and visual styles for the **Object List Editor**.
Scripting	Settings for the script engine. Discussed in more detail in a later chapter.
Web Template Editor	Defines the path to the working folder for Siebel web templates as well as the path to an external text editor executable, which can be launched from within Siebel Tools to edit a Siebel web template file.
Debug	Entries in this tab define the command line to invoke the Siebel Mobile or Developer Web Client when the Script Debugger or Workflow Process Simulator is launched.
Visualization	Style settings for the various viewers such as the **View Details** window.
Object Explorer	Allows defining which object types (and child types) appear in the Object Explorer window.
Database	Specialized settings to accommodate IBM DB2 server databases.

The development process

Developers are typically given clear instructions about the required modifications from the solution architects and business analysts. For example, a new field should be added to the **Contact** business component and the **Contact Form Applet** should expose the new field as a new textbox control.

When implementing the preceding example and during all other development cycles, the developer has to adhere to a process that can be depicted as follows:

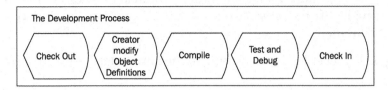

In the following sections, we will refer to the preceding example while we discuss each of the process steps in detail.

Checking out

When a developer, connected to the local database in Siebel Tools, wants to establish write access to an object, she or he has to use the **Check Out** functionality of Siebel Tools. There are two choices: Checking out single object definitions or entire projects.

Since Siebel CRM version 8.0, the Siebel Repository is preconfigured to support single object locking. In technical terms, the majority of projects have the **Allow Object Locking** flag set to true. This flag can only be changed to false when we log in to Siebel Tools as SADMIN to the **Server** data source. We can then right-click a project and select **Toggle Allows Object Locking** to switch the flag between its true and false values.

When a project has the Allow Object Locking flag set to true, we can only check out individual object definitions from that project. If the flag is set to false, we can only check out the entire project. The development team should decide early which check out technique to use in order to avoid confusion.

During the Check Out process, the selected objects are copied from the server database to the local database. All **local data is overwritten** during this process. This is similar to the *Get* functionality we have discussed earlier in this chapter. The difference between *Get* and *Check Out* is that after the data is copied during a Check Out, the **Locked** flag is set to true in **both** server and local databases on either the individual object or the entire project. Here are the outcomes:

- Setting the Locked flag to true in the **server** database makes the object or project **unavailable for check out** by other developers
- Setting the Locked flag to true in a **local** database enables **write access** to the object or all objects in the project

In summary, the Check Out process ensures that an individual developer has exclusive write access to the selected objects.

The following procedure is intended to demonstrate the process of disallowing object locking for a given project. Following our simple preceding example, we disallow object locking for the **Contact** project in order to be able to check out the entire project. We can identify the project to check out by inspecting the **Project** property of any object definition:

1. Log on to Siebel Tools, connecting to the **Server** database as SADMIN.

 In a real-life environment, you may not have access to the SADMIN password and may need assistance from an administrator to execute the following steps.

2. In the **Object Explorer** window, select the **Project** object type.
3. Query for the **Contact** project in the **Object List Editor**.
4. Right-click the **Contact** project and select **Toggle Allows Object Locking** in the context menu.
5. Use the **Exit** command in the **File** menu to close the server session of Siebel Tools.

The preceding procedure is only needed when we wish to toggle the Allows Object Locking flag for a project.

The next procedure describes the process of checking out a project using the Contact project (which contains the Contact business component) as an example:

1. If necessary, log on to Siebel Tools, connecting to the **local** database.
2. Select the **Check Out...** option in the **Tools** menu (or press *F10*).
3. In the **Projects** list of the **Check Out** dialog, select the **Contact** project.

 You can type the name of the project on the keyboard to locate the project faster.

4. Click the **Check Out** button.
5. A progress dialog is displayed. Wait for the check out process to finish.
6. Navigate to the **Contact** business component and verify that a pencil icon appears in the **W** column, indicating write access.

The process for checking out a single object definition, such as the **Contact Form Applet**, is similar to checking out a project. The next steps describe the process of checking out an object definition using the Contact Form Applet as an example:

1. In the **Object Explorer**, select the **Applet** type.

2. In the **Object List Editor**, query for the **Contact Form Applet**.

3. Right-click the object definition and select **Check Out Object**.

4. In the dialog box, click the **Check Out** button.

5. Wait for the process to finish.

At the end of the Check Out process, a Siebel Tools archive file (.sif) is created automatically in the TEMP folder of the Siebel Tools installation directory. The file represents the original state of each checked out object or project at the moment of check out.

These files are used for comparing the modified version of an object against the original and can be used to restore an object or project to its original state.

Working with Siebel Tools archive files will be covered in detail later in this chapter.

Creating or modifying object definitions

Once we have successfully checked out an existing project (or created a new project locally as described earlier in this chapter), we can start creating new object definitions. The following sections describe commonly used techniques to create new object definitions. We will have the opportunity to practice these techniques during the upcoming chapters of this book.

New Object Wizards

We can use the **New Object...** option in the **File** menu or click the **New** button in the **Edit** toolbar to launch the **New Object Wizards** selection dialog. It is highly recommended to use a graphical wizard rather than attempt to create the object definition from scratch. The following screenshot shows the **General** tab of the **New Object Wizards** dialog:

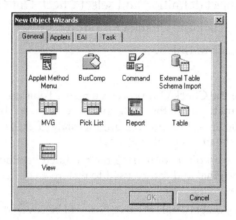

The following table lists all available wizards in the different tabs of the **New Object Wizards** dialog:

General	Applets	EAI	Task
Applet Method Menu	Chart Applet	Integration Object	Task
Business Component (BusComp)	Form Applet	OLEDB Rowset (obsolete)	Task Form Applet
Command	List Applet	Web Service	Task List Applet (8.1 and above)
External Table Schema Import	MVG (Multi Value Group) Applet	Data Access Service	Task View
Multi Value Group (MVG)	Pick Applet		Transient Business Component
Pick List	Tree Applet		
Report (Actuate)			
Table			
View			

Creating new records

For simple object types such as Links or Business Objects, we can use the **New Record** functionality in the **Object List Editor**. To do so, we ensure that we have write access to at least one project, select the desired object type in the **Object Explorer**, and then use the *Ctrl+N* keyboard shortcut in the **Object List Editor**.

We can then use either the **Object List Editor** or the **Properties** window to enter the necessary data to define the new object.

Copying existing object definitions

Under some circumstances it is easier to copy an existing object definition rather than create a new one. For example, it takes less effort to copy an existing applet and change the copy to create a slightly modified version than to create a new applet from scratch.

To copy an existing record, we must ensure that we have write access to at least one project and then use the *Ctrl+B* keyboard shortcut on a selected item in the **Object List Editor**.

The new object is an exact copy of the original. It includes all child records that eventually exist. We have to rename the copy to a unique name (following our naming convention) before we can begin to modify it.

Creating a new version of existing object definitions

Two object types—Tasks and Workflow Processes—support **versioning**. We can use the **Revise** button in the WF/Task Editor Toolbar to create a new version of a selected Task or Workflow Process definition.

The new version has the same name as the original but its **Version** property is incremented by one. In addition, the **Status** property of the new version is set to **In Progress**, which indicates write access when the object or the project it belongs to is checked out.

Modification techniques

The **Properties** window or the **Object List Editor** are the basic means of editing new or existing object definitions. Changes are made by entering text (aided by drop-down lists in many cases) or setting flags. The **implicit save** feature of Siebel CRM ensures that modifications on the individual record are saved once the user *steps off* the record.

Siebel Tools provides graphical editors for many object types such as Applets, Views, or Workflow Processes. Changes made in these editors must be saved **explicitly** either by using the *Ctrl+S* keyboard shortcut or by clicking the **Save** button in the toolbar.

Using the **Comments** property to record all modifications as well the username and date when they occurred is highly recommended. This practice ensures that other members of the project team can follow the modification history of any given object clearly.

Validating object definitions

It is good practice to use the Siebel Tools **validation utility** to verify that all settings on the object definitions are correct. We can right-click an object definition such as an applet and select **Validate** from the menu to invoke the **Validate** dialog.

Oracle provides pre-built rules that perform various checks against different object types. In order to inspect these rules and to control whether rules should be enforced or ignored we can click the **Options** button in the Validate dialog. The **Validation Options** dialog is shown in the following screenshot:

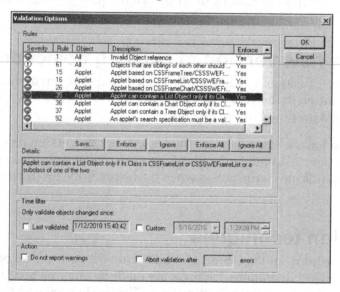

Once the options are set, we click the **OK** button to go back to the Validate dialog. Clicking the **Start** button invokes the validation process. The results are displayed in the dialog (selecting a message shows the full text in the Details field) and can be saved to a text file.

If validation errors are reported on an object, we must ensure that the problem is rectified before we continue in the configuration process.

Compiling object definitions

The **Siebel Repository File** (**SRF**) contains all repository objects in a structured format, which is optimized for consumption by the Siebel executable. In order to be able to test modifications locally we must change the SRF file, which is used by the Siebel Mobile or Developer Web Client, by compiling the modified objects or projects.

To do so, we can select one or more object definitions in the Object List Editor and press *Ctrl+F7* to launch the **Object Compiler**. To compile entire projects we use the *F7* key or the **Compile Projects** command in the **Tools** menu.

In the **Siebel Repository File** field or the **Object Compiler** dialog, we should use the **Browse** button to select the SRF file path, which typically points to a language-specific subdirectory in the OBJECTS folder of a Siebel Mobile or Developer Web Client installation directory. The following is an example of a typical SRF file path for the American English (ENU) version of **Siebel Industry Applications** (**SIA**).

```
C:\siebel\8.1\Client_1\OBJECTS\ENU\siebel_sia.srf
```

After we click the **Compile** button, all client instances that are currently using the SRF file are brought into a state where the file can be modified (indicated by the color of the Oracle icon in the Windows system tray changing from red to gray). The compiler then writes all selected object definitions to the SRF file, using the current Siebel Tools language to retrieve localized attributes such as applet labels. At the end of the process, the client instances are brought up again so we can continue to test.

Testing and debugging

A developer uses the local instance of the Siebel Mobile or Developer Web Client on her or his workstation to verify that the modifications in the Siebel Repository are valid. This is also called a **unit test**. Depending on the range of modifications the test cycle could simply consist of checking the visual layout of a new applet. But usually testing has to go a bit deeper and could include the creation of test data and debugging of workflow processes or scripts.

Both the workflow process simulator and the script editor support full range debugging. For example, developers can inspect the values of script variables and step through the code line by line.

To enable the debugging functionality in Siebel Tools, we must set the runtime parameters in the **Debug** tab of the **Development Tools Options** dialog. We can access this dialog by selecting the **Options...** command in the **View** menu. The following screenshot shows the **Debug** tab:

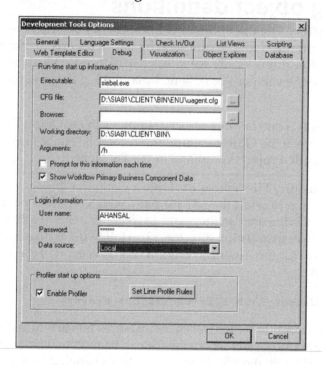

The following table provides descriptions and example settings to be made in the **Debug** tab:

Parameter	Description	Example Value
Executable	The name of the Siebel executable to invoke.	`siebel.exe`
CFG file	The full path to a Siebel client configuration file (`.cfg`).	`D:\SIA81\CLIENT\BIN\ENU\ uagent.cfg`
Browser	The full path to a browser executable. Leaving this parameter empty will result in the Windows default browser being used.	Typically left empty when Internet Explorer is the Windows default browser.
Working directory	The directory where the Siebel executable file is located.	`D:\SIA81\CLIENT\BIN\`

Parameter	Description	Example Value
Arguments	Must specify /h for debug mode. Other arguments such as /s for SQL spooling can be added.	`/s D:\TEMP\spool.sql/h`
User name	The username for the database specified via the Data source parameter.	AHANSAL
Password	The password for the data source.	(hidden)
Data source	The name of the data source (typically Local).	Local
Enable Profiler	Enable or disable the script profiler utility.	checked

Once these settings are saved, we can use the *F5* key to launch the Siebel Mobile or Developer Web Client in script debug mode or start the Workflow Process simulator. Both techniques will be discussed in detail later in this book.

 When the `siebel.exe` program connects to a local database, we refer to it as the **Mobile Web Client**. When the connection is made to a server database via the network, it is called a **Developer Web Client**.

Checking in

Once the changes are tested and verified locally, we must use the **Check In** functionality to copy the local projects or object definitions to the server database. This is the reverse process for checking out. As a result, the data in the server database is overwritten and the Locked flags are **unchecked** on **both** databases, server and local, resulting in the loss of local write access for the developer.

Other developers can then use the *Get* or *Check Out* functionality to obtain the changes from the server database.

The following steps describe the Check In process:

1. Press *Ctrl+F10* or select **Check In...** from the **Tools** menu.

2. In the **Check In** dialog, select one or more projects or objects in the list.

3. Click the **Check In** button.

4. Wait for the process to finish.

The following screenshot shows the **Check In** dialog.

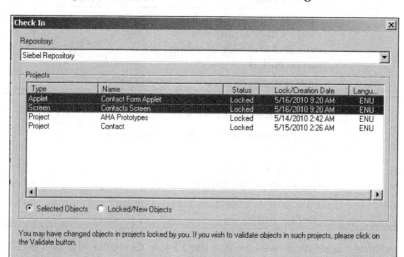

The **Check In** dialog has several options and functionalities, which are described in the following table:

Option	Description
Locked/New Objects	Changes the selection to all objects or projects that are locked in both databases or that have been newly created in the local database.
Maintain lock	When this option is checked, the Locked flag is not set to false on both databases, thus maintaining exclusive write access for the developer.
Undo Check Out	Removes the locking information in the server database but keeps the Locked flag in the local database. As a result the object can no longer be checked in.
Validate	Invokes the validation utility for all selected objects or projects.
Diff...	Invokes the Compare Objects dialog, which allows visual comparison between the server and local versions of the selected objects or projects.

At the end of the Check In process, the archive files (.sif) created by the Check Out process in the Siebel Tools TEMP directory are deleted automatically.

Local locking and prototyping

Under certain circumstances we only need local write access. These circumstances include prototyping or evaluation of object behavior. We can right-click any object definition and select **Lock Object** from the context menu to set the Locked flag only in the database that we are currently connected to.

Alternatively we can use the *Alt+L* keyboard shortcut to lock the entire project that the currently selected object definition belongs to.

Objects that are locked in only one database cannot be checked in. If we wish to keep the changes we must create an archive file of the object. The next section discusses how to create archive files.

Archiving object definitions

Siebel Tools supports the creation of archive files, with a .sif suffix, for selected object definitions or entire projects. As indicated in the previous sections, these archive files are created during the Check Out process automatically to provide easy comparison and restoring capabilities. A .sif file contains the XML representation of the archived objects.

Archive files can also be created manually and have proven very useful for backup purposes or to quickly provide fellow developers with object prototypes.

We can use the **Add to Archive…** command in the context menu to add one or more objects to a list of objects to be archived. The **Export to Archive File** dialog is displayed on the first invocation of the command.

It is possible to use the Object Explorer and Object List Editor to select additional object definitions for the archive file. The following screenshot shows the **Export to Archive File** dialog:

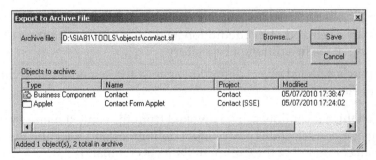

When the selection process is finished, we specify the path to the .sif file in the **Archive file** field and click the **Save** button.

Importing archived object definitions

The Import Wizard of Siebel Tools allows importing object definitions from one or more archive files. The wizard can be invoked from the Tools menu. The following example process describes how to use the Import Wizard:

1. In the **Tools** menu, select **Import from Archive...**.
2. In the **Select Archive to Import** dialog, browse to a .sif file.
3. Click the **Open** button.
4. In the **Preview** window of the Import Wizard we can select and delete objects from the list to exclude them from importing.
5. In the **Conflict Resolution** section we choose a suitable conflict resolution strategy. If we are in doubt, we should keep the default setting (Merge).
6. Click **Next**.
7. In the **Review Conflicts and Actions** window of the Import Wizard, we can inspect each object and its attributes and control the conflict resolution behavior by right-clicking in the Object differences or Attribute differences list.
8. Click **Next**.
9. Click **Yes** to confirm the summary message.
10. Wait for the import process to finish.
11. In the **Summary** window, click **Finish** to close the Import Wizard.

Comparing object definitions

As indicated in the section on the Check In process, a comparison utility exists that allows visual comparison of object definitions in the following ways:

- Compare two selected object definitions of the same type
- Compare a selected object definition against an object definition of the same type and name in a different repository
- Compare a selected object definition against the content of an archive (.sif) file

The **Compare Objects** window can be invoked from the context menu by right-clicking one or a selection of two object definitions and selecting the appropriate subcommand of the **Compare Objects** command.

In addition to visualizing the differences between the two selections, the Compare Objects window supports **copying** of child objects between the selected parent objects. Two arrow buttons in the middle of the window serve this purpose. The target object must be locked for this feature to work.

 The copy feature of the Compare Objects window is especially useful when we wish to avoid repetitive work such as placing the same button on multiple applets.

Searching the Siebel Repository

Siebel Tools provides a text search utility, which can be invoked from the **Search Repository...** option in the **Tools** menu. The utility allows selecting one or more object types and executes a full text search on all attributes of the selected object types. Due to the fact that the average Siebel Repository contains millions of records and the search is therefore very time consuming, this option should only be used as a last resort when the standard query option is not applicable.

Integrating external source control systems

In the **Check In/Out** tab of the **Development Tools Options** dialog we can enable integration of Siebel Tools with an external source control system. When this feature is enabled, Siebel Tools will execute the batch file specified in the options every time a developer performs a Check In process.

The batch file—a sample for Microsoft Visual SourceSafe is provided with the Siebel Tools installation—must be prepared by the development team to invoke the source control system's specific commands.

When source control integration is enabled, the developer will be prompted for a comment on each Check In process and an archive file (.sif) will be checked in as a new version in the source control system.

Automating developer tasks using command line options

The following tasks can be automated by running the Siebel Tools executable (`siebdev.exe`) and other utilities on the command line:

- Validate the entire repository
- Compile the entire repository
- Compare two SRF files
- Import from and export to archive (`.sif`) files
- Convert custom labels to symbolic strings
- Export object definitions for **Application Deployment Manager (ADM)**

To run a validation for the entire repository, a quite lengthy process, we have to invoke the Siebel Tools executable (`siebdev.exe`) from the command line similar to the following example:

```
C:\SIA8\Tools\BIN\siebdev.exe /d Local /u AHANSAL /p tzU87tr /bv
```

The `/d` switch specifies the data source while the `/u` and `/p` switches provide the username and password for that data source. Apart from these switches, the `/bv` (batch validation) switch will launch the validation utility automatically after Siebel Tools is started.

To compile the entire repository, also called a **Full Compile**, we use a command similar to the following:

```
C:\SIA8\Tools\BIN\siebdev.exe /d Local /u AHANSAL /p tzU87tr /bc "Siebel
Repository" new.srf /tl ENU
```

The `/bc` (batch compile) switch must be followed by the name of the repository and the name of the new SRF file. If no path is given for the new SRF file, it will be written to the OBJECTS directory of the Siebel Tools installation folder. The `/tl` (tools language) switch defines the language that will be used to compile the translatable strings.

The `/srfdiff` switch can be used to invoke the SRF comparison utility. This utility can also be invoked manually from the **Tools** menu. The purpose of SRF comparison is to identify differences between to releases.

In addition to the command line options described previously, Siebel Tools supports automating the export and import of object definitions into and from archive files (`.sif`). These two command line options /batchexport and /batchimport, are typically used while applying maintenance releases. They are documented in the *Using Siebel Tools* guide in the Siebel bookshelf.

A specialized command line utility named `consoleapp.exe` is available to automate tasks such as converting custom labels to symbolic strings and exporting object definitions for migration to test or production environments with **Application Deployment Manager (ADM)**.

Keeping the upgrade in mind

Almost every Siebel CRM project is bound to undergo an upgrade to a newer major release in the long term. For example, a project team that may have started with Siebel CRM version 7.8 could have to face the challenge of upgrading to version 8.2 (or later versions).

Every time when the first two digits of the version number change, which is considered an **upgrade** as opposed to a **patch**, which only increases the last two digits, a new version of the Siebel Repository is delivered from Oracle.

The main effort of a Siebel CRM upgrade project is the so-called **Repository Merge** process during which the changes made by customers and Oracle engineers to the prior standard repository are analyzed and applied to the new customer repository. The following diagram depicts the merge process using versions 7.8 and 8.1 as an example:

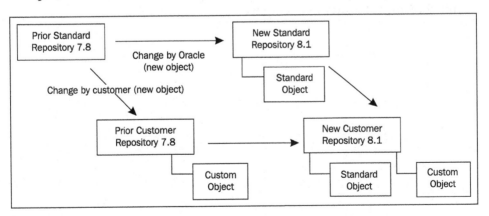

We can observe that any object definition created by custom developers is copied to the New Customer Repository, which is the working repository in the next version.

To avoid excess effort during an upgrade project, we should keep the following in mind during design and implementation of any change to the current version:

- Adhere to **strict naming conventions**. Use a project-specific prefix for any new object definition (including child level objects such as business component fields).

- **Never delete** objects defined by Oracle engineering from the repository. Use the **Inactive** flag to mark them as inactive.

- When changing standard objects (defined by Oracle engineering) use the **Comments** field to document the modification history.

- Try to keep the following to an **absolute minimum**:
    - Changes to the physical schema
    - Scripting on Applications and Applets
    - Implementing logic on the **user interface (UI)** layer in general (this violates the definition of the UI layer in any programming environment)

- Try to use as much of the **preconfigured** functionality as possible. It is a fact, proven by thousands of upgrade projects that every modification made to the Siebel Repository adds to the complexity and the effort needed to complete the upgrade process.

- When implementing new application functionality is inevitable, follow the example of Oracle engineering and create **business services** and **workflow processes**.

- Avoid **reinventing the wheel** or rebuilding Siebel CRM to match the functionality of legacy applications.

Summary

In this chapter, we discussed the most important pieces of Siebel Tools functionality that developers typically use in their daily work.

Initializing and populating the developer's database is a mandatory step to establishing the local development environment.

We followed a typical development process to identify tasks such as checking out, modifying, and creating new object definitions as well as validating, compiling, and testing the changes using the Mobile or Developer Web Client.

In addition, Siebel Tools supports development teams with archiving and search features as well as integration with external source control systems.

In order to achieve a professional and upgradeable implementation of the customer's requirements we have to follow basic principles that have been laid out in the section *Keeping the upgrade in mind*.

In the next chapter, we will introduce the case study scenario, which provides real-life examples for the remainder of the book.

3

Case Study Introduction

This chapter introduces the case study that provides input for all configuration examples throughout the remainder of the book. We will describe **All Hardware (AHA)**, a fictitious corporation specializing in consumer electronics, its business processes, and the requirements for the new Siebel CRM system that originate from these processes.

This chapter intends to establish the (fictitious) business context for the requirements, which will be implemented throughout the remaining chapters of this book and will be structured as follows:

- Background of All Hardware (AHA)
- Description of AHA's Business Processes
- Requirements for AHA

Background of All Hardware (AHA)

Since its founding in the nineties, UK based All Hardware (AHA) has been continually expanding into the European and eastern markets of consumer electronics. AHA sells all types of devices such as washing machines, dishwashers, stereos, TVs, as well as computers and peripherals.

AHA runs its own stores (AHA markets) in large cities across Europe some of which are only opened to registered retailers. In addition, AHA runs several luxury branded flagship stores and has a well-established internet shop.

One of the businesses with the highest growth rates in the past few years was the exclusive supply of high-end audio, video, and computer equipment to luxury hotel chains, driven especially by AHA's investments in the Arabic countries.

AHA has decided to purchase Oracle's Siebel CRM in order to streamline its IT systems into a single source of truth. The implementation project has several phases and spans over several years, after which, so is the intention, AHA's implementation of Siebel CRM will provide all customer and product-related information to the sales, service, and marketing departments.

Description of AHA's business processes

The following business processes will serve as requirement sources for this book:

- Sales—Update Customer
- Sales—Retail Order
- Marketing—Campaign Tracking

Sales—Update Customer

Customers, for example, who wish to communicate their new address to AHA can do so via various channels such as the internet, AHA's customer service line and the information desks in the AHA markets. AHA strives to make each customer contact as smooth and positive as possible. In addition, the AHA representative who processes the data change should also be able to verify all relevant customer information and, if appropriate, inform the customer about new campaigns and offers.

A team of business analysts has conducted a series of workshops with key employees of AHA's customer care, sales, and marketing departments and has created the following high level outline of the **Sales — Update Customer** business process:

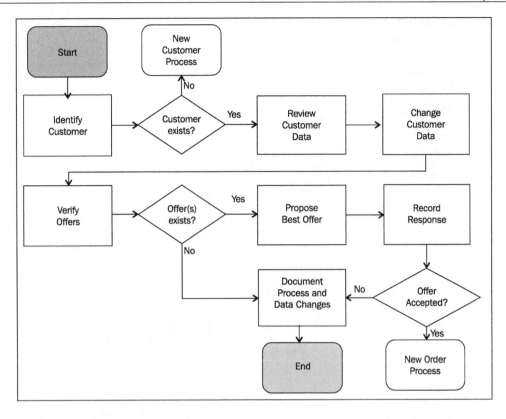

The agent executes a query to identify the customer. If no customer record can be found, the *New Customer Process* is triggered. If a customer record is found, it must be reviewed and changed according to the customer's communication. The agent then verifies offers for the customer. If one or more offers are displayed, the agent will propose the offer marked as *best offer* to the customer and record the customer's response. If the customer accepts the offer, the *New Order Process* is triggered. The process information (start time, end time, and executed steps) as well as data changes on key fields must be documented during or at least at the end of the process.

Sales—Retail Order

Retailers can use AHA's specialized stores and web shops to purchase bulk items. Often, these items are slightly damaged and therefore very low priced. Many retailers specialize in refurbishing these items and sell them on to their local markets.

AHA offers a partner program for high-volume retail customers (AHA Priority Partners) and wishes to allow both the partner employees and its own employees to collaborate efficiently during the ordering process.

The business analyst team has defined the following high level outline of the
Sales – Retail Order business process:

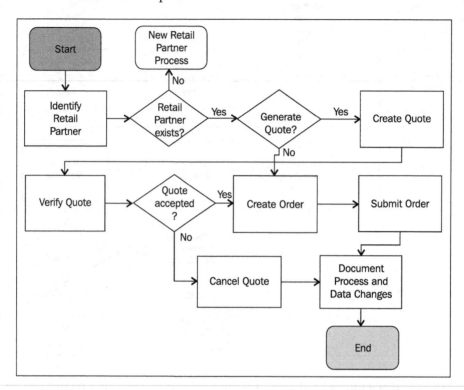

The agent uses a query to identify the retail partner. If no record is found, the *New
Retail Partner Process* is triggered. If the retail partner exists and has the *Always
Generate Quote* flag set to *Yes*, a quote will be created. Before giving the quote to the
customer, it must pass validation rules. When the customer accepts the quote, an
order is generated and submitted. If the customer does not accept the quote, the
quote must be canceled. The process information (start time, end time, and executed
steps) as well as data changes on key fields must be documented during or at least at
the end of the process.

Marketing—Campaign Tracking

In the past, AHA's marketing division has relied on third-party agencies to conduct
the marketing campaigns. Due to the different customer segments (consumers,
retailers, and luxury hotel chains), and in order to have a consistent view on the
customer responses to marketing treatments, the marketing division has joined the
Siebel CRM project.

In an effort to completely redesign the marketing strategy, the following high level business process for **campaign tracking** was defined with the business analyst team:

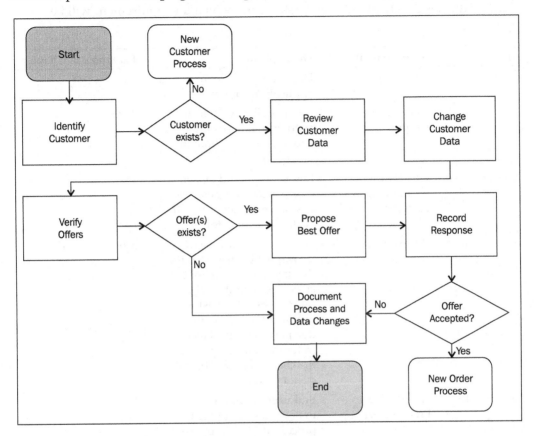

The agent identifies the active campaign. Depending on the customer type, different response information is required and entered by the agent. For retail partners, an opportunity must be generated in case the response is positive. For responses from hotel chains, a task must be generated that identifies the need for a personal follow-up call or meeting. The account manager for the hotel chain must be notified that a new task has been generated. The process information (start time, end time, and executed steps) as well as data changes on key fields must be documented during or at least at the end of the process.

Requirements for AHA

The business analyst team has worked with the business users and a group of technical solution architects to identify process-related and non-process-related requirements that the CRM application should fulfill for the first project phase.

The following table describes the general, non-process-related requirements that will serve as examples in the upcoming chapters. The *Examples in Chapter* column indicates the chapter in this book during which the requirement will be implemented:

Area	Requirement	Description	Examples in Chapter
User Interface	AHA Logo	Display the AHA Logo in the application banner.	15
User Interface	Multi-Language support	Provide all display texts as translatable strings to support future rollout in other countries.	4, 23
User Interface	Create orders for business customers	End users should be able to create orders for business customers directly from the customer profile form.	16
User Interface	Process start page	For each process, a start view must be provided that displays a summary of the customer. The start view must display the customer profile information, the documents for the customer (refer the following), and the change history for the customer data.	5, 6, and others
User Interface	Navigate to Process start page	End users should be able to navigate quickly to the process start view by using keyboard shortcuts or the application toolbar.	16
Reporting	Sales representative report	Provide the data in the sales representative info page to the reporting system.	18
Data Model	Last update	Show the full name of the person who committed the last update on a record. Clicking on the name should open an e-mail form.	7
Data Model	Constrained lists	Limit the amount of data visible in pick applets.	10
Data Model	Field validation	Set validation rules for key attributes of customer, quote, and order data.	7

Area	Requirement	Description	Examples in Chapter
Data Model	Indicators	For each customer record, the number of open service requests and the number of campaign contacts in active campaigns should be displayed.	7
Data Model	Courtesy traffic light	A traffic light icon should indicate the level of courtesy to avoid loss of high value customers.	8, 15
Data Model	Document list	AHA wishes to use a single entity named *Customer Document* to contain all opportunities, quotes, orders, and campaign responses in a single list.	9 and others
Data Model	Provide the ability to associate public notes with any customer record	Change the existing one-to-many (1:M) relationship to many-to-many (M:M).	11
Security	Read only data source	Ensure that a *read-only* version of customer, address, and order data exists.	7
Security	Provide a list of sales tools that have been created by the user	A new view titled *Sales Tools created by me* must be created.	12
Process Monitoring	View hit counter	Log all view hits and provide the data to an analysis tool.	17

Sales—Update Customer

The Sales—Update Customer business process has been proposed by the AHA business analyst team to ensure the complete auditing of customer interaction. The following special requirements must be met in the prototype. The numbers in parentheses identify the chapters in this book during which the requirement will be implemented:

Documentation of offer presentation. Each time an offer is made to the customer, this should be documented with the name of the employee, the product offered, the time of the offer, and the response of the customer. (8, 9)

Sales—Retail Order

The Sales—Retail Order business process should be facilitated by the **Siebel Task UI** module. AHA has made it clear that the following requirements are key acceptance criteria. The number in parentheses identifies the chapter in this book during which the requirement will be implemented.

- Allow data entry for queries in free form. The system should map the data entered by the user to the correct fields. (21)
- The price list field for a quote or order must not be empty. (7)

Summary

In this chapter, we introduced the fictitious company *All Hardware* (AHA) and some of its key business processes and resulting business requirements.

In the remainder of this book, we will use the requirements described in this chapter to provide real-life examples for configuring Siebel CRM applications.

4
Symbolic Strings

Localization is one of the great challenges in software development. It is one thing to translate text but a much more complex endeavor to ensure that a software application is capable of being localized for multiple languages and regional settings (locales). Oracle's Siebel CRM is fully localizable, which ensures that end users can work with a user interface in their language. In addition all system messages, help files, and reports can be translated. Dates and numeric information are displayed in the correct formatting of the end user's locale.

In this chapter, we introduce the centerpiece of Siebel localization — the concept of **symbolic strings**. This allows us to ensure that our project adheres to the Siebel standard of multi-language support. Even if our Siebel application is currently only deployed in a single language, it is beneficial to apply multilingual techniques from the start.

The chapter will be structured as follows:

- Understanding Symbolic Strings
- Creating and using Symbolic Strings
- Using Message Categories
- Localizing Siebel Applications

Understanding symbolic strings

Symbolic strings are an object type in the Siebel Repository. We can understand how symbolic strings support the multi-language capabilities of Siebel CRM by looking at the following example:

Every list or form applet in a Siebel application exposes a button with the text **Query** as its caption. There are thousands of applets, and therefore thousands of instances of the Query button control, in the repository.

Let us imagine that our customer wishes to change the caption text from **Query** to **Search**.

If the caption was stored along with each individual button definition, a developer would have to check out and manipulate thousands of objects. To avoid this time-consuming and error-prone effort, each object that displays a text in the user interface **references** a **Symbolic String** definition. The following diagram illustrates this:

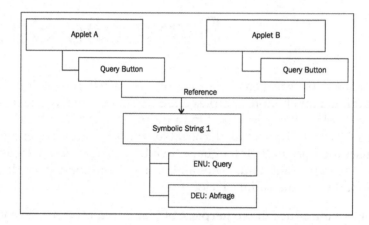

We can observe that each query button references the same symbolic string that contains the text for each supported language (American English - ENU - and German - DEU - in the example). A developer who needs to change the caption of all buttons from **Query** to **Search** would only have to update the symbolic string's English locale record. After compilation, the buttons will show the new caption.

Siebel Tools provides three properties for each display text. An applet control, such as the query button in the preceding example, has the following properties to define its caption:

- **Caption-String Reference**: The reference to a symbolic string object definition.

- **Caption-String Override**: A manually entered text, overriding the text from the symbolic string.

- **Caption**: The text to be displayed in the user interface. When a string override is present, the caption property will be set to the override text.

The following screenshot shows the object definitions for the Contact Form Applet and its Query button in Siebel Tools:

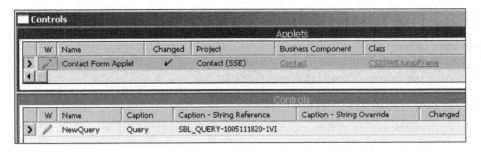

We can see that the control with the name **NewQuery** has its **Caption** property set to **Query**. Because the **Caption - String Override** property is empty, the **Caption** property uses the text stored in the symbolic string referenced in the **Caption—String Reference** property (**SBL_QUERY-1005111820-1VI**).

In order to inspect, modify, or manually create symbolic strings, we must expose the Symbolic String object type in the **Object Explorer**. As discussed in a previous chapter, this can be achieved by using the **Object Explorer** tab in the **Siebel Tools** options dialog. We can access the options dialog by selecting the **Options…** command in the **View** menu.

After enabling the display of the Symbolic String object type, we can click it in the **Object Explorer** window and inspect the symbolic string that served as the example above. The following screenshot shows the **SBL_QUERY-1005111820-1VI** symbolic string:

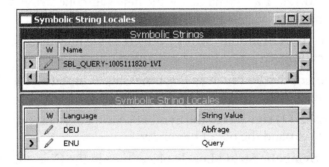

We observe that the symbolic string has two child records—one for German (DEU) and one for American English (ENU)—which define the language-specific string value. The translations are imported into the Siebel Repository during the installation of the language packs, which are available for more than 20 languages.

When compiling the **Siebel Repository File** (SRF) for multiple languages we must first set the **Siebel Tools Language** using either the options dialog or a command line switch. One individual SRF file must be compiled for each deployed language.

Creating and using symbolic strings

Developers can use the predefined symbolic strings, making use of the standard library of translated display texts, or create additional custom symbolic strings. We have two options of creating symbolic strings:

- Manual creation in Siebel Tools
- Automatic creation using batch scripts provided by Oracle

In the following we will explore both scenarios.

Creating symbolic strings manually

We should follow the procedure described as follows to create custom symbolic string definitions in Siebel Tools. We will create a new symbolic string to be used in a later section of this chapter:

1. If necessary, use the **Options** dialog to expose the **Symbolic String** object type in the **Object Explorer** window.
2. Create a new project named **AHA Symbolic Strings** and lock it.
3. In the **Object Explorer**, navigate to the **Symbolic String** object type.
4. In the **Object List Editor**, use the *Ctrl+N* keyboard shortcut to create a new record.
5. Enter **X_ERROR_1** as the name for the new symbolic string definition, keeping the **X_** prefix.
6. Assign the **AHA Symbolic Strings** project to the new object definition using the **Project** property.
7. Enter a descriptive text such as **Error message template 1 for AHA** in the **Definitions** property.
8. Click the plus (**+**) sign left to the Symbolic String object type in the **Object Explorer** to expand the object hierarchy.
9. Select the **Symbolic String Locale** object type in the Object Explorer.
10. In the **Object List Explorer**, use *Ctrl+N* to create a new record in the lower list.
11. Enter ENU in the **Language** property.
12. Enter The following error occurred: %1 as the **String Value** (without the double quotes).

13. Repeat steps 10 to 12 to create a German translation with the following properties:

    ° Language: DEU

    ° String Value: Der folgende Fehler ist aufgetreten: %1

14. **Compile** the X_ERROR_1 symbolic string.

15. Check in or unlock the project (optional).

 Note: The processes of creating and locking objects and projects as well as checking out, checking in, and compiling have been described in *Chapter 2*. If you use the Siebel Sample Database to follow the procedures in this book, you can only lock and unlock objects or projects. Check in and check out functionality is not available for the Siebel Sample Database.

A Siebel Tools archive file (Symbolic_String__X_ERROR_1.sif) is provided with this chapter's code files. The file represents the new symbolic string definition created in the section previously.

For instructions on how to import the code files in your self-study environment, please refer to *Chapter 2, Developer Tasks* or *Appendix B, Importing Code Files* of this book.

Did you know?
The prefix for custom symbolic string names (X_ by default) can be set using the SymStrPrefix parameter in the [Siebel] section of the Siebel Tools configuration file (tools.cfg).

Oracle recommends using X_ as the prefix for custom symbolic strings.

Associating symbolic strings with objects

The following steps describe how to associate symbolic strings with any object definition that carries a translatable display text. The example uses an applet control (Birth Date), which needs a different caption:

1. In the **Object Explorer**, click the **Applet** object type.

2. In the **Object List Editor**, query for the **Contact Form Applet**.

3. Check out or lock the **Contact Form Applet**.

4. Expand the **Applet** type in the **Object Explorer** and click the **Control** type.

5. In the **Object List Editor**, query for the control named **Birth Date**.

6. Observe that the control's caption is currently **Date of Birth**. We will change this to **Birth Date**.

7. Copy the current value of the **Caption - String Reference** property to the clipboard for later use in the Comments.

8. In the **Caption - String Reference** column, click the drop-down list to open the pick dialog.

9. In the **Starting with** field, enter `*Birth*` and press *Enter*.

10. Select the record for **Birth Date** and click the **Pick** button.

11. The caption for the Birth Date control is now set to **Birth Date**.

12. Enter a comment for the Birth Date control to indicate the change. The Comments property should read similar to this:

    `AHA: Changed Caption - String Reference from SBL_DATE_OF_BIRTH-1009094343-5YQ to SBL_BIRTH_DATE-1004225653-00F.`

13. Compile the **Contact Form Applet**.

14. Check in or unlock the **Contact Form Applet**.

    A Siebel Tools archive file (`Applet__Contact_Form_Applet.sif`) is provided with this chapter's code files. The file represents the Contact Form Applet after the changes in the preceding section.

Using batch scripts to create symbolic strings automatically

As an alternative to the manual creation of symbolic strings, developers can use the **string override** properties to type in the display text directly. This approach saves the developer time and effort. However this approach introduces potential spelling errors and inconsistencies of display texts across the user interface.

When we use the string override property, the text will be stored as a new child **locale** object associated with the original object. For example, using the string override technique to create a customized caption such as *Find a Person* for the query button in the Contact Form Applet results in a new **Control Locale** record associated with the button as shown in the following screenshot:

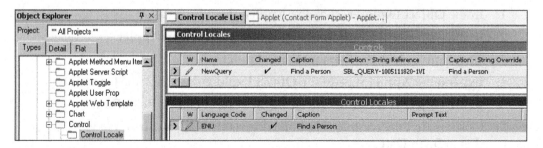

We can observe that inserting a value in the Caption - String Override property of a control results in a separate Control Locale record being created automatically for the current working language of Siebel Tools.

When developers use the technique described previously, translatable texts reside in multiple locations. This violates the concept of a central library as established by the Symbolic String object type.

Did you know?

The compiler detects the separate locale records when an override is used. From the compiler's perspective, it does not matter whether the translated string is a child of a symbolic string or of the object itself.

It is however recommendable to use symbolic strings because of easier administration and maintenance.

Oracle provides two batch scripts that can be used by customers to convert individual locale records into symbolic strings. The scripts can be found in the BIN subdirectory of the Siebel Tools installation folder and are named strconv.bat (for **string conversion**) and strcons.bat (for **string consolidation**).

In the following sections, we will describe how to use these batch files.

Using strconv.bat to generate symbolic strings

Before using the batch files for the first time, we must open them in a text editor of our choice and provide parameter values. The following table describes the necessary parameter settings for the strconv.bat file:

Parameter	Description	Example Value
TOOLS_INSTALL	Full path to the BIN directory of the Siebel Tools installation folder.	D:\SIA81\TOOLS\BIN
CONFIG_FILE	Full path to the tools.cfg file.	D:\SIA81\TOOLS\BIN\ENU\tools.cfg
TEST_LOCATION	Full path to an existing directory to hold temporary files generated by the utility.	D:\TEMP\SYMBOLIC_STRINGS

The following screenshot shows the respective portion of the `strconv.bat` file after the modifications:

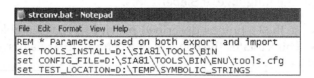

The `strconv.bat` file must be invoked from the Windows command line. The syntax for the command is as follows:

```
strconv "Object Type" "Action" "Username" "Password"
```

Downloading the example code for this book

You can download the example code files for all Packt books you have purchased from your account at http://www.PacktPub.com. If you purchased this book elsewhere, you can visit http://www.PacktPub.com/support and register to have the files e-mailed directly to you.

Object Type is the full name of the object type from which the locale records will be collected. To convert the caption of the button in the preceding example, we must use **Control** as the object type. The utility must be invoked once for each object type that has translatable properties. Examples for such object types are Applet, Control, List Column, and Business Service Method.

The second input parameter is the name of the **action**. The conversion process is split into two separate actions, namely **export** and **import**. During the export action, to be invoked first, the utility exports information about the locale objects into text files in the temporary directory specified by the TEST_LOCATION parameter. These text files can optionally be modified before we invoke the import action. Potential modifications include for example applying a spellcheck or style conventions to the collected strings.

The import action, executed after the export and optional modification of the exported files, reads the files, creates new symbolic string object definitions in the Siebel Repository, and associates them with the object to which the original locale record was associated.

The **Username** and **Password** parameters must be set to valid credentials for the database, which is specified by the **DataSource** parameter in the [Siebel] section of the `tools.cfg` file (typically set to **Local**).

A command similar to the following executes the export action of the string conversion utility for the **Control** object type.

```
D:\SIA81\TOOLS\BIN\strconv "Control" export AHANSAL tzU87tr
```

Once the command is complete, which could take a considerable amount of time, a set of text files can be located in the directory specified by the TEST_LOCATION parameter in the strconv.bat file.

Did you know?

The strconv and strcons batch files provided by Oracle serve as a wrapper for the consoleapp.exe utility. This program can be used to invoke business service methods from the command line.

As indicated previously, the exported files may optionally undergo some corrective manipulation. After this, we can invoke the import action by using a command similar to the following:

```
D:\SIA81\TOOLS\BIN\strconv "Control" import AHANSAL tzU87tr
```

This command reads all files related to the **Control** object type from the temporary directory and creates one new symbolic string object definition for each distinct text. Furthermore, the symbolic string object will be associated with the object definition — the Control in the above example — that carried the original string as a locale record.

Using strcons.bat to consolidate duplicate symbolic strings

The strcons.bat file works in a similar way to the strconv.bat file. The main difference is that it exports all custom symbolic string texts to temporary files, allowing for final spellchecks or manipulation. The import action then consolidates all duplicate strings into a single symbolic string and corrects the object associations that point to deleted duplicate strings.

To prepare the strcons.bat file for first use, we have to set the same parameters that have already been described above for the strconv.bat file.

A command similar to the following invokes the export action for string consolidation:

```
D:\SIA81\TOOLS\BIN\strcons export AHANSAL tzU87tr
```

The two parameters following the **export** command must be a correct username and password combination for the database specified by the **DataSource** parameter in the `[Siebel]` section of the `tools.cfg` file.

The preceding command produces a set of text files in the temporary directory. We can optionally apply corrective action to these files. A command similar to the following invokes the final import action:

```
D:\SIA81\TOOLS\BIN\strcons import AHANSAL tzU87tr
```

The result of this command is a consolidated (de-duplicated) library of symbolic strings. The utility also corrects the association of objects to symbolic strings that have been deleted in the process by associating the object to the surviving symbolic string.

Using message categories

Symbolic strings not only provide static translatable text snippets for the Siebel user interface. With the **Message Category** object type, we find a valuable resource to store dynamic message text templates in the Siebel Repository.

Messages can be combined with message categories for easier classification. We can reference the messages in custom scripts, enabling us to adhere to professional programming standards by avoiding hardcoded text in the program.

Messages can include placeholders for dynamic text replacement at runtime. These placeholders are specified by the percentage sign (`%`) followed by a sequential number. A valid placeholder would be for example `%1`. At runtime, the developer can submit arguments to the script functions, which retrieve the message text and replace the text in the arguments in the sequence identified by the placeholder number.

The following screenshot shows an example message with a placeholder:

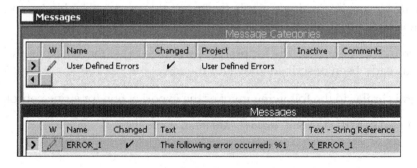

The following procedure describes how to create the example message:

1. If necessary, follow the instructions in the section **Creating symbolic strings manually** to create a new symbolic string definition named **X_ERROR_1** with an English text of **The following error occurred: %1**.

   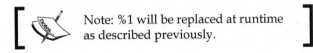

   Note: %1 will be replaced at runtime as described previously.

2. If necessary, use the options dialog to expose the **Message Category** object type in the **Object Explorer** window.

3. In the Object Explorer window, click the Message Category object type.

4. In the **Object List Editor**, query for the **User Defined Errors** message category. This is an empty category for customer use.

5. Ensure that you have write access to the User Defined Errors message category by checking it out or locking it locally (if you use the Siebel Sample Database for self-study purposes).

6. In the Messages list, create a **new** record (using *Ctrl+N*).

7. Enter AHA_ERROR_1 in the **Name** property.

8. Type X_ERR in the **Text - String Reference** column and press the *Tab* key to navigate to the next column.

   Observe that the value in the Text - String Reference column is automatically completed to **X_ERROR_1** because X_ERR was unambiguous. Using the auto-complete feature for pick list fields is recommended to increase productivity.

9. Compile and check in (or unlock) the **User Defined Errors** message category.

We will discuss how to use repository messages in detail in a later chapter.

A Siebel Tools archive file (Message_Category__User_Defined_Errors.sif) is provided with this chapter's code files. The file represents the User Defined Errors message category after the changes in the above section.

Localizing Siebel applications

It is a quite common situation that a Siebel CRM application is deployed to users in foreign countries with different language requirements during later phases of the project. This means that all objects that have been created by the custom developers must be translated into one or more additional languages.

Siebel Tools provides the **Locale Management Utility (LMU)**, which assists developers and business users in the process of translating content. The following screenshot shows the LMU user interface.

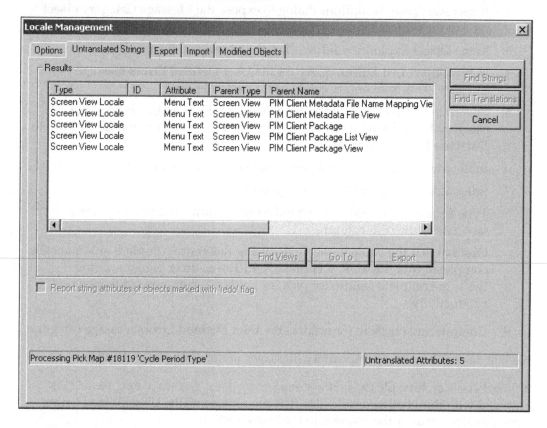

The following procedure describes the localization process from a high level perspective:

1. Select **Tools | Utilities | Locale Management...** to invoke the LMU.

2. In the **Options** tab, select a source and target language and select applications or projects from which the strings should be exported.

3. In the **Untranslated Strings** tab, click the **Find Strings** button.

4. The LMU will now scan the repository for all strings that have not been translated into the target language. Wait for the process to finish.

5. In the **Export** tab, click the **Export** button and select a file name and file type. The LMU supports text files and the **XML Language Interchange File format (XLIFF)**.

6. The files can now be submitted for translation.

7. After translation, we use the **Import** tab in the LMU dialog to import the translated files.

8. The LMU will create the according locale object definitions with the translated text.

The LMU assists in translating repository content. We must bear in mind that a full localization of a Siebel application is a time-consuming endeavor and additionally includes the localization of help files, reports, and List of Values data, to name the most important resources to be translated. These tasks are out of the scope of this book.

Summary

Symbolic strings are important object definitions. They are referenced by almost any object that holds translatable display values such as applet controls or error messages.

In this chapter, we learned how symbolic strings work and how they can be created. Developers can create symbolic strings manually or by **collecting** overridden strings using the string conversion and string consolidation batch utilities.

The chapter also showed how to create custom message templates and gave an overview on how to use the **Locale Management Utility (LMU)** to export strings for translation and import the translated files.

In the next chapter, we will learn how to create and modify applets.

5

Creating and Configuring Applets

In this chapter, we introduce the major user interface elements of Siebel CRM, namely applets. We will focus on how to create and modify form and list applets. Other applet types such as pick applets, tree applets, and chart applets are introduced as well. The case study, introduced in *Chapter 3, Case Study Introduction*, will provide input for hands-on practices.

The chapter is structured as follows:

- Understanding applets and web templates
- Creating and modifying form applets
- Creating and modifying list applets
- Other applet types

Understanding applets and web templates

A Siebel applet can be defined as a **user interface (UI)** element that enables the visual display and manipulation of data provided by a single business component.

The following table describes the applet types in Siebel CRM:

Applet Type	Description
Form Applet	Displays one record at a time and provides a great variety of controls such as text boxes, text areas, check boxes, radio groups, and images.
List Applet	Defines a sequence of list columns and displays a data set delivered by its associated business component in rows. The control types are limited to text, check box, and image. The list layout provides the end user with more flexibility in sorting data and arranging the list columns.
Pick Applet	A specialized list applet and supports dynamic pick lists. End users can query and sort data in order to find the right record to associate with the original record. Example: associate an account to an opportunity.
Multi-Value-Group (MVG) Applet	A type of list applet used to display the list of records associated with the original record in a one-to-many (1:M) or many-to-many (M:M) relationship.
Association Applet	Used to display the available records for association in a M:M relationship. Typically displayed together with the MVG applet in a *shuttle applet*.
Chart Applet	Displays data from a business component graphically as bar, line, or pie charts.
Tree Applet	Displays data in hierarchical (tree) style.
Task Applet	Allows entering transient data in the Siebel Task UI.
Playbar Applet	Contains the navigation buttons (Next, Previous, and so on) for the Siebel Task UI.
Detail Applet	Specialized applets such as the *About View* dialog.

Applet web templates

Each applet definition is associated with one or more **Web Templates** to define the visual layout in the browser. Web Template object definitions act as repository-side pointers to external text files, the **Siebel Web Template (SWT)** files.

SWT files define the common boilerplate layout for applets, views, and common web pages such as the application login page. Most applets use the same set of SWT files. This is the reason why so many standard applets have the same look and feel.

SWT files are situated in the WEBTEMPL subdirectory of the Siebel application installation folder. Siebel Tools, the Siebel Mobile, Developer Web Client, and each Siebel Server have a separate WEBTEMPL directory.

We can use the **Web Template Explorer** in Siebel Tools to inspect the SWT files and their hierarchy. To open the Web Template Explorer, we navigate to **View | Windows | Web Templates Window** in the Siebel Tools menu bar. The following screenshot shows the Web Template Explorer for the CCAppletList_B_EL.swt file:

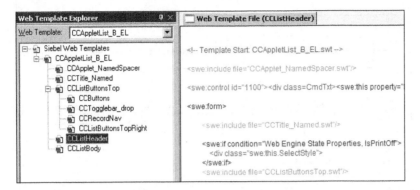

The file shown in the screenshot is the main template for list applets. It contains references to other nested files, which define the different sections of a list applet such as the list header (**CCListHeader**) and the list body (**CCListBody**).

The syntax of SWT files is an extended variant of the Hypertext Markup Language (HTML). Engineers at Siebel Systems created proprietary <swe:> tags, which allow dynamic generation of HTML content at runtime.

An SWT file mainly consists of so-called placeholders or **web template items**. Siebel Tools renders these placeholders as drop targets in the graphical layout editors and allows the developer to position components such as list columns and applet buttons.

Did you know?

Oracle recommends refraining from modifications to the SWT files. This is because changing one template file typically affects a lot of objects and any modification would have to be reapplied after an upgrade to a higher version of Siebel CRM.

The following diagram depicts the relationships between applets, web templates, and SWT files:

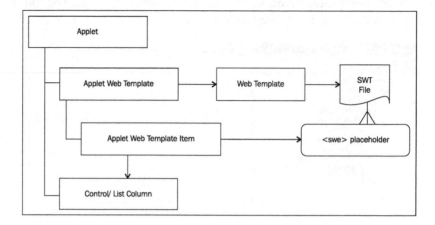

From the diagram we can derive the following facts:

- Each Applet has one or more **Applet Web Templates**
- Each Applet Web Template references a **Web Template**, which points to an SWT file (external to the repository)
- Each Applet Web Template has one or more **Applet Web Template Items**, which bind a Control or List Column of the Applet to a placeholder in the SWT file

Applet web template types

Siebel Tools allows the definition of different types of Applet Web Templates as described in the following table:

Type	Description
Base	When an applet is rendered using the **Base** web template type, the data displayed by the applet is read-only. To create or modify records, an end user must bring the applet in Edit, New, or Query mode by issuing the respective commands via buttons or keyboard shortcuts.
Edit	This web template type typically uses a **form**-based layout to provide the fields to edit an existing record. It is also used when the applet is used to create new records or to enter query criteria, if no New or Query type templates are defined for the applet.
	The Edit type is the standard web template type for form applets.
New	The New web template type is used when a user creates a new record. It typically uses a **form**-based layout.

Type	Description
Query	The Query web template type is used when the user has started a query. Creating different layouts for queries is a common practice to provide only a limited set of input fields for query criteria.
Edit List	This is the standard web template type for list applets and it allows the direct manipulation of data in the list.

Creating and modifying form applets

Form applets are the main UI vehicle to display data of a single record. They are typically used when end users need to view a large number of fields at a time or during data and query criteria entry.

Because the Siebel Repository already contains hundreds of preconfigured form applets, we have the following choices when it comes to configuration of the Siebel UI:

- Copy existing applets and modify the copy.
- Create new form applets using the Form Applet Wizard.

The first option typically means less effort when the majority of controls can be reused.

Case study example: Creating a form applet

In *Chapter 3* we described the following user interface requirements for the **Process Start Page** for the AHA (All Hardware) project:

For each process, a start view must be provided that displays a summary of the customer. The start view must display the customer profile information, the documents for the customer, the campaign history (graphically), and the change history for the customer data.

The business analyst team has worked with the end user community to create the following mock-up diagram for the Process Start Page view:

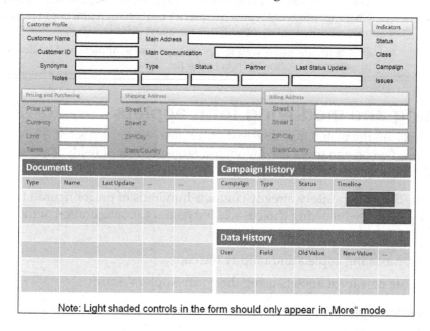

Note: Light shaded controls in the form should only appear in „More" mode

The form in the upper half of the preceding mock-up diagram will be implemented as a form applet in Siebel Tools. As an additional piece of information, the business analyst team has provided the following mapping document, which defines the fields in the **Account** business component used for the new form applet:

Control Caption	Business Component Field	Comments
Customer Name	Name	
Customer ID	CSN	
Synonyms	Synonym	MVG; use *Synonym Mvg Applet* as MVG Applet.
Notes	(implemented in later chapter)	Must create new multi-value fields to allow association of public notes to the account.
Main Address	Full Address-ENU	Calculated Field (read only).
Main Communication	Email Address	MVG; to be developed in a later phase.
Type	Type	
Status	Account Status	

Control Caption	Business Component Field	Comments
Partner	Partner Flag	Display as Checkbox.
Last Status Update	Account Status Date	Must implement business logic to populate the field with the current timestamp when the Account Status field is updated.
Status (Indicator)	Status Indicator	Must be read only.
Class (Indicator)	Revenue Class	Must create Icon Map (implemented in a later chapter).
Campaign Members (Indicator)	(implemented in a later chapter)	Show the number of incomplete campaign contacts for the customer.
Issues (Indicator)	(implemented in a later chapter)	Show the number of open service requests for the customer.
Price List	Price List	The price list associated with the customer.
Currency	Currency Code	The currency code of the customer's price list.
Limit	Credit Auto Approval Limit	
Terms	Payment Type	Standard payment terms for the customer.
Shipping Address: Street 1	Ship To Street Address	MVG; Use Bill To Address Mvg Applet.
Shipping Address: Street 2	(implemented in later phase)	Must create a secondary address field for shipping address.
Shipping Address: ZIP/City	Ship To Postal Code/ Ship To City	Align text fields without padding.
Shipping Address: State/ Country	Ship To State/ Ship To Country	Align text fields without padding.
Billing Address: Street 1	Bill To Street Address	MVG; Use Ship To Address Mvg Applet.
Billing Address: Street 2	Bill To Street Address 2	
Billing Address: ZIP/City	Bill To Postal Code/Bill To City	Align text fields without padding.
Billing Address: State/ Country	Bill To State/Bill To Country	Align text fields without padding.

The business analyst team has also indicated that an existing applet—the **Account Profile Applet**—can be used as the base for the development of the new form applet, which should go by the name of **AHA Customer Profile Form Applet**.

The following procedures use examples from the preceding requirements to describe different techniques that are useful when we create a new form applet in Siebel Tools. For the sake of brevity, we will use the string override technique for non-existing symbolic strings. As discussed in *Chapter 4*, we can later convert the overrides to symbolic strings using command line utilities.

Copying an existing applet

A procedure similar to the following can be applied to copy an existing applet:

1. Create a **new project** named AHA User Interface and lock it.

 Note: The project is created to hold all UI objects created in this and upcoming chapters.

2. Navigate to the **Account Profile Applet** and use the *Ctrl+B* keyboard shortcut to create a copy of it.

3. Rename the copy to **AHA Customer Profile Form Applet**.

4. Enter AHA User Interface in the **Project** column.

5. In the **Comments** property, enter a descriptive text such as Created for the AHA user interface prototype. Add a date and your username to the comment.

6. Right-click the new applet and select **Edit Web Layout** to open the applet in the layout editor.

Changing caption text using symbolic strings

We can use a procedure similar to the following to change the caption of controls when needed:

1. Click the gray **HTML Form Section** labeled **Account Information**.

2. In the **Properties** window, click the drop-down icon in the **Caption** field to open the **String Reference** dialog.

3. Use the **Starting with** field to locate the string with the value **Customer Profile**.

4. Click the **Pick** button.

The following screenshot shows the Caption - String Override dialog for the form section's caption:

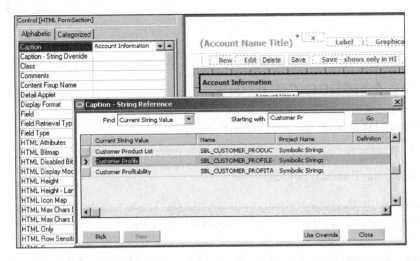

5. Use the *Ctrl+S* keyboard shortcut or click the **Save** button in the toolbar to save the changes.

Note: If there is no symbolic string available, we can use the **Caption - String Override** property to enter the text manually. We should use the utilities described in *Chapter 4* to convert the overrides to symbolic string in later phases of the project. Alternatively we can add a new symbolic string and use it.

Changing the association to a business component field

We can keep a control in a copied applet and change the **Field** property to display data from a different business component field. This is described in the following procedure. We should only use this technique with text fields that have **no value** in the Pick Applet or MVG Applet property:

1. Select the control labeled **Site** (click the text box - not the label-in the editor).

2. In the **Properties** window, change the **Field** property to **CSN**.

3. Change the **Caption** property to **Customer ID**.

4. Change the **Name** property to AHA Customer ID.

[Note: Renaming the control is a recommended practice to
avoid confusion.]

5. Save the changes.

Deleting existing controls

We can use a procedure similar to the following to remove a control and its
accompanying label from the web layout:

1. Right-click the checkbox next to the Public label and select **Delete**.
2. Delete the Public label also.

If you accidentally delete a control, you can use the Undo functionality (*Ctrl+Z*) or
retrieve the control from the **Controls/Columns** docking window.

Moving an existing control to a different location

We can use the mouse to drag controls to different locations in the grid layout.
However, using the keyboard as described below can prove more exact:

1. Use *Ctrl+Click* to select both the **Synonyms** control (textbox) and its
   accompanying label.
2. Use the *arrow* keys (you can hold down the key) to position the selected items
   below the **Customer ID** control.
3. Save the changes.

Creating new controls

To create new controls and an accompanying label we use the **Palettes** window as
described in the following procedure:

1. Drag a Field object from the **Palettes** docking window to the editor canvas.
2. Drop the object at the location of the **Last Status Update** control in the
   mock-up diagram.

   The following screenshot depicts the drag and drop operation:

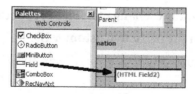

3. In the **Properties** window, change the **Name** of the new control to **AHA Account Status Date**.

4. Set the **Field** property to **Account Status Date**.

5. In the **Caption - String Override** property, enter Last Status Update.

6. From the **Controls/Columns** window, drag the **AHA Account Status DateLabel** control to the left of the new field.

 Note: The label control has been generated automatically-with the suffix **Label** appended after the control name-and serves to display the control's caption text. We should never create a separate label object for an existing control.

7. Arrange the label and the field according to the mockup diagram.

8. Save the changes.

Creating new form sections

Form sections allow arranging a form applet's controls into groups. A procedure similar to the following describes how to create new form sections:

1. Drag a **Form Section** object from the **Palettes** window to the editor's canvas.

2. Drop the object at the upper-right corner of the canvas (the location of the Indicators form section in the mock-up diagram).

3. In the **Properties** window, change the **Name** of the form section to **AHA Indicators Form Section**.

4. In the **Caption - String Override** property, enter Indicators.

5. Save the changes.

Formatting and aligning multiple controls

To efficiently resize and align multiple controls at once, we can multi-select the controls and use the **Format** toolbar as described in the following procedure:

1. Use *Ctrl*+Click to select multiple controls at once, selecting the control that should act as a reference (regarding size and relative positioning) last. The last selected control is indicated by a **red border**.

2. Use the buttons in the **Format Toolbar** to modify the alignment, width, height, and spacing of all selected objects as needed.

The following screenshot shows the **Format Toolbar** (in floating mode):

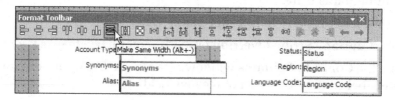

Hovering the mouse cursor over a toolbar button opens a tool tip which shows a brief explanation of the button's functionality and - if defined - the associated keyboard shortcut.

3. Save the changes.

Setting the tab order

To set the sequence to be used to set focus on controls when an end user navigates through the form using the *Tab* key we use the **HTML Sequence** property of the control.

To allow easier modification when new controls are added to the form applet at a later stage in the project it is recommended that we use a sequence with **gaps** such as 5,10,15, and so forth.

Copying controls from other applets using the compare objects window

We can use the technique described in the following procedure whenever we need to copy one or more child objects between two objects of the same type:

1. Close the applet editor (right-click the tab and select **Close**).
2. In the applet list, execute a query that retrieves the **AHA Account Profile Form Applet** and the **SIS Account Entry Applet** (using the **OR** operator).
3. Use *Shift*+Click to select both applet definitions in the list.
4. Right-click the list and select **Compare Objects | Selected** from the menu.
5. In the **Compare Objects** window, expand the **SIS Account Entry Applet** and its child node elements until you can select the **Control** named **Account Status Indicator**.
6. The following screenshot shows the Compare Objects window with the Account Status Indicator selected in the SIS Account Entry Applet (right):

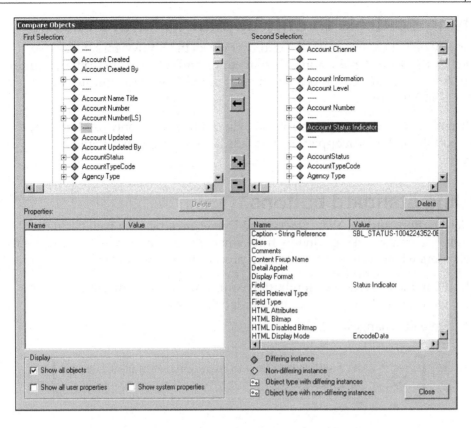

7. Click the second arrow button from the top (pointing to the AHA Account Profile Form Applet) to copy the control to the other applet.

8. Click **Yes** to continue.

9. Click **Close** to close the **Comparison** window.

10. Open the **AHA Account Profile Form Applet** in the web layout editor.

11. Drag the **Account Status Indicator** control and its accompanying label from the **Controls/Columns** window as described in the preceding section on creating new controls.

12. Save the changes.

Adding a show more/show less button

We can use the **Compare Objects** window as described in the previous section to copy the **ToggleLayout** control-which implements the **Show More/Show Less** button for form applets-and the corresponding **Applet Web Template Item** to the new applet.

Setting controls to only appear in "more" mode

To display only a control when the end user clicks the **Show More** button we right-click the control in the applet layout editor and select **More** from the context menu. A down arrow icon appears to the left of the control to indicate that the control is in **More** mode.

It is beneficial to arrange the controls that should be shown only in **More** mode at the bottom of the form applet. This avoids layout gaps, which could confuse the end user.

Adding standard buttons

Standard buttons such as New, Query, and Delete are typically available in the Controls/Columns docking window from where we can drag them to the respective placeholders when needed. The following procedure serves as an example for this task:

1. Drag the **NewRecord** minibutton control from the **Controls/Columns** window to the button placeholder labeled **New**.

2. Save the changes.

 We will discuss how to create custom buttons later in this book.

Displaying data in the applet title

To display fields of the current record in the applet title bar, we can use the **Compare Objects** window to copy the **AppletTitle** control and the according Applet Web Template Item to the new applet. The **SIS Account Entry Applet** can be used as a source. The **AppletTitle** control can be associated with any field in the business component in order to display its value as meaningful header information.

Setting applet properties for data operations

The following applet properties control what data operations (delete, insert, merge, or update) are available to end users:

Property	Description
No Delete	When set to TRUE, deleting records is not allowed.
No Insert	When set to TRUE, no new records can be created.
No Merge	When set to TRUE, merging of records is disallowed.
No Update	When set to TRUE, no updates can be made to existing records.

In order to allow all data operations on the **AHA Account Profile Form Applet**, we set all of the properties described in the preceding table to **FALSE**.

Did you know?

By pressing the *F1* key, we can open the Object Types Reference document from the **Siebel Tools Online Help**. The document is opened in context with the currently selected object type and provides detailed descriptions for the properties of the object type.

The following screenshot shows the **AHA Account Profile Form Applet** in the layout editor after the modifications required by the business analyst team:

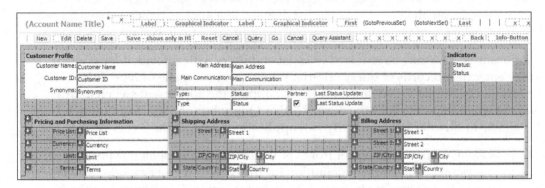

As indicated in the requirements table, some of the applet features will be implemented in later chapters.

Compiling the new applet

To prepare for testing the applet we close all open editors and select the **AHA Account Profile Form Applet** in the object list editor. Pressing *Ctrl+F7* opens the Compile dialog for the selected object.

In the **Siebel Repository file** field we must specify the full path to an existing SRF file in the client's OBJECTS/ENU subdirectory.

Clicking the **Compile** button starts the compilation process.

Note: We are not able to test the applet in the Siebel Developer Web Client because the applet is not yet part of a View. We will create the necessary View object definition in a later chapter.

A Siebel Tools archive file (AHA Customer Profile Form Applet.sif) is provided with this chapter's code files. The file represents the AHA Customer Profile Form Applet after the changes in the preceding sections.

Creating and modifying list applets

List applets are used to display multiple records at once. Specialized web templates are used to create the visual style for list display. List applets typically have more than one web template in order to control their appearance in certain work modes.

For example, one may be required to assist end users with a detailed form when they enter new records or query criteria. When a web template of type **Edit** - using a form web template - is defined for the list applet, the applet will switch to this layout when the user clicks the **New**, **Edit**, or **Query** button. The **Edit** button is only available in **Standard-Interactivity (SI)** applications such as the Siebel Partner Portal.

To provide more fine-grained control over the layout of an applet it is possible to define a separate web template definition for the **New** and **Query** modes as well. When one of these template types is defined for an applet it will switch to the **New** layout template when the user clicks the **New** button and to the **Query** layout when the user clicks the **Query** button.

List applets support end users with the following tasks:

1. Resize list columns for better data visibility.
2. Rearrange list columns using the **Columns Displayed** dialog.
3. Freeze list columns by double-clicking the column header for easier horizontal scrolling.
4. Sort data.
5. Compare data.
6. Select and change multiple records at once.
7. Export and print lists.
8. Save and apply target lists for use in marketing campaigns.

Case study example: Creating a list applet

The mock-up diagram by the business analyst team - shown in the preceding section - includes a **Data History** list applet. The business analyst team indicated that they wish to create a new list applet based on the **Audit Trail Item 2** business component, which exposes the history of changes recorded in the Siebel Audit Trail tables. The applet should provide read-only access to the audit trail data. Furthermore, only the **Date** and **Field** controls should be available in **Query** mode to avoid performance problems, which may occur when end users execute queries that include other fields.

Creating a new list applet using the Siebel Tools new object wizard

Siebel Tools includes **wizards** for creating new objects, including all types of applets. In the following example procedure, we will describe the process of creating a new list applet using the Siebel Tools Wizard. The process for creating other types of applets such as form or pick applets is similar:

1. In the **Object Explorer** window, select the **Applet** type.
2. Right-click in the **Object List Editor** and select **New Object Wizards... | List Applet** from the menu.
3. In the **General** page of the wizard enter the following information:
    - **Project**: AHA User Interface
    - **Name for the applet**: AHA Data History List Applet
    - **Display title**: Data History
    - **Business component**: Audit Trail Item 2
    - **Upgrade behavior**: Preserve

> The upgrade behavior for custom objects should always be set to *Preserve*.

4. Click **Next**.
5. In the **Web Layout - General** page of the wizard select the **Applet List (Base/ Edit List)** template in the upper list.
6. Click the uppermost arrow button to associate the selected web template with the **Base** mode of the new applet.
7. In the lower list, select the **Applet Form Grid Layout** web template.
8. Click the lowermost arrow button to associate the selected web template with the **Edit** mode of the new applet.

The following screenshot shows the **Web Layout - General** page of the wizard with the correct settings:

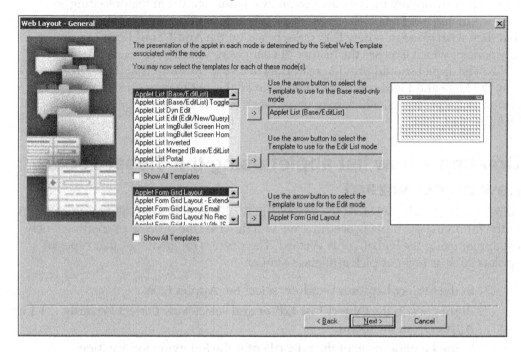

Audit trail data will only be displayed in read-only mode. This is why we do not select a template for the Edit List mode. We will modify the Edit web template later to create a form for querying only dedicated fields.

9. Click **Next**.

10. In the **Web Layout - Fields** page, select the following business component fields and use the right arrow button to add them to the list of selected fields:

    ° Employee Login

    ° Field

    ° Old Value

    ° New Value

    ° Date

    ° Operation

    ° Audit Source

11. Click **Next**.

12. Use the left arrow button to remove the following button controls from the list of selected controls:

    ° DeleteRecord

    ° EditRecord

    ° NewRecord

    ° QueryAssistant

    ° UndoRecord

    ° WriteRecord

13. Click **Next**.

14. Review the information in the finish page and click **Finish**.

The new object wizard creates the new list applet and opens it in the layout editor. As the wizard does not create a 100% complete version, we must edit the two layout templates. We will describe these procedures in the following sections.

Editing the base layout template

The following procedure describes how to edit the base layout template of a list applet:

1. In the **Controls/Columns** window, select **1:Base** in the **Mode** field.

2. Drag the button controls to the respective placeholders as follows:

    ° **NewQuery → Query**

    ° **ExecuteQuery → Go**(ExecuteQuery)

    ° **UndoQuery → Cancel**(Query)

3. Set the **Show In List** property for the following list columns to **FALSE**:

    ° **Employee Login**

    ° **Operation**

    ° **Audit Source**

Did you know?

The **Show In List** property controls - when set to **TRUE** - whether the list column will be part of the default set of visible columns. If the value is set to **FALSE**, the column will be part of the *Available* list in the **Columns Displayed** dialog.

4. Use the **Compare Objects** window as described in the form applet section to copy the **ToggleListRowCount** control - which implements the Show More/Show Less button for list applets - and the respective Applet Web Template Item from the **SIS Account List Applet** to the **AHA Data History List Applet**.

5. Set the **HTML Number of Rows** property to **5** to show only five records when the applet is loaded.

6. Right-click the layout editor and select **Preview**.

   Compare your work with the following screenshot:

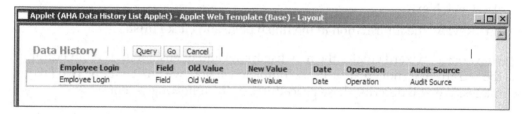

7. Right-click the editor and select **Preview** again to leave the preview mode.

8. **Save** all changes and close the layout editor.

Now that we have finalized the first web template, we can continue to modify the other web template definitions.

Editing the query layout template

The following procedure describes how to modify the base template of a list applet:

1. In the **Object Explorer** window, expand the **Applet** type and select the **Applet Web Template** type.

2. Change the **Name** and **Type** property of the **Edit** web template to **Query**. This creates the query template we need to fulfill the requirement described previously.

3. Right-click the new **Query** template and select **Edit Web Layout**.

4. Delete all controls and accompanying labels except for the **Date** and **Field** control.

5. Rearrange the **Date** and **Field** control so that they are aligned in one row.

6. Compare your work with the following screenshot:

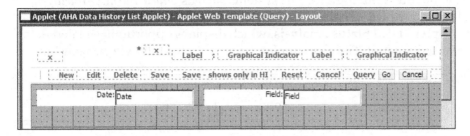

7. Save all changes and close the layout editor.
8. Compile the **AHA Data History List Applet**.

A Siebel Tools archive file (AHA Data History List Applet.sif) is provided with this chapter's code files. The file represents the AHA Data History List Applet after the changes in the previous sections.

Other applet types

While most of the applets in a Siebel application are of either the form or list type, there are various other applet types available. In this section, we will discuss the following applet types using examples from Siebel CRM standard applications:

*   Chart applet
*   Tree applet
*   Pick applet
*   Multi-Value-Group (MVG) and associate applet

Configuring chart applets

Chart applets display business component data in a graphical manner. Examples for typical charts are vertical or horizontal bar charts, line charts, and pie charts. Siebel CRM is pre-integrated with the JAVA-based charting engine of *VisualMining* to deliver the charting functionality.

Siebel chart applets fill the gap between displaying and exporting data in lists and full-scale **business intelligence** (BI) systems such as *Oracle Business Intelligence*. In the following, we will use the preconfigured applet named **FINCORP Investor Chart Applet - Lead Status Analysis**, which displays opportunity-related data for a selected account. The chart applet is shown in the following screenshot:

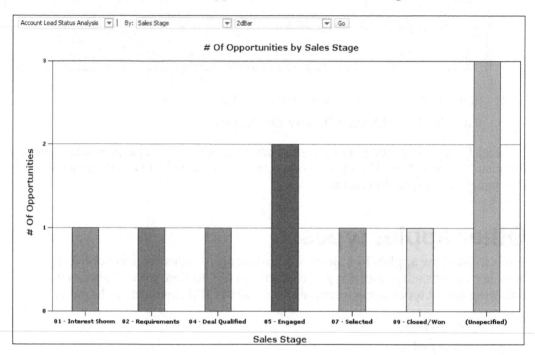

The chart shows the distribution of sales stages across the opportunities for the selected account (not visible). Drop-down lists allow the end user to toggle to other applets, select other categories for the X-axis, and select the chart type such as pie or bar chart.

The most important building block of a chart applet is the **Chart** child object with its **Chart Elements**. The following screenshot shows the Chart object of the **FINCORP Investor Chart Applet - Lead Status Analysis** applet in Siebel Tools:

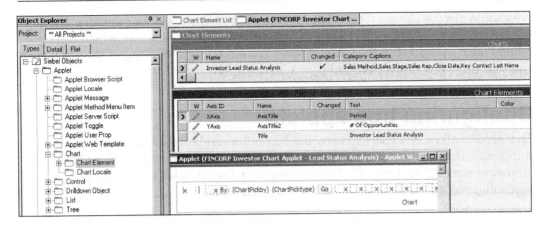

The Chart object type defines the fields for the X and Y-axis of the chart as well as the captions along with color and size information.

The following table describes the most important properties of the Chart object type.

Property	Description	Example Value
Category Field	Defines the business component fields for the (horizontal) **X-axis** of the chart. Must be entered as a comma separated list and is rendered as a drop-down list in the applet.	Sales Stage,Sales Rep,Close Date,Key Contact Last Name
Data Point Field	Defines the business component field for the (vertical) **Y-axis** of the chart. Default value is "Id" (the primary key of the business component).	Id
Data Function	The aggregation operation to perform against the data point field. Valid values are COUNT, SUM, AVERAGE and PLOT.	COUNT
Type	The chart type to be displayed when the applet is loaded.	2dBar
Picklist Type	A comma separated list of valid chart types. Rendered as a drop-down list in the applet.	3dBar,3dHorizBar,2dBar,2dHorizBar

We should always use the **Chart Applet Wizard** to create new chart applets. The wizard ensures that the correct settings are made for an initial setup, which can be refined later. We can start the Chart Applet Wizard by right-clicking in the applet list and selecting **New Object Wizards... | Chart Applet**.

Configuring tree applets

Tree applets allow end users to view the hierarchical relationships of business component data in the typical and commonly known style of a file explorer. The following screenshot shows the **Pharma Account Tree Applet**, one of the many preconfigured tree applets in Siebel CRM applications:

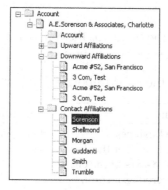

Expandable folder icons define the entities while file icons are used to display the records. End users can quickly view associations between records by using tree applets.

The main component of a tree applet definition is the **Tree** object type and its associated **Tree Node** elements. The following screenshot shows the **Pharma Account Tree Applet** in the Siebel Tools layout editor:

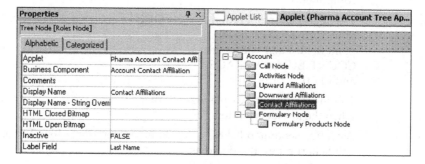

The **Contact Affiliations** tree node is selected. As we can see in the **Properties** window in the preceding screenshot, a tree node's purpose is to define a **business component**, one of its **fields** (in the **Label Field** property) and an **applet** to display the business component data when the node is selected in the user interface.

It is recommended that the **Tree Applet Wizard** is used to create new tree applets. However, the wizard only produces a boilerplate tree, so we have to manually modify the wizard's result and add tree nodes as required.

Configuring pick applets

Pick applets are a special type of list applet that are used to display business component data when an end user clicks the *pick icon* (a select button with one dot and a check mark) in a list or form applet. End users can work with the controls in the pick applet to query or modify the data set.

The following screenshot shows the **FINCORP Deal Account Pick Applet** in the Siebel user interface:

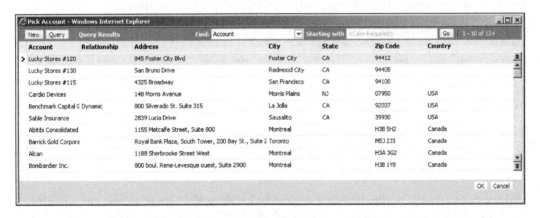

By double-clicking a record or clicking the **OK** button, the selected record will be associated with the record in the originating applet.

Apart from a set of special controls such as the **Find** drop-down list, the **Starting with** field, and the **OK** and **Cancel** buttons, we can treat pick applets as any other list applet.

We will discuss the process of creating the necessary business layer objects to enable pick applets later in this book.

Configuring multi-value-group (MVG) and associate applets

Multi-Value-Group (**MVG**) applets serve the purpose of displaying a list of records that are associated with an existing record. To open the MVG applet, the end user has to click the MVG icon (a select button with two dots and a check mark) in the user interface.

MVG applets are used for 1:M or M:M relationships. In the case of M:M relationships, MVG applets reference an additional applet, which is called an **associate applet**. The associate applet displays a list of available data from which the end user can choose one or more records to associate them with the original record.

An MVG and its associate applet are always displayed in the same browser popup window. This is also called a *Shuttle Applet* because of the buttons between the two applets, which allow end users to work with the data associations.

The following screenshot shows the **Account Team Mvg Applet** (right) and the **Team Member Assoc Applet** (left) in the Siebel CRM user interface:

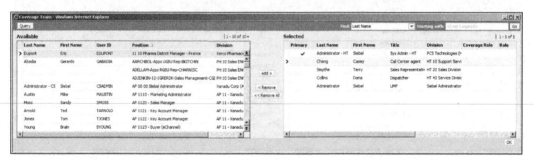

End users can query in the associate applet to locate one or more positions. Clicking the **Add >** button associates the records selected in the associate applet to the originating record, making the records visible in the MVG applet. The *shuttle buttons* are control definitions of the MVG applet.

We can apply our knowledge of creating or modifying list applets to MVG and associate applets alike. Siebel Tools also provides a New Object Wizard for the MVG applet type but not the associate applet type.

We will discuss how to create the necessary business layer objects to support MVG and associate applets later in this book.

Summary

Applets are the major building blocks of the Siebel CRM user interface. We can distinguish between form, list, chart, and tree applets.

Form applets provide enough space to display multiple fields of a single record at once with the widest variety of controls such as text boxes, checkboxes, images, and radio groups.

List applets, including the specialized pick, MVG, and associate applets, allow end users to work in table style, selecting columns for display and sorting data.

Chart applets support graphical display of business component data in the form of bar charts, line charts, or pie charts.

Tree applets allow end users to visualize the hierarchical relationships of business component data.

From the developer's perspective, we find a lot of support by means of the New Object Wizard for all applet types and graphical editors for form, list, and tree applets.

In this chapter, we used two applet definitions from the case study scenario. As a result, we can use the form and list applets we produced in this chapter in the next one where we will discuss how to create and modify View and Screen object definitions.

6
Views and Screens

Views and screens are the foundation for the Siebel CRM user interface. In this chapter, we will learn how to create and configure both object types. The chapter is structured as follows:

- Understanding views and screens
- Creating and modifying views
- Adding a view to a screen
- Registering a new view

Understanding views and screens

From the discussion of Siebel Repository objects in *Chapter 1*, we know that a screen is a set of views and a view is a container for one or more applets. To deepen our understanding of views and screens, we will discuss these object definitions and their related objects in greater detail in the following sections.

Understanding views

Views define the largest visible area in the Siebel UI. The following screenshot shows the preconfigured **All Service Request List View**. The two applets in the view consume most of the screen estate:

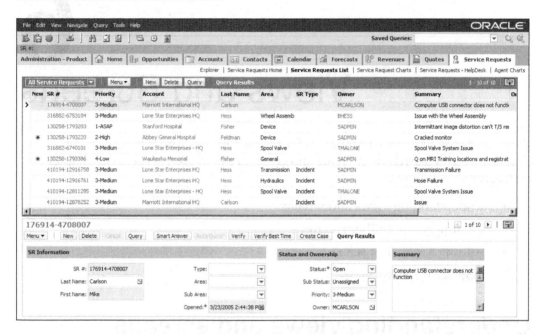

From a **business process perspective**, a view is the UI element that must be available to the end user at a certain step in the process. Only then can a user accomplish the tasks defined in that step.

Views are made available to end users by administering **responsibilities**. A responsibility is a group of users who must execute the same business processes. A responsibility also defines a list of views that its associated users have access to. The following diagram depicts the relationships between business processes, users, views, and responsibilities.

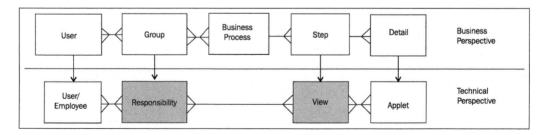

From the preceding diagram we can learn the following:

- A business process is a set of steps, each of which can be executed in a Siebel view

- Detailed task descriptions of the business process steps reference applets in this view

- Groups of users are assigned to one or more business processes

- Responsibilities enable the availability of views to users in Siebel CRM

From the **developer's perspective**, we can explore the **View** object type in Siebel Tools. The following diagram shows the major elements of a view and their relationships to other objects in the Siebel Repository:

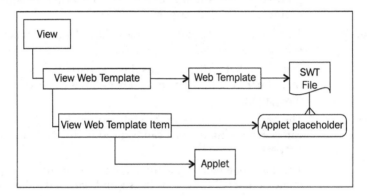

The following can be said about the View object type:

- A View typically contains one **View Web Template** object definition

- The View Web Template references a **Web Template** object definition which points to a **Siebel Web Template (SWT)** file outside of the repository

- SWT files for views contain **applet placeholders**

- An applet is **bound** to a placeholder by means of a **View Web Template Item**

Siebel Tools provides a graphical editor for views. Developers can arrange applets in the layout defined by the SWT file using familiar drag and drop techniques.

The following table describes the most important properties of the View object type:

Property	Description
Business Object	The name of the business object definition that provides the data context for the view.
Add To History	When set to **TRUE**, the view will be added to the browser history. When set to **FALSE**, the view will not appear in the browser history.
Admin Mode Flag	When set to **TRUE**, the view becomes an administration view, providing an extended range of privileges to the user, including full data access. When set to **FALSE**, the view is a standard view.
	Administration views are typically only made accessible to a small group of administrators. Using these views, administrators can for example verify data import processes.
Default Applet Focus	The name of the applet that should have UI focus when the view is loaded.
Thread Title	Static text that is displayed as the first part of an entry in the thread bar in the UI. The thread bar allows quick backward navigation.
Thread Applet	The name of an applet in the view. Any field of the business component of that applet can be used in the Thread Field property.
Thread Field	The name of a field in the thread applet's business component. The value of that field becomes the second part of the thread bar entry.
Visibility Applet	The name of an applet in the view. The business component of that applet will control the data visibility in the view. When a visibility applet is specified, the view is considered a **visibility context view** and links to it appear in the **visibility drop-down list** situated in the parent list applet. If no value is specified, the view is considered a detail view and links to it appear in the view tab bar.
Visibility Applet Type	Defines the level of data visibility from *personal* to *organization*. Data visibility, also known as **Access Control**, will be discussed in a later chapter.

Understanding screens

A screen is a container for views. The **Screen** object type contains one or more **Screen View** items, which define the list of views as well as their sequence, hierarchy, and captions for view tabs and site map entries in the UI.

The **site map** in the Siebel Web Client displays all views that are available to the current user. The views are arranged hierarchically for each screen as can be seen in the following screenshot, which shows the site map entry for the **Administration - Data Validation** screen as an example:

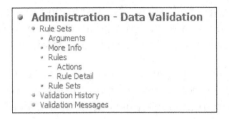

A screen is divided into three navigational levels:

- **Level 1: Aggregate categories** (for example **Rule Sets** in the preceding screenshot). An aggregate category can contain one or more aggregate views, detail categories, or detail views.

- **Level 1 and 2: Aggregate views** (for example **Validation History** in the preceding screenshot). When an aggregate view is situated in the first level of a screen it is displayed as a link underneath the screen bar. When an aggregate view is part of an aggregate category, it can be accessed by the visibility drop-down list in the upper list applet of the view.

- **Level 2: Detail categories** (for example **Rules** in the preceding screenshot). Detail categories are optional. Detail views such as the **More Info** view in the above screenshot can exist at this level as well.

- **Level 2 and 3: Detail views** (for example **Rule Detail** in the preceding screenshot). If a detail view is a member of a detail category, it is displayed at the lowest navigational level as a link underneath the view bar.

The following graphic illustrates this concept:

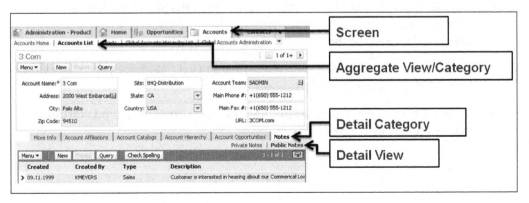

When end users click on a tab in the **screen bar** the application navigates to the view which is defined as the screen's **default view** in the Siebel Repository. The **link bar** below the screen tab allows end users to access aggregate views or aggregate categories.

The **view bar**, typically displayed below the first applet in a view, allows access to detail views or detail categories. When a detail category is opened, a **link bar** appears below the view bar, providing links to the detail views.

Developers can view and modify the sequence of views in a screen in the **Screen View Sequence Editor** in Siebel Tools. To open the editor, we can right-click the screen object definition in the object list editor and select **Edit Screen View Sequence**. The following screenshot shows the **Administration - Rule Sets** screen in the **Screen View Sequence Editor** in Siebel Tools:

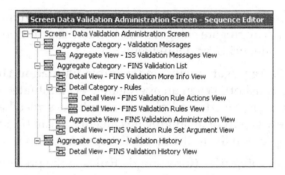

The first part of the captions (to the left of the hyphen) in the sequence editor is the type of the screen view object.

View web templates

Siebel CRM provides many pre-built web templates for views. These templates are described in the *Siebel Developer's Reference* guide in the Siebel bookshelf documentation library. The list of view templates for employee-facing applications such as Siebel Call Center can be found at the following URL:

```
http://download.oracle.com/docs/cd/E14004_01/books/ToolsDevRef/
ToolsDevRef_EmployeeTemplates50.html
```

The **View Detail** template is most commonly used and serves as a good starting point when we create new views.

Creating and modifying views

Siebel Tools provides developers with the **New View wizard** to quickly create views. The **View Editor** allows us to inspect and modify existing views. We will use both utilities in the following section. The high level process of creating a new view can be laid out as follows:

- Create the view using the New View wizard
- Arrange the applets on the view layout as needed
- Set the applet mode property as needed
- Set the thread bar properties
- Add the view to a screen
- Compile all new and modified repository objects
- Register the view in the web client
- Associate the view with one or more responsibilities
- Test the view

Case study example: Ceating a new view

In *Chapter 5*, we introduced the requirements around the new **AHA Customer Process Start View** and created a form and a list applet to be placed in that view. The basic view layout has been designed by the business analyst team as shown in the following diagram:

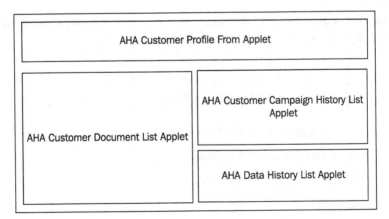

AHA Customer Profile From Applet

AHA Customer Document List Applet

AHA Customer Campaign History List Applet

AHA Data History List Applet

As we have only created two applets so far, we will use preconfigured applets to occupy the placeholders of the missing applets. The **AHA Customer Document List Applet** as well as the necessary business layer objects to support the **AHA Data History List Applet** will be created during case study examples in later chapters.

Creating a view using the new view wizard

To create the new view we can follow this procedure:

1. Click the **New** button in the toolbar. Alternatively select **New Object...** from the **File** menu.

2. In the **General** tab of the **New Object Wizards** selection dialog, double-click the **View** icon.

3. In the first page of the wizard enter the following information:

    °   **Project**: AHA User Interface
    °   **Name**: AHA Customer Process Start View
    °   **Title**: Customer Process Start
    °   **Business Object**: Account
    °   **Upgrade Behavior**: Preserve

4. Click **Next**.

5. In the **View Web Layout - Select Template** page select the **View Detail** web template.

6. Click **Next**.

7. In the **Web Layout - Applets** page use the arrow button pointing to the **Selected Applets** list to select the following applets:

    [Note: We will add one applet later for demonstration purposes.]

    °   AHA Customer Profile Form Applet
    °   Account Contact List Applet
    °   Account Category List Applet

8. Click **Next**.

9. Click **Finish**.

10. The layout of the new view is automatically displayed in the **View Editor**.

The New View wizard places the applets on the first available placeholders beginning from the top of the template. These placeholders use the entire width of the screen. We must modify the view layout to conform to the requirements from the business analyst team where only the top form applet should consume the entire screen width and the other applets should use only half of the screen width.

Modifying a view in the view web layout editor

The following procedure explains how to move applets to different placeholders in the view editor:

1. Drag the **Account Contact List Applet** from its current position (below the form applet) and drop it on the first placeholder that consumes only the left half of the view area. This placeholder is situated on the bottom of the layout, so we have to move the mouse cursor below the lower edge of the editor to scroll down while dragging.

2. Repeat the previous step for the **Account Category List Applet**, dropping it on the first placeholder that consumes only the right half of the view area.

3. Save all changes.

Adding applets to a view in the view web layout editor

The following procedure describes how to add an applet to an existing view. We will use the AHA Customer Process Start View for illustration and add the **Account Activity List Applet**.

1. From the **Applets** window, drag the **List Applet** icon to the placeholder below the **Account Category List Applet** and drop it there.

2. In the **Pick Record** dialog box, select **Name** in the **Find** field and type **Account Act*** in the **Starting with** field.

3. Click the **Go** button.

4. Select the **Account Activity List Applet** in the list and click the **Pick** button.

5. Save all changes.

Setting the applet mode property

The **Applet Mode** property of a **View Web Template Item** controls which of the available layout modes of an applet is initially displayed when the view is loaded.

The following procedure describes how to set the applet mode property for the AHA **Customer Process Start View**:

1. In the **View Web Layout Editor**, select the **Account Category List Applet**.
2. Right-click the applet and select **View Properties Window**.
3. In the **Properties** window, set the **Applet Mode** property to **Edit List**.
4. Repeat steps 1 to 3 for the **Account Activity List Applet**.
5. Save all changes.
6. Close the editor window.
7. Compile the **AHA Customer Process Start View**.

A Siebel Tools archive file (AHA Customer Process Start View.sif) is available with this chapter's code files. The file represents the AHA Customer Process Start View after the changes in the preceding sections.

Setting the thread bar properties of a view

The thread bar properties control the text that is displayed in the link bar on top of a view that documents the drilldown path that the end user has chosen to navigate. Clicking an item in the thread bar allows the end user to quickly navigate back to previous steps or the beginning of the drilldown path.

Configuring the thread bar properties of a view is discussed in *Chapter 14*.

Did you know?

Using the **Tools | Utilities | Export View Previews** command, we can create a set of HTML files that can be used for proofreading the view and applet layout early in the development process.

The export feature however does not distinguish the applet layout for different applications, indicated by the **Expression** property of the Applet Web Template Items, and therefore renders form applets distorted when these applets use the Expression property.

Adding a view to a screen

To be able to test the view in the Mobile or Developer Web Client, we must add it to a screen and register it with at least one of the responsibilities we hold. We will describe these processes in this and the following section.

The following procedure explains how to add the **AHA Customer Process Start View** to the **Accounts** screen:

1. Navigate to the **Accounts Screen** object definition in the **Object List Editor**.

2. Check out or lock the Accounts Screen.

3. Expand the Screen object type in the **Object Explorer** and select the **Screen View** object type.

4. In the list of screen view object definitions, use *Ctrl+N* to create a new record.

5. Set the following properties (using the *Tab* key to navigate to the right in the list):

    ° **View**: AHA Customer Process Start View

    ° **Parent Category**: Account List

    ° **Viewbar Text - String Override**: Process Start Page

    ° **Menu Text - String Override**: Process Start Page

6. Right-click the **Accounts Screen** object definition in the upper list and select **Edit Screen View Sequence**.

7. In the **Sequence Editor** select the **AHA Customer Process Start View**.

8. Use the *Ctrl+*down arrow keyboard shortcut to move the **AHA Customer Process Start view** below the **Account Detail View**.

9. Click the **Save** button in the toolbar.

10. Close the **Sequence Editor** window.

11. Compile the **Accounts Screen**.

A Siebel Tools archive file (Accounts Screen.sif) is available with this chapter's code files. The file represents the Accounts Screen after the changes in the preceding section.

Registering a new view

The process of registering a view is executed in the **Administration - Application** screen in the Siebel Web Client. The following procedure describes how to register and test the AHA Customer Process Start View. Note that during the process we will create a new responsibility named **AHA Prototype**, which will hold all new views created in the case study examples. This is a typical procedure during early development phases and only needs to be carried out once:

1. In Siebel Tools, copy the name of the view (AHA Customer Process Start View) to the **clipboard**.

2. Ensure that all new and modified object definitions (screens, views, and applets) are compiled to the local client's SRF file.

3. Start the **Siebel Mobile Web Client** and log in with your developer account to the local database. When you use the Siebel Sample Database, log in as SADMIN.

4. Navigate to the **Site Map**.

5. Navigate to **Administration - Application | Responsibilities**.

6. In the **Responsibilities** list, create a new record and enter AHA Prototype as the name.

7. In the **Users** list in the lower-right corner of the view, click the **Add** button.

8. Select your own user account from the pick list.

9. Click **OK**.

10. Navigate to **Administration - Applications | Views**.

 The **Views** link is located in the drop-down list at the right end of the link bar below the screen bar.

11. In the **Views** list, create a new record.

12. Paste the view name from the clipboard in the **View Name** field.

13. Enter AHA UI Prototype in the **Description** field.

14. In the **Responsibilities** list, in the lower half of the view, click the **New** button.

15. In the **Add Responsibilities** dialog, use the **Starting with** field and the **Go** button to find the **AHA Prototype** responsibility.

16. Click the **OK** button to associate the **AHA Prototype** responsibility with the **AHA Customer Process Start View**.

17. From the application menu, select **File > Log Out** to log out of the application.

Two ADM data files (`Chapter_6_View.xml` and `Chapter_6_Responsibility.xml`) are provided with this chapter's code files. The files represent the registered AHA Customer Process Start View and the AHA Prototype responsibility after the changes in the preceding section. Please refer to the instructions in *Appendix B* for how to import ADM data files. The file `Chapter_6_View.xml` must be imported first.

Testing a new view

Developers must ensure that the new view can be loaded without errors. In addition, developers should execute typical data operations such as inserting new records and navigating between records to verify that the view behaves as intended. This is commonly known as a **unit test**.

The following procedure describes the unit test cycle for a new Siebel view using the new AHA Customer Process Start View as an example:

1. Log in to the Siebel Mobile Web Client.

2. Navigate to the **Site Map**.

3. Navigate to the **Accounts** screen.

4. Scroll down until you find the entry labeled **Process Start Page**. (This is the text entered as the **Menu Text**. Entries in the Site Map are sorted alphabetically.)

Did you know?
You can use the browser's text search feature to find entries in the site map. To open the text search dialog in Internet Explorer, click the **Find (on This Page)...** item in the **browser's Edit** menu.

5. Click the **Process Start Page** entry in the site map.

6. Verify that the view is loaded without errors and displays the form applet on top and the three list applets side by side below the view tab bar.

7. Click the **Show More** button in the upper form applet. Verify that all controls appear.

8. Click **New** in the form applet and enter an arbitrary name (for example **AHA Test Account 1**) for a test account.

9. Scroll down to the **Activities** list and create a new record for testing purposes.

10. Create a second test account.

11. Navigate back to the first test account and verify that all associated records appear.

12. Delete the test data if necessary.

If you followed the procedures in this chapter you may want to compare your work with the following screenshot:

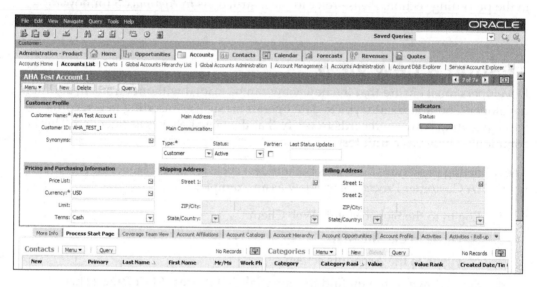

The screenshot only shows the upper half of the new view.

Summary

Views are the major user interface element of Siebel CRM applications. They serve as a container for applets and support the end users in their daily tasks by providing the functionality for the business process steps.

Screens define a hierarchical order of views so that end users can quickly navigate from one view to the other if needed.

In this chapter, we discussed how to create and modify views, add them to a screen, and register them with a responsibility in the Siebel Client.

In the next chapter, we will learn how to configure business components and their fields.

7

Business Components and Fields

Business Components and their child object types such as **Fields** and **Joins** constitute the focal point of the **Siebel business logic layer**. In this chapter, we will introduce the concepts of business components as well as techniques to implement business components and define the required business logic.

The chapter is structured as follows:

- Understanding Business Components
- Creating Joins and Fields
- Controlling Field Level behavior
- Controlling Business Component behavior

Understanding business components

A business component definition represents a single business entity such as the customer, the products that a company sells, and the orders that customers make. When solution architects design business models they often use **entity relationship diagrams (ERDs)** to describe entities and their relationships to each other. The following diagram is an example for an ERD:

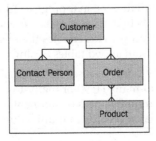

The diagram defines the entities *Customer*, *Contact Person*, *Order*, and *Product*. The **crow's feet** endpoints of the lines between the entity shapes represent a **to many** relationship. A customer can be associated with multiple contact persons while the same person can be associated with multiple customers. Relationships of this type are called many-to-many (M:M) and the typical graphical representation is a line with a **crow's foot** at each end. The preceding diagram also defines that a customer can place one or more orders each of which can consist of multiple products.

When the previous simplistic business model would have to be implemented in Siebel CRM, a technical analyst would map each entity to existing business components in the Siebel Repository. When an appropriate business component does not exist, the technical analyst would define a business component to be created.

Did you know?

Siebel Tools provides a graphical Entity Relationship Diagram designer, which can be used by business analysts or solution architects to create ERDs and map the entities and attributes to existing business components and fields.

The Business Component type defines a set of child object types, which are described in the following table:

Child Object Type	Description
Field	Fields define the attributes of the business entity implemented by their parent business component. Examples for fields are the first or last name of a person. **Single Value Fields (SVF)** map to columns in database tables or can be calculated at runtime. **Multi Value Fields (MVF)** map to fields in other business components. A field definition has many properties that control its runtime behavior. These properties will be discussed in detail in this chapter.
	Calculated fields use the **Siebel Query Language** to derive a value from calculation expressions or other fields. It is important to understand that calculated fields may have a negative impact on application performance.
Join	Joins define the mappings to additional tables that contain records that are in a many-to-one (M:1) relationship with the base record. This enables the business component to display data from joined tables as single value fields.
Multi Value Link (MVL)	A MVL defines a secondary business component that is in a one-to-many (1:M) or many-to-many (M:M) relationship with its parent business component. MVLs allow the display of a set of related records in multi value fields.

Child Object Type	Description
BusComp View Mode	This specialized object type defines the filters for data access control (*also known as visibility*). The concept of data access control will be discussed in a separate chapter.
Business Component User Prop	User properties allow developers to define advanced runtime behavior. The availability of user properties is defined by the business component's class. User properties will be discussed in a separate chapter.
Business Component Server Script	A business component has multiple event handlers where developers can place custom scripts. The concept of scripting will be discussed in a separate chapter.

The following diagram depicts the hierarchy of business component child object types and their relationships to other major object types in the Siebel Repository.

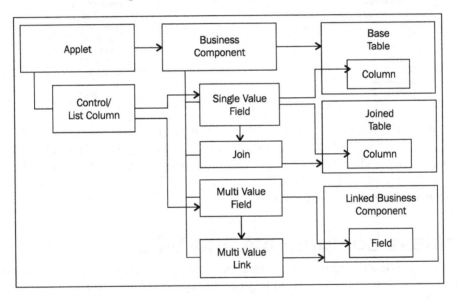

We can see that a business component references one base table and multiple joined tables as well as other business components. Single value fields can reference columns of the base table directly or use a join definition to reference columns in joined tables. Multi value fields use multi value link definitions to reference fields in linked business components. From the discussion of the Siebel Repository metadata model in *Chapter 1* we know that one business component can be accessed by multiple applets.

Visualizing business component definitions

The **View Details** window in Siebel Tools is a useful utility and provides insight into the mapping of the business component's single value fields to columns in the base and joined tables as well as the mapping of the multi value fields to fields in linked business components. We can open the **View Details** window by right-clicking a business component definition in the **Object List Editor** and selecting **View Details** from the menu.

The following screenshot shows a portion of the **View Details** window for the **Loc Mgmt - Location** business component, which implements venue locations:

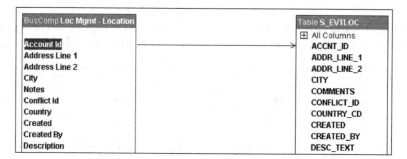

The **View Details** window allows selecting of the business component, the tables, and the joins (not visible in the screenshot) as well as the fields and columns. The **Properties** window displays the properties of the selected item. An arrow indicates the mapping of a selected field to either a column in a base or joined table or to a field in a linked business component.

Business components and SQL

The metadata defined by business components is interpreted by the Siebel executable at runtime and is used to dynamically generate SQL statements, which are issued to the underlying relational database.

The following simple scenario uses fields of the **Service Request** business component to illustrate how the Siebel executable generates the necessary SELECT statement to query for service request data in the database.

The following fields, shown in a partial screenshot of the **Service Request Detail Applet**, are used for the scenario:

- **SR Number**
- **Contact Id** (not shown in the applet)
- **Contact Last Name**

- **Contact First Name**

The **Contact Id** field is not visible in the user interface but defined by the **Join Specification** object associated with the **Join** object, which is used to fetch data about the contact person for the service request.

The mapping from the applet controls to business component fields and from there to columns in tables in the database can be described with the following table:

Applet Control Caption	Business Component Field	Table	Column
SR #	SR Number	S_SRV_REQ (Base Table)	SR_NUM
(Field not exposed in applet)	Contact Id	S_SRV_REQ (Base Table)	CST_CON_ID
Last Name	Contact Last Name	S_CONTACT	LAST_NAME
First Name	Contact First Name	S_CONTACT	FST_NAME

The following pseudo SELECT statement would be generated if only these fields would have to be fetched for display. Comments are used to describe the location in the Siebel Repository where the information for the SELECT statement comes from.

```
SELECT
S_SRV_REQ.SR_NUM,            //Field: SR Number
S_CONTACT.LAST_NAME,         //Field: Contact Last Name
S_CONTACT.FST_NAME           //Field: Contact First Name
FROM
S_SRV_REQ,                   //Property: (Base) Table
S_CONTACT                    //Join: S_CONTACT
WHERE
S_SRV_REQ.CST_CON_ID =       //Join Specification: Source Field
S_CONTACT.PAR_ROW_ID         //Join Specification: Destination Column
```

From the preceding pseudo SELECT statement, we can learn that a **Join** defines the name of the **table** to join while the associated **Join Specification** defines the **columns** that should be matched in the WHERE clause of the statement.

The following screenshot shows the **S_CONTACT** Join and its associated Join Specification used in the previous example:

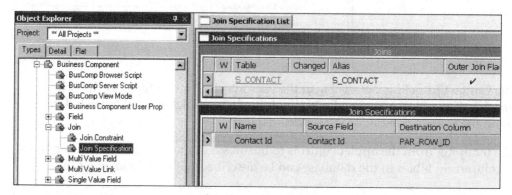

The Join Specification references the **Source Field (Contact Id)**, which maps to the **CST_CON_ID** foreign key column in the **S_SRV_REQ** table. The **Destination Column** property contains the name of the column (**PAR_ROW_ID**) in the joined table (**S_CONTACT**), which will be used in the WHERE clause to match with the column referenced by the source field.

Creating joins and fields

A **Single Value Field** can be mapped either to a column in the business component's base table, specified by the **Table** property of the business component, or to a column in a joined table. In addition, we can use the **Siebel Query Language** syntax to create calculated fields.

In this section, we will use a scenario from the case study introduced in *Chapter 3, Case Study Introduction* to demonstrate how to create single value fields.

Case study example: Displaying data from joined tables

As stated in the requirements list in *Chapter 3*, the customer wishes to display the full name of the person who committed the last update on a record as a link that opens an e-mail form. The following procedure describes how to implement this requirement for the **Service Request** business component.

Case study example: Creating a join

In order to implement the preceding requirement, we must start with creating a new **Join** object definition in the **Service Request** business component. The Join and its Join Specification will provide the necessary metadata information to get the first and last name of the user who last updated the record from the S_CONTACT table:

1. Navigate to the **Service Request** business component.

2. Check out or lock the **Service Request** business component.

3. In the **Object Explorer** window, expand the **Business Component** type and select the **Join** type.

4. Use the *Ctrl+N* keyboard shortcut to create a new Join definition.

5. Enter the following values in the **Object List Editor** columns:
    - **Table**: S_CONTACT
    - **Alias**: AHA Updated By - S_CONTACT
    - **Outer Join Flag**: Checked
    - **Comments**: Created for AHA prototype

6. In the **Object Explorer** window, expand the **Join** type and select the **Join Specification** type.

7. Use the *Ctrl+N* keyboard shortcut to create a new **Join Specification** definition.

8. Enter the following values in the **Object List Editor** columns:
    - **Name**: AHA Updated By
    - **Source Field**: Updated By
    - **Destination Column**: PAR_ROW_ID

Case study example: Creating single value fields

The following procedure describes how to create new fields in the Service Request business component to support the display of the first and last name of the person who last updated the service request. The new fields will use the join definition created in the previous section:

1. In the **Object Explorer**, select the **Business Component** type.

2. In the **Object List Editor**, query for the **Service Request** business component.

3. In the **Object Explorer**, expand the **Business Component** type and select the **Field** type.

4. Use the *Ctrl+N* keyboard shortcut to create a new **Field** definition.

5.   Enter the following values in the **Object List Editor** columns:
  ○   **Name:** AHA Updated By First Name
  ○   **Join:** AHA Updated By - S_CONTACT
  ○   **Column:** FST_NAME
  ○   **Comments:** Created for AHA prototype

6.   Create a second Field definition with the following values:
  ○   **Name:** AHA Updated By Last Name
  ○   **Join:** AHA Updated By - S_CONTACT
  ○   **Column:** LAST_NAME
  ○   **Comments:** Created for AHA prototype

7.   Create a third Field definition to get the e-mail address of the person:
  ○   **Name:** AHA Updated By Email Address
  ○   **Join:** AHA Updated By - S_CONTACT
  ○   **Column:** EMAIL_ADDR
  ○   **Comments:** Created for AHA prototype

Case study example: Creating calculated fields

The AHA business analyst team has defined the following requirements, which can be fulfilled by using calculated fields:

• Business users wish to display the full name of the person who last updated a service request record in a single text field. Clicking the name of the person should open an e-mail form.

• The Indicators form section in the **AHA Customer Profile Form Applet**, created in *Chapter 5*, should show the number of open service requests and the number of campaign contacts in active campaigns for the customer.

The following procedures describe how to use the **Siebel Query Language** and its calculation expressions to implement these requirements. We will inspect the functionality provided by the Siebel Query Language in more detail later in this chapter.

Using a calculation expression to create an e-mail link

1. Navigate to the **Service Request** business component.

2. In the **Object Explorer** window, expand the **Business Component** type and select the **Field** type.

3. In the **Fields** list, create a new record and enter the following values:

    -   **Name**: AHA Updated By Full Name Mailto
    -   **Calculated**: Checked
    -   **Comments**: Created for AHA prototype
    -   **Calculated Value**: "<a href=mailto:" + [AHA Updated By Email Address] + ">" + [AHA Updated By First Name] + " " + [AHA Updated By Last Name] + "</a>"

By clicking the ellipsis icon (three dots) in the **Calculated Value** column, we can access the **Expression Editor** which should be our favorite location, to select fields from the **Elements** list rather than typing the expression. The following screenshot shows the Expression Editor with the value for the new calculated field:

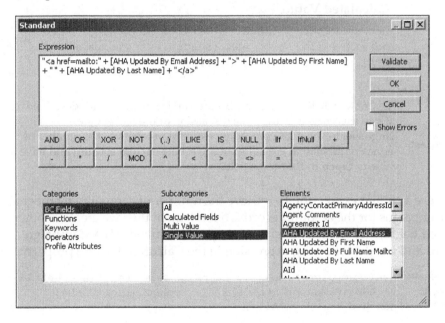

The expression uses the plus (+) sign to concatenate HTML text snippets with the values of the newly created fields in order to fulfill the requirement of allowing end users to click on the name of the person to send an e-mail.

A Siebel Tools archive file (`Service Request BC.sif`) is available in this chapter's code file. The file represents the Service Request business component after the changes made in the previous sections.

Using calculation expressions to show the number of related records

The following procedure describes how to create a calculated field which implements the requirements for showing the number of open service requests and campaign members for a customer:

1. Navigate to the Account business component.

2. Create a new calculated field for the Account business component and enter the following values:

   - **Name**: AHA Issue Indicator
   - **Calculated**: Checked
   - **Comments**: Created for AHA prototype
   - **Calculated Value**:
     ```
     GetNumBCRows("Account","Service Request","[Account
     Id]='" + [Id] + "' AND [Status]='" + LookupValue('SR_
     STATUS','Open') + "'","All")
     ```

 The GetNumBCRows() and LookupValue() functions are described later in this chapter during the discussion of the Siebel Query Language. In short, the preceding expression retrieves the number of service requests that are associated with the current account and have a value of **Open** in the Status field.

We can use a similar expression to retrieve the number of campaign members in active campaigns for the account record. To implement this, we create another calculated field in the **Account** business component named **AHA Campaign Indicator** and use the following expression in the **Calculated Value** property:

```
GetNumBCRows("Campaign Members","Campaign Members","[Account Id]='"
+ [Id] + "' AND [Campaign Status]='" + LookupValue('CAMPAIGN_
STATE','Launched') + "'","All")
```

The expression retrieves the number of people that are associated with the current account and are in the target member list of any campaign that has a status of **Launched** (which indicates that the campaign is active).

After the changes we must compile the Account business component.

A Siebel Tools archive file (`AccountBC.sif`) is available in this chapter's code file. The file represents the Account business component after the changes made in the preceding section.

Case study example: Exposing a new field in an applet

To test the modifications at the business component layer we must expose the new calculated fields in the presentation layer.

The following procedure outlines the steps to modify the **Service Request Detail Applet** in order to show the new calculated field for the e-mail link:

1. Navigate to the **Service Request Detail Applet**.

2. Check out or lock the **Service Request Detail Applet** if necessary.

3. Right-click the **Service Request Detail Applet** and select **Edit Web Layout**.

4. In the **Controls/Columns** window, select the **active Edit** mode template.

5. Drag and drop a **Field** item from the **Palettes** window below the **First Name** field.

6. Enter the following values in the **Properties** window:

   ◦ **Name:** AHA Updated By Full Name Mailto

   ◦ **Comments:** Created for AHA prototype

   ◦ **Caption:** Last Updated By

   ◦ **Field:** AHA Updated By Full Name Mailto

   ◦ **HTML Display Mode:** DontEncodeData

   ◦ **HTML Type:** PlainText

   By setting the **HTML Display Mode** property to **DontEncodeData** we ensure that the HTML string generated by the calculated field is rendered as a link in the browser. Setting the **HTML Type** property to **PlainText** ensures that the value is displayed as a text string in the form applet.

7. Drag the accompanying **label** item (named **AHA Updated By Full Name Mail to Label**) from the **Controls/Columns** window to the left of the new control.

8. Save all changes.

9. Close the applet editor.

10. Compile the **Service Request Detail Applet**.

11. Compile the **Service Request** business component.

12. Log on to the Siebel Developer/Mobile Web Client and navigate to the **Service Requests screen**.

13. Navigate to the **My Service Requests** view.

14. Create a test record if needed.

15. Verify that the name of the person who did the last update appears and that it is rendered as a **mailto** link.

 To successfully verify the configuration, the test user must have an e-mail address.

The following screenshot shows the new control in the Service Request Detail Applet. The browser status bar showing the **mailto** link is also visible.

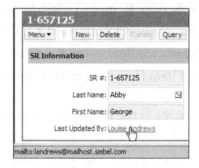

A Siebel Tools archive file (`Service Request Detail Applet.sif`) is available in this chapter's code file. The file represents the Service Request Detail Applet after the changes made in the preceding section.

The procedure to expose the new indicator fields in the **Account** business component in the **AHA Customer Profile Form Applet** is similar to the preceding description and is therefore not laid out in detail.

The following screenshot shows the **Indicators** form section of the AHA Customer Profile Form Applet after the modification.

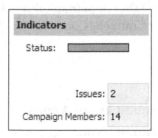

A Siebel Tools archive file (AHA Customer Profile Form Applet.sif) is available in this chapter's code file. The file represents the AHA Customer Profile Form Applet after the changes made in the preceding section.

Controlling field level behavior

There are many additional properties of a Field object that drive its behavior at runtime. The following table describes the most important Field properties:

Field Property	Description
Join	References a Join object definition to use for a single value field. If this property is empty and the field is neither a calculated nor a multi value field, the base table of the business component is used by the field.
Column	The column in the joined or base table to which the single value field refers.
Calculated	When set to TRUE, the field is a calculated field and must have an expression in the **Calculated Value** property. Examples for calculated fields have been provided earlier in this chapter.
Calculated Value	The expression to be computed for a calculated field.
Disable Sort	When set to **TRUE**, sorting on the field is not possible.
Force Active	When set to **TRUE**, the SQL statement generated at runtime will always include the column referenced by the field regardless of it being exposed by the applet or not. Setting this property to TRUE negatively affects the application performance.
Force Case	When set to **UPPER**, all characters entered in the field are converted to uppercase. When set to **LOWER**, all characters are converted to lowercase. A value of **FIRSTUPPER** results in each first character of a word being converted to uppercase.
Pre Default Value	A value (or expression) that is applied as the initial field value when a new record is created.
Post Default Value	A value (or expression) that is applied when a new record is saved and no value has been entered into the field.
Read Only	When set to **TRUE**, the field is write-protected.
Required	When set to **TRUE**, a value must be provided for the field. Form applets exposing this field will display a red asterisk in the control label text.
Type	The logical data type for the field. An example value is **DTYPE_BOOL**, which interprets a single character column with a value of Y as true and a value of N as false.

Field Property	Description
Validation	An expression that defines a validation rule to be applied when the record is saved.
Validation Message-String Reference	A reference to a Symbolic String definition that carries the translatable text to be displayed when the expression in the Validation property evaluates to FALSE.
PickList	A reference to a Pick List definition that implements the available values for the field. Pick Lists are discussed in a later chapter.

Case study example: Field properties

As outlined in *Chapter 3*, All Hardware (AHA) requires that key attributes of customer, quote, and order data should be validated. In addition, the price list field for a quote or order must not be empty.

The validation rules for customer attributes are described by the AHA business analyst team in the following table.

Field	Validation	Message to be displayed
Customer Name	Must be at least three characters long.	Please enter at least three characters for the customer name.
Founded Date	Must be in the past or set to the current day.	Please enter a valid date in the Founded Date field.

The following procedures describe how to fulfill the requirements described previously.

Creating translatable validation messages

To support localization of the validation message text, we should create Symbolic Strings first.

1. If necessary, create a new project **named AHA Symbolic** Strings and lock it.

2. In the **Object Explorer**, select the **Symbolic String** type. (If it is not visible, use the **Object Explorer** tab in the **Siebel Tools Options** dialog to make it visible.)

3. In the **Object List Editor**, create a new record and provide the following values:

   ○ **Name:** X_AHA_VALIDATION_ACCOUNT_NAME

   ○ **Project:** AHA Symbolic Strings

4. In the **Object Explorer**, expand the **Symbolic String** type and select the **Symbolic String Locale** type.

5. Create a new record in the lower list and enter the following values:

   ○ **Language:** ENU

   ○ **String Value:** Please enter at least three characters for the customer name

6. Repeat steps 3 to 5 to create another Symbolic String definition with the name X_AHA_VALIDATION_ACCOUNT_FOUNDED_DATE, which implements the message for the Founded Date field.

A Siebel Tools archive file (Symbolic Strings.sif) is available in this chapter's code file. The file represents the symbolic string definitions created in the preceding section.

Implementing field validation

The following procedure describes how to set the **Validation** property for the Name field of the Account business component:

1. In the **Object Explorer**, select the **Business Component** type.

2. Query for the **Account** business component in the list.

3. Check out or lock the **Account** business component if necessary.

4. In the **Object Explorer**, expand the **Business Component** type and select the **Field** type.

5. Query for the **Name** field in the lower list.

6. Enter the following values in the list editor:

   ○ **Validation:** Len([Name])>=3

   ○ **Validation Message - String Reference:** X_AHA_VALIDATION_ACCOUNT_NAME

7. Compile the **Account** business component.

We can repeat the preceding procedure for the Date Formed field of the Account business component. In order to ensure that only the current date or dates in the past are entered, we must set the **Validation** property to `<=Today()`. The **Validation Message - String Reference** property should be set to `X_AHA_VALIDATION_ACCOUNT_FOUNDED_DATE`.

To test the changes, we launch the Siebel Mobile or Developer Web Client and navigate to the **More Info** view in the **Accounts** screen. There we create a new test record with a name which only has two characters. Attempting to save the record should result in an error message showing the text we defined in the symbolic string value.

The **Founded** date field is situated in the large applet on the lower half of the **More Info** view. Any attempt to enter a future date and save the record should result in an error message as well.

A Siebel Tools archive file (`Account BC.sif`) is available in this chapter's code file. The file represents the Account business component after the changes made in the previous section.

Case study example: Creating a required field

The following procedure describes how to fulfill the requirement for not allowing the **Price List field** of the Quote business component to be empty by setting the **Required** property of the field to TRUE.

1. Navigate to the **Quote** business component.
2. Check out or lock the **Quote** business component.
3. Navigate to the **Price List** field.
4. In the **Properties** window, set the **Required** property to **TRUE**.
5. Compile the **Quote** business component.

To test the preceding change, we can start the Siebel Mobile or Developer Web Client and navigate to the **Quotes** screen. The form applet in the **My Quotes** view should now display a **red asterisk** in the label caption of the **Price List** control, which indicates that Price List is now a required field. Any attempt to save a quote record without a price list should result in an error message.

A Siebel Tools archive file (`Quote BC.sif`) is available in this chapter's code file. The file represents the Quote business component after the changes made in the preceding section.

The Siebel Query Language

The syntax for expressions in calculated fields and validations that were used in the previous example procedures is based on the **Siebel Query Language**, an expression language that is used in many locations in Siebel CRM.

The following table describes the locations in Siebel Tools where the Siebel Query Language can be used:

Location	Description
Queries	The name-determining application for the Siebel Query Language. The functions and operators of the Siebel Query Language can be used to query for data in both Siebel Client and Siebel Tools.
Business Component/ Applet: Search Specification	Search Specifications define filter criteria for applets and business components.
Calculated fields	As described in the previous example procedures, the Siebel Query Language provides many functions and operators for creating calculation expressions.
Field: Pre Default and Post Default properties	When default values for fields should be generated dynamically using the Siebel Query Language, we must prefix the expression with the keyword **Expr:** followed by a space. The expression itself must be enclosed in single quotes.
Field: Validation property	As described in the previous example procedures, Siebel Query Language syntax can be used to construct validation expressions.
User properties	User properties allow developers to add extended business logic to various object definitions such as business components and fields. Many user properties support the Siebel Query Language. User properties will be discussed in a separate chapter.
Expressions in workflow processes and tasks	Developers can use the capabilities of the Siebel Query Language to process data in workflow processes and task flows. Workflow processes and tasks will be discussed in separate chapters of this book.

The following client-based modules of Siebel CRM also make extended use of the Siebel Query Language:

- Predefined Queries
- Personalization
- Runtime Events

- State Models
- Data Validation Manager
- EAI Data Maps
- iHelp

We can find the full documentation of the Siebel Query Language in the **Siebel Developer's Reference** document, which can be found in the Oracle Siebel CRM online documentation. Version 8.1 of this document can be found at the following URL: `http://download.oracle.com/docs/cd/E14004_01/books/ToolsDevRef/booktitle.html`.

The Developer's Reference and other guides are also available in the Siebel Tools online help from the **Contents** command in the **Help** menu.

The **Functions in Calculation Expressions** section in the **Operators, Expressions and Conditions** chapter of the Siebel Developer's Reference guide describes all available functions of the Siebel Query Language.

The following table describes important functions of the Siebel Query Language and provides examples:

Function	Description	Example and Explanation
[Field reference]	We must use square brackets to reference business component fields.	[Id] References the business component's ID field.
Today()	Returns the current date.	Expr: 'Today() + 7' Can be used in a pre or post-default value to set a date field to one week (seven days) in the future by default.
Timestamp()	Returns the current date and time.	Expr: 'TimeStamp()' Often used to create pre-default values with the current date and time.
IIf(expression,return1,return2)	Returns the value of the return1 expression when the expression evaluates to TRUE. Otherwise, the value of the return2 expression is returned.	IIf([Ship Date]>Today(),0, Today()-[Ship Date]) If the shipping date is in the future, return 0 (zero), otherwise return the number of days between the shipping date and today.

Function	Description	Example and Explanation
ParentFieldValue (fieldname)	Returns the value of the field in the parent business component. The **Link Specification** property of the parent field must be set to **TRUE to** enable this functionality.	See next row for an example.
IfNull(expression1, expression2)	When expression1 returns a value other than NULL, the IfNull function returns the first expression's return value. Otherwise, the value of the second expression is returned.	`IfNull(ParentFieldValue ("Commit Time"),Timestamp())` Returns the value of the parent business component's *Commit Time* field. If that field is empty, the function returns the current date and time.
Len(text)	Returns the length of the text string. Other string manipulation functions include Left() and Right() to truncate strings.	`Len([Name])>=3` Can be used as a field validation expression to force users to enter at least three characters for the Name field. See the case study example earlier in this chapter.
+ (String Concatenation)	The plus (+) sign can be used to concatenate strings.	`[First Name] + " " + [Last Name]` Concatenates the value of the First Name field, a space character and the value of the Last Name field.
LookupValue(LOV_Type, Language Independent Code)	The Siebel Query Language supports various "Lookup" functions to query the List Of Values table. When a field references a Pick List definition, the LookupValue() function should always be used to avoid localization issues.	`LookupValue('SR_ STATUS','Open')` Returns the translated value for the user's current language of the "Open" entry in the *SR_STATUS* type of the **List Of Values** table.

Function	Description	Example and Explanation
GetNumBCRows(business object, business component, search expression, view mode)	Uses the search expression to query the business component in the business object context. The view mode parameter controls the level of access control (personal, team, organization). The function returns the number of records matching the search expression.	`GetNumBCRows("Ac count","Service Request"," [Account Id]='" + [Id] + "'","All")` The previous example has been implemented in a similar fashion earlier in this chapter. The Service Request business component (linked as a child in the Account business object) is queried for all records that have the value of the Account's **Id** field in their **Account Id** field. The search expression is concatenated using **double quotes** to separate strings and **single quotes** to be used inside the search string. The search expression for an example value of 1-2 for the Id field would evaluate to: *[Account Id]= '1-2'* The **All** view mode specifies that all records for which a valid owner is specified are retrieved regardless of organization visibility.
Julian calendar functions	Various functions starting with the name **Julian** allow developers to do calculations using the Julian Date format.	`JulianYear(Today())-4713` Calculates the current year number. The Julian calendar starts 4713 B.C. For the 1st of January 2011, the JulianYear function returns 6724 (the number of years since 4713 B.C. Subtracting 4713 from the return value yields the year number of the Gregorian calendar (2011).

Syntax for pre and post-default values

The syntax for supplying pre or post-default values for fields differs slightly from the other properties. The following table describes the most important concepts and enables us to set pre or post-default values correctly:

Scenario	Example and Explanation
Using expressions in Siebel Query Language	`Expr: 'Today() + 7'`
	Expressions in Siebel Query Language must be preceded by the keyword Expr followed by a colon and a space. The expression itself must be enclosed in single quotes.
	The previous example has been explained in a previous section.
Using values of other fields	`Field: 'Id'`
	We can provide the value of another single value field that does not use a join as a pre or post-default value. The keyword **Field** must be followed by a colon and a space. The field name must be enclosed in single quotes.
	The previous example passes the value of the Id field.
Using field values of parent business components	`Parent: 'Account.Id', 'Service Request.Account Id'`
	To use values of fields in parent business components, we must specify the Parent keyword (followed by a colon and a space) and provide a comma separated list of business component fields. The business component name and the field name are separated by a dot (*dot notation*).
	Previous example: When the current parent is the Account business component, the value of the Account's Id field is passed. When the parent business component is Service Request, the value of the Account Id field is passed.

Scenario	Example and Explanation
Using system properties	System: Creator
	To access values of system properties we can use the System keyword followed by a colon and a space. The name after the space can be one of the following reserved system properties:
	• **Creator** (returns the login name of the current user)
	• **CreatorId** (returns the unique Id of the current user)
	• **Currency** (returns the current division's currency code)
	• **LocalCurrency** (returns the currency of the local **machine)**
	• **OrganizationName** (returns the name of the user's current organization)
	• **OrganizationId** (returns the unique Id of the user's current organization)
	• **Position** (returns the name of the user's currently active position)
	• **PositionId** (returns the unique Id of the user's current position)
	• **Timestamp** (returns the current date and time)
	• **Today** (returns the current date)

It is important to consider that the data type of the field that defines the pre or post-default value must match the data type of the return value. For example, we can only use the System: Today pre-default value on a field that has a logical data type of **DTYPE_DATE** or one of the other date related data types.

Source: Siebel Developer's Reference Version 8.1

```
http://download.oracle.com/docs/cd/E14004_01/books/ToolsDevRef/
ToolsDevRef_Operators13.html
```

Using the Siebel Query Language

When we use the Siebel Query Language for calculated fields, default values, or other purposes, we must bear in mind that each calculation that the Siebel executable has to process decreases the application's performance. For example, when a list applet exposes a calculated field that uses the GetNumBCRows() function, an additional query is executed once for each record in the list. Depending on the amount of records in the respective database tables, this could dramatically increase the load time of the view.

We must therefore consider each additional calculation expression very carefully and design our solutions **with performance in mind**.

Controlling business component behavior

When we inspect business component definitions in the Siebel Repository we find that the runtime behavior of a business component is defined by a set of properties. The most important properties are described in the following table.

Property	Description
Table	The name of the base table of the business component. Fields of the business component can reference columns in the base table without the need for a join.
Search Specification	A filter definition—in Siebel Query Language—that is used to fetch only a subset of records from the database.
Sort Specification	A comma separated list of field names and the sort order in which the data should be sorted when the business component queries the database.
No Delete	When set to **TRUE**, records cannot be deleted by this business component.
No Insert	When set to **TRUE**, no new records can be inserted by this business component.
No Merge	When set to **TRUE**, the merge functionality is not available in this business component.
No Update	When set to **TRUE**, updates to existing records are not possible.
Owner Delete	When set to **TRUE**, only the owner of a record (the person who holds the primary position on the Team field) can delete it.
Class	The C++ class behind the business component defines the base functionality. Some business components use specialized classes. The class property must not be changed by customers.

Case study example: Business component properties

As described in *Chapter 3*, one of the requirements for All Hardware's Siebel CRM implementation is to provide secure read-only access to customer, address, and order data for external systems.

The AHA business analyst team has identified the following business component definitions that implement these three entities:

- Account
- CUT Address
- Order Entry-Orders

The following procedure describes how we can copy existing object definitions and modify the copies to create customer-owned business components for special purposes. This process is often referred to as **cloning**. The example procedure uses the Account business component to illustrate the process, which is similar for all other business components.

1. Create a new project named AHA Business Components and lock it.
2. Navigate to the **Account** business component.
3. Use the *Ctrl+B* keyboard shortcut to copy the **Account** business component.

> This is a *deep* copy that includes all child object definitions and takes a while.

4. Modify the copy by entering the following values in the **Object List Editor**.
   - **Name**: AHA Account Read Only
   - **Comment**: Created for AHA Prototype; Copy of Account BC
   - **Project**: AHA Business Components
   - **Upgrade Ancestor**: Account (see the following for details on the Upgrade Ancestor property)
5. Set the following values in the **Properties** window to disallow all data operations except queries on the **AHA Account Read Only** business component:
   - **No Delete: TRUE**
   - **No Insert: TRUE**
   - **No Merge: TRUE**
   - **No Update: TRUE**
6. Compile the AHA Account Read Only business component.
7. Repeat steps 2 to 6 for the CUT Address and Order Entry-Orders business component. Rename the copies to **AHA CUT Address Read Only** and **AHA Order Entry - Orders Read Only**.

Siebel Tools archive files representing the three new business component definitions (AHA Account Read Only BC.sif, AHA CUT Address Read Only BC.sif, and AHA Order Entry - Orders Read Only BC.sif) are available in this chapter's code file.

Did you know?

The **Upgrade Ancestor** property references the original object definition and should be used when an object defined by Oracle engineering (a **standard** object) is copied and the project team wishes that changes made by Oracle engineering to the ancestor are propagated to the clone during the process of upgrading to a newer version of Siebel CRM.

There may be circumstances where this behavior is not desirable, so setting the Upgrade Ancestor property for every cloned object without prior consideration may not be the best idea.

By setting the four properties starting with **No** in step 5 of the preceding procedure to **TRUE** we prohibit delete, insert, merge, and update operations on any record accessed by the new business component thus creating a read-only version of the Account business component.

Summary

Business components and their child object definitions such as joins and fields are among the most important members of the business logic layer of the Siebel CRM metadata model.

In this chapter, we learned how business components work and how to create joins and single value fields.

In addition, we explored how to use expressions in the Siebel Query Language to define calculated fields and apply validation rules.

Finally, we learned how to create custom instances of business components for the purpose of supporting read-only data access.

In the next chapter, we will explore the data layer of the Siebel Repository and learn how to configure its object types.

8

The Data Layer

The data layer of the Siebel Repository defines the physical schema of tables,
columns, and indexes for storing customer, administrative, and repository data.
Developers must understand how the objects of this layer and their relationships
establish the physical foundation for the business layer. Configuration activities
on this layer are limited to additive changes. This means that developers are only
allowed to create new tables or columns but not to modify data layer objects defined
by Oracle engineering.

This chapter is structured as follows:

- Understanding tables, columns, and indexes
- Considerations for custom schema changes
- Using preconfigured extension tables
- Creating custom columns
- Creating custom indexes
- Creating custom tables
- Applying schema changes to local and server databases

Understanding tables, columns, and indexes

As already outlined in *Chapter 1*, the data layer of the Siebel Repository consists of
the following object types:

- Table
- Column
- Index
- User Key

It is important to understand that the information in the Siebel Repository metadata defines the physical schema in the relational database and not the other way round. A developer must, for example, define a new table in the Siebel Repository **first** using **Siebel Tools** and then use the **Apply** functionality to physically create the table in the database.

The *Apply* functionality and the ddlsync utility can be used to synchronize the *logical schema* (the data layer object definitions in the Siebel Repository) with the *physical schema* (the tables and indexes in the relational database).

Both the *Apply* functionality and the ddlsync utility will be discussed in detail later in this chapter.

In the following section, we will dive a little bit deeper into the data layer object types and their properties.

Understanding table types

Besides a unique name, a table object definition must also have a type. The **Type** property of a table defines the purpose of the table. The following table describes the most important table types:

Table Type	Description	Example Tables
Data (Public)	Typical Siebel data tables, which are used to store records such as customer accounts, assets, service requests, activities, and so on. One-to-many (1:M) extension tables also are of this type.	S_ASSET S_SRV_REQ S_ASSET_XM
Data (Private)	Tables of this type are directly related to Siebel CRM core modules such as Audit Trail, List of Values, and Siebel Configurator.	S_AUDIT_TRAIL S_LST_OF_VAL
Data (Intersection)	Tables that support many-to-many (M:M) relationships between other data tables such as the persons (contacts) associated with a campaign.	S_CAMP_CON
Extension	Preconfigured one-to-one (1:1) extension tables for customer use. These tables are discussed in greater detail in the next section of this chapter.	S_ASSET_X
Extension (Siebel)	1:1 extension tables that are used by Oracle engineering for industry-specific functionality or the so-called Party Data Model. Extension tables always reference the table that they extend in their **Base Table** property.	S_CONTACT_FNX S_CONTACT

Table Type	Description	Example Tables
Interface	Tables for exclusive use by the **Enterprise Integration Manager (EIM)**. They can also be recognized by their common prefix *EIM_*.	EIM_ACCOUNT
External	Table definitions that reference tables in external relational databases or presentation tables of the Oracle BI Server. The prefix for external tables is *EX_*.	EX_MKT_REVENUE
Repository	These tables store the Siebel Repository metadata such as applets and business components.	S_APPLET

Understanding columns

Each table definition has multiple column definitions. Each column must have a distinguished name. The most important properties of a column object definition are described in the following table:

Column Property	Description
Type	Normal data columns have a type of *Data (Public)*. In addition, each table has a set of system columns, which are described later in this section.
Primary Key	When set to **TRUE**, the column serves as the primary key column in foreign key - primary key relationships between two tables. This information is only present in the Siebel Repository metadata and not in the relational database.
Nullable	When set to **TRUE**, the column can be empty (NULL). When set to **FALSE**, the column cannot be empty (NULL). This setting is propagated to the relational database as *NOT NULL*.
Required	When set to **TRUE**, the Siebel application logic enforces a non-NULL value for the column.
Foreign Key Table	When a column references a table in its **Foreign Key Table** property, it serves as a foreign key. This metadata information is not carried forward to the relational database. The Siebel application logic fully caters for referential integrity.
Physical Type	The data type that is used by the relational database to store values for the column. Typical physical types are **Varchar** (for arbitrary text), **UTC Date Time** (for time zone relative timestamps) and **Number** (for numerical values).
Length	The maximum number of characters to store for text columns.
Precision	The maximum number of digits to store for numeric columns.
Scale	The maximum number of decimal digits to store for numeric columns.
Default	The value to be written to the column when no value is entered. Typically used for *flag* columns which use *N* to indicate the Boolean state of FALSE and *Y* to indicate the Boolean state of TRUE.

The following screenshot shows selected column definitions of the **S_SRV_REQ** table in Siebel Tools:

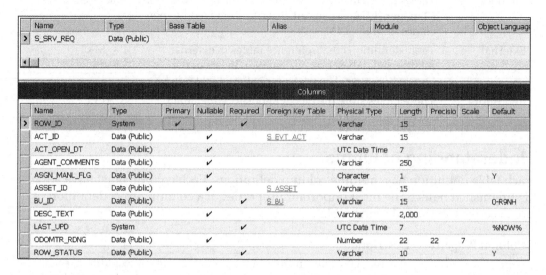

Name	Type	Base Table	Alias		Module		Object Language
> S_SRV_REQ	Data (Public)						

						Columns					
Name	Type	Primary	Nullable	Required	Foreign Key Table	Physical Type	Length	Precisio	Scale	Default
> ROW_ID	System	✔		✔		Varchar	15			
ACT_ID	Data (Public)		✔		S_EVT_ACT	Varchar	15			
ACT_OPEN_DT	Data (Public)		✔			UTC Date Time	7			
AGENT_COMMENTS	Data (Public)		✔			Varchar	250			
ASGN_MANL_FLG	Data (Public)		✔			Character	1			Y
ASSET_ID	Data (Public)		✔		S_ASSET	Varchar	15			
BU_ID	Data (Public)			✔	S_BU	Varchar	15			0-R9NH
DESC_TEXT	Data (Public)		✔			Varchar	2,000			
LAST_UPD	System			✔		UTC Date Time	7			%NOW%
ODOMTR_RDNG	Data (Public)		✔			Number	22	22	7	
ROW_STATUS	Data (Public)			✔		Varchar	10			Y

The screenshot shows examples for system and public data columns of various types.

System columns

As indicated previously, each table in the Siebel CRM schema has a set of columns of type **System**. The following table describes the system columns. The *System Field Mapping* column in the following table identifies the business component system field name that maps to the column:

System Column	Description	Example Value	System Field Mapping
ROW_ID	Flagged as **Primary Key** in more than 99 percent of all tables. The value in the ROW_ID column is unique across all tables in the enterprise (including mobile clients).	1-7TW9	Id
CREATED	Stores the timestamp (in Greenwich Mean Time - GMT) when the record has been created.	2005-07-01 16:11:28	Created

System Column	Description	Example Value	System Field Mapping
CREATED_BY	A foreign key column to the S_USER table. Stores the ROW_ID of the user who created the record.	1-Y0GP	Created By
LAST_UPD	Stores the timestamp (GMT) when the record was last been updated.	2010-10-25 05:45:02	Updated
LAST_UPD_BY	A foreign key column to the S_USER table. Stores the ROW_ID of the user who last updated the record.	1-Y0GP	Updated By
MODIFICATION_ NUM	The number of updates made to the record.	38	Mod Id
CONFLICT_ID	Used to identify a record that caused a conflict during the Siebel Remote synchronization process. A value of 0 (zero) indicates no conflict.	0	Conflict Id
DB_LAST_UPD	The GMT timestamp of the last update in the current database. Different from LAST_UPD when the record originated in another database and was - for example - imported into the current database.	2010-08-25 05:45:02	(Not mapped as a system field)
DB_LAST_UPD_SRC	The source of the last update in the current database. If the value is different from *User*, the update originates from a Siebel internal process such as Assignment Manager.	User	(Not mapped as a system field)
PAR_ROW_ID	This column is only present in extension tables and serves as a foreign key to the base table.	1-AF8	(Not mapped as a system field)

The View Details window, which we can open by right-clicking a business component definition, shows the system field mappings. System fields are not visible in the Fields list and have no properties. The following screenshot shows the View Details window for the Contact business component:

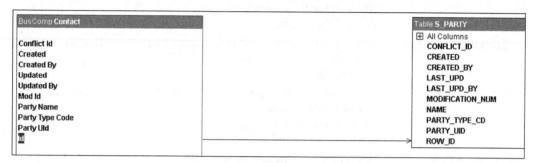

The **Id** system field is selected and the arrow indicates the mapping to the **ROW_ID** column of the business component's base table—**S_PARTY**.

> **Did you know?**
>
> Siebel applications use a proprietary mechanism to generate unique values for the **ROW_ID** column. **ROW_ID** values are composed of a prefix that identifies the database, a hyphen, and a suffix that is incremented alphanumerically.
>
> The **S_SSA_ID** table is used by the object manager to store the next suffix value. **ROW_ID** values are only used once, which means that when a record is deleted from the database, the **ROW_ID** value will not be generated again.

Understanding indexes

Indexes are typically created to increase query and sorting performance. A typical Siebel CRM table such as S_CONTACT has dozens of **Index** object definitions associated. An Index object definition has one or more **Index Column** definitions each of which references a column in the table and defines a sort order and sequence.

The following screenshot shows the **S_CONTACT_M14** index and its associated index columns:

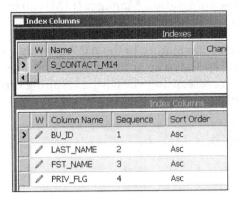

This particular index supports queries on the BU_ID, LAST_NAME, FST_NAME, and PRIV_FLG columns of the S_CONTACT table and supports ascending sorting on these four columns in the sequence defined by the **Sequence** property.

The Siebel CRM schema for Industry Applications (SIA) version 8.1 contains more than 20,000 indexes for more than 4,000 tables.

While indexes speed up query and sorting performance, they decrease the performance for insert, update, and delete operations because each of these operations requires an update to all indexes that reference the affected columns.

When we decide to create new tables or columns, we should investigate the query and sorting behavior of the business components, applets, EAI interfaces, and end users to determine the best definition of indexes.

Understanding user keys

A table can contain one or more associated **User Key** object definitions. A user key is an index that is used to define a set of columns that uniquely define a record. In relational databases, these objects are also known as *unique indexes*.

A popular example for a user key is the S_ORG_EXT_U1 definition on the S_ORG_ EXT table. It defines the following columns:

- BU_ID (the ROW_ID value of the account's primary organization)
- NAME (the name of the account)
- LOC (the location or **site** of the account)

The combination of values in these three columns must be unique. This is enforced by the database, so neither end users nor processes that access the database tables directly such as **Enterprise Integration Manager** (EIM) can create records that violate this unique index.

We can test this behavior by navigating to the **All Accounts** view in the Siebel Web Client and trying to create and save an account that has the same values for name and location. The following screenshot shows the resulting error message, which indicates that the same values already exist:

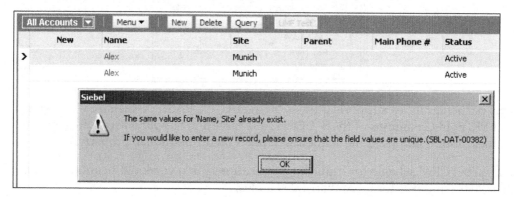

Creating table reports

A table report is a formatted document that enables implementation team members to review information about the selected table, its columns, and their purpose as well as the table's indexes.

Because of the shift from **Actuate Reports** to **Oracle BI Publisher** between Siebel 8.0 and Siebel 8.1, there are two different ways to create table reports. In Siebel **8.0**, Table reports can be created from the **Reports** menu in **Siebel Tools**. In Siebel **8.1 and above**, table reports can only be created from the **Siebel client**. The following procedure describes how to generate a table report in Siebel 8.1 and later:

1. In the Siebel Web Client, navigate to the **Administration - Application** screen (using the **Site Map**).
2. Navigate to the **Tables** view.
3. Execute an exact query (using double quotes to enclose the search string) such as **S_CONTACT** to locate a table.
4. Click the **Reports button** in the application toolbar and select the **Tables Report**.
5. Select an output format such as **PDF**.

6. Click the **Submit** button.

7. The report is made available for download.

8. Save the report or open it.

The following screenshot shows the table report for the **S_CONTACT** table:

SIEBEL Generated by		Repository Tables				Report Date: 06-DEC- 2009 Page 1 of 20

Name	S_CONTACT		User Name	Person		
Status	Active		Type	Extension (Siebel)	Base Table	S_PARTY
Comments	(Pharma Modified) A Person is any individual involved in the sales process. A person may be part of the selling organization or external to the selling organization; an external person is considered a Contact and may be affiliated with the customer account or a business partner. A Contact need not be affiliated with an organization. Used by Siebel Pharma for Professionals					

Columns

Name	Not Null	Data Type	Domain Type	Domain	Comments
ACTIVE_CTI_CFG_ID	N	Varchar 15	FK	S_CTI_CFG	The active Communication Server Configuration
ACTIVE_FLG	Y	Character 1			Active Flag.
ACTIVE_TELESET_ID	N	Varchar 15	FK	S_CM_TELESET	The active teleset for a user

In addition to table reports that describe one table at a time by formatting the information that is already available in the Siebel Repository, Oracle also makes the complete data model documentation with entity-relationship - diagrams available to its Siebel customers.

These documents named **Siebel Data Model Reference** can be downloaded for each Siebel version by licensed customers on the My Oracle Support portal (http://support.oracle.com).

Considerations for custom schema changes

The preconfigured data layer objects, which we discussed in the previous sections—tables, columns, indexes, and user keys - which are defined in the out of the box Siebel Repository by Oracle, are protected against modifications.

This means that developers are not allowed to make changes to the standard data layer objects by any means. This includes direct or indirect manipulation of tables or indexes using SQL scripts, which results in an unsupported state of the Siebel Repository and could lead to severe problems at runtime and during upgrades to newer versions of Siebel CRM.

The only changes allowed are additive in nature, including the following:

- Creating custom tables
- Creating custom columns in standard tables
- Creating custom indexes on custom and standard tables

 Note that creating additional user keys on standard tables is also not supported.

All these changes must be made by creating or modifying object definitions in Siebel Tools rather than issuing **data definition language (DDL)** scripts directly against the relational database. Siebel Tools provides the necessary mechanisms to create the respective tables, columns, and indexes from the repository metadata.

A diligent developer or solution architect should always bear in mind that the task is not complete by just creating additional tables and columns. Depending on the Siebel CRM technology used in our project, we could find ourselves in the situation of having to apply additional modifications to the Siebel Repository. The following list describes these modifications:

- **Schema changes must be propagated to all databases (mandatory)**: Every additional data layer object, be it a single column, an entire table, or an index must be physically created in all databases. This includes the local databases of all developers, the server databases for the development, test, and production systems as well as local databases for mobile users.

- **EIM table mappings (optional)**: If **Enterprise Integration Manager (EIM)** is used to import, update, export, merge, or delete Siebel data in base tables, additional EIM table columns or entire EIM tables must be created for custom columns and tables.

- **Docking rules for Siebel Remote synchronization (optional)**: If Siebel Remote is used to support mobile users, we must create additional metadata, so-called Dock Objects, to enable routing and synchronization of data in custom columns or tables.

- **Indexes and user keys (optional)**: In the very likely event that the custom columns or tables are used heavily for queries, additional effort must be made to create the corresponding Index and User Key object definitions.

The repository modifications described in the previous list require a very high level of expertise and should only be carried out by seasoned professionals.

Because of the high level of effort that results from custom schema changes, it is highly recommendable to explore alternatives first before undertaking the changes. Alternatives include preconfigured columns and tables, which will be discussed in the next section.

Using preconfigured extension tables

Because extending the standard database schema is often associated with high effort and therefore costs, the Siebel data model designers have catered for so-called extension tables.

These tables are preconfigured to provide physical storage space for additional custom business component fields and even custom child business components without the need to create new columns or tables.

The following types of extension tables exist in the Siebel CRM schema:

- One-to-one (1:1) extension tables, supporting custom fields
- One-to-many (1:M) extension tables, supporting custom child business components

In the following section, we will discuss these table types and provide case study examples, how to use them to create new custom business component fields and custom child business components.

Using 1:1 extension tables

We can describe a 1:1 extension table with the following attributes:

- The **Type** property of the table object definition is **Extension** or **Extension (Siebel)**.
- The **Base Table** property is not empty and references an existing table.
- The **Name** property of an 1:1 extension table for customer use has a **suffix** of _X.
- An extension table has a system column named **PAR_ROW_ID**, which serves as a foreign key to the base table.
- Each extension table for customer use has a set of columns for each major data type, which are **not** mapped to fields in any existing standard business component. The names of these columns have a prefix of ATTRIB_ followed by a sequential number.

The following screenshot from Siebel Tools shows the **S_ORG_EXT_X** table, which serves as the 1:1 extension table for the **S_PARTY** table (the base table for business components such as Account) thus providing additional storage for customer data:

Name	Type	Base Table	Alias
S_ORG_EXT_X	Extension	S_PARTY	S_ORGANIZATION_EXTERNAL

Columns

W	Name	Physical Type	Length	Comments
	ATTRIB_01	Varchar	100	Used to store "Description of Key Competitors".
	ATTRIB_02	Varchar	100	Used to store "Description of Partners".
	ATTRIB_03	Varchar	30	Used to store "Line of Business".
	ATTRIB_04	Varchar	30	Used to store "Fin Acct - Trade Name"
	ATTRIB_05	Varchar	30	Used to store "Fin Acct - Business Type"
	ATTRIB_06	Varchar	30	Used to store "Fin Acct - Nature of Business"
	ATTRIB_07	Varchar	30	Extension Attribute
	ATTRIB_08	Character	1	Used to store "Public Company Flag".
	ATTRIB_09	Character	1	Extension Attribute
	ATTRIB_10	Character	1	Extension Attribute
	ATTRIB_11	Character	1	Extension Attribute

In order to identify free columns in a 1:1 extension table we can inspect the **Comments** property. If the text begins with *Used to store...* then the column is already in use by a business component field. Siebel engineers at Oracle use the Comments property to mark columns in 1:1 extension tables that are already used by standard business component fields.

In the preceding screenshot, the ATTRIB_07 column has a Comment text of *Extension Attribute*, which marks it as free. However, developers at our site could already have mapped the column in a business component field without having updated the Comments text.

The following procedure describes how we can use the **Flat** tab in the **Object Explorer** window in Siebel Tools for a secure identification of unused columns in 1:1 extension tables. We use the **ATTRIB_07** column in the **S_ORG_EXT_X** table as an example:

1. In the **Object Explorer** window, select the **Flat** tab.
2. The **Object Explorer** now shows all object definitions without their hierarchical context, allowing us to see all object definitions in a *flat* list.
3. Select the **Field** object type in the **Object Explorer**.
4. In the **Object List Editor**, create the following query:
   - Join = S_ORG_EXT_X
   - Column = ATTRIB_07

5. Press *Enter* to execute the query.

6. The query result list is empty. This indicates that no business component field exists that references the ATTRIB_07 column in the S_ORG_EXT_X table.

The previous procedure can be applied to any column for which we need the information by which business component fields are referenced.

Did you know?

Because of the fact that Oracle engineering obviously makes extended use of the existing 1:1 extension table columns, many architects at customer sites argue that it is safer to create custom extension columns or custom 1:1 extension tables.

This argument is valid when the customer plans to create a large number of additional fields in existing business components. Quite often the number of new custom fields exceeds the number of available columns in 1:1 extension tables.

However, these extensions must be thoroughly planned especially when the customer also uses **Enterprise Integration Manager** (**EIM**) or Siebel Remote.

In the following case study example, we will show how to use an existing column in a 1:1 extension table to create a new custom field in an existing business component.

Case study example: Creating a new field based on an existing 1:1 extension table column

As indicated in the requirements list for All Hardware (AHA) in *Chapter 3*, a traffic light icon should indicate the willingness of AHA to act courteous when a customer for example has outstanding payments. The business analyst team at AHA has already done some research and they decided to create a new field in the Account business component named **AHA Courtesy Indicator**. The data for the new field should be stored in the ATTRIB_07 column of the S_ORG_EXT_X table.

The following procedure describes how to create a new field that references an existing column in a 1:1 extension table of the business component's base table. We will also ensure that the **Comments** property of the extension table column is updated accordingly:

1. Navigate to the **Account** business component.

2. If necessary, check out or lock the Account business component.

3. In the **Object Explorer**, expand the Business Component type and select the **Field** type.

4. In the Fields list for the Account business component, create a new record with the following values:
   - **Name:** AHA Courtesy Indicator
   - **Join:** S_ORG_EXT_X
   - **Column:** ATTRIB_07
   - **Comments:** AHA Prototype; used for courtesy traffic light

5. In the **Object Explorer** window, select the **Table** type.

6. In the **Object List Editor**, query for the **S_ORG_EXT_X** table.

7. Check out or lock the **S_ORG_EXT_X** table.

8. In the **Object Explorer**, expand the Table type and select the **Column** type.

9. In the **Columns** list, query for the **ATTRIB_07** column.

10. Set the **Comments** property of the **ATTRIB_07** column to **AHA: Used to store "AHA Courtesy Indicator"** to indicate that the column is in use by the AHA project.

11. Compile the **S_ORG_EXT_X** table and the Account business component.

> Additional requirements exist for the AHA Courtesy Indicator field such as the creation of a graphical traffic light icon. These procedures will be covered in later chapters of this book.

Siebel Tools archive files (Account BC.sif and S_ORG_EXT_X.sif) are available in this chapter's code file. The files represent the Account business component and the S_ORG_EXT_X table after the changes made in the previous section.

Using 1:M extension tables

One-to-many (1:M) extension tables are provided in the standard Siebel CRM schema to enable developers to create **any amount** of custom child business components for each major business entity such as Account, Asset, and Contact.

1:M extension tables can be described by the following attributes:

- The **Name** property of a 1:M extension table has a suffix of _XM.

- 1:M extension tables have a **PAR_ROW_ID** column, which serves as the foreign key to the parent entity for the child records.

- The **TYPE** column allows storing the purpose (child entity) for each record.

- The **NAME** column together with the **TYPE** and **PAR_ROW_ID** column is part of a **User Key** definition that ensures uniqueness of the combined values of these columns.

- Each 1:M extension table has a set of preconfigured attribute columns for each major data type to hold the child entity data. The name prefix for these columns is ATTRIB_.

In contrast to 1:1 extension tables, there is no reason to fear *competition* with Oracle engineering in using preconfigured 1:M extension table columns because the **TYPE** column allows exact distinction of each record.

In the next chapter, we will use a case study example to demonstrate the creation of a new child business component on top of a preconfigured 1:M extension table.

Creating custom columns

There are certain circumstances when using preconfigured columns or tables is not an option. For example, the number or additional custom attributes could exceed the number of available columns in existing extension tables.

To support a large number of additional custom business component fields it is common practice to create custom extension columns in one of the tables that are already in use by the business components. By doing so, we avoid additional joins and therefore we cause only a minor performance impact.

The following procedure describes how to create a custom extension column in an existing table, using the S_ORG_EXT table as an example:

1. Navigate to the **S_ORG_EXT** table.
2. Check out or lock the **S_ORG_EXT** table if necessary.
3. Navigate to the **Columns** list for the **S_ORG_EXT** table.
4. Create a new column definition with the following values:
   - **Name** (example): AHA_EXT_1

   [X_ will be added as a name prefix automatically.]

   - **Physical Type**: Varchar
   - **Length**: 100
   - **Comments**: Created for AHA prototype

5. Compile the **S_ORG_EXT** table.

6. Apply the database changes (see upcoming section).

As discussed previously, we must consider the following additional tasks when we create custom columns or tables:

- Applying Database Changes
- Creating EIM table mappings
- Creating docking rules for Siebel Remote
- Creating custom indexes and user keys

In the following sections, we will learn how to create custom indexes and apply schema changes to local and server databases.

Creating custom indexes

The following procedure describes how to create a custom index definition to support faster queries and sorting operations on one or more custom columns:

1. Navigate to the **S_ORG_EXT** table.

2. Check out or lock the table if necessary.

3. In the **Object Explorer**, expand the **Table** type and select the **Index** type.

4. In the **Indexes** list create a new record.

5. Set the **Name** to S_ORG_EXT_AHA1.

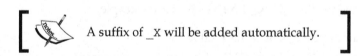 A suffix of _X will be added automatically.

6. In the **Object Explorer**, expand the Index type and select the **Index Column** type.

7. In the Index Columns list, create a new record with the following values:
   - **Column Name**: X_AHA_EXT_1
   - **Sequence**: 1
   - **Sort Order**: Asc

8. Compile the **S_ORG_EXT** table.

9. Apply the database changes (see upcoming section).

A Siebel Tools archive file (S_ORG_EXT.sif) is available in this chapter's code file. The file represents the **S_ORG_EXT** table after the changes made in the preceding sections.

Creating custom tables

To support entirely new business entities or a very large number of extension columns, Siebel Tools provides the ability to create custom table definitions using the **New Table wizard**. The following types of tables can be created:

- Standalone tables
- 1:1 extension tables for existing tables
- 1:M extension tables for existing tables
- Intersection tables to support many-to-many (M:M) relationships

The New Table wizard creates the table and all required system columns as well as some index and user key definitions. However, any additionally required attribute columns as well as any required indexes or user keys must be created manually.

Case study example: Creating a custom standalone table

One of the key requirements of the All Hardware Company is to provide a unified list of all customer documents (opportunities, quotes, orders, and campaign responses) to their employees.

The technical architects have determined that a custom table must be created to support the storage of the document keys. Additional objects will have to be created in the business and user interface layers (these tasks will be discussed in later chapters).

The following procedure describes how we can use the New Table wizard to create a new standalone table to fulfill the requirement:

1. Create a **new project** named **AHA Tables** and lock it.
2. Click the **New** button in the Format **toolbar**.
3. Double-click the **Table** icon in the **General** tab of the **New Object Wizards** dialog.
4. In the **General** tab of the **New Table** wizard, enter the following:
   - **Name**: CX_AHA_DOC

The CX_ (Custom e**X**tension) prefix should be kept for all custom tables.

- ° **Project**: AHA Tables
- ° **Table type**: Stand-alone Table (keep the default)

5. Click **Next**.
6. Click **Finish**.

The wizard generates the table definition and navigates to the Tables list to display it.

When we inspect the newly created standalone table more closely, we find that it also contains the following child object definitions:

- Nine system columns
- An index on the ROW_ID column

The following table, provided by the technical analyst team of AHA, describes the additional attribute columns, which must be created manually:

Column Name	Data Type	Length	Foreign Key Table	Description
ACCOUNT_ID	Varchar	15	S_ORG_EXT	The foreign key to the document's parent account.
DOC_ID	Varchar	15		The unique key of the document.
DOC_TYPE	Varchar	30		The type of the document such as "Quote".
DOC_STATUS	Varchar	30		The status of the document such as "Active".
DOC_USER_ID	Varchar	15	S_USER	Foreign key to "responsible user".
DOC_VER_FLG	Character	1		A flag to indicate whether the document has been verified by the user.

The process of creating columns has already been described in an earlier section so it is not laid out here in detail. For the sake of simplicity, we are not creating indexes for the case study example but this should be strongly considered for real-life implementations.

In addition, the generation of EIM mappings and docking objects could become mandatory when a new table is created. This depends on the decision to use the respective modules (Enterprise Integration Manager and Siebel Remote) in conjunction with the new table object.

The following screenshot shows the complete **CX_AHA_DOC** table with the system columns generated by the New Table wizard and the data columns, which were added manually:

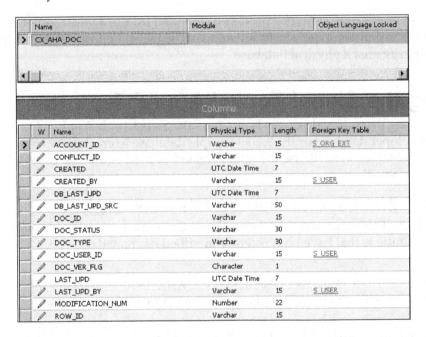

A Siebel Tools archive file (`CX_AHA_DOC.sif`) is available in this chapter's code file. The file represents the **CX_AHA_DOC** table after the changes made in the preceding sections.

Applying schema changes to local and server databases

All additions and modifications to data layer object types such as tables, columns, indexes, and user keys must become manifest in the physical database.

To accomplish this, Oracle provides two utilities, which we will discuss in this section:

- Siebel Tools **Apply** feature
- Synchronize Schema Definition process (ddlsync)

The Siebel Tools **Apply** feature is typically used by developers against their local databases but it also works against server databases.

The *Synchronize Schema Definition* process is intended for use against server databases and helps in automating the synchronization of the Siebel Repository metadata information against a physical database.

Using the Siebel Tools "Apply" feature

The following procedure describes how to use the Siebel Tools **Apply** feature against a local developer database or the Siebel Sample database to create new columns, indexes, and tables. We will use the tables created or modified in the case study examples of this chapter:

1. In Siebel Tools, navigate to the **Table** object type.
2. In the **Tables** list, use the **Changed** column to query for all table object definitions that have been recently modified or created.

 The **S_ORG_EXT** table and the **CX_AHA_DOC** table should appear in the result set. If not, query for them using the Name column.

3. Click the **Apply/DDL** button on top of the list.
4. In the **Choose Option** dialog, select the **Apply** option.
5. Click **OK** in the warning message that indicates that you are connected to a local database.
6. If you are using a local developer database, continue with step 7. If you are using the **Siebel Sample** database, proceed to step 8.
7. For a local developer database, set the following options in the **Apply Schema** dialog:
   - **Tables:** Current Query
   - **Database user:** SIEBEL

SIEBEL is the default table owner.

- ○ **Database user password**: (enter your local password)

 The table owner password in local developer databases is the same as for the mobile user.

- ○ **ODBC Data Source**: (keep the default)

8. For the **Siebel Sample** database, set the following options in the **Apply Schema** dialog:
    - ○ **Tables**: Current Query
    - ○ **Database user**: DBA

 DBA is the default administrator account for Sybase databases.

- ○ **Database user password**: SQL
- ○ **ODBC Data Source**: SEAW Samp Db default instance

 Replace the default value with the name of the ODBC DSN for the Siebel Sample database.

9. Click **Apply**.
10. Wait for the process to finish.
11. Click **OK** in the message that indicates that all changes were successfully applied.
12. Check in or unlock the new and modified table object definitions.

Did you know?

The Generate DDL option in the Choose Options dialog allows saving the **data definition language (DDL)** statements to a file rather than executing them directly against the database. Nonetheless, the ODBC connection must be made to compare the Siebel Repository metadata against the current schema of the database.

The Siebel Tools **Apply** feature can also be used against server databases. To do this we have to log in to Siebel Tools against the server database and use the table owner password for the server database in the Apply Schema dialog.

After applying database schema changes against a server database we also have to click the **Activate** button on top of the tables list. This ensures that the schema version information in the **S_APP_VER** system table is updated. The **S_APP_VER** table is used by several server components to verify that the schema information in the so-called data dictionary file (diccache.dat) on the server is correct. When the schema version number in the **S_APP_VER** table and the diccache.dat file are different, a new diccache.dat file is created by reading the current physical schema from the database.

Verifying the application of local database changes

The local databases used for Siebel developers and remote users as well as the Siebel Sample database are **Sybase Adaptive Server Anywhere** databases. We can use Sybase's **Interactive SQL** utility, which is delivered with Siebel Tools to connect to the database and verify that the physical changes have been applied. We must also use this utility to execute DDL scripts generated by Siebel Tools (as described in the information box above).

The following procedure describes how to use Interactive SQL to connect to the local developer database:

1. Use **Windows Explorer** to navigate to the BIN subdirectory of the Siebel Tools installation folder.

2. Double-click the dbisql.exe program.

3. In the **Connect to Adaptive Server Anywhere** dialog, click the **Database** tab.

4. Click the **Browse** button.

5. In the **Files of type** drop-down at the bottom of the browse dialog, select **All Files (*.*)**.

6. If you are using a local developer database, continue with step 7. If you are using the Siebel Sample database, proceed to step 8.

7. To connect to a local developer database, execute the following steps:

   i.   Browse to the LOCAL subdirectory of the **Siebel Tools** installation folder.

   ii. Select the sse_data.dbf file and click **Open**.

   iii. Click the **Login** tab in the Connect to Adaptive Server Anywhere dialog.

   iv. Enter **SIEBEL** as the **User ID**.

   v.   Enter your local database password in the **Password** field.

   vi. Click **OK**.

8. To connect to a Siebel Sample database, execute the following steps:

   i.   Browse to the SAMPLE\UTF8 subdirectory of the **Siebel Client** installation folder.

   ii. Select the sse_samp.dbf file and click **Open**.

   iii. Click the **Login** tab in the **Connect to Adaptive Server Anywhere** dialog.

   iv. Enter DBA as the **User ID**.

   v.   Enter SQL in the **Password** field.

   vi. Click **OK**.

9. In the **Command** window in the bottom area of the Interactive SQL utility, enter an SQL statement similar to the following:

```
select * from CX_AHA_DOC
```

10. Click the **Execute** button.

11. Verify that no **Table not found...** error is displayed and that the columns of the table appear in the **Data** window. We can scroll right in the Data window to verify the existence of all columns we defined in Siebel Tools.

12. Close the Interactive SQL utility.

The following screenshot shows the Interactive SQL utility after the example SQL statement execution:

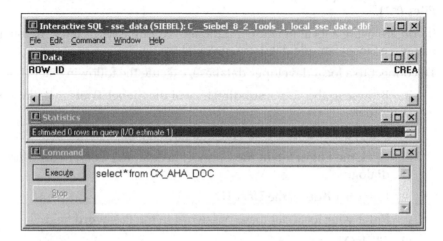

Using the synchronize schema definition process

As indicated previously, the Synchronize Schema Definition process provides the ability to automate the synchronization of the data layer object definitions in the Siebel Repository, also known as the **logical schema**, with the physical schema of server databases.

The process is part of the **Siebel Database Server Utilities** which are typically installed on at least one Siebel Server in the Enterprise. For details on how to install the Database Server Utilities, please refer to the book *Oracle Siebel CRM 8 Installation and Management* by the same author. In addition, the *Installation Guide* in the Oracle Siebel documentation library can be recommended (`http://download.oracle.com/docs/cd/E14004_01/books/SiebInstWIN/booktitle.html`).

The Synchronize Schema Definition process is also part of the **Repository Migration** process (covered in a later chapter), which is offered as well by the Siebel Database Server Utilities. It is important to understand that any new or modified data layer object definition must exist in the Siebel Repository in the same database that the utility acts upon.

For development environments this means that we must **check in** the respective tables before starting the utility. For test and production environments the Repository Migration process should be used to import the new repository metadata and synchronize the logical and physical schema.

The following procedure describes how to execute the Synchronize Schema Definition process against an Oracle database. In the example procedure, we execute the wizard on a Microsoft Windows operating system. The procedure is similar on Linux and other UNIX-based operating systems:

Step	Description	Tasks and Example Values
1	Start the Siebel Configuration Wizard.	Click the **Database Server Configuration** shortcut in the Windows start menu.
2	Siebel Server directory	Provide the path to the Siebel Server's installation directory.
		Typically, the default can be kept.
		Click **Next**.
3	Siebel Database Server Utilities directory	Provide the path to the Siebel Database Server Utilities installation folder.
		Typically, the default can be kept.
		Click **Next**.
4	Database Platform	Select **Oracle Database Enterprise Edition**.
		Click **Next**.
5	Task selection	Select **Run Database Utilities**.
		Click **Next**.
6	Action selection	Select **Synchronize Schema Definition**.
		Click **Next**.
7	UNICODE selection	Select whether the database is operating on a UNICODE codepage or not.
		Click **Next**.
8	Select base language	Select **English (American)**.
		Click **Next**.
9	ODBC Data Source Name (source)	Example: SIEBELEVAL_DSN
		This is the name of the System DSN for the source enterprise which can be found in the Windows ODBC Administration console.
		Click **Next**.
10	Siebel Database User Name and Password	**User Name**: SADMIN
		Example Password: TJay357D
		Click **Next**.

Step	Description	Tasks and Example Values
11	Siebel Database Table Owner and Password	**Table Owner:** SIEBEL
		Example Password: dQ7JXufi
		Click **Next**.
12	Source and target repository name	Keep the defaults (**Siebel Repository**)
		Click **Next**.
13	Index and data tablespace names	Example Index Table Space Name: SIEBELDB_IDX
		Example (Data) Table Space Name: SIEBELDB_DATA
		Click **Next**.
14	Repository Name	Typically **Siebel Repository** can be kept.
		Click **Next**.
15	Oracle parallel indexing	Keep the default (**Does not use...**)
		Click **Next**.
16	Security group and log output directory	Keep the defaults.
		Note the log output directory will become a subdirectory of the Siebel Server's LOG directory.
		Click **Next**.
17	Apply configuration changes	Select **Yes apply configuration changes now**.
		Click **Next**.
18	Summary	Review the summary information.
		Click **Next**.
19	Do you want to execute configuration?	Click **Yes**.
20	The Siebel Upgrade Wizard is displayed.	Click **OK** in the Siebel Upgrade Wizard dialog.
21	During the process, several command windows are opened	Ensure that you do not close or make selections in any of the command windows.
		Wait for the Siebel Upgrade Wizard to complete.
22	The configuration wizard displays a message **Execution successful**	Click **OK** to confirm successful execution of the configuration wizard.
23	The configuration wizard jumps to the Siebel Server directory selection	Click **Cancel** in the **Siebel Configuration Wizard** dialog.

Step	Description	Tasks and Example Values
24	Confirm exiting the configuration wizard	Click **Yes**
25	Siebel Upgrade Wizard displays **Complete**	Click **OK** in the **Siebel Upgrade Wizard** dialog.

We can verify the successful creation of new tables, columns, or indexes by issuing DDL statements such as `desc` against the server database. On Oracle databases we can use Oracle's **SQL*Plus** utility to log in as the SIEBEL table owner to the server database and execute a statement similar to the following:

```
desc CX_AHA_DOC;
```

If we see the column listing for the CX_AHA_DOC table then the schema changes have been successfully applied.

Summary

In this chapter, we learned to understand the object types that define the data layer in the Siebel Repository, namely tables, columns, indexes, and user keys. In addition, we discussed the implications of changes to the physical schema and that it is beneficial to use alternative solutions such as preconfigured extension tables instead of creating custom tables or columns.

Of course, company requirements will exist which that physical schema changes necessary. In this chapter, we also learned how to create new columns, tables, and indexes and synchronize the Siebel Repository metadata with the physical schema of the relational database.

In the next chapter, we will expand on the topic of 1:M extension tables and learn how to create the necessary business layer objects to support new child entities.

Business Objects and Links

9

This chapter introduces the concept of Business Objects and Links. Both object definitions are important members of the Siebel business layer and establish relationships between business components. In addition, we will learn how to create child business components based on 1:M extension tables and incorporate them into business objects.

The chapter is structured as follows:

- Understanding business objects and links
- Creating child business components on a 1:M extension table
- Creating child business components on a standalone table
- Creating links
- Configuring business objects

Understanding business objects and links

In order to understand business objects and links and how these object types support relationships between business components, we can investigate views in a Siebel application using the **About View** option in the **Help** menu.

For example, we can navigate to the **Contacts Screen** and drill down on a contact's last name to open the **Contact Detail View**, which shows all activities associated to the selected person.

We then select the **About View** command in the **Help** menu of the Siebel application to open a dialog similar to the following screenshot:

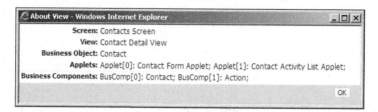

Besides the technical names of the screen (**Contacts Screen**) and view (**Contact Detail View**) that is currently open, the dialog also conveys to us the name of the **business object** referenced by the view (**Contact**). The applet list uses indexes, in square brackets, allowing us to easily identify which business component is referenced by what applet. In the previous example, the Contact Form Applet references the **Contact** business component and the Contact Activity List Applet references the **Action** business component.

Closer inspection of this view's functionality reveals that the activity list only displays activity records that are associated to the contact displayed in the contact form on top of the view. This can be verified by using the **Next Record** or **Previous Record** button in the form applet to display different contact records. When we click the **New** button in the activity list, a new activity record is created and automatically associated to the contact displayed in the form on top of the view.

The two entities—contact and activity—implemented as the **Contact** and **Action** business components, are arranged in a parent—child relationship that can be visualized as follows:

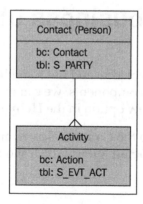

A person—represented by the **Contact** business component—can be associated with many activities, represented by the Action business component.

We can use the information collected with the **About View** dialog to continue our examination in Siebel Tools. The following procedure describes how to examine the Contact **business object** in Siebel Tools:

1. In the **Object Explorer**, select the **Business Object** type.

2. In the **Object List Editor**, query for the **Contact** business object.

3. In the **Object Explorer**, expand the Business Object Type and select the **Business Object Component** type.

4. In the Business Object Components list, query for the **Action** business component.

5. Observe that the **Link** property references a link object definition named **Contact/Account**.

The following screenshot shows the result of the preceding query:

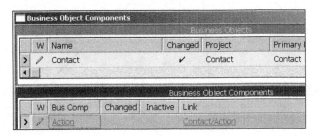

A business object can be described by the following characteristics:

- A business object is a list of business components

- The relationship between business components in a business object are established by links

- A business object has a primary business component, which is the parent for all other linked business components

- The primary business component does not use a link

The relational hierarchy of a business object's business components can be visualized in Siebel Tools by right-clicking the business object and selecting **View Details**. The resulting diagram may be difficult to view when a large number of business components is involved.

The following screenshot shows a diagram for the **Account - ESP** business object generated by the **View Details** functionality of Siebel Tools:

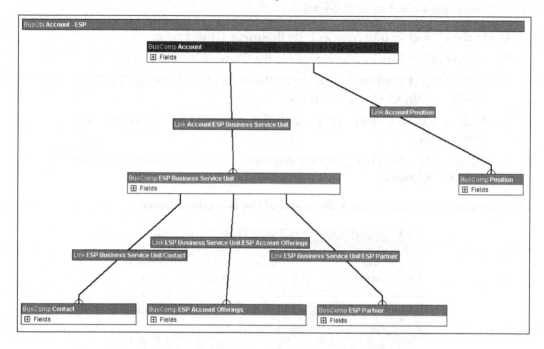

The connection of business components by means of links and the hierarchical parent—child relationships are clearly visible in the previous diagram.

Link object definitions

In the preceding example, we investigated the Contact business object and how the Contact business component is linked to the Action business component by means of a link object definition named **Contact/Action**.

In the following section we will learn more about links by investigating the Contact/Action link more closely.

Did you know?

Siebel Tools supports a **naming convention** for links by using the name of the parent (upper) business component for the first part of the name and the name of the child (lower) business component for the second part of the name. The names are separated by a slash (/). This naming convention is automatically applied when we create new link definitions.

It is however not enforced; developers can rename the link once it is created.

The following procedure describes how to review the properties for a link object definition in Siebel Tools:

1. In the **Object Explorer**, select the **Link** object type.
2. In the **Object List Editor**, query for the **Contact/Action** link.
3. Open the **Properties** window to inspect the properties of the link.

The following screenshot shows a portion of the **Properties** window for the **Contact/Action** link:

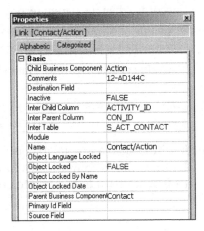

The following table describes the most important properties of the Link object type:

Property	Description
Parent Business Component	The name of the business component that is the parent in the relationship defined by the link.
Child Business Component	The name of the business component that acts as the child in the relationship defined by the link.
Inter Table	The name of the intersection table used for the relationship.
	Important: If this property is populated, the relationship defined by the link is a many-to-many (M:M) relationship. If not, the relationship is a one-to-many (1:M) relationship.
Inter Parent Column	The column in the intersection table that stores the primary key (ROW_ID) of the parent record. Only required for M:M links.
Inter Child Column	The column in the intersection table that stores the primary key (ROW_ID) of the child record. Only required for M:M links.

Property	Description
Source Field	In the case of a **1:M** relationship, this property defines the name of the field in the **parent** business component that serves as the primary key. If this property is empty, the **Id** field (which maps to the ROW_ID column) is used.
Destination Field	In the case of a **1:M** relationship, this property defines the name of the field in the **child** business component that maps to the foreign key column.
Cascade Delete	For **1:M** links, this property controls what happens to child records when the parent record is deleted.
	A value of **None** indicates that child records remain untouched when the parent record is deleted.
	A value of **Clear** enforces that the foreign key column of the child records is set to NULL.
	A value of **Delete** means that child records are deleted when the parent record is deleted.

Driven by additional properties, links also allow us to control the **filtering** and **sorting** of child records. Similar to business components, links also have properties such as **No Insert**, which controls whether it is allowed to create a child record through the link or not.

Creating a child business component on a 1:M extension table

When business requirements dictate the creation of new child entities, developers can rely on 1:M extension tables in order to avoid modifications of the physical schema. 1:M extension tables have been described in the previous chapter. In the following case study example, we will practice the creation of a new child business component based on a 1:M extension table. Later in this chapter, we will learn how to create a new link and insert the new business component in an existing business object using the new link.

Case study example: Creating a custom child business component

As indicated in the description of the **Sales – Update Customer** business process in *Chapter 3, Case Study Introduction*, AHA wants to store the date, employee, product, and the customer response of each product offering to a customer. The AHA business analyst team has identified the preconfigured **S_ORG_EXT_XM** table as the best place to store this data.

The analyst team has created the following table to describe the new business component definition named **AHA Customer Offer** and its field mappings:

Field	Column	Remarks
Account Id	PAR_ROW_ID	The foreign key field must map to PAR_ROW_ID.
Type	TYPE	Set the **pre default value** to AHA_CUST_OFFER.
		Set this as a **required** field.
Identifier	NAME	Set the **pre default value** to Field: 'Id' to ensure uniqueness of the user key.
		Set this as a **required** field.
Offer Date	(Empty)	This is a calculated field.
		Set **Calculated Value** to [Created].
		Set the **Data Type** property to DTYPE_UTCDATETIME.
User Login Name	S_USER.LOGIN (Joined)	Create a **join** to **S_USER** using the **Created By** system field.
Product Id	ATTRIB_03	Used to store the ROW_ID of the product being offered.
Product Name	S_PROD_INT.NAME (Joined)	Displays the name of the product being offered.
		Create a **join** to **S_PROD_INT** using the **Product Id** field.
		Create a pick list that only shows products marked as orderable.
		A new read-only pick applet must be created on top of the Internal Product business component.
		(See the following for instructions on creating pick lists and pick applets).

Field	Column	Remarks
Response Type	ATTRIB_04	Used to store the type of the customer's response to the offer.
		Create a new static pick list with the following values:
		Purchase
		Tentative
		Positive
		Negative
		(See the following for instructions on creating pick lists.)
Response Text	ATTRIB_47	Allows 255 characters.

[The pick list definitions referenced in the preceding tables will be implemented and explained in detail in the next chapter.]

Business Components that are based on 1:M extension tables must provide a default value for the **Type** field. This ensures that every new record created by this business component has a value in the TYPE column of the 1:M extension table by which it can be identified as a member of the entity represented by the business component.

In order to retrieve only records of the type associated with the new business component, we must set its **Search Specification** property to a value similar to the following:

```
[Type] = "AHA_CUST_OFFER"
```

This search expression ensures that only records that have a value of **AHA_CUST_OFFER** in the **TYPE** column are retrieved by the new business component.

The following procedure describes how to create a new child business component based on a 1:M extension table using the **New Business Component wizard**:

1. Create and lock a new project named AHA Business Components if necessary.
2. Click the **New** button in the **Edit** toolbar to open the **New Object Wizards** selection dialog.
3. In the **General** tab, double-click the **BusComp** icon to start the **New Business Component** wizard.

4. Provide the following values in the first wizard page:
    - ○ **Project**: AHA Business Components
    - ○ **Name**: AHA Customer Offer
    - ○ **Table**: S_ORG_EXT_XM

5. Click **Next**.

6. In the **Single Value Fields** page, select **PAR_ROW_ID** in the **column** drop-down list.

7. Enter Account Id in the **name** field below the drop-down list (overwrite the default name).

8. Click the **Add** button to write the new field definition to the **list** at the bottom of the page.

9. Repeat steps 6 to 8 for each non-joined and non-calculated field in the preceding table. The following screenshot shows the wizard page before adding the last column mapping:

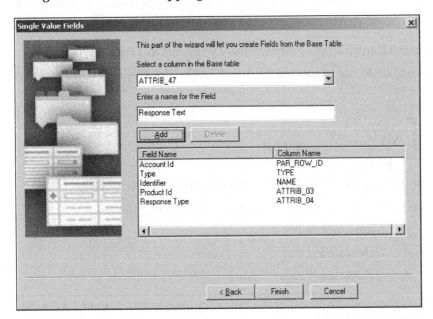

10. Click the **Finish** button.

11. The new business component definition is created and Siebel Tools navigates to it automatically.

12. In the **Properties** window for the new business component make the following entries:
    - ° **Search Specification:** [Type] = "AHA_CUST_OFFER"
    - ° **Comments:** Created for AHA prototype to store customer offers
    - ° **No Delete:** TRUE

    [Note: This prevents deletion of the offer history.]

13. Navigate to the **Type** field and set the **Pre Default Value** property to AHA_CUST_OFFER.

    [The value in the **Pre Default Value** property of the **Type** field must match the quoted string in the business component's Search Specification property exactly (case is important). It is therefore recommendable to copy and paste this value rather than typing it twice.]

14. Set the **Required** property for the **Type** field to **TRUE**.

15. Navigate to the **Identifier** field and set the **Pre Default Value** property to Field: 'Id'.

    [This ensures that the user key in the S_ORG_EXT_XM table is satisfied.]

16. Set the **Required** property for the **Identifier** field to **TRUE**.

17. Create a new calculated field with the following values:
    - ° **Name:** Offer Date
    - ° **Calculated:** TRUE
    - ° **Calculated Value:** [Created]

Now that we have created the new child business component definition and the majority of fields, we can use the following procedure as a guide to create the joined fields as requested by the AHA business analyst team. As we have already discussed joined fields in a previous chapter, the instructions in the procedure are less explicit.

18. Create two new Join object definitions for the AHA Customer Offer business component as per the following table:

Table	Alias	Outer Join Flag
S_USER	Created By - S_USER	Checked
S_PROD_INT	Product - S_PROD_INT	Checked

Did you know?

It is recommendable to use the **Alias** property of a Join object definition to indicate the usage and the joined table name. This allows for easier identification of the table from the Fields list.

Setting the **Outer Join Flag** to **TRUE** ensures that records are fetched for the business component regardless of the existence of a corresponding record in the joined table.

19. For the **Created By - S_USER** join object definition, create a new Join Specification definition with the following properties:

   ○ **Name**: Created By
   ○ **Source Field**: Created By
   ○ **Destination Column**: PAR_ROW_ID

Because the S_USER table is an extension table, we should use PAR_ROW_ID instead of ROW_ID as the destination column. This ensures data integrity.

20. For the **Product - S_PROD_INT** join object definition, create a new Join Specification definition with the following properties:

   ○ **Name**: Product Id
   ○ **Source Field**: Product Id
   ○ **Destination Column**: ROW_ID

21. Create two new joined Field definitions for the AHA Customer Offer business component as per the following table:

Name	Join	Column
User Login Name	Created By - S_USER	LOGIN
Product Name	Product - S_PROD_INT	NAME

22. Right-click the AHA Customer Offer business component and select **Validate** from the context menu.

23. Click the **Start** button to initialize the validation.

24. Observe the status bar of the Validate dialog. After a few seconds it should indicate *Total tests failed: 0*. If any errors or warnings appear in the dialog, click each of them to facilitate reading the message in the Details text box. All configurations leading to errors should be corrected and the validation process should be repeated until no errors are reported.

25. Close the **Validate** dialog.

26. Compile the **AHA Customer Offer** business component. This finalizes the definition of a new child business component based on a preconfigured 1:M extension table.

As indicated previously, the required Pick List and Pick Map object definitions for the Response Type and Product Name fields will be implemented in the next chapter.

A Siebel Tools archive file (AHA Customer Offer BC.sif) is available in this chapter's code file. The file represents the AHA Customer Offer business component after the changes made in the previous section.

We must also create a new list applet for the AHA Customer Offer business component. Please refer to the instructions in *Chapter 5, Creating and Configuring Applets* to create an applet with the following characteristics:

- **Project**: AHA User Interface
- **Name**: AHA Customer Offer List Applet
- **Title**: Customer Offers
- **Business Component**: AHA Customer Offer
- **Upgrade Behavior**: Preserve
- **Web Templates**: Edit List only using the Applet List (Base/EditList) template
- **Columns**: Offer Date, Product Name, Response Type, Response Text, User Login Name

For the **Response Text** list column, set the following properties:

- **HTML Type: Text Area**
- **Show Popup: TRUE**

Save all changes and compile the AHA Customer Offer List Applet.

A Siebel Tools archive file (`AHA Customer Offer List Applet.sif`) is available in this chapter's code file. The file represents the AHA Customer Offer List Applet after the changes made in the preceding section.

Case study example: Creating child business components on a standalone table

The following procedure extends the case study example of *Chapter 8, The Data Layer* where we created the **CX_AHA_DOC** table in order to allow the unified display of all documents such as quotes, opportunities, and campaign responses of a customer in a single list.

The AHA technical architecture team has provided a planning document for the new **AHA Customer Documents** business component with the following fields (mapping to the CX_AHA_DOC base table):

Field	Column	Remarks
Account Id	ACCOUNT_ID	The foreign key to the document's parent account.
Account Name	S_ORG_EXT.NAME	Uses Join to S_ORG_EXT. Use Account Id for Join Specification.
Document Id	DOC_ID	The unique key of the document.
Document Type	DOC_TYPE	The type of the document such as *Quote*.
Document Status	DOC_STATUS	The status of the document such as *Pending*.
Responsible User Id	DOC_USER_ID	Foreign key to responsible user.
Responsible User Login Name	S_USER.LOGIN	Uses Join to S_USER. Use Responsible User Id for Join Specification.
		Add the dynamic pick list *PickList Login Name*.
Verified Flag	DOC_VER_FLG	A flag to indicate whether the document has been verified by the user.
		Set the Post Default Value property to *N*.

 Pick lists will be covered in greater detail in *Chapter 10, Pick Lists*.

Please refer to the previous section for detailed instructions on how to create a new business component using the New Business Component wizard.

In addition to the AHA Customer Documents business component, we should also create a new list applet named `AHA Customer Documents List Applet`. Please refer to *Chapter 5* for detailed instructions how to create list applets. To fine-tune the applet we can specify the **Employee Notification Pick Applet** in the **Pick Applet** property for the **Responsible User Login Name** list column and set the **HTML Icon Map** property for the **Verified Flag** list column to **CHECK**.

Siebel Tools archive files (`AHA Customer Documents BC.sif` and `AHA Customer Documents List Applet.sif`) are available in this chapter's code file. The files represent the AHA Customer Documents business component and the AHA Customer Documents List Applet after the changes made in the preceding section.

Case study example: Creating links

Continuing with the case study example, we must now ensure that the Siebel application is able to link the **Account** business component with the new **AHA Customer Offer** business component in a 1:M relationship.

The following procedure describes the steps necessary to create a new link object definition to support this relationship:

1. In the **Object Explorer**, select the **Link** object type.
2. In the **Object List Editor**, create a new record and enter the following properties:
   - **Project**: `AHA Business Components`
   - **Parent Business Component**: `Account`
   - **Child Business Component**: `AHA Customer Offer`
   - **Source Field**: `Id`
   - **Destination Field**: `Account Id`
   - **Comments**: `Created for AHA Prototype`
3. Observe that the **Name** property is automatically populated with **Account/ AHA Customer Offer**.
4. Step off the record to save the new link.
5. Compile the Account/AHA Customer Offer link.
6. Repeat steps 1 to 5 to create a new link between the **Account** and the **AHA Customer Documents** business component.
7. Repeat steps 1 to 5 to create a new link between the **Account** and the **Audit Trail Item 2** business component, using the **Record Id** field as the **Destination** field.

These three new link definitions support the case study requirements described in *Chapter 3*.

A Siebel Tools archive file (`Chapter 9 Links.sif`) is available in this chapter's code file. The file represents the new link object definitions created in the preceding section.

Case study example: Configuring business objects

We can now use the links created in the previous section to augment the Account **business object**. By doing so we will be able to place applets based on the child business components created in this chapter in any view that is based on the Account business object.

The following procedure describes how to add a business component and link to an existing business object:

1. In the **Object Explorer**, select the **Business Object** type.

2. In the **Object List Editor**, query for the **Account** business object.

3. Check out or lock the Account business object if necessary.

4. In the **Object Explorer**, expand the **Business Object** type and select the **Business Object Component** type.

5. In the Business Object Components list, create a new record and provide the following property values:

    ○   **Bus Comp**: `AHA Customer Offer`

    ○   **Link**: `Account/AHA Customer Offer`

    ○   **Comments**: `Created for AHA Protoype`

6. Repeat step 5 for the **AHA Customer Documents** business component and the **Account/AHA Customer Documents** link.

7. Repeat step 5 for the **Audit Trail Item 2** and the **Account/Audit Trail Item 2** link.

8. Compile the Account business object.

We will describe how to test the configurations made in this chapter's case study examples in upcoming chapters.

A Siebel Tools archive file (`Account BO.sif`) is available in this chapter's code file. The file represents the Account business object after the changes made in the previous section.

Summary

While business components provide the complete set of business logic for a given business entity, business objects group them together in hierarchical relationships by establishing the context of a primary business component and using link object definitions to glue one parent and one child business component together.

So-called 1:M links use foreign key — primary key relationships. M:M links reference intersection tables to support the storage of related primary keys.

When we wish to establish new child business components for existing parent business components, we must first create the new child business component, then a new 1:M link definition, and finally add the new child business component to the business object where the parent business component is the primary business component.

In the next chapter, we will discuss the concept of static and dynamic pick lists.

10
Pick Lists

Pick Lists ensure that end users can only select valid values for a field. This is a major boost for data quality and usability. It is important for developers to understand how pick lists work in Siebel CRM and how they can be configured.

In this chapter, we will learn the following:

- Understanding pick lists
- Creating a new static pick list for an existing field
- Administering the List of Values table
- Creating dynamic pick lists
- Creating pick applets
- Constrained and hierarchical pick lists

Understanding pick lists

Siebel CRM supports two types of pick lists—static and dynamic. The preconfigured applications are replete with examples for both types. In the following, we will use the **Opportunity** entity as an example to examine static and dynamic pick lists.

Static pick lists

A static pick list is rendered in the **user interface** (**UI**) as a simple one column drop-down box. The following screenshot shows the **Lead Quality** pick list in the **More Info** form applet for opportunities:

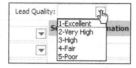

Static pick lists like the previous one are typically **bounded**, that means that end users are only allowed to enter values provided by the drop-down list. An **unbounded** pick list allows the end user to enter values which are not displayed in the pick list. The **Probability** field of an opportunity is an example for an unbounded pick list in preconfigured Siebel CRM applications.

On the business component level, we find that each field that exposes the behavior described previously has the following characteristics:

- The field **references a Pick List** object definition
- The field has **one or more Pick Map** child records

The following Siebel Tools screenshot shows these characteristics for the **Quality** field of the **Opportunity** business component. This field is exposed as the Lead Quality drop-down box in the previous example:

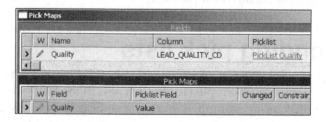

The **Picklist** property of the Quality field is set to **PickList Quality**, the name of a Picklist object definition, and there is one entry in the **Pick Maps** list for the Quality field.

A pick map defines the list of fields in the **pick business component**, defined by the pick list object definition, and fields in the **originating business component** to which the values are **copied** when the user makes the selection in the pick list.

The majority of static pick lists retrieve their values from a single table—**S_LST_OF_VAL**, also known as *List of Values*—by means of a specialized business component named **PickList Generic**. The administration of data in the List of Values table will be discussed in detail later in this chapter.

The pick list object type

The Picklist object type serves to define the behavior of the pick list at runtime as well as the pick business component that provides the data displayed in the pick list. We can imagine a picklist object definition as a data provider for the field it is associated with. A picklist references a business component from which it pulls data. In addition, a picklist object definition can define additional filtering and sorting behavior.

The following table describes the most important properties for the Picklist object type:

Property	Description
Business Component	The name of the business component that provides the data for the pick list.
Bounded	When set to **TRUE**, only values from the pick list can be selected. When set to **FALSE**, the pick list accepts other values as well.
Static	When set to **TRUE**, the pick list is rendered as a drop-down list and the values are typically provided by the **PickList Generic** or **PickList Hierarchical** business component that access the Siebel List of Values table (**S_LST_OF_VAL**).
	When set to **FALSE**, the values in the pick list typically come from a commonly used business component such as Account. Pick lists with a value of *FALSE* in the Static property are called **dynamic** pick lists.
Type Field	The name of a field in the pick list's business component that is used to retrieve a subset of data. For static pick lists that use the *PickList Generic* or *PickList Hierarchical* business components, this property is typically set to **Type**.
Type Value	Used in conjunction with the **Type Field** property. When both properties are set, a simple filter expression (Field = Value) is formed. For static pick lists this property contains the name of the List of Values type to distinguish a list of values for a single drop-down box.
Search Specification	Developers can use the **Siebel Query Language** to create an **optional** search expression to filter the data retrieved from the pick list's business component.
Sort Specification	Can be used to define the sorting of data retrieved from the pick list's business component.

Pick maps

Every field that references a Picklist object definition **must** also provide a pick map. Pick maps are implemented as child object definitions for the respective field. Pick map entries are used by the runtime engine for the following purposes:

- Determine the list of fields in the pick business component and the corresponding fields in the originating business components to copy the data to when the user makes a selection (also known as *copy pick maps*).

- Determine additional filters for the values in the pick list (also known as *constrained pick maps*).

- Use a field in the originating business component to determine if the copy or filter should be executed. This is implemented as the pick map's child entity named **Pick Map UpdOnlyIfNull** (*update only if null*). A pick map that has one or more of these child entries will only be executed when the fields in the **UpdOnlyIfNull** list have a NULL value.

In the following sections we will provide examples of both types (copy and constrain) of pick map entries.

Dynamic pick lists

Dynamic pick lists can be easily recognized in the Siebel CRM user interface by the typical **select icon** with one dot and a check mark. When end users click this icon, officially named **Select button**, a pick applet is opened in a pop-up window to provide a more convenient way to search and select values.

The following screenshot shows the **Account** field in the Opportunity form applet and the pick applet for Accounts:

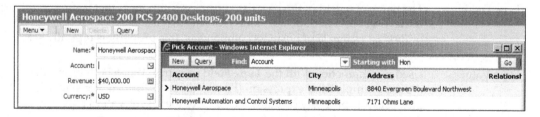

The following facts distinguish dynamic from static pick lists:

- End users can typically add entries to dynamic pick lists, hence the name **dynamic**.

- Applet controls or list columns for dynamic pick list fields must reference a pick applet.

- Dynamic pick lists typically retrieve data from *normal* business components (as opposed to the PickList Generic business component for static pick lists).

Did you know?

Pick lists allow for automatic completion of values entered by the end user. When an end user enters for example *1* in the Lead Quality field of an opportunity and then uses the *Tab* key to go to the next field, the value is automatically completed to *1-Excellent* because there is only one value in the list that starts with *1*.

In dynamic pick lists, end users can use wildcards such as the asterisk (*) symbol when they type in values. For example, typing *Hon*S** in the Account field of an Opportunity and leaving the field with the *Tab* key opens the Account Pick Applet displaying only accounts whose names start with *Hon* and contain an uppercase *S*.

Repository object types for pick lists

The following diagram describes the object types and their relationships that define the functionality around pick lists in the Siebel Repository:

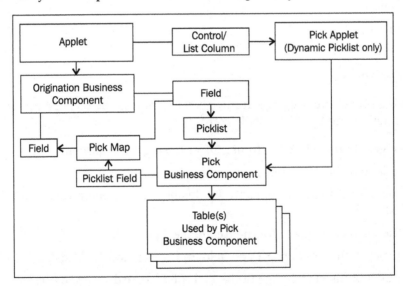

We can summarize the functionality as follows:

- The controls or list columns in an applet reference fields in the originating business component
- For dynamic pick lists, the applet's controls or list columns also reference a pick applet

- The field in the originating business component references a Picklist object definition and has at least one Pick Map entry
- The Picklist references the pick business component that provides data
- A pick map entry defines the copy path from a pick list field to a field in the originating business component

Case study example: Creating a new static pick list for an existing field

Developers are supported in the task of creating pick lists by the **Pick List Wizard** in Siebel Tools. In the following case study example, we will use this wizard to create a new static pick list for a field.

In *Chapter 9, Business Objects and Links*, we created a new child business component named **AHA Customer Offer**. As indicated in the field level requirements, a new static pick list should be created for the **Response Type** field with the following values:

- Purchase
- Tentative
- Positive
- Negative

The following procedure describes how to create a new static pick list for a business component field using the **Pick List Wizard**:

1. Navigate to the **AHA Customer Offer** business component.
2. Check out or lock the business component if necessary.
3. In the **Object Explorer**, expand the Business Component type and select the **Field** type.
4. In the Fields list, query for the **Response Type** field.
5. Right-click the **Response Type** field and select **Add Pick List...**
6. In the **Pick List Type** page of the **Pick List Wizard** select **Static**.
7. Click **Next**.
8. In the **Pick List Definition** page select **Create new Pick List**.
9. Click **Next**.
10. Provide a name for the new **Pick List**, for example AHA Customer Response Pick List.

11. Select **Create new List of Values**.

12. Click **Next**.

13. In the **List of Values** page, enter a name for the new **List of Values type**, for example AHA_CUST_RESPONSE.

14. In the **Enter a value** text box type Purchase.

15. Click the **Enter** button in the dialog to add **Purchase** to the **Current values** list box.

16. Repeat steps 13 and 14 for the values **Tentative**, **Positive**, and **Negative**.

    The following screenshot shows the List of Values page of the Pick List Wizard with all four values entered:

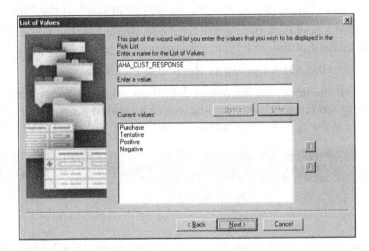

17. Click **Next**.

18. In the **Pick List Definition** page enter a comment such as Created for AHA prototype in the second text box.

19. Check the **Bounded Pick List** checkbox.

20. Click **Next**.

21. Click **Finish**.

22. Compile the **AHA Customer Offer** business component.

23. In the **Object Explorer**, select the **Pick List** type.

24. In the **Object List Editor**, query for the **AHA Customer Response Pick List**.

25. Compile the AHA Customer Response Pick List.

Verifying object definitions created by the pick list wizard

The following steps are optional but should be executed in order to verify that the wizard has generated all object definitions and List of Values data as intended:

1. Navigate to the **AHA Customer Offer** business component.

2. In the **Fields** list, execute the query for the **Response Type** field again to refresh the list.

3. Verify that the Response Type field now references the **AHA Customer Response Pick List** in the **PickList** property.

4. In the **Object Explorer**, expand the Field type and select the **Pick Map** type.

5. Verify that a new pick map entry has been created by the wizard that copies the **Value** field of the pick business component to the **Response Type** field.

6. Navigate to the **AHA Customer Response Pick List**.

7. Verify that the new pick list object definition exists and compare it with the following screenshot. Note the **Static** and **Bounded** flags and the **Type Value** referencing the type for the entries in the **List of Values (LOV)** table:

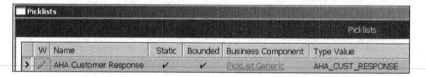

8. In the **Screens** menu of Siebel Tools, navigate to **System Administration | List of Values**.

9. In the **List of Values** list, query for the AHA_CUST_RESPONSE type.

10. Verify that four entries exist and compare them with the following screenshot:

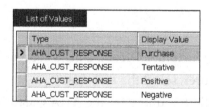

In summary, we can observe that the Pick List wizard creates and modifies the following repository metadata objects:

- **PickList property** of the selected **field** in the originating business component
- **Pick Map** child object definitions for the selected field
- **Pick list** object definition

When executed for **static** pick lists, the wizard also creates new records in the **List of Values (LOV)** table. Data in this table is **not** part of the Siebel Repository and as such it can neither be compiled to the SRF file nor checked in to the development server database to make it available to fellow developers. We have the following options to synchronize the LOV data (and other non-Repository data) with the development server database:

- Use the **Synchronize Database** option in the Mobile Web Client (if Siebel Remote is fully enabled on the development server).
- Log in to the server database and **manually** enter List of Values data (not recommended).
- Create an **Application Deployment Manager (ADM)** project for LOV data and deploy it on the development server. Using ADM functionality for deployment of administrative data such as LOVs is discussed in a separate chapter of this book.

Administering the list of values table

The data for static pick lists is stored in the S_LST_OF_VAL table as we have learned previously. The data set for a single pick list is defined by the **Type** value. Administrators and developers have two options to administer data in the S_LST_OF_VAL table:

- Use the List of Values list in Siebel Tools
- Use the List of Values view in the Siebel Web Client

Both applications allow us to add, modify, or deactivate entries in the List of Values data pool. In the following example procedure we describe how to undertake these tasks in the Siebel Web Client. For example purposes we will deactivate the *Purchase* entry in the AHA_CUST_RESPONSE type and create a new entry with a value of *Decided to buy*:

1. Log in to the **Siebel Developer Web Client** to the **same database** that you used to create the AHA Customer Response Pick List in the previous section.
2. Navigate to the site map.

Hint: Click the globe icon on the toolbar or press *Ctrl+Shift+A*

3. Navigate to the **Administration - Data** screen.

4. Click the hyperlink for the **List of Values** view.

5. Query for **AHA_CUST_RESPONSE** in the **Type** column.

6. Verify that four records are retrieved.

7. Select the **Purchase** entry and press *Ctrl+B* to copy the record.

 Copying records is a recommended practice to save time during data entry. However, we must be aware that some values such as the order sequence are copied as well, which may not be desirable.

8. In the **Display Value** column of the new record enter Decided to buy.

9. Press *Ctrl+S* to save the record. Note that the Language-Independent Code column is set to **Decided to buy** automatically.

10. Uncheck the **Active** flag for the **Purchase** entry and save the record.

11. Click the **Clear Cache** button on top of the list to reload the application's LOV cache.

The following screenshot shows the **List of Values** administration view after the changes described in the preceding procedure:

Type	Display Value	Orde	Active	Language-Independent Code
> AHA_CUST_RESPONSE	Decided to buy	0	✓	Decided to buy
AHA_CUST_RESPONSE	Purchase	0		Purchase
AHA_CUST_RESPONSE	Tentative	1	✓	Tentative
AHA_CUST_RESPONSE	Positive	2	✓	Positive
AHA_CUST_RESPONSE	Negative	3	✓	Negative

An ADM import XML file (Chapter_10_LOV.xml) is provided in this chapter's code file. This file represents the AHA_CUST_RESPONSE LOV type after the changes in the previous section.

The following table describes the most important columns in the List of Values administration view:

Column	Description
Type	Records for a single pick list are combined by the same type value. LOV Types are administered in the S_LST_OF_VAL table itself and have **LOV_TYPE** as the type value.
	To create a new LOV type, we must therefore create a new LOV entry with **LOV_TYPE** as the type value.
Display Value	The value displayed to the end user. When the *Multilingual List of Values (MLOV)* feature is implemented, the **Language Name** field identifies the language for the display value.
	Note: Administration of MLOV data is discussed in the book **Oracle Siebel CRM 8 Installation and Management**.
Language-Independent Code	The value stored in the database. When MLOV is implemented, this value is used to look up the language-dependent display value in the user's UI language.
Order	Used to specify the **sort order** for the values. When LOV entries for the same type have the same order number, they are sorted alphabetically.
Active	When the Active flag is checked, the entry is displayed in the pick list. When the Active flag is unchecked, the entry is not displayed in the pick list.
Language Name	The name of the language for multilingual List of Values entries.
Parent LIC	Used to create hierarchical pick lists (discussed in a later section of this chapter). **LIC** is short for **Language-Independent Code**.
Translate	When this flag is checked, the LOV entry can be translated into additional languages. Used by Oracle engineering to indicate that references to the LOV entry are language agnostic (using the LookupValue function rather than using hardcoded field values).
Multilingual	When this flag is checked, the LOV entry has been configured for multilingual (MLOV) behavior. This means that the application will use the user's application language to look up the display value.
Replication Level	When set to **All** (default), the entry is synchronized with mobile clients.
Low, High	Used to provide exact representations of data ranges for special purposes such as data analysis. Example: The display value of *> 100M* for the Account Revenue dropdown has a **High** value of 100000000, which can be better used for comparison in analytical scenarios.

Case study example: Creating dynamic pick lists

The process of creating dynamic pick lists is similar to that of creating static pick lists. The major exceptions are that dynamic pick lists reference commonly used business components such as Account or Internal Product and that a pick applet must be specified in the applet control or list column.

As indicated in the previous chapter, the solution architect team of AHA has defined the following requirements for the **Product Name** field of the **AHA Customer Offer** business component:

- Create a new pick list that only displays products marked as orderable
- Create a new read-only pick applet

We will describe example procedures for these tasks in this and the following section.

The following procedure describes how to create a new dynamic pick list for the Product Name field of the AHA Customer Offer business component:

1. Navigate to the **AHA Customer Offer** business component.
2. In the **Object Explorer**, expand the Business Component type and select the **Field** type.
3. In the **Fields** list, query for the **Product Name** field.
4. Right-click the **Product Name** field and select **Add Pick List...**
5. In the **Pick List Type** page of the Pick List Wizard select **Dynamic**.
6. Click **Next**.
7. In the **Pick List Definition** page select **Create new Pick List**.
8. Click **Next**.
9. In the **Pick List Definition** page enter the following values:
   - **Business Component**: Internal Product
   - **Field to sort**: Name
   - **Name for the pick list**: AHA Orderable Product Pick List
   - **Search Specification**: [Orderable]="Y"
   - **Comment**: Created for AHA prototype
10. Click **Next**.

11. In the **Pick List Specifications** page, check all flags (**No Delete, No Insert, No Merge, No Update**).

12. Click **Next**.

13. In the **Pick Map** page, select the **Product Name** field in the first drop-down list (originating business component field).

14. Select the **Name** field in the second drop-down list (pick business component field).

15. Click the **Add** button to add the pick map to the list box.

16. Repeat steps 13 to 15 for the **Product Id** field in the originating business component and the **Id** field in the pick business component.

17. Click **Next**.

18. Click **Finish**.

19. Compile the **AHA Customer Offer** business component.

20. Compile the **AHA Orderable Product Pick List**.

Siebel Tools archive files (AHA Customer Offer BC.sif and Chapter 10 Pick Lists. sif) are available in this chapter's code file. The files represent the AHA Customer Offer business component and the new pick list definitions after the changes made in the above sections.

Case study example: Reusing existing pick lists

To finalize the work started in *Chapter 9* and subsequently fulfill AHA's requirements, we can use the following procedure to reuse an existing pick list for the **Responsible User Login Name** field in the **AHA Customer Documents** business component. The AHA technical architect team has identified *PickList Login Name* as the pick list definition to reuse:

1. Navigate to the **AHA Customer Documents** business component.

2. Check out or lock the business component if necessary.

3. Navigate to the **Responsible User Login Name** field.

4. Right-click the field and select **Add Pick List...**

5. In the **Pick List Type** page of the Pick List Wizard select **Dynamic**.

6. Click **Next**.

7. In the **Pick List Definition** page, select **Use existing Pick List**.

8. In the **Existing Pick Lists** list, select the **PickList Login Name** pick list.

 For easier navigation in the list, you can type the name on the keyboard (case not required) after clicking inside the list.

9. Click **Next**.

10. In the **Pick Map** page, map the following fields from the **originating** and the **pick** business component:
    ○ **Responsible User Login Name**: Login Name
    ○ **Responsible User Login Id**: Id

11. Click **Next**.

12. Click **Finish**.

13. Compile the **AHA Customer Documents** business component.

A Siebel Tools archive file (AHA Customer Documents BC.sif) is available in this chapter's code file. The file represents the AHA Customer Documents business component after the changes made in the preceding section.

Case study example: Creating pick applets

The second requirement stated in the previous case study example is to create a new pick applet that displays the product data to end users so they can select one product.

Developers have the following options for pick applets (sorted from least to most effort):

- Reuse existing pick applets based on the same pick business component
- Copy an existing pick applet and modify the copy
- Create a new pick applet using the Pick Applet wizard

 Did you know?
Because the Pick Applet wizard does not place all typical pick applet controls such as the *Find* combo boxes on the web layout, these must be copied from an existing pick applet using the **Compare Objects** window in order to avoid placing them on the wrong placeholders.

The following procedure describes how to copy an existing pick applet and modify the copy. Copying an existing pick applet ensures that all typical pick applet controls such as the Find functionality are present in the custom pick applet on the correct placeholders. In the example, we will copy the **Product Pick Applet** that is used to select products for an opportunity:

1. Navigate to the **Product Pick Applet**.

2. Copy the **Product Pick Applet** by selecting the record and pressing *Ctrl+B*.

3. Set the following values for the copied applet:

    ○ **Name**: AHA Product Pick Applet

    ○ **Project**: AHA User Interface

    ○ **Comments**: Created for AHA prototype, copy of Product Pick Applet

4. Right-click the **AHA Product Pick Applet** and select **Edit Web Layout**.

5. In the layout editor, select the **Part #** list column and press *Delete* to delete it.

6. Repeat step 5 for the **Service Length Period** column.

7. Save the changes by pressing *Ctrl+S*.

8. Close the editor window.

9. Compile the **AHA Product Pick Applet**.

We now have created a new pick applet. In order to invoke the pick applet from another applet, we must add a reference to the pick applet to another applet's controls or list columns. In continuing the case study example, the following procedure describes how to modify the Product Name list column of the AHA Customer Offer List Applet (created in an earlier chapter) to reference the AHA Product Pick Applet:

1. Navigate to the **AHA Customer Offer List Applet**.

2. Navigate to the **Product Name** list column of the AHA Customer Offer List Applet.

3. Set the **Pick Applet** property of the Product Name list column to **AHA Product Pick Applet**.

4. Set the **Runtime** property of the Product Name list column to **TRUE**.

5. Compile the AHA Customer Offer List Applet.

Did you know?

The **Runtime** property should always be set to **TRUE** for controls or list columns that have specialized behavior such as launching popup applets or calendar controls at runtime. For example, to ensure that the calendar control is available in both the High-Interactivity and Standard Interactivity UI modes, we should set the Runtime property for each date control to **TRUE**.

A Siebel Tools archive file (`Chapter 10 Applets.sif`) is available in this chapter's code file. The file represents the applet definitions created and modified made in the previous section.

Case study example: Testing pick list configurations

In order to test the business layer and applet modifications, we must be able to view the applets in the Siebel Web Client. In early phases of the project (such as in this chapter), it may be necessary to create a simple test view that exposes the modified applets.

The procedure to create and register new views has already been laid out in *Chapter 5*, so only brief instructions are given here for creating a test view for the AHA Customer Offer List Applet and the AHA Customer Documents List Applet:

1. Use the **New View wizard** to create a view with the following characteristics:

    ○ **Project**: AHA User Interface

    ○ **Name**: AHA UI Test View

    ○ **Title**: Test View

    ○ **Business Object**: Account

    ○ **Upgrade Behavior**: Preserve

    ○ **Web Template**: View Detail

    ○ **Applets**: AHA Customer Profile Form Applet, AHA Customer Offer List Applet, AHA Customer Documents List Applet

    ○ **Applet Mode for all list applets**: Edit List

2. Arrange the list applets side by side by positioning them on the 50 percent placeholders on the bottom of the view template.

3. Add the AHA UI Test View to the **Accounts screen** and register it with the **AHA Prototype** responsibility.

4. Use the test view to verify that the following pick lists work as expected:
   ° Product Name (dynamic) and Response Type (static) on the Customer Offers list
   ° Responsible Employee Login Name (dynamic) on the Customer Documents list

A Siebel Tools archive file (`Chapter 10 Test View.sif`) is available in this chapter's code file. The file represents the view and screen definitions as created or modified in the above section.

ADM import XML files (`Chapter_10_View.xml` and `Chapter_10_Responsibility.xml`) are provided in this chapter's code file. These files represent the AHA UI Test View and the AHA Prototype Responsibility type after the changes in the previous section. The `Chapter_10_View.xml` file must be imported first.

Constrained and hierarchical pick lists

Because of the fact that pick lists are based on the feature set of business components, developers can limit the record set visible to the end user in the pick list. This technique is called **constrained pick lists** and applies to static and dynamic pick lists alike.

Hierarchical pick lists are a special type of static pick lists where the end user has to follow a defined sequence of selection. For example, the area field of a service request has to be filled before the subarea field. The subarea dropdown will only display values suitable for the selected area.

Filtering the record set for a pick list can be required for various reasons. Usability and data quality are among the typical reasons. Another reason can be data security.

We have the following options to filter the record set for a pick list:

- Constrained pick maps (discussed in this section)
- Specify a search specification on the pick business component, the pick list, or the pick applet (discussed earlier in this chapter)
- Siebel State Model (not discussed in this book)

Exploring a constrained dynamic pick list

We can find many examples of constrained dynamic pick lists in the preconfigured Siebel CRM applications. For instance, we can navigate to the **Agreements screen** and associate an agreement with an account. When we then click the select button in the **Last Name** field to select a contact person for the agreement, the pick list only displays contacts that are associated with the account.

The following screenshot shows this behavior for an agreement record in the Siebel Sample Database:

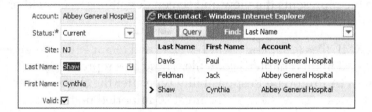

This behavior is implemented by declaring a so-called *constrained pick map* entry. The pick map for the Contact field in the Agreement business component is displayed in the following screenshot. Note the **Constrain flag** for the **Account Id** field:

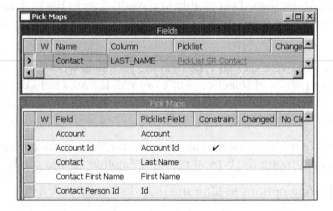

Checking the Constrain flag defines that when the pick map is executed, the pick list will only display records that match the filter criteria. In the previous example, the pick list will only display records where the value in the **Account Id** field in the pick list's business component matches the value in the Account Id field of the **Agreement** business component.

Exploring hierarchical static pick lists

The preconfigured Siebel CRM applications provide useful examples of hierarchical static pick lists. For instance, we can log in to a Siebel Demo application, using the sample database, and navigate to the **Service Request** screen. There we can investigate the behavior of the **Type**, **Area**, and **Sub Area** drop-down boxes in the form applets for service requests. When we select **Automotive** in the **Type** drop-down list, we can only select values related to the automotive industry in the **Area** drop-down list, for example **Engine**. The **Sub Area** drop-down list will then only display values related to engine problems such as **Check Engine Light**.

We can also observe that when we change a field in a group of hierarchical pick lists, the fields that are below that field in the hierarchy are emptied automatically.

When we investigate the fields behind these three drop-down lists in the **Service Request** business component we can learn how multi-level hierarchical pick lists work. The following table describes the fields involved in our example:

Applet Display Name	Field	Constrain Pick Map Fields	Picklist	LOV Type of Pick list	Pick Business Component
Type	**INS Product**	(None)	INS PickList SR Product	SR_AREA	PickList Hierarchical
Area	**INS Area**	Parent = INS Product	INS PickList SR Area	SR_AREA	PickList Hierarchical
Sub Area	**INS Sub-Area**	Parent INT = INS CurrentArea	INS PickList SR Hierarchical Sub-Area	SR_AREA	PickList Hierarchical Sub-Area

The main characteristics of hierarchical pick lists can be described as follows:

- They share the same **List of Values (LOV)** type.
- They use the **PickList Hierarchical** business component, or a copy thereof, which uses a self join to define a **Parent** field. This field is labeled **Parent LIC** in the List of Values administration view.
- The pick map for any but the first field in the hierarchy contains one **constrained** entry that matches the current entry of the upper level to the parent of the current level.
- The List of Values entries for the type, SR_AREA in the preceding example, use the **Parent LIC** field to define which hierarchy level they belong to.

The following screenshot shows the List of Values administration view with the three values for the service request's type, area, and sub area that we used in the previous example:

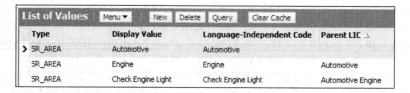

Type	Display Value	Language-Independent Code	Parent LIC
SR_AREA	Automotive	Automotive	
SR_AREA	Engine	Engine	Automotive
SR_AREA	Check Engine Light	Check Engine Light	Automotive Engine

As we can see, the *Engine* entry defines *Automotive* as its parent and the *Check Engine Light* entry defines *Automotive Engine* as its parent.

Summary

Static and dynamic pick lists ensure that high levels of usability and data quality can be easily achieved in Siebel CRM applications.

Simple drop-down boxes are implemented as static pick lists. The values for these pick lists are administered in a central List of Values table.

Relationships between entities, such as the account for an agreement, are supported by dynamic pick lists and pick applets, which allow the user to search and modify the data set.

Pick maps define the values to copy between the pick and the originating business components as well as the rules to constrain the entries in the pick list.

Finally, pick lists can be organized hierarchically to support multi-level selections.

In the next chapter, we will learn how to configure multi value fields.

11
Multi Value Fields

Multi value fields are widely used in Siebel CRM applications and enable end users to view and edit data relationships such as one-to-many (1:M) or many-to-many (M:M). Developers must be aware of the technical intricacies of multi value fields in order to configure them efficiently.

In this chapter we will learn the following:

- Understanding Multi Value Fields
- Creating many-to-many (M:M) relationships
- Creating multi value links
- Creating multi value fields
- Creating **multi value group** (**MVG**) Applets

Understanding multi value fields

As discussed in previous chapters, links connect a parent and a child business component in a 1:M or M:M relationship. The usual way to display data in such relationships to the end user is a view with one applet per business component, displaying the parent record on top and the list of child records below. These views are also called *detail views*.

The following screenshot shows the **Opportunity Detail - Contacts View** as an example of a detail view:

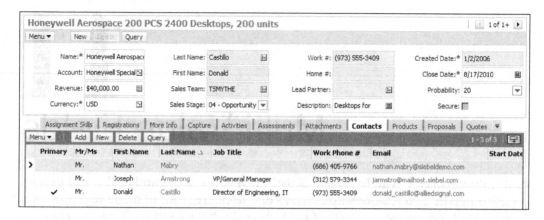

The view displays one opportunity record on top using a form applet and a list of contact persons associated to the opportunity using a list applet.

When we examine this example further we find the following considerations:

- A separate view means additional effort with regard to the administration of access control and responsibilities

- End users may only be interested in the information displayed by the form applet but the database has been instructed to fetch the contact data as well, which can impact performance when there are a lot of contact records in the database

- It is impossible to find all opportunities where a selected person, for example Mr. Castillo, is a member of the contact list

Multi value fields provide a solution for these considerations. With multi value fields we can implement the following:

- A single applet control or list column, instead of an entire view, displaying the related child records only when the end user clicks the select icon

- Minimal performance impact because the data is only fetched from the databases when the user opens the multi value group applet

- The possibility to query for all parent records that have a certain child record associated

Preconfigured Siebel CRM applications often use both mechanisms, detail views and multi value fields, at the same time. This is the case in our example view. When we have a closer look at the opportunity form applet on top of the view, we find the **Last Name** field, which can be identified as a multi value field because the select icon has two dots and a checkmark. Clicking this icon opens the so-called **multi value group (MVG)** applet associated with the originating applet control or list column. MVG applets are implemented as list applets in a pop-up browser window. In case of a M:M relationship, a second list applet, the Associate applet, is rendered on the left half of the pop-up window. The combination of MVG applet (right) and Associate applet (left) is called a *Shuttle Applet*.

The following screenshot shows the **Last Name** field for the example opportunity record and the Contacts shuttle applet:

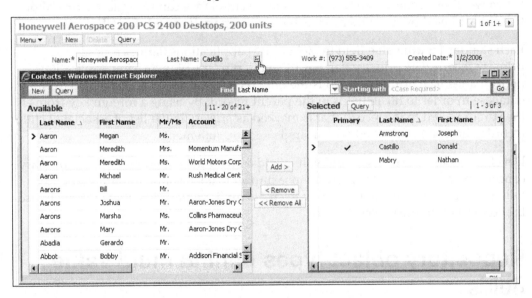

End users can search the list of available contact persons in the associate applet on the left. Clicking the **Add >** button associates the selected contact records with the parent opportunity and displays them in the MVG applet on the right.

End users can also use the multi value field for queries in order to find all parent records that are associated with a certain child record. In following our above example, we could click the **Query** button in the opportunity form applet and enter Castillo in the **Last Name** field. When we press the *Enter* key to execute the query, the Siebel application issues the necessary SQL statements against the database to retrieve all opportunity records that have a contact with a last name of *Castillo* associated.

Did you know?

The Siebel Query Language provides the EXISTS() function to query multi value fields. In **Siebel Industry Applications (SIA)**, any search term entered in a multi value field is automatically wrapped by the EXISTS() function.

Developers and administrators can use the EXISTS() function to create complex search specifications or predefined queries, or generally use the function when dealing with multi value fields.

The "Primary" concept

When we observe the above screenshots more closely we can see that one record of the list displayed by the child applets has the **Primary flag** set to **TRUE**.

Each standard multi value field in Siebel CRM applications defines a single primary record. The primary flag has the main purpose of increasing application performance. The primary record is the only record that needs to be fetched from the database in order to fill all fields in the parent record. By using a foreign key from the parent record to the record that is marked as *primary* in the list of associated child records, this can be achieved with a single select statement.

Developers who create new multi value fields must understand and use the primary concept in order to keep the performance impact to an absolute minimum. In the following sections, we will learn how to create multi value fields, that effectively use the concept of primary records.

Repository object types behind multi value fields

To successfully create multi value fields we must understand the object types that are needed in the Siebel Repository. The following object types are the foundation for multi value fields:

- Link
- Multi Value Link
- Multi Value Field
- **Multi Value Group (MVG)** and Association List applets

We introduced the concept of the link object type in *Chapter 9, Business Objects and Links,* so we do not need to discuss it here. In the following sections, we will discuss the other object types in the previous list.

Multi value link

Multi Value Links are child object definitions to business components. They can be appropriately described as references to **business components** and the **links** used to establish a parent—child relationship from the parent business component to the child business component.

The Opportunity business component for example uses a multi value link definition named **Contact** to establish a connection between itself as a parent and the Contact business component as a child. The *Contact* multi value link is used by the **Contact Last Name** field to display the last names of the contact persons associated with the opportunity. The following screenshot shows the relevant portion of the **View Detail** window for the Opportunity business component that visualizes this relationship:

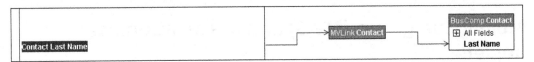

The key properties of the multi value link object type can be described as follows:

Property	Description
Destination Business Component	The name of the child business component that the multi value link refers to.
Destination Link	The name of a link that connects the destination business component (as a child) to a parent business component.
Primary Id Field	The name of a field in the multi value link's parent business component that is used to store the unique identifier (typically the ROW_ID) of the primary child record.
Auto Primary	Controls the way to set the primary flag.
	When set to **DEFAULT**, the first record entered in the multi value field becomes the primary.
	When set to **NONE**, the end user must manually designate a primary child record.
	SELECTED is only applicable when there are multiple multi value links for the same destination business component. Selecting one record as the primary will then also cause the respective record to become primary in all other multi value link relationships when it has not yet been set as such.
Popup Update Only	When set to **TRUE**, changes can only be made through the MVG applet.

Multi value field

Multi value fields are fields that use a multi value link to retrieve data from other business components. The Object Explorer window in Siebel Tools allows distinguishing between Single Value Fields and Multi Value Fields by selecting the respective type in the hierarchy. When the Field object type is selected, the Object List Editor displays all fields and we can use the **Multi Valued** property, set to **TRUE** for multi value fields, to distinguish between single and multi value fields.

Did you know?

The term Multi Value Group comes from the fact that a **group** of multi value fields typically refers to a single multi value link.

Multi value group (MVG) and association list applets

To allow end users to efficiently associate child records through a multi value field, specialized MVG applets are provided. These applets are list applets with additional controls. They are linked to the originating applet via the **MVG Applet** property of the control or list column exposing the multi value field.

In the case of a M:M relationship, an additional list applet is needed to display all available records. These applets have their type property set to **Association List** and are commonly referred to as *Assoc applets*. They are linked to an MVG applet by means of the **Associate Applet** property.

Relationships between repository objects for multi value fields

The following diagram depicts the relationships between the objects related to multi value field functionality in the Siebel Repository:

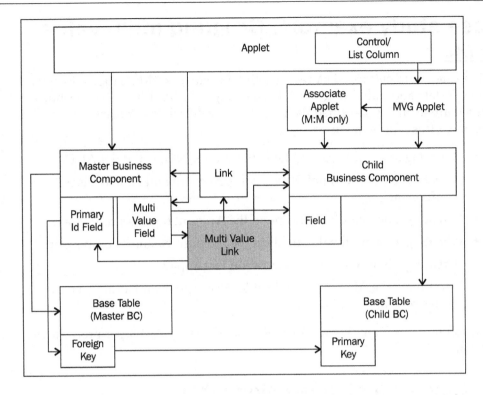

From the preceding diagram we can learn the following:

- A control or list column that refers to a multi value field in the applet's business component also references a MVG applet
- In case of a M:M relationship, the MVG applet references an associate applet
- Both the MVG and associate applet reference the child business component
- Multi value fields use a multi value link to establish a connection to a field in a child business component
- Multi value links reference the child business component and define a link that connects the parent and child business component
- In addition, multi value links reference a primary ID field, which acts as the foreign key to a single record in the child business component

  For the sake of readability the above diagram does not depict intersection tables for M:M relationships.

Case study example: Creating multi value fields

As indicated in *Chapter 3*, AHA requires that the current 1:M relationship between customer data and public notes should be changed to M:M. The AHA technical architecture team has identified the following modifications as necessary to implement this requirement:

- Creating a new intersection table between S_NOTE and S_PARTY
- Creating a new M:M link between the Account and Note business component
- Creating a new multi value link in the Account business component
- Creating new multi value fields in the Account business component
- Creating a new MVG and Association List applet
- Modifying the AHA Account Profile Form applet and adding a new Notes control

In the following sections, we will describe the necessary developer procedures in detail.

Creating a new intersection table

Because the process of creating new tables has already been discussed in *Chapter 8*, we will not repeat this content here.

Please refer to *Chapter 8, The Data Layer* for the exact step-by-step description to create a new table. It is recommendable to use the New Table wizard to create a table with the following characteristics:

- **Name:** CX_AHA_PTY_NOTE
- **Project:** AHA Tables
- **Type:** Intersection Table
- **First parent table:** S_PARTY
- **Foreign key column to first parent table:** PARTY_ID
- **Second parent table:** S_NOTE
- **Foreign key column to second parent table:** NOTE_ID
- **Comments:** Created for AHA prototype

The table must be applied and compiled.

In order to support the primary concept, we must also create a new foreign key column to S_NOTE in the S_PARTY table. The new column should have the following characteristics:

- **Name**: X_AHA_PR_NOTE_ID
- **Foreign Key Table**: S_NOTE
- **Physical Type**: Varchar
- **Length**: 15
- **Comments**: Created for AHA prototype

Changes to the S_PARTY table must be applied and compiled.

 Extending the S_PARTY table might not be the best solution when there are large volumes of data stored in the Siebel database. The AHA technical architecture team has indicated that this is not the case for AHA.

A Siebel Tools archive file (Chapter 11 Tables.sif) is provided with this chapter's code file. The file represents the new intersection table and modified S_PARTY table after the modifications in the previous section.

To finalize the procedure, we have to create a new field in the **Account** business component that maps to the new foreign key column in the S_PARTY table. The new field should have the following characteristics:

- **Name**: AHA Primary Note Id
- **Column**: X_AHA_PR_NOTE_ID
- **Comments**: Created for AHA prototype

The Account business component must be compiled after this modification.

Creating a new M:M link

Links are the foundation for multi value fields. We can create a multi value field on top of any 1:M or M:M link. In *Chapter 9*, we learned how to use the link object type to create one-to-many (1:M) relationships between a parent and a child business component.

In this section, we will learn how to create a M:M link between two business components in order to support a many-to-many relationship.

Because the concept of links and business objects has already been discussed in detail in *Chapter 9*, the procedure to create a new M:M link between the **Account** and **Note** business component is less explicit. Please refer to *Chapter 9* for step-by-step instructions on how to create links and child business components.

The new link definition for the case study example should have the following characteristics:

- **Project**: AHA Business Components
- **Parent Business Component**: Account
- **Child Business Component**: Note
- **Inter Table**: CX_AHA_PTY_NOTE
- **Inter Parent Column**: PARTY_ID
- **Inter Child Column**: NOTE_ID
- **Comments**: Created for AHA prototype

To complete the procedure, we must modify the Account business object and add the Note business component using the new Account/Note link. Finally, we have to compile the new Account/Note link and the Account business object.

Creating multi value fields using the MVG wizard

Siebel Tools provides a MVG wizard to facilitate the process of creating multi value fields and multi value links. The following procedure describes how to use the MVG wizard to create a series of new multi value fields for the preceding case study example:

1. Check out or lock the **Account** business component if necessary.
2. Click the **New** button in the Siebel Tools toolbar.
3. In the **New Object Wizards** dialog, double-click the **MVG** wizard.
4. In the **Multi Value Group** dialog provide the following values:
   - **Project**: Account (the project that contains the master business component)
   - **Master business component**: Account
5. Click **Next**.

6. Provide the following values in the dialog:
    - **Detail business component**: Note
    - **Name for the multi value link**: AHA Note

7. Click **Next**.
8. In the **Direct Links** dialog, select the **Account/Note** link.
9. Click **Next**.
10. In the **Primary ID Field** dialog, provide the following values:
    - **Primary ID Field**: AHA Primary Note Id
    - **Auto Primary**: Default
    - **Use Primary Join**: Checked
    - **Check No Match**: Unchecked

11. Click **Next**.
12. In the **Multi Value Link** dialog, leave all checkboxes unchecked.
13. Click **Next**.
14. In the **Multi Value Fields** dialog, select the **Note** field from the drop-down list.
15. Modify the name to AHA Note.
16. Click the **Add** button to add the new multi value field definition to the list on the bottom of the dialog.
17. Repeat steps 14 and 16 for the following fields:

 Skip step 15 and keep the auto-generated names.

    - **Area**
    - **Created By Name**
    - **Sub-Area**
    - **Type**

18. Click **Next**.
19. Click **Finish**.
20. The **MVG Applet wizard** is launched automatically because no MVG applet exists for the new multi value fields.

21. Click **Cancel** to close the MVG Applet wizard.

> We will discuss creating MVG and Association List applets in the next section.

We have now created the main repository object definitions for a new multi value link and five new multi value fields on the Account business component. In order to satisfy the requirements of AHA such as to limit the multi value group to public notes and provide pick lists in the MVG applet, we must follow this procedure to fine-tune the object definitions:

1. Navigate to the **Account/Note** link.

2. Set the following properties:
   - **Search Specification**: [Private]<>'Y'
   - **Sort Specification**: Created (DESC)

3. Compile the **Account/Note** link.

4. Navigate to the **Multi Value Field list** for the **Account** business component.

5. Set the **Picklist** property for the following multi value fields as indicated in the following list:
   - **AHA Note Area**: Com PickList Note Area
   - **AHA Note Sub-Area**: Com PickList Note Hierarchical Sub-Area
   - **AHA Note Type**: Com PickList Note Type (SIA)

6. Compile the Account business component.

A Siebel Tools archive file (Chapter 11 Business Components.sif) is provided with this chapter's code file. The file represents the Account business component, the new Account/Note link, and the Account business object after the changes in the preceding section.

Case study example: Creating multi value group (MVG) and association list applets

The process of implementing multi value fields requires the creation (or reuse) of multi value group (MVG) applets and, in the case of M:M relationships, association list applets. Both applet types are specialized list applets that include extra controls to provide a higher level of usability to the end user.

Because of the fact that the MVG applet wizard provided by Siebel Tools produces only a half-done artifact, it is recommendable to copy an existing MVG applet and modify the copy.

The following procedure describes how to create a new MVG applet for the previous case study example by copying an existing MVG applet:

1. Navigate to the **Industry Mvg Applet**.

2. Use the *Ctrl+B* keyboard shortcut to copy the Industry Mvg Applet.

3. Modify the copy as follows:

    ○ **Name:** AHA Notes Mvg Applet

    ○ **Project:** AHA User Interface

    ○ **Business Component:** Note

    ○ **Title:** Public Notes

    ○ **Associate Applet:** (empty)

    ○ **Comments:** Created for AHA prototype; Copy of Industry Mvg Applet

4. Right-click the **AHA Notes Mvg Applet** and select **Edit Web Layout**.

5. Delete all list columns except the **Primary** column from the **Base** web template.

6. In the **Controls/Columns** window switch to the **Edit List** web template and delete the same list columns as in step 5.

7. Press *Ctrl+S* to save the changes.

8. Close the **Web Layout Editor**.

9. In the **Object Explorer**, expand the **Applet type**.

10. Expand the **List** type and select the **List Column** type.

11. Delete all List Column definitions except the list column named **SSA Primary Field**.

Did you know?

To support the *Primary* feature, MVG applets can expose a system field named **SSA Primary Field**. This field is only available in applets of the MVG type.

12. In the **Object Explorer**, select the **Applet** type.

13. Right-click the **AHA Notes Mvg Applet** and select **Edit Web Layout**.

14. Ensure that the **Base** web template is selected in the **Controls/Columns** window.

15. Drag a **Text List Column** object from the **Palettes** window to the column placeholder to the right of the Primary column.

16. In the **Properties** window set the following properties for the new list column:

    ○ **Name**: AHA Note Text
    ○ **Field**: Note
    ○ **Display Name**: Note
    ○ **HTML Type**: TextArea
    ○ **Runtime**: TRUE
    ○ **Show Popup**: TRUE

17. Repeat steps 15 and 16 to create four additional list columns with the following characteristics:

Name	Field	Display Name	Runtime
AHA Created By	Created By Name	Created By	FALSE
AHA Type	Type	Type	TRUE
AHA Area	Area	Area	TRUE
AHA Sub-Area	Sub-Area	Sub-Area	TRUE

18. Press *Ctrl+S* to save the changes.

19. In the **Controls/Columns** window switch to the **Edit List** web template.

20. Drag the five new list columns from the **Controls/Columns** window to the column placeholders in the same sequence as in the Base template.

21. Save the changes.

22. Right-click the layout editor and select **Preview**.

23. Compare the layout with the following screenshot.

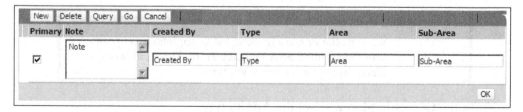

24. Close the applet layout editor.

Creating association list applets

There is no wizard available in Siebel Tools to create association list applets. Therefore, it is recommendable to use the copy technique.

The following shortened procedure describes how to create a new association list applet for the case study example:

1. Copy the **Industry Assoc Applet** and modify the copy as follows:
    - **Name**: AHA Notes Assoc Applet
    - **Project**: AHA User Interface
    - **Business Component**: Note
    - **Title**: Add Notes
    - **Comments**: Created for AHA prototype; Copy of Industry Assoc Applet

2. Delete all list column mappings from both web templates in the applet layout editor.

3. Delete all list column definitions.

4. Refer to steps 14 to 17 in the previous procedure to create five list columns for the **Edit List** web template in the applet layout editor.

5. Refer to steps 19 and 20 in the previous procedure to add the new list columns to the **Query** web template.

6. Save all changes and close the applet layout editor.

7. Navigate to the **AHA Notes Mvg Applet**.

8. Set the **Associate Applet** property to **AHA Notes Assoc Applet**.

9. Compile the **AHA Notes Mvg Applet** and the **AHA Notes Assoc Applet**.

Creating MVG controls

The final step in the process of creating multi value fields is to modify one or more applets that are based on the master business component. We can add a new control (or list column) to the applet as usual with the important additional modification to reference a MVG applet in the **MVG Applet** property. To continue our case study example we can modify the **AHA Customer Profile Form Applet** and add a new Field control with the following characteristics:

- **Name**: AHA Notes MVG
- **Field**: AHA Note

- **Caption - String Override**: Customer Notes
- **MVG Applet**: AHA Notes Mvg Applet
- **Runtime**: TRUE

Due to the length of the notes text, we should provide more space for the new control.

To test our configuration, we must ensure that all data layer changes have been applied and all new or modified object definitions have been compiled.

We can then use the Siebel Developer Web Client to navigate to the Process Start Page view and verify that the Account profile form applet now has a functional multi value group control to create new notes or select existing notes for a customer.

A Siebel Tools archive file (Chapter 11 Applets.sif) is provided with this chapter's code file. The file represents the new MVG and Associate applets as well as the AHA Customer Profile Form Applet after the changes in the preceding section.

Summary

This chapter introduced us to the concepts behind multi value fields in Siebel CRM. Multi value fields allow us to create links between parent and child business components and provide a high level of usability to the end user by means of MVG and association list applets.

The chapter also provided a full case study example that demonstrated how to create a new M:M relationship between two business components and how to create the necessary repository object definitions in the data layer, business layer, and user interface.

In the next chapter, we will learn how to configure data security with Siebel access control.

12
Configuring Access Control

Siebel Access Control is a major element of the Siebel CRM architecture. Laid out for multi-organization implementations, the Siebel CRM business layer provides row level data security across the entire data model. This means that individual end users have access to different sets of data from the same view. In this chapter, we will discover the following topics:

- Understanding Siebel Access Control
- Configuring View properties for Siebel Access Control
- Defining business component view modes
- Configuring additional object types for Access Control

Understanding Siebel access control

The Siebel sample database is most suitable for exploring how Siebel access control works. We can follow the procedure below to examine how the visibility of service request data is managed by Siebel access control. In the example we will use two different sample user accounts—Casey Cheng, Call Center Agent, and Fred Roberts, Service Engineer—to simulate a typical service center scenario:

1. Log in to the **Siebel Call Center Demo** application as Casey Cheng, using CCHENG as username and password.
2. Navigate to the **Service** screen.
3. Click the **Service Request List** link below the screen bar.
4. The **My Service Requests** list is displayed.
5. Observe that all records in the list have the **Owner** field set to **CCHENG**.
6. In the **Help** menu, select the **About View** command.

7. In the About View dialog, note the name of the current view (**Personal Service Request List View**) and the name of the list applet (**Service Request List Applet**).

8. Click **OK** to close the **About View** dialog.

9. In the service request list, click the **New** button to create a new service request record.

10. In the new record, provide the following field values:
    ○ **Owner**: FROBERTS
    ○ **Summary**: Testing Siebel access control

11. Press *Ctrl+S* to save the record.

12. Press *Alt+Enter* to refresh the list.

13. Observe that the service request record is no longer visible to Casey Cheng.

14. In the **File** menu, select **Connect**.

15. In the login dialog enter FROBERTS as username and password and press *Enter*.

16. Navigate to the **My Service Requests** list view.

17. In the **Saved Queries** drop-down list in the upper-right corner of the application select **New SRs** to filter the list.

18. Observe that the service request record created earlier using Casey Cheng's account is visible to Fred Roberts among other service requests.

19. Open the **About View** dialog and observe that the names of the view and the list applet are the same as in step 7.

20. Press *Ctrl+Shift+X* to log out of **Siebel Call Center**.

The previous example demonstrates that the same view provides completely different data sets to different end users. Siebel CRM has several types of preconfigured *visibility views* of which the *My View* is widely used for individual data access.

When we are logged in to the Siebel sample database as the Siebel Administrator (SADMIN) we have the broadest responsibility. Therefore, we can use all available views. When we navigate to the **My Service Request** list view as SADMIN, we can click the drop-down icon in the list applet title to see the other available visibility views as shown in the following screenshot:

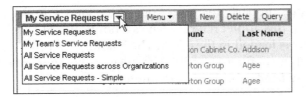

As we can observe, there are numerous other visibility views such as **My Team's...**, **All...**, and **All ... across Organizations**.

Selecting one of the entries in the visibility drop-down list navigates to a different view that typically contains the same applets as the other views in the list. Selecting the **All Service Requests** entry, for example, opens the **All Service Request List View**.

View properties for access control

The technical difference between the visibility views is that each of them has different values in its *visibility* properties. For example, the **Personal Service Request List View**, labeled **My Service Requests**, and the **All Service Request List View**, labeled **All Service Requests**, only differ in name, labeling, and the **Visibility Applet Type** property.

The following screenshot shows the two views in Siebel Tools for comparison:

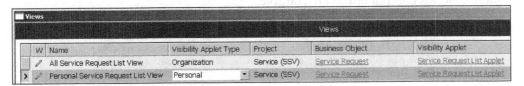

We can confirm that the **Visibility Applet Type** property is set to **Organization** for the All Service Request List View and to **Personal** for the **Personal Service Request List View**.

Did you know?

When the **Visibility Applet Type** and **Visibility Applet** properties are set for a view, we refer to this view as a *visibility view*.

The **Visibility Applet** property references one of the view's applets. The business component to which this applet refers receives a notification to apply a data filter when the view is loaded in the client. The **Visibility Applet Type** property value specifies the type of filter to apply. The business component must have a corresponding **View Mode** child object definition.

Business component view modes

Business component view mode objects have the following key properties:

- **Reserved Name** (see following table).

- **Owner Type**: Identifies the user attribute to use for filtering data. For example, an owner type of **Person** means that the user's **login ID** is used for the filter. Other values are Position, Organization, Group, and Catalog Group (see table below for explanations).

- **Visibility Field**: The name of a single value field or multi value field (and the corresponding multi value link) that is used as the counterpart of the user attribute, identified by the Owner Type property, for the data filter. For example, if the owner type is **Person** and the visibility field is **Owner Id**, the business component will only display records where the Owner Id field contains the current user's login ID.

The following screenshot shows the view mode object definitions for the Service Request business component as an example:

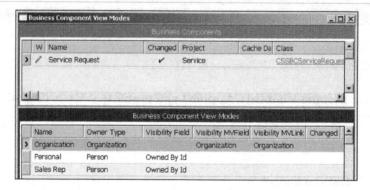

To view or modify view mode object definitions, we can navigate to the business component in Siebel Tools, expand the Business Component type in the Object Explorer, and select the **BusComp View Mode** type.

The following table describes the preconfigured visibility view types and the corresponding Visibility Applet Type and business component view mode names. Note that some view types can use different visibility applet types depending on the data objects:

Visibility View Type	Visibility Applet Type (View Mode)	Description
"My View"	Personal, Sales Rep	When set to **Personal**, the business component referenced by the visibility applet uses the user's login ID to filter records.
		When set to **Sales Rep**, the user's currently active position is used to filter records.
"All View"	Organization	The **Organization** view mode is configured to display only records that belong to the user's currently active organization.
"My Team's…"	Manager	The filter is applied based on the user's login ID or position. In addition, records belonging to users that have a child position below the current user's position are also displayed. Because this applies to management positions, the name of the view mode is **Manager**.
"All … across My Organizations"	Sub-Organization	Similar to the *My Team's* view but takes the organization hierarchy into account. Displays records that belong to the user's organization and to all its descendant organizations.
Catalog Views	Group, Catalog	Views that use Group or Catalog as the visibility applet type provide access control based on the user's membership to so-called **access groups**. Access groups can be associated to **catalogs** and **categories** and are typically used for product and literature display.
"All … across Organizations"	All	When the Visibility Applet Type property is set to **All**, the business component does not use a view mode definition. Instead, all records are displayed that have at least one organization associated regardless of the user's current organizational membership.

Repository object definitions for access control

The following diagram depicts the relationships between the repository object types involved in Siebel access control.

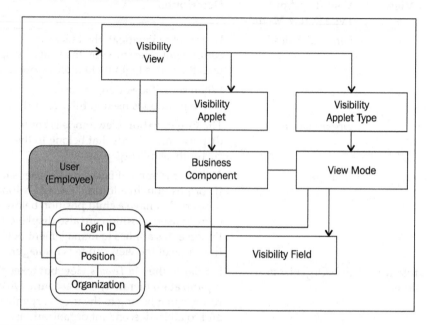

From the preceding diagram we can derive the following information:

- A visibility view specifies a visibility applet and a visibility applet type
- The visibility applet type refers to one of the **view mode** definitions in the business component referenced by the visibility applet
- A view mode object definition references a field in its parent business component and one of the user's (or employee's) access control attributes such as login ID, position, or organization

 For the sake of readability, the diagram does not include access groups and catalogs.

 Did you know?

In Siebel terms, an employee is a user who holds at least one position in an organization.

Configuring view properties for Siebel access control

During a Siebel CRM project it is very likely that a new Siebel view should define the correct access control settings. The following case study example demonstrates how to create a new visibility view.

Case study example

As indicated in *Chapter 3, Case Study Introduction* AHA requires that a new view titled **All Sales Tools created by me** should be made available to end users. The technical architects at AHA have already identified a *My Literature* list view, which can be used as the base for the new view. The new view should only display literature records, or sales tools, that the user has created her-or himself.

The following procedure describes how to copy the existing view (named *FINS Sales Tool List View - My*) and modify the copy:

1. Navigate to the view named **FINS Sales Tool List View - My**.

2. Copy the view using the *Ctrl+B* shortcut.

3. Modify the copy as follows:

   ○ **Name**: AHA My Sales Tools List View

   ○ **Project**: AHA User Interface

   ○ **Visibility Applet Type**: Personal

   ○ **Comments**: Created for AHA prototype

4. Compile the **AHA My Sales Tools List View**.

5. Navigate to the **Literature Screen** object definition.

6. Ensure that you have **write access** to the Literature Screen by checking it out or locking it.

7. In the **Screen Views** list, add a **new** record and enter the following values:

   ○ **View**: AHA My Sales Tools List View

   ○ **Type**: Aggregate View

   ○ **Parent Category**: Sales Tool List

   ○ **Viewbar Text - String Override**: All Sales Tools created by me

   ○ **Menu Text - String Override**: All Sales Tools created by me

   ○ **Comments**: Created for AHA prototype

8. Right-click the **Literature Screen** and select **Edit Screen View Sequence**.

9. In the **Screen View Sequence Editor**, select the item that represents the AHA My Sales Tools List View.

10. Use *Ctrl+Down* to move the view below the view named FINS Sales Tool List View-My.

11. Press *Ctrl+S* to save the changes.

12. Close the **Screen View Sequence Editor**.

13. Compile the **Literature Screen**.

A Siebel Tools archive file (`Visibility.sif`) is available with this chapter's code file. The archive file represents the new AHA My Sales Tools List View and the Literature Screen after the changes made in the above section.

Registering the new view

We can refer to the instructions in *Chapter 6, Views and Screens* for details on how to register a view and associate it to a responsibility.

In short we have to do the following to make the view visible to our test user account:

- Create a new record for the **AHA My Sales Tools List View** in the Views list of the **Administration - Application** screen

- Associate the AHA My Sales Tools List View with the **AHA Prototype** responsibility

In addition we should add the **Admin Sales Tools List** view to the AHA Prototype responsibility in order to be able to create test literature records.

Defining business component view modes

The new view created in the previous section specifies **Personal** as the value for the **Visibility Applet Type** property. As an additional configuration step we must now ensure that the business component behind the **Sales Tool List Applet** (referenced in the Visibility Applet property) has an accompanying view mode definition.

The following procedure describes how to create a new view mode definition for the **Sales Tool** business component:

1. Navigate to the **Sales Tool** business component.

2. Ensure that you have write access to the Sales Tool business component.

3. In the Object Explorer, expand the **Business Component** type and select the **BusComp View Mode** type.

4. In the Business Component View Modes list, create a new record with the following values:

   ○ **Name:** Personal

   ○ **Owner Type:** Person

   ○ **Visibility Field:** Created By

   ○ **Comments:** Created for AHA prototype

5. Compile the Sales Tool business component.

A Siebel Tools archive file (Sales Tool BC.sif) is available with this chapter's code file. The archive file represents the Sales Tool business component after the changes made in the preceding section.

Testing the access control configuration

To test the filtering capacity of the new configuration we should follow the procedure given here:

1. Log in to the Siebel Developer Web Client.

2. Open the site map (*Ctrl+Shift+A*) and navigate to the **Administration - Document** screen.

3. Click the link for the **Literature** view.

4. Click the **New File** button and browse to a test document. Alternatively we can drag and drop a file from a Windows Explorer window to the list applet in the Literature administration view.

5. Step off the new record (or press *Ctrl+S*) to save it.

6. Open the site map and navigate to the **Literature** screen.

7. Click the link for the **All Sales Tools created by me** view.

8. Verify that the view is displayed in the visibility drop-down list in the upper-left corner of the list applet.

9. Verify that the view only displays records created by the current user.

Did you know?

We can use the *Ctrl+Alt+K* keyboard shortcut to open the **About Record** dialog for the selected record. This dialog reveals the system fields of the record including the name of the user who created the record.

The following screenshot shows the new **AHA My Sales Tools** list view:

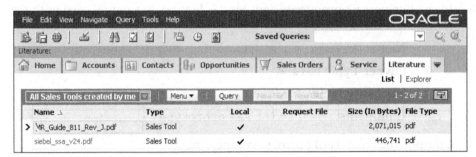

Configuring additional object types for access control

The following object types in the Siebel Repository can be configured to support the Siebel Access Control functionality:

- Pick List
- Link
- Drilldown Object

The following sections describe the visibility-related properties of these object types.

Visibility settings for pick list object definitions

We can define the following properties, which influence the data set displayed in pick lists, by applying Siebel Access Control mechanisms:

- **Visibility Auto All**: When this property is set to **TRUE** and the user has access to data from the pick list's business component by means of a view that uses **All** as the **Visibility Applet Type** then the data in the pick list is filtered in the same way as in an **All** view. When this property is set to **FALSE**, the data set of the pick list is governed by the Visibility Type property.

- **Visibility Type**: When this property is empty, no visibility rules apply. When it is set to any of the valid visibility modes (Personal, Sales Rep, All, Manager, Organization, Sub-Organization, Catalog, or Group) then the underlying business component will filter the data accordingly.

Visibility settings for link object definitions

Similar to pick lists, links can be configured using the Visibility Auto All and Visibility Type properties. The data filter determined by these properties applies to the link's child business component.

In addition, links have a property named **Visibility Rule Applied**. When this property is set to **Always**, any view using the link will have access control enforced on the child business component as specified by the **Visibility Type** property. When this property is set to **Never**, access control on the child records is disabled. However, when an end user drills down on a child record that she or he is not allowed to see in the target view, an error message is displayed.

Visibility settings for drilldown object definitions

Drilldown objects are child object definitions of applets, and as such are covered in greater detail in *Chapter 14, Configuring Navigation*. In general, a drilldown object defines a target view that is opened when the user clicks the hyperlink generated by the drilldown object.

We can specify a valid view mode for the **Visibility Type** property of a drilldown object to control the level of access control in the drilldown object's target business component.

Summary

Siebel Access Control is a strong and secure filter mechanism that ensures that end users only see records that they are supposed to see. The filter is applied by matching a single or multi value field of a business component against the value of one of the visibility-related user attributes (login ID, position, organization, or access group membership).

The main developer tasks of creating visibility views and defining business component view modes have been laid out in this chapter.

In addition, we discussed how access control mechanisms can be used for pick lists, links, and drilldown objects.

In the next chapter, we will learn how to configure specialized behavior of repository object definitions with user properties.

13
User Properties

Many business requirements are very detailed and complex. For example, the end user community could demand that one field is updated automatically when another field has been changed. To solve this kind of requirement in Siebel CRM, developers can define so-called **user properties** as an extension to the standard properties of object types such as business components, fields, and applets. In this chapter, we will discuss the following topics:

- Understanding user properties
- Business component and field user properties
- Applet, control, and list column user properties
- Viewing user properties

Understanding user properties

User properties are child object types that are available for the following object types in the Siebel Repository:

- Applet, Control, List Column
- Application
- Business Service
- Business Component, Field
- Integration Object, Integration Component, Integration Component Field
- View

To view the User Property (or *User Prop* as it is sometimes abbreviated) object type we typically have to modify the list of displayed types for the Object Explorer window. As discussed in the previous chapter, this can be achieved by selecting the **Options** command in the **View** menu. In the **Object Explorer** tab of the Development Tools Options dialog, we can select the object types for display as shown in the following screenshot:

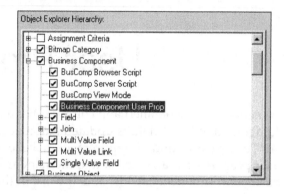

In the preceding example, the **Business Component User Prop** type is enabled for display.

After confirming the changes in the Development Tools Options dialog by clicking the **OK** button, we can for example navigate to the **Account** business component and review its existing user properties by selecting the **Business Component User Prop** type in the Object Explorer.

The following screenshot shows the list of user properties for the Account business component:

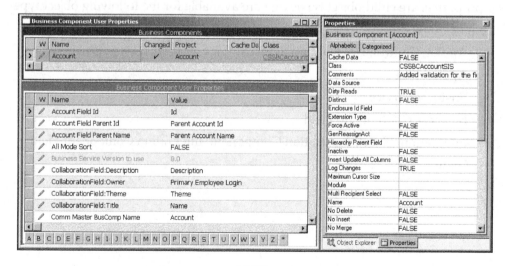

The screenshot also shows the standard Properties window on the right. This is to illustrate that a list of user properties, that mainly define a Name/Value pair can be simply understood as an extension to an object type's usual properties, which are accessible by means of the Properties window and represent Name/Value pairs as well.

Because an additional user property is just a new record in the Siebel Repository, the list of user properties for a given parent record is theoretically infinite. This allows developers to define a rich set of business logic as a simple list of Name/Value pairs instead of having to write program code.

The **Name** property of a user property definition must use a reserved name—and optional sequence number—as defined by Oracle engineering. The **Value** property must also follow the syntax defined for the special purpose of the user property.

Did you know?

The list of available names for a user property depends on the object type (for example Business Component) and the C++ class associated with the object definition. For example, the business component **Account** is associated with the `CSSBCAccountSIS` class, which defines a different range of available user property names than other classes.

Many user property names are officially documented in the **Siebel Developer's Reference** guide in the Siebel Bookshelf. We can find the guide online at the following URL:

```
http://download.oracle.com/docs/cd/E14004_01/books/ToolsDevRef/
ToolsDevRef_UserProps.html
```

The user property names described in this guide are intended for use by custom developers. Any other user property that we may find in the Siebel Repository but that is not officially documented should be considered an internal user property of Oracle engineering. Because the internal user properties could change in a future version of Siebel CRM in both syntax and behavior without prior notice, it is highly recommended to use only user properties that are documented by Oracle.

Another way to find out which user property names are made available by Oracle to customers is to click the drop-down icon in the **Name** property of a user property record. This opens the user property pick list, which displays a wide range of officially documented user properties along with a description text.

Multi-instance user properties

Some user properties can be instantiated more than once. If this is the case a sequence number is used to generate a distinguished name. For example, the **On Field Update Set** user property used on business components uses a naming convention as displayed in the following screenshot:

Name	Value
On Field Update Set 1	"Currency Code", "Price List", ""
On Field Update Set 2	"Managers Review", "Last Manager Review Date", Timestamp()
On Field Update Set 3	"Managers Review", "Last Review Manager Id", LoginName()
On Field Update Set 4	"Name", "Party Name", "[Name]"

In the previous example, we can see four instances of the On Field Update Set user property distinguished by a sequential numeric suffix (1 to 4).

Because it is very likely that Oracle engineers and custom developers add additional instances of the same user property while working on the next release, Oracle provides a *customer allowance gap* of **nine** instances for the next sequence number. In the previous example, a custom developer could continue the set of On Field Update Set user properties with a suffix of 13. By doing so, the custom developer will most likely avoid conflicts during an upgrade to a newer version of Siebel CRM. The Oracle engineer would continue with a suffix of five and upgrade conflicts will only occur when Oracle defines more than eight additional instances. The gap of nine also ensures that the sequence of multi-instance user properties is still functional when one or more of the user property records are marked as inactive.

In the following sections, we will describe the most important user properties for the business and user interface layer. In addition, we will examine case study scenarios to identify best practices for using user properties to define specialized behavior of Siebel CRM applications.

Business component and field user properties

On the business layer of the Siebel Repository, user properties are widely used to control specialized behavior of business components and fields. The following table describes the most important user properties on the business component level. The *Multiple Instances* column contains **Yes** for all user properties that can be instantiated more than once per parent object:

User Property Name	Description	Multiple Instances
Active Field Active Value	These two user properties define the name of a **business component field** and a value of that field. When the field has the value defined in the Active Value user property then the record is considered *Active* and can be updated. Otherwise, the record is considered *Inactive* and cannot be updated.	No
Admin NoDelete Admin NoUpdate	When the value of these user properties is set to **Y**, the business component prevents deletions or updates (respectively) even when the business component is in Admin mode.	No
All Mode Sort View Mode Sort	Allows developers to control how data is sorted for views that potentially display a large number of records (for example, Manager, All, Organization view modes). A value of **Normal** indicates that the business component's sort specification will be used for sorting. A value of **TRUE** switches the sort order to the U1 index of the underlying table. A value of **FALSE** results in no sorting. The **View Mode Sort** user property allows defining a sort specification for various view modes when All Mode Sort is set to **FALSE**.	No
BC Read Only Field	The value of this user property is typically the name of a calculated field that returns Y or N. When the value is Y the record is read-only, otherwise the record can be updated as usual.	No
Currency Field	Specifies the name of a field in its parent business component. When the currency of this field is changed, a new value for this field is calculated based on the exchange rates stored for the currency pair in the Siebel database.	Yes

User Property Name	Description	Multiple Instances
Deep Copy Deep Delete Deep Copy/Delete Link Recursive Link	These user properties control the behavior of the parent business component and child business components when a parent record is copied or deleted. **Deep Copy** specifies the name of the child business component in a 1:M relationship with the parent business component whose records are copied to the parent copy. **Deep Delete** defines the name of a child business component whose records will be deleted when the parent record is deleted. The **Deep Copy/Delete Link** and **Recursive Link** user properties allow defining the link object definitions that should be used to determine the set of child records for the deep copy or delete operations.	Yes
Disable Automatic Trailing Wildcard Field List	The value of this user property is a list of field names for which the automatic trailing wildcard behavior, automatically appending an asterisk sign (*) to the query string, should be disabled.	No
Field Read Only Field: fieldname	A reference to a Boolean field. When the field returns Y, the field specified in the *fieldname* suffix of the user property's name becomes read-only.	Yes
Named Method	Allows developers to specify an action to be executed when a method is invoked on the business component. This user property is discussed in greater detail in the following section.	Yes
No Clear Field	The value of this user property is the name of a field in the parent business component. When set, the field cannot be set to NULL.	Yes
NoDelete Field	Can be specified once per parent business component. When the field specified by the user property returns Y then the entire record is protected from being deleted.	No

User Property Name	Description	Multiple Instances
On Condition Set Field Value	The value of this user property specifies a condition, a target field name, and a value to which the target field is set when the condition evaluates to TRUE.	Yes
On Field Update Invoke	Specifies a field in the parent business component, a target business component, and a target method, which is invoked on the target business component when the field is updated.	Yes
On Field Update Set	Specifies a field in the parent business component, a target field, and a value to which the target field is set when the field is updated. Example Value: `"Primary Owner Id", "Manual Asgn Flag", "Y"`	Yes
Parent Read Only Field	Specifies a field in a business component to which the current business component has a child relationship. When that field returns *Y*, all records in the current business component are read-only.	No
Recipient …	The user properties with a name starting with *Recipient* allow controlling the behavior of Siebel CRM applications during communication with customers such as sending e-mail or fax messages.	Yes

Source: Siebel Developer's Reference, Version 8.1:

```
http://download.oracle.com/docs/cd/E14004_01/books/ToolsDevRef/
booktitle.html
```

Named method user property

The Named Method user property can be specified on the business component and applet level. It is of major importance for implementing automated event flows in Siebel CRM applications.

For example, we can expose a button on a sales order form applet that allows the end user to send the current sales order to an external system. The complex processing of the order data and the invocation of the EAI interface are implemented as a Siebel workflow process. The invocation of the workflow process can be implemented with the **Named Method** user property on the business component level thus providing business logic support for all applets that are based on the business component.

The syntax for the Named Method user property on the business component level is as follows:

- **Name**: `Named Method N`
- **Value**: `"Method Name", "Action Type", "Object", "Action Parameters"`

The key words in the **Value** field must be enclosed in double quotes and must be separated by a comma followed by a space. In the following section, we will discuss the key words in greater detail:

- **N**: An integer number that defines the sequence in case there are multiple definitions for the Named Method user property. As indicated above, Siebel CRM does not allow sequence gaps greater than nine. In addition, only two-digit sequence numbers are allowed. So the maximum number of instances for a single user property name is 99.

- **Method Name**: The name of the method. When the method is invoked the action defined by the following parameters is executed.

- **Object**: Depending on the action type, the object can be a business component field or a business component against which the action is executed.

- **Action Parameters**: Except for the `INVOKESVC` action type (described as follows), only one action parameter is required. The action parameter is typically a value or an expression, in Siebel Query Language, that returns the value for the action.

- **Action Type**: The Siebel CRM framework provides three major types of actions, `SET`, `INVOKE`, and `INVOKESVC`, which are described in the following table:

Action Type	Description	Example Value and Explanation
SET	Allows setting a field, specified as the object, to the return value of an expression, specified as the action parameter.	`"ViolationTrue"`, `"SET"`, `"Protocol Violation"`, `"'Y'"` Explanation: When the *ViolationTrue* method is invoked, the *Protocol Violation* field is set to Y.
INVOKE	With this action type, the object is the name of a business component and the action parameter is the name of a method to invoke on the object business component.	`"Ungroup"`, `"INVOKE"`, `"Quote Item"`, `"WriteRecord"` Explanation: When the *Ungroup* method is invoked on the current business component, the *WriteRecord* method is invoked on the *Quote Item* business component.
INVOKESEL	Similar to INVOKE but invokes the method for all selected records of the object business component.	
INVOKEALL	Similar to INVOKE but invokes the method for all records of the object business component.	`"UpdateOptyProdQty"`, `"INVOKEALL"`, `"Opportunity Product"`, `"UpdateOptyProdQty"` Explanation: When the *UpdateOptyProdQty* method is invoked on an *Opportunity* record, the same method is invoked on all associated *Opportunity Product* records.

Action Type	Description	Example Value and Explanation
INVOKESVC	The INVOKESVC action type is used to invoke **business service methods** and pass input **arguments** for these methods. The object is a business component. The action parameters are the name of the business service, the name of the method, and a list of name/value pairs for the input arguments.	`"UpdateProgram",` `"INVOKESVC", "LOY` `Program", "Workflow` `Process Manager",` `"RunProcess",` `"ProcessName", """LOY` `Update Program Process""",` `"RowId", "[Id]"` Explanation: When the *UpdateProgram* method is invoked, the *Workflow Process Manager* business service's *RunProcess* method will be invoked. The input argument *ProcessName* will be set to *LOY Update Program Process*. The input argument *RowId* will be set to the value of the *Id* field of the current record in the *LOY Program* business component. Note: To provide a double quote as the input, for example to enclose a string that contains spaces such as *LOY Update Program Process* in the preceding example, we must specify two double quotes in order to **escape**. This explains why the process name is enclosed in three double quotes.

Action Type	Description	Example Value and Explanation
INVOKESVCSEL	Similar to the INVOKESVC action type but invokes the business service method for the currently selected records of the object business component.	`"CalculateRoomBlockRates",` `"INVOKESVCSEL", "TNT SHM` `Sub Opportunity", "TNT` `SHM Recurring Events",` `"CalculateRoomBlockRates"` Explanation: When the *CalculateRoomBlockRates* method is invoked, the *CalculateRoomBlockRates* method of the *TNT SHM Recurring Events* business service will be invoked for all selected records of the *TNT SHM Sub Opportunity* business component.
INVOKESVCALL	Similar to the INVOKESVC action type but invokes the business service method for all records of the object business component.	

We will learn how to use the Named Method user property in an upcoming chapter.

Case study example: Using the On Field Update Set user property

In *Chapter 5, Creating and Configuring Applets* we created the AHA Customer Profile Form Applet. One of the controls in this applet should display the timestamp when the customer's status was last updated. We have already placed the control, which maps to the **Account Status Date** field in the **Account** business component, on the applet but it is not yet functional.

The following procedure describes how we can create a new instance of a business component user property named **On Field Update Set** in the Account business component. This user property will enforce an update with the current timestamp on the **Account Status Date** field when the **Account Status** field has been updated:

1. If necessary, configure the **Object Explorer** window so that the **Business Component User Prop** type is exposed.

2. Navigate to the **Account** business component.

3. Ensure that you have write access to the account business component.

4. In the **Object Explorer,** navigate to the **Business Component User Prop** type.

5. Query for all user properties that have names starting with *On Field Update Se*.

6. Copy the existing user property named **On Field Update Set 2**.

 This user property has a value of "Managers Review", "Last Manager Review Date", Timestamp() in the Siebel 8.1.1 SIA repository.

7. Rename the copy to **On Field Update Set 14**.

 The highest sequence number of active *On Field Update Set* user properties is **5**, so we can add the *customer allowance gap* of nine to it. If the sequence numbers in your working repository should be different for any reason, please adjust the numbering accordingly.

8. Modify the value of the new user property as follows:

"Account Status", "Account Status Date", Timestamp()

 Ensure that each comma is followed by a space.

9. Set the **Comments** to **Created for AHA prototype**.

10. Step off the record to save it.

11. Navigate to the **Account Status Date** field and set the following properties:
    - **Type**: DTYPE_DATETIME
    - **Comments**: Changed Type from DTYPE_DATE to DTYPE_DATETIME for AHA prototype

12. Compile the Account business component.

To test the changes, we can launch the **Siebel Developer Web Client** and navigate to the **Process Start Page** view in the **Accounts** screen. It may be necessary to create a test customer account.

We can then continue the test cycle by modifying the customer's **Status** field and using the *Tab* key to move to the next control. We should be able to observe that the **Last Status Update** control now displays the current date and time.

The following screenshot shows the **Last Status Update** field after changing the customer's status to **Contract Pending**:

A Siebel Tools archive file (`Account BC.sif`) is provided with this chapter's code files. The file represents the Account business component after the changes in the preceding section.

Field user properties

The following table describes prominent user properties that we can use to control the behavior of individual business component fields:

User Property	Description
DisableSearch	When set to **TRUE**, wildcard searches using an asterisk (*), which may negatively impact query performance on the parent field, are not possible.
	The value can be delivered by a calculated field or an expression to dynamically enable or disable wildcard searches.
DisableSort	When set to **TRUE**, sorting is disabled on the parent field. This is indicated to the end user by the text **Not Sortable** displayed in the tool tip on the list column.
	The value can be delivered by a calculated field or an expression to dynamically enable or disable sorting.
Encrypt... Display Mask Char	Several user properties allow defining field level encryption as well as masking of field values, for example credit card numbers, in the user interface.
Required	The value of this user property is typically the name of a calculated field. When this field returns Y, the parent field of the user property cannot be empty.
Text Length Override	When this user property is present, the **Text Length** property of its parent field determines the maximum possible length of the field text. The value of this user property is irrelevant.
	The maximum possible text length of a field is normally determined by the physical length of the underlying database table column.

Source: Siebel Developer's Reference, Version 8.1 `http://download.oracle.com/docs/cd/E14004_01/books/ToolsDevRef/booktitle.html`

Applet, control, and list column user properties

The Applet object type provides user properties on the applet level itself as well as on the control and list column level (for list applets only).

The following table describes some of the most important applet user properties:

User property	Description
CanInvokeMethod: methodname	This user property allows controlling whether a button or menu item on the applet is enabled (clickable) or disabled (grayed out and not clickable). The name of the method invoked by the button or by the command behind the menu item is specified as the second part of the name (after a colon and a space).
	The value of this user property can be either a string—**TRUE** or **FALSE** or eventually Y or N—or an expression that must evaluate to TRUE or FALSE.
	Example:
	Name: CanInvokeMethod: CancelFunction
	Value: [Freeze Flag] <> "Y"
	Explanation:
	Buttons or menu items exposing the *CancelFunction* method will only be clickable when the value of the *Freeze Flag* field is not Y.
Default Applet Method	The value of this applet user property is the name of a method that is provided by the applet's buttons or menu items. The end user can simply press the *Enter* key to invoke the method.
Default Focus...	It is possible to set the focus of a control or list column that is not the first in the display sequence by using the *Default Focus* user properties. This may allow faster access to the control or list column for end users. The user property can be defined individually for each template type such as Edit, New, and Query.
Named Method N: methodname	The syntax for the Named Method user property on the applet level differs slightly from the business component level: the name of the method is defined as the second part of the user property name (after a colon and a space).
NoDataHide	When the value of this user property is set to Y, the applet will not be displayed when there is no data to display.

Control user properties

The most notable user properties for **Control** objects are related to navigation events. The **Url** user property must be added to a button control that invokes the **GotoUrl** method and specifies the target URL. The **View** user property is a child object definition of a button control that invokes the **GotoView** method and defines the view to which the Siebel application navigates when the button is clicked.

List column user properties

The **List Column** object type supports the **DisableSort** user property that allows controlling the presence or absence of sorting functionality for a specific list column rather than for all list columns in potentially many applets (when defined on the field level).

View user properties

The only officially documented user property for the View object type is **DefaultAppletFocus**. The value of this user property is the name of one of the view's applets. The applet will have focus when the view is loaded.

Summary

User properties are a powerful resource for defining special application behavior and business logic. They are provided as an alternative to writing custom script code by Oracle engineering.

Because user properties are often limited to certain classes, in the case of business components and applets, their functionality is not always easy to understand.

In this chapter, we introduced the most important user properties for business components, fields, applets, controls, list columns, and views.

In the next chapter, we will learn how to support navigation concepts such as drilldowns, applet toggles, and the thread bar.

14
Configuring Navigation

The Siebel CRM user interface supports the end user's desire to quickly navigate forward and backward while carrying out tasks. This chapter introduces the concept of drilldowns, the thread bar, and toggle applets and shows us how these navigation elements can be configured in Siebel Tools. The chapter is structured as follows:

- Understanding drilldown objects
- Creating static drilldowns
- Creating dynamic drilldowns
- Configuring the thread bar
- Configuring toggle applets

Understanding drilldown objects

In Siebel CRM, a **drilldown** is the activity of clicking on a hyperlink, which typically leads to a more detailed view of the record where the hyperlink originated. The standard Siebel CRM applications provide many examples for drilldown objects, which can mainly be found on list applets such as in the following screenshot that shows the Opportunity List Applet:

The Opportunity List Applet allows the end user to click on the opportunity name or the account name. Clicking on the **Opportunity Name** navigates to the **Opportunity Detail - Contacts View** in the same screen while clicking on the **Account** name navigates to the **Account Detail - Contacts View** on the Accounts screen.

Siebel CRM supports both **static** and **dynamic** drilldown destinations. The Opportunity List Applet (in Siebel Industry Applications) defines dynamic drilldown destinations for the opportunity name column depending on the name of the product line associated with the opportunity.

We can investigate this behavior by creating a test opportunity record and setting its **Product Line** field (in the **More Info** view) to **Equity**.

When we now drill down on the **Opportunity Name**, we observe that the **FINCORP Deal Equity View** is the new navigation target, allowing the end user to provide detailed equity information for the opportunity.

 To test this behavior, we must use the Siebel Sample Database for **Siebel Industry Applications (SIA)** and log in as SADMIN.

We can now inspect the Opportunity List Applet in Siebel Tools. Every applet that provides drilldown functionality has at least one definition for the **Drilldown Object** child type. To view the Drilldown Object definitions for the Opportunity List Applet we can follow the following procedure:

1. Navigate to the **Opportunity List Applet**.

2. In the **Object Explorer**, expand the **Applet** type and select the **Drilldown Objects** type.

3. Inspect the list of **Drilldown Object Definitions**.

The following screenshot shows the drilldown object definitions for the Opportunity List Applet:

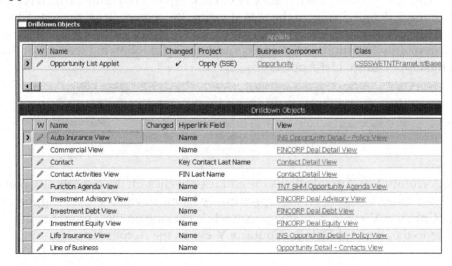

We can observe that a drilldown object defines a **Hyperlink Field** and a (target) **View**. These and other properties of drilldown objects are described in more detail later in this section. There are various instances of drilldown objects visible in the previous screenshot that reference the **Name** field. One instance—named **Line of Business** defines dynamic drilldown destinations that can be verified by expanding the **Drilldown Object** type in the Object Explorer and selecting the **Dynamic Drilldown Destination** type (with the **Line of Business** drilldown object selected).

The following screenshot shows the dynamic drilldown destination child object definitions for the **Line of Business** drilldown object:

The child list has been filtered to show only active records and the list is sorted by the Sequence property.

Dynamic Drilldown Destinations define a **Field** of the applet's underlying business component and a **Value**. The Siebel application verifies the **Field** and **Value** for the current record and—if a matching dynamic drilldown destination record is found—uses the **Destination Drilldown Object** to determine the target view for the navigation. When no match is found, the view in the parent drilldown object is used for navigation.

When we investigate the drilldown object named **Primary Account**, we learn that it defines a **Source Field** and a **target business component**, which is a necessity when the drilldown's target **View** uses a different business object than the View in which the applet is situated. In order to enable the Siebel application to retrieve the record in the target **View**, a source field that carries the **ROW_ID** of the target record and the business component to query must be specified.

The following table describes the most important properties of the Drilldown Object type:

Property	Description
Hyperlink Field	A field of the applet's underlying business component that is exposed as a list column or control. The list column or control is automatically rendered as a hyperlink when a drilldown object references it.
View	The target view for the navigation.
Business Component	The name of the target business component. Must be set when the target view uses a different business object than the view that contains the parent applet.
Source Field	The name of a field in the applet's underlying business component that is used to match with the destination field in the target business component.
Destination Field	The name of a field in the target business component.
Sequence	Used for dynamic drilldowns. When more than one drilldown object reference the same hyperlink field, the one with the lowest sequence number must define dynamic drilldown destinations.
Visibility Type	Allows the developer to specify the view mode for the target business component.

The following table describes the most important properties for the Dynamic Drilldown Destination type:

Property	Description
Field	A field of the applet's underlying business component. This field does not need to be exposed on the applet.
Value	A possible value for the field. When the value of the current record matches the value in the dynamic drilldown destination, the application uses the destination drilldown object to define the target view.
Destination Drilldown Object	The name of one of the applet's drilldown objects.
Sequence	Controls the sequence in which the application evaluates the conditions defined by the field/value pairs.

Creating static drilldowns

In the following section, we will learn how to create static drilldowns from list and form applets.

Case study example: Static drilldown from list applet

In earlier chapters, we created the AHA Customer Documents List Applet, which provides a unified view for all quotes, orders, opportunities, and so on, associated with an account. The applet should provide drilldown capability to the documents and the employee details of the responsible person.

In the following procedure, we describe how to create a static drilldown from the AHA Customer Documents List Applet to the Relationship Hierarchy View (Employee), which displays the reporting hierarchy and employee details:

1. Navigate to the **AHA Customer Documents List Applet**.

2. Check out or lock the applet if necessary.

3. In the **Object Explorer**, expand the **Applet** type, and select the **Drilldown Object type**.

4. In the **Drilldown Objects list**, create a new record and provide the following property values:

    ° **Name:** Responsible Employee

    ° **Hyperlink Field:** Responsible User Login Name

    ° **View:** Relationship Hierarchy View (Employee)

    ° **Source Field:** Responsible User Id

    ° **Business Component:** Employee

    ° **Destination Field:** Id

    ° **Visibility Type:** All

5. Compile the **AHA Customer Documents List Applet**.

We will continue to work on the AHA Customer Documents List Applet later in this chapter.

Creating drilldown hyperlinks on form applets

Sometimes it is necessary to provide a drilldown hyperlink on a form applet. The following procedure describes how to accomplish this using the SIS Account Entry Applet as an example. The applet will provide a hyperlink that allows quick navigation to the **Account Detail - Activities View**:

1. Navigate to the **Account business** component.

2. Check out or lock the business component if necessary.

3. Add a new field with the following properties:
   - ° **Name:** AHA Drilldown Field 1
   - ° **Calculated:** TRUE
   - ° **Calculated Value:** "Drilldown 1" (include the parentheses)

4. Compile the **Account business** component.

> **Did you know?**
> We should create a dummy field like in the previous example to avoid interference with standard fields when creating drilldowns on form applets. This field will be referenced in the drilldown object and control.

5. Navigate to the **SIS Account Entry** Applet.

6. Check out or lock the applet if necessary.

7. In the **Object Explorer**, expand the **Applet type** and select the **Drilldown Object** type.

8. Create a new entry in the **Drilldown Objects list** with the following properties:
   - ° **Name:** AHA Activity Drilldown
   - ° **Hyperlink Field:** AHA Drilldown Field 1
   - ° **View:** Account Detail - Activities View

9. In the **Object Explorer**, select the **Control** type.

10. In the **Controls** list, create a new record with the following properties:
    - ° **Name:** AHA Activity Drilldown
    - ° **Caption:** Go to Activities
    - ° **Field:** AHA Drilldown Field 1
    - ° **HTML Type:** Link
    - ° **Method Invoked:** Drilldown

11. Right-click the **SIS Account Entry** Applet in the top list and select **Edit Web Layout** to open the layout editor.

12. Drag the **AHA Activities Drilldown** control from the **Controls | Columns** window to the grid layout and drop it below the **Zip Code** text box.

13. Save the changes and close the web layout editor.

14. Compile the **SIS Account Entry** Applet.

15. Log in to the Siebel client and navigate to the **Account List** view.

16. Click on the **Go to Activities** link in the form applet and verify that the activities list is displayed for the selected account.

The following screenshot shows the result of the previous configuration procedure in the Siebel Web Client:

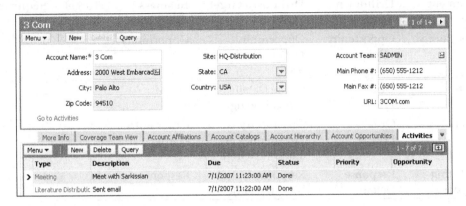

Clicking the **Go to Activities** hyperlink on the form applet will navigate the user to the activities list view for the current account.

Creating dynamic drilldowns

In the following section, we will learn how to configure dynamic drilldown objects for a list applet.

Case study example: Dynamic drilldown destinations for a list applet

The AHA technical architect team has defined the drilldown behavior for the AHA Customer Documents List Applet so that clicking on the document Id should navigate to a detail view depending on the document type. Clicking on a quote Id should for example navigate to the quote pricing view while clicking on an opportunity Id should navigate to the opportunity product view.

The following procedure describes how to configure the AHA Customer Documents List Applet for dynamic drilldowns:

1. Navigate to the **AHA Customer Documents List Applet**.

2. Check out or lock the applet if necessary.

3. In the **Object Explorer**, expand the Applet type and select the **Drilldown Object** Type.

4. In the **Drilldown Objects list**, create four records—one for each drilldown destination—for the **Document Id** field (set as **Hyperlink Field** and **Source Field**) according to the following table:

Document type	Drilldown name	Drilldown target view	Business component	Target field	Sequence
Opportunity	Opportunity - Products	Opportunity Detail - Products View	Opportunity	Id	1
Quote	Quote - Pricing	Quote Detail View (Pricing)	Quote	Id	2
Order	Order - Pricing	Order Entry - Line Items View (Sales)(Pricing)	Order Entry - Orders	Id	3
Marketing Response	Response - Detail	Response Detail View (Detail)	Response	Id	4

5. In the **Drilldown Objects list**, select the **Opportunity - Products** entry.

6. In the **Object Explorer**, expand the **Drilldown Object type** and select the **Dynamic Drilldown Destination** type.

7. In the **Dynamic Drilldown Destinations** list create four records—one for each drilldown destination—with the **Field** property set to **Document Type**. The following table provides the details for the records to be created:

Name	Value	Destination Drilldown Object	Sequence
Opportunity	Opportunity	Opportunity - Products	1
Quote	Quote	Quote - Pricing	2
Order	Order	Order - Pricing	3
Response	Response	Response - Detail	4

8. Compile the **AHA Customer Documents List** Applet.

> The AHA Customer Documents List Applet will be added to the AHA Customer Process Start View in a later chapter. Because the mechanism to populate the AHA Customer Documents business component is not yet implemented, we cannot yet test the drilldown configuration.

The Siebel Tools archive file (AHA Customer Documents List Applet.sif) in this chapter's code files represents the applet after the changes in this chapter.

Configuring the thread bar

The thread bar is a navigation utility that allows the end user to identify the current drill path and to navigate back to views and records she or he has previously visited.

Did you know?

The name **thread bar** is an analogy to the legendary ball of red wool thread that the Greek goddess Ariadne gave to Theseus, who was supposed to kill the tyrannical Minotaur in his maze hideout. Theseus attached the thread at the entrance of the maze and safely found his way out again.

In a similar manner — albeit with less bloodshed — the end user can find her or his way out of the *maze* of views.

The following screenshot shows the thread bar in the Siebel Web Client:

The end user has used drilldowns to navigate from the **Account** named **3Com** to the contact Todd Sarkissian. He then drilled down on a **service request (SR)** and on one of the SR's activities. By clicking the hyperlinks in the thread bar, the end user can navigate backwards in the drilldown history.

The hyperlinked text in a thread bar entry is composed of two parts, which are separated by a colon (:). The first part is a static text and the second part is the value of a field in the business component referenced by one of the view's applets.

The following properties of the **View** object type define the thread bar text:

Property	Description
Thread Title	The static first portion of the thread bar entry for the view. Symbolic Strings can be used to provide translatable text.
Thread Applet	A reference to one of the view's applets. Typically the upper applet, exposing the primary business component, is used.
Thread Field	The name of a field in the thread applet's business component. The value of this field will be displayed in the second portion of the thread bar entry.

Case study example: Configuring the thread bar

In previous chapters we created and modified the AHA Customer Process Start View. The following procedure describes how to configure the thread properties of this view:

1. Navigate to the **AHA Customer Process Start View**.

2. Check out or lock the view if necessary.

3. In the **Object List Editor**, set the following properties:
   - **Thread Title - String Override: AHA Customer**
   - **Thread Applet: AHA Customer Profile Form Applet**
   - **Thread Field: Name and Location**

4. Compile the AHA Customer Process Start View.

5. Test the changes by logging in to the Siebel client and clicking any drilldown in the **AHA Customer Process Start View**.

6. Observe that the thread bar displays the text **AHA Customer** followed by a colon and the name and location of the current account record.

Configuring toggle applets

Toggle applets are applets that are associated with an original applet and appear instead of the original applet, either when the end user selects the toggle applet (manual toggle) or dynamically depending on the value of a field in the applet's business component.

Manual applet toggle

The first situation—the static or manual toggle—is that an end user can use a drop-down list or tabs to select a different applet. The following screenshot shows an example in the Siebel standard application:

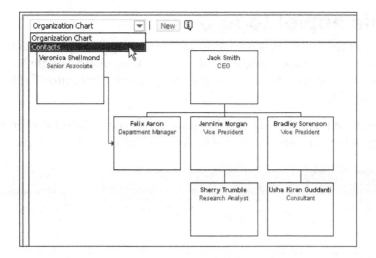

The **Organizational Analysis** view (ESP Business Service Unit Contacts View) in the **Enterprise Selling Process** category of the **Accounts** screen uses a specialized applet (ESP BSU Organization Analysis Applet) that allows the end user to switch between the organization chart graphic and the standard list applet (ESP BSU Contact List Applet) by means of a drop-down list.

When we inspect the **ESP BSU Organization Analysis Applet** in Siebel Tools, we find that the ESP BSU Contact List Applet is listed in the **Applet Toggles** list as shown in the next screenshot:

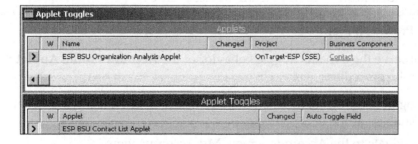

We can observe that the only property with a value is the Applet property. The drop-down list in the UI is populated automatically by the system using the applet's Title property value.

The process of configuring a manual applet toggle is therefore very simple and only consists of adding new records for the toggle applets to the original applet. The only consideration is that all applets must reference the same business component.

Dynamic applet toggle

As we can see in the previous screenshot, an Applet Toggle object definition optionally specifies an **Auto Toggle Field** along with an **Auto Toggle Value** (not visible in the screenshot), which allow the system to determine the toggle applet dynamically.

A good example in the Siebel standard application is the **Account Profile Applet**. The following screenshot shows the list of **Applet Toggles** for this applet:

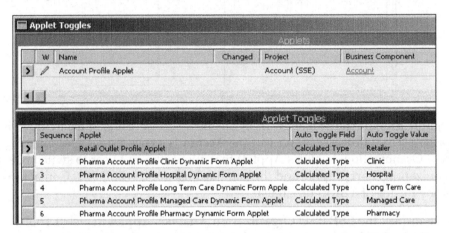

As we can observe in the previous screenshot, the **Account Profile Applet** will be replaced automatically with the **Retail Outlet Profile Applet** when the **Calculated Type** field's value is **Retailer**. There are a total of six toggle applets defined for the **Account Profile Applet**.

We can observe the dynamic toggle behavior of the **Account Profile Applet** by following the procedure:

1. Log in to the Siebel Mobile Web Client as SADMIN, using the Siebel Sample Database as the data source.

2. Navigate to the **Accounts** screen, **My Accounts** view.

3. Drill down on the first record in the list.

4. Click the **More Info** view tab. The lower applet in this view is the **Account Profile Applet**.

5. In the upper form applet, set the **Account Type** field to **Retailer** and press the *Tab* key to leave the field.

6. Observe that the **Account Profile Applet** is replaced with the **Retail Outlet Profile Applet** automatically.

Use the **About View** dialog from the **Help** menu to verify the applet name.

7. Observe the behavior for other values of the **Account Type** field such as **Hospital**.

When we wish to configure dynamic toggling for an applet, we have to follow the procedure described:

1. Navigate to the applet.
2. Check out or lock the applet if necessary.
3. In the **Object Explorer**, expand the **Applet type** and select the **Applet Toggle type**.
4. In the **Applet Toggles** list create a new record for each toggle applet and provide values for the following properties:
   - **Applet**: Name of the toggle applet
   - **Auto Toggle Field**: Name of a field in the parent applet's business component (can be a calculated field)
   - **Auto Toggle Value**: The value of the auto toggle field to indicate the matching record
   - **Sequence**: The numeric sequence to check the dynamic toggle conditions
5. Compile the applet.
6. Test your changes in the Siebel Mobile or Developer Web Client.

Summary

Assisting end users while they are navigating the Siebel CRM user interface is an important task for developers.

The classic navigation utility is the drilldown, which can be defined as static, targeting the same view all the time, or dynamic, allowing for decision logic to be applied before selecting the target view for the drilldown.

Drilldowns are always displayed as hyperlinks to the end user and are tightly coupled with the thread bar. The thread bar content can be configured at the view level by defining the static and dynamic portions to display.

Toggle applets allow either manual or automatic selection of a replacement applet.

In the next chapter, we will learn how to customize the look and feel of the Siebel CRM user interface.

15

Customizing the Look and Feel of Siebel Applications

The visual appearance — also referred to as *Look and Feel* — of Siebel web applications can be customized by modifying Siebel web template files, cascading style sheets, and image files. This chapter discusses the techniques to apply these changes in a safe and upgradeable manner.

The chapter is structured as follows:

- Understanding Siebel web templates
- Customizing Siebel web templates
- Customizing web pages
- Customizing style sheets
- Configuring bitmaps and icon maps
- Replacing the application logo

Understanding Siebel web templates

Siebel Web Template (SWT) files are proprietary files that combine typical **Hypertext Markup Language (HTML)** tags with processing instructions for the **Siebel Web Engine (SWE)**. The SWE is responsible for rendering applets, views, and web pages at runtime. The main categories for web templates are:

- Applet web templates
- View web templates
- Web Page web templates

In previous chapters, we have learned a lot about applets and views but not web pages. A web page can be described as any page that is neither an applet nor a view. Examples of web pages are the login page and the banner frame (containing the menu and logo of an application).

SWT files are stored in a directory named WEBTEMPL. This directory is present in each Siebel Server, Mobile or Developer Web Client, and Siebel Tools installation folder.

In order to get a deeper understanding of SWT files and their structure we can inspect the CCFrameBanner.swt file, which defines the banner displaying the application menu and the application logo as shown in the following screenshot:

This part of the application is defined in the CCFrameBanner.swt file, which is shown in the following screenshot:

```
<!-- Template Start: CCFrameBanner.swt -->

<HTML dir="swe:dir">
<head>
<title><swe:this property="Title"/></title>
<swe:include file="CCStylesChoice.swt"/>
</head>
<BODY class="poweredBy" topmargin="0" leftmargin="0" marginheight="0" marginwidth="0">
  <table width="100%" cellpadding='0' cellspacing='0' border='0'>
    <swe:switch>
      <swe:case condition="Web Engine State Properties, IsHighInteractive">
        <tr valign="top" style="position:absolute;left:-2;">
      </swe:case>
      <swe:default>
        <tr valign="top">
      </swe:default>
    </swe:switch>

    <td class="applicationMenu" nowrap><swe:menu type="Default" width="275" height="20" bgcolor="#123783" fgcolor="#ffffff" /></td>
      <td class="applicationMenu"><img src="images/spacer.gif" height="25" width="1"></td>

      <swe:pageitem id="11"><td nowrap><swe:this property="FormattedHtml" /><span class="bannerDiv"> | </span></td></swe:pageitem>
      <swe:pageitem id="12"><td nowrap><swe:this property="FormattedHtml" /><span class="bannerDiv"> | </span></td></swe:pageitem>
      <swe:pageitem id="13"><td nowrap><swe:this property="FormattedHtml" /><span class="bannerDiv"> | </span></td></swe:pageitem>
      <swe:pageitem id="14"><td nowrap><swe:this property="FormattedHtml" /><span class="bannerDiv"> | </span></td></swe:pageitem>
      <swe:pageitem id="15"><td nowrap><swe:this property="FormattedHtml" /><span class="bannerDiv"> | </span></td></swe:pageitem>

      <td width="100%"><div id="MsgLayer"> </div></td>
      <td align="right"><a href="http://www.oracle.com" target="_blank"><swe:image name="POWERED_BY" category="HTML Control Icons"/></a></td>
```

The previous screenshot was taken from the Web Template Explorer, which can be opened in Siebel Tools by selecting **View | Windows | Web templates Window** from the menu. The benefit of the Web Template Explorer is that it provides color coding to easily distinguish the elements of the file.

The CCFrameBanner.swt file and its siblings not only contain both standard HTML tags such as <table> and <a> but also a variety of proprietary <swe:> tags. These tags represent instructions for the Siebel Web Engine, which replaces them with HTML code and data at runtime. The most important <swe:> tags are described in the following table:

SWE tag	Description
<swe:this>	Refers to the current object that uses the template. Used to display properties of that object.
<swe:include>	Uses the file attribute to reference another SWT file. This is also referred to as *nested templates* and provides a high level of reusability.
<swe:switch> <swe:case> <swe:default>	Used to create conditional sections in the SWT file. The <swe:case> tag can be used in conjunction with business services to determine conditions dynamically.
<swe:menu>	A specialized tag that is replaced with the application menu at runtime. The tag also allows defining the foreground and background color as well as the dimensions of the menu.
<swe:pageitem>	Page items are placeholders, identified by an ID number, which can be replaced with content that is mapped as web template items in Siebel Tools.
<swe:image>	Defines the category and name of a bitmap image — defined in the Siebel Repository — that replaces the tag at runtime. Used for the application logo.

Did you know?
We can find a detailed description of all <swe:> tags in the Siebel Web Engine Tags section of the *Siebel Developer's Guide* in the Siebel bookshelf.

The following table describes the most important <swe:> tags for applet web templates:

SWE tag	Description
<swe:control>	A placeholder — identified by an ID number — to which a control such as a button, text box, or list column can be bound in the applet web layout editor.
<swe:for-each>	Allows the implementation of loops. Typically used to render a large number of repeating elements such as list columns. Specifies a start value, a count, and the name of a variable that holds the current value.

The following table describes the most important `<swe:>` tags for view web templates:

SWE tag	Description
`<swe:applet>`	Placeholder for applets—identified by an ID number. Applets can be bound as View Web Template Item object definitions to the placeholders in the view web layout editor.
`<swe:threadbar>`	This tag is replaced with the thread bar at runtime.
`<swe:viewbar>` `<swe:viewlink>`	Placeholders for the view tab bar and its subordinate link bar.

Web template definitions

SWT files are stored outside of the Siebel Repository. To be able to reference them from repository-based object definitions such as applets, views, and web pages, developers use the Web Template object type.

A Web Template object definition has an associated Web Template File object definition, which contains the name of the file in the WEBTEMPL directory. Web Template object definitions can therefore be described as outward references because they point from the Siebel Repository to a file outside of it.

The following screenshot shows the **View Detail** web template as an example:

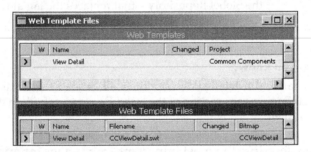

We can see that the **Web Template File** object definition associated with the **View Detail** Web Template references the CCViewDetail.swt file.

As we have learned in previous chapters, Web Template object definitions are referenced as child object definitions in the applet, view, and web page object types.

In summary, we can state the following about Siebel Web Templates:

- SWT files contain HTML markup and <swe:> tags
- **Web Template** object definitions serve as references to SWT files from within the Siebel Repository
- Applets, views, and web pages use web templates to link to the SWT files
- The <swe:> tags are interpreted at runtime by the SWE, which resides in the Application Object Manager
- The SWE resolves the nesting and logic such as decisions or loops and replaces the <swe:> tags with HTML content and data at runtime
- The result of the SWE's work, the *page*, is delivered to the browser

Considerations for customizing the look and feel of Siebel applications

While many Siebel projects keep customization of the look and feel of the applications to a minimum (replacing the Oracle logo in the upper-right corner of the application window with the company logo is often the only change) there are situations that make customization a necessity.

Such situations are for example:

- Company style guides and branding rules (especially for customer-facing applications published on the Internet)
- Adherence to requirements imposed by norms and regulations for accessibility for the visually impaired
- Data model configurations that impact the amount of data displayed on applets

In the following sections, we will discuss several techniques related to customizing Web Templates, cascading style sheets, and image files for Siebel CRM applications.

Did you know?

The term *customization* is used in this chapter mainly because Oracle frequently reminds customers that changes made to Web Templates, style sheets, and image files must typically be executed repeatedly when an upgrade to a newer version of Siebel CRM is applied.

In the software industry, *customization*, as opposed to *configuration*, refers to changes made by customers to pre-built applications such as Siebel CRM when these changes are not supported directly by the upgrade logic.

We will discuss the following example scenarios in the next sections:

- Increasing the number of columns that can be displayed in a list applet
- Creating a custom view web template
- Changing the appearance of the login page
- Modifying the color schema of Siebel applications
- Configuring bitmaps for static images
- Configuring icon maps to display data values graphically
- Replacing the company logo

In real life, we have to take into consideration that changes to the aforementioned files have a wide range of impact. For example, changing the color code in the application's main style sheet will affect the entire application.

In addition, following this book's *configure with the upgrade in mind* approach, we will provide solutions that have the least level of effort during a Siebel upgrade.

Using an external text editor for web template customization

Siebel Tools can be configured to invoke an external text editor to modify Web Template files that reside in the WEBTEMPL directory of Siebel Tools. The following procedure describes how to prepare Siebel Tools for Web Template customization:

1. In the **View** menu, select the **Options...** command.
2. Click on the **Web Template Editor** tab.
3. Click on the **Browse** button.
4. Navigate to a folder that contains the executable file of the text editor. For example, we can choose C:\WINDOWS\NOTEPAD.EXE or point to any other text editor of our choice.

5. Select the executable file and click on the **Open** button.

6. Click **OK** to close the **Options** dialog.

We can now load SWT files into the text editor from the following places in Siebel Tools:

- **Web Template Explorer**: Right-click the template viewer and select **Edit Template**

- **Applet Editor**: Click the **Edit Template** button in the **Controls/Columns** docking window

- **View Editor**: Click the **Edit Template** button in the **Applets** docking window

- **Web Page Editor**: Right-click the layout window and select **Edit Template**

The text editor will open the respective SWT file from the WEBTEMPL directory in the Siebel Tools installation folder. When changes are saved in the text editor, Siebel Tools prompts to reload the web template file once the text editor is closed.

To test the changes we must manually copy the modified files to the WEBTEMPL directory of the Siebel Mobile or Developer Web Client installation folder and subsequently to the WEBTEMPL directories on all Siebel Server machines.

It is a recommended practice to create a backup copy before we start modifying the files.

Customizing pre-built web templates

The following example scenario shows how to increase the number of columns that can be displayed in a list applet. Techniques shown in this chapter can be applied to any type of customization to SWT files.

The SWT file used in the example is CCAppletList_B_EL.swt and files that are referenced by it. This file is referenced in the Siebel Repository as the Web Template named Applet List (Base/EditList). This Web Template is the base for the majority of list applets:

1. In the **View** menu, select **Windows | Web templates Window** to open the **Web Template Explorer**.

2. In the drop-down box on top of the **Web Template Explorer** window, select the **CCAppletList_B_EL** template.

We can type the name of the template after opening the drop-down box for faster location of the template.

3. In the **Web Template Explorer**, expand the **CCAppletList_B_EL** template and select the **CCListHeader** template.

 This is the SWT file that defines the column header row.

4. Right-click on the **CCListHeader** template in the lower half of the web template viewer and select **Edit Template**.

The following screenshot illustrates step 4:

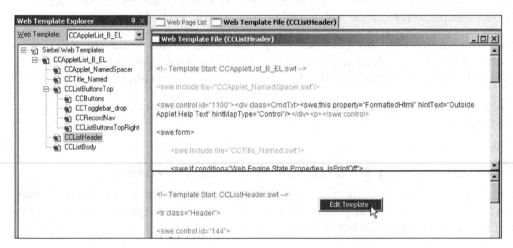

5. In the text editor window, use the **Save As** functionality to create a backup copy named CCListHeader_Original.swt.

6. Use the **Open File** functionality of the text editor to open the CCListHeader. swt file again in case the editor has closed it as a result of the procedure of saving the backup copy.

7. Use the **Text Search** functionality of the text editor to locate the last <swe: for-each> tag.

8. Select the entire element enclosed by <swe:for-each> and </swe:for-each> tags.

9. Copy the selection to the clipboard by pressing *Ctrl+C*.

10. Position the cursor below the selection.

11. Create a new line (press *Enter*).

12. Enter a comment similar to the following:

```
<!-- Customization for AHA UI prototype: Added 10 columns -->
```

13. Create a new line (press *Enter*)

14. Paste the content of the clipboard by pressing *Ctrl+V.*

15. In the pasted text, change the value of the `startValue` attribute to `701`.

16. In the pasted text, change the value of the `count` attribute to `10`.

17. Position the cursor below the new element.

18. Create a new line (press *Enter*).

19. Enter a comment similar to the following:

```
<!-- End of customization -->
```

20. Compare your work with the following screenshot:

```
CCListHeader.swt - Notepad
File  Edit  Format  View  Help
        </swe:for-each>

        <swe:for-each startValue="611" count="40" iteratorName="currentId">
         <swe:control id="swe:currentId">
          <th align="swe:this.TextAlignment" width="swe:this.HtmlWidth" class
         </swe:control>
        </swe:for-each>
<!-- Customization for AHA UI prototype: Added 10 columns -->

        <swe:for-each startValue="701" count="10" iteratorName="currentId">
         <swe:control id="swe:currentId">
          <th align="swe:this.TextAlignment" width="swe:this.HtmlWidth" class
         </swe:control>
        </swe:for-each>
<!-- End of customization -->
```

21. Save the changes and close the text editor.

22. Click on **OK** in the **File Changed** dialog in Siebel Tools to reload the file.

23. Scroll down in the **Web Template Viewer** if necessary to verify the changes.

24. Use the syntax-based color coding to verify that all changes are correct.

25. Copy the `CCListHeader.swt` file from the Siebel Tools `WEBTEMPL` directory to the same directory in the Siebel Mobile or Developer Web Client installation folder.

26. Repeat steps 3 to 25 for the **CCListBody** template.

 This is necessary because this template defines the body section of the list applets and needs the same column placeholders as the **CCListHeader** template.

The files `CCListHeader.swt` and `CCListBody.swt` in this chapter's code files contain the changes applied in the previous section.

Modifications similar to the ones described in the previous procedure can be applied to all SWT files shipped by Oracle. However, we should document the changes diligently (using at least the comments feature) and be prepared to manually merge the changes into the newer version of the respective files after an upgrade to a newer version of Siebel CRM.

Alternatively, we can create custom SWT files and register them in the repository. This technique is shown in the following section:

Creating custom web templates

The following sample procedure uses the `CCViewDetail_ParentPntr.swt` file, which is used for the majority of detail views. The example scenario is that the developers need an additional pair of applets that consume 50 percent of the screen width. The respective applet placeholders should be situated at the end of the template. Because there is only a limited number of views that will display a grid of six smaller applets, the developers decided to create a custom template to avoid problems after a potential upgrade:

1. Open the `WEBTEMPL` directory of the **Siebel Tools** installation folder in **Windows Explorer**.

2. Locate the `CCViewDetail_ParentPntr.swt` file and copy it.

3. Rename the copy to `AHA_ViewDetail_ParentPntr.swt`.

4. Open the `AHA_ViewDetail_ParentPntr.swt` file in a text editor.

5. Locate the `<table>` HTML element in the main content section. The element should look similar to the following snippet (only the first few lines are shown):

    ```
    <table width="100%" border="0" cellspacing="0"
                   cellpadding="3">
    <tr valign="top">
    <td width="50%">
    ```

6. Select the lines from `<table...` to the first occurrence of the `</table>` element (the entire table definition) and copy them to the clipboard.

7. Position the cursor below the last `</swe:for-each>` tag.

8. Enter a new line and a comment similar to the following:

    ```
    <!-- Customization for AHA UI prototype: added 2 applets -->
    ```

9. Enter a new line and paste the code from the clipboard.

10. In the pasted code, change the value of the `first startValue` attribute to 18.

11. Change the value of the first **count** attribute to 1.

12. Repeat steps 10 and 11 for the `second startValue` attribute (setting its value to 19) and `count` attribute (setting it to 1).

13. Add a **comment** at the end of the custom code, similar to the following:

```
<!-- End of customization -->
```

14. Compare your work with the following screenshot:

```
AHA_ViewDetail_ParentPntr.swt - Notepad
File  Edit  Format  View  Help
          <swe:applet hintMapType="Applet" id="swe:currentId" hintText="Grandchild Applet"
</swe:for-each>

<!-- Customization for AHA UI prototype: added 2 applets -->

<table width="100%" border="0" cellspacing="0" cellpadding="3">
        <tr valign="top">
                <td width="50%">
                        <swe:for-each count="1" iteratorName="currentId" startValue="18">
                                <swe:applet hintMapType="Applet" id="swe:currentId" hintTe
                        </swe:for-each>
                </td>

                <td width="50%">
                        <swe:for-each count="1" iteratorName="currentId" startValue="19">
                                <swe:applet hintMapType="Applet" id="swe:currentId" hintTe
                        </swe:for-each>
                </td>
        </tr>
</table>

<!-- End of customization -->
```

15. Save and close the file.

16. Copy the `AHA_ViewDetail_ParentPntr.swt` file to the client's `WEBTEMPL` directory.

The file `AHA_ViewDetail_ParentPntr.swt` is available with this chapter's code files.

Registering a custom web template file

The following procedure describes how to register a custom SWT file—similar to the one created in the previous section—as a new Web Template object definition in the Siebel Repository. After registering the file as a Web Template, we can associate it with any suitable object, for example a `View`:

1. In Siebel Tools, navigate to the **Web Template** type in the **Object Explorer**.

2. In the **object list** editor, create a new record with the following property values:
   - **Name: AHA View Detail (Parent with Pointer)**
   - **Project: AHA User Interface**

        °   **Type: View Template**

        °   **Comments: Created for AHA prototype**

3. In the **Object Explorer**, expand the **Web Template type** and select the **Web Template File Type**.

4. In the **Web Template Files** list create a new record with the following property values:

        °   **Name: AHA View Detail (Parent with Pointer)**

        °   **Filename: AHA_ViewDetail_ParentPntr.swt**

5. Compile the AHA View Detail (Parent with Pointer) web template.

Customizing web pages

As mentioned in the previous section, a web page is a repository object type that is neither an applet nor a view. The Siebel application login page is a perfect example of a web page. Web pages are referenced by application object definitions from the following properties:

- **Container Web Page**: The name of a web page that defines the overall frameset for the Siebel application.

- **Login Web Page**: The name of a web page that is used as the login page.

- **Acknowledgement Web Page**: The name of a web page that is shown when the user has successfully logged on. Typically empty in favour of the Acknowledgement Web View property.

- **Error Web Page**: The name of a web page that is shown in case of an error.

- **Logoff Acknowledgement Web Page**: The name of a web page that is shown after the user has logged off.

The following are among the most common customization scenarios for web pages:

- Modify the SWT file associated with the web page to change the overall layout or references to image files.

- Modify the captions of the web page items associated with the web page. However we are not allowed to change or deactivate the Oracle copyright notice on the login page.

- Create new web page items and place them on newly created placeholders in the SWT file. For example, a link to a help file could be placed on an error web page.

Customizing style sheets

Similar to many other web-based applications, Siebel CRM also uses cascading style sheet (CSS) files to define its visual appearance in the web browser. CSS is a commonly used technology in web development.

Developers who are requested to customize the CSS files shipped with Siebel CRM applications should consider the following:

- We should have a thorough understanding of the CSS syntax before we manipulate the files
- Changes to Siebel CSS files affect the entire application
- We must establish a clear backup and documentation strategy because all changes must be reapplied after an upgrade to a newer version of Siebel CRM

The following example procedure describes how to customize the look and feel of the thread bar by modifying the `main.css` file. This file is the primary resource for employee-facing high-interactivity applications such as Siebel Call Center and Siebel Sales:

1. On the developer workstation, navigate to the `public|enu|files` directory in the installation folder of the Siebel Developer Web Client.

2. Make a backup copy of the `main.css` file and name the copy `main.css.original`.

3. Open the `main.css` file in a text editor.

> There are a number of open source and commercial CSS editors on the market that facilitate the task of inspecting and modifying cascading style sheets. In this simple scenario, a text editor such as Microsoft Notepad is sufficient.

4. Use the text search functionality of the text editor to locate the section for the thread bar formatting. Sections in the Siebel CSS files can be identified by comments such as `/* Threadbar    */`.

5. Copy the entire threadbar section (including the header comment) and paste it again after the original to create a backup copy of the original data.

6. Edit the header comment of the copy to `/* Original Threadbar    */`.

7. Use the `/*` and `*/` characters to enclose the original threadbar formatting instructions in comments. Compare your work with the following screenshot:

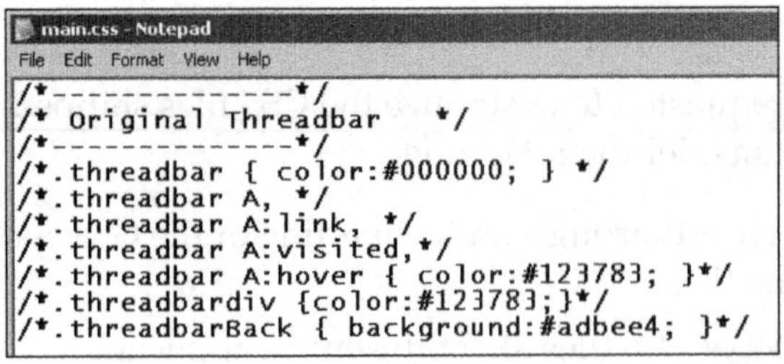

```
main.css - Notepad
File  Edit  Format  View  Help
/*----------------*/
/* Original Threadbar    */
/*----------------*/
/*.threadbar { color:#000000; } */
/*.threadbar A, */
/*.threadbar A:link, */
/*.threadbar A:visited,*/
/*.threadbar A:hover { color:#123783; }*/
/*.threadbardiv {color:#123783;}*/
/*.threadbarBack { background:#adbee4; }*/
```

8. Edit the remaining threadbar section so that it contains the following instructions:

```
/*--------------*/
/* Threadbar     */
/* Customized for AHA prototype          */
/*--------------*/
.threadbar { font-size: 8pt;font-weight:bold;color:#123783; }
.threadbar A,
.threadbar A:link { color:#123783; }
.threadbar A:visited,
.threadbar A:hover { text-decoration:none;background-
                     color:#FFFFFF; }
.threadbardiv { font-weight:bold;color:#123783; }
.threadbarBack { background:#e0e5f5; }
```

These formatting instructions define the following look and feel:

- ○ The thread bar text will be 8 points large and bold
- ○ When the mouse cursor hovers over the thread bar text, it will not get underlined and it will have a white background
- ○ The background color of the thread bar is set to the same color code as the toolbar's background

9. Save the `main.css` file

10. Launch the Siebel Developer Web Client to test. If the changes are not visible, use the *F5* key to refresh the browser cache.

The following screenshot shows the thread bar before the changes:

The next screenshot shows the thread bar after the changes to the `main.css` file have been applied:

We can observe that the browser applies the formatting instructions correctly.

Configuring bitmaps and icon maps

The Siebel CRM web applications use graphic files to enhance the visual appearance of the user interface. Examples of these files are:

- The company logo in the upper-right corner
- Bitmaps on toolbar buttons and screen tabs
- Control icons such as calendar and calculator
- Folder icons in hierarchical tree views
- Data visualization icons in list and form applets

The graphic files reside in the `images` folder in the `PUBLIC` folder of the SWSE or client installation directory. This is necessary so that the browser can download them. For easier management of the graphic files, the Siebel Repository contains the `Bitmap Category` type, which organizes Bitmap object definitions into categories.

A **Bitmap object definition** mainly defines the name of the file, which is in turn referenced in the HTML code rendered by the browser.

The following screenshot shows the **Bitmap Category** named **HTML Command Icons**, which contains the bitmaps used in the Siebel application toolbars:

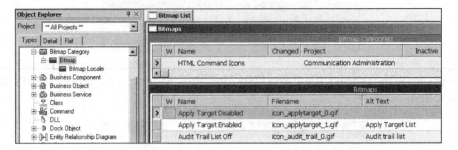

An **Icon Map** is an object definition that associates a bitmap with a value. It can be referenced by controls and list columns so that, instead of the plain text, a graphic is displayed in the browser. The property of list columns or controls that defines this reference is named as **HTML Icon Map**.

The following screenshot shows a portion of the **Order Entry - Order List Applet (All)** applet:

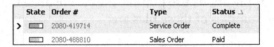

The **State** column uses a guage to give a graphical representation of the order status.

Case study example: Using an icon map

As defined by AHA business analysts, the AHA Customer Profile Form Applet should display a graphical indicator to allow employees to determine the level of courtesy in order to avoid loss of valuable customers. In previous chapters we have already created the AHA Courtesy Indicator field in the Account business component.

In the following example procedure we will use an existing icon map to visualize the courtesy level in the AHA Customer Profile Form Applet:

1. Navigate to the AHA Customer Profile Form Applet.
2. Check out or lock the applet if necessary.
3. Open the AHA Customer Profile Form Applet in the **web layout editor**.

4. Create a new field control in the **Indicators** form section with the following properties:

  ° **Name: AHA Courtesy Indicator**

  ° **Field: AHA Courtesy Indicator**

  ° **Caption - String Override: Courtesy**

  ° **HTML Type: PlainText**

  ° **HTML Icon Map: LS Pharma Market Potential**

5. Save and compile the AHA Customer Profile Form Applet.

6. Launch the Siebel Developer Web Client and navigate to the **Process Start View** to test your changes. Use the following screenshot to verify your results:

 Test data like **High**, **Low**, and **Medium** has to be entered manually in the AHA Courtesy Indicator field. This can be achieved by exposing the AHA Courtesy Indicator field a second time as a standard text field.

We can observe that the icon changes when the AHA Courtesy Indicator field has different values. The existing icon map named LS Pharma Market Potential which was chosen for the example, displays different constellations of yellow dollar ($) signs to represent the values **Low**, **Medium**, and **High**.

Case study example: Replacing the application logo

The following example procedure explains how we can replace the Oracle logo in the upper-right corner of the Siebel CRM application window with our company logo. The logo graphic file must be 24 pixels in height to fit into the Siebel application banner frame. In the example, we use the file `All_Hardware_Logo.png`, which is available with this chapter's code files:

1. Copy the `All_Hardware_Logo.png` file to the `public|enu|IMAGES` directory of the Siebel Developer Web Client installation folder.

2. In **Siebel Tools**, expose the **Bitmap Category** object type in the **Object Explorer** if necessary.

3. Navigate to the **HTML Control Icons** bitmap category.

4. Check out or lock the bitmap category.

5. In the **Object Explorer**, expand the **Bitmap Category type** and select the **Bitmap type**.

6. In the Bitmaps list, create a new record with the following properties:
   - **Name: AHA_LOGO**
   - **Filename: All_Hardware_Logo.png**
   - **Alt Text — String Override: All Hardware Logo**
   - **Comments: Created for AHA prototype**

7. Compile the **HTML Control Icons** bitmap category.

8. Navigate to the `WEBTEMPL` directory of the Siebel Developer Web Client installation folder.

9. Create a backup copy of the `CCFrameBanner.swt` file.

10. Open the `CCFrameBanner.swt` file in a text editor.

11. Locate the line that contains the following text:
    ```
    <swe:image name="POWERED_BY"
    ```

12. Copy the line and paste it again below itself.

13. Edit the copied text so that it reads as follows (changes are in **bold** text):
    ```
    <td align="right"><a href="http://www.all-hardware.com"
    target="_blank"><swe:image name="AHA_LOGO" category="HTML Control
    Icons"/></a></td>
    ```

The URL www.all-hardware.com only serves as an example. At the moment of writing this book, the URL was not registered and should not be used for any productive deployment of Siebel CRM applications.

14. Position the cursor before the original line and type a comment, without the closing tag, similar to the following:

```
<!-- Begin of Customization - AHA Logo
```

15. Position the cursor at the end of the original line and press *Enter* to create a new line.

16. Type a comment `closing tag -->` so that the original line is now enclosed in the comment.

17. Enter a comment below the new line to indicate the end of customization.

18. Compare your work with the following screenshot:

```
<!-- Begin of Customization - AHA Logo
<td align="right"><a href="http://www.oracle.com" target
-->
<td align="right"><a href="http://www.all-hardware.com"
<!-- End of Customization - AHA Logo -->
```

The previous screenshot does not show the full text. The file CCFrameBanner.swt is available in this chapter's code files for your reference. In addition, a Siebel Tools archive file (HTML Control Icons.sif) is available in this chapter's code file representing the repository changes made in this section.

19. Launch the Siebel Developer Web Client to test your changes. Use the *F5* key to refresh the browser cache if needed.

The following screenshot shows the result of the preceding procedure:

The logo of **All Hardware** is now displayed in the Siebel application banner frame. To deploy these changes to test or production servers we must ensure that the image file, the SWT file, and the repository content are fully deployed.

Summary

There are various techniques to manipulate the look and feel of Siebel CRM applications. In this chapter, we discussed how SWT files define the visual appearance of applets, views, and web pages and how customizations can be applied.

Cascading Style Sheet (CSS) files control the formatting of all elements of a Siebel CRM application. We learned how to customize CSS files using the thread bar as an example.

Graphic files are used to enrich the user experience in the browser application. In this chapter, we learned how to work with bitmap categories and icon maps, and how to customize the application logo.

In the next chapter, we will learn how to configure menus and buttons in Siebel CRM applications.

16
Menus and Buttons

The Siebel event framework allows developers to implement simple or complex processes and provide user interface elements such as menus and buttons to the end user. In this chapter, we will learn how the Siebel event framework works and how to configure buttons and menus in Siebel CRM applications.

The chapter is structured as follows:

- Understanding the Siebel event framework
- Creating applet buttons
- Configuring command objects
- Configuring application menu items
- Configuring toolbar buttons
- Configuring applet menu items

Understanding the Siebel event framework

To understand how the Siebel application engine processes events such as a click on a button or a menu item, we can inspect one of the various pre-built objects in standard Siebel CRM applications.

A commonly used button in Siebel CRM applications is the **Site Map** button. End users frequently navigate to the site map to access screens and views. Navigation to the site map can be triggered by clicking the **Site Map** command in the **Navigate** menu, pressing *Ctrl+Shift+A* on the keyboard, or by clicking the toolbar button with the globe icon.

In Siebel Tools, we can execute a procedure similar to the following to inspect the definition for the Site Map menu item and toolbar button:

1. Expose the **Command, Menu,** and **Toolbar** object types in the **Object Explorer** if necessary.

2. In the **Object Explorer** window, select the **Menu** type.

3. In the **Object List Editor**, select the **Generic WEB** menu.

4. In the **Object Explorer**, expand the **Menu** type and select the **Menu Item** type.

5. Use the **Caption** column to query for the menu item labeled **Site Map**.

6. Inspect the **Command** property and observe that the **Command** object definition used by the menu item is named **Sitemap**.

7. In the **Object Explorer**, select the **Flat** tab.

8. In the **Flat** tab, select the **Toolbar Item** type.

9. Use the **Display Name** column to query for toolbar items that are labeled **Site Map**.

10. Observe that there are various instances (in different toolbar definitions) but they all refer to the same command object named Sitemap.

11. In the **Object Explorer**, select the **Types** tab to go back to the hierarchical object list.

12. Navigate to the **Command** object named **Sitemap**.

13. Inspect the **Method** property and observe that the method invoked by this command is named **GotoPage**. When invoked, this method navigates to a web page object in the browser.

14. Inspect the **Method Argument** property and observe that the name of the web page is **CC Site Map**.

15. In the **Object Explorer**, expand the **Command** type and select the **Accelerator** type.

16. Observe that the **Key Sequence** property is set to *Ctrl+Shift+A*. This defines the keyboard shortcut.

We have completed the inspection of the menu item and the toolbar button that navigates to the Siebel application's site map page. We have learned that **command** object definitions are referenced by menu items and toolbar buttons alike. The command object defines the method or action to be invoked as well as the keyboard accelerator. We will learn more about command object definitions later in this chapter.

Event handling in Siebel applications

There are many circumstances during which the Siebel application must react to events that are not directly triggered by end users. For example, an external interface could update hundreds-of-thousands of records during a nightly batch and it is required to validate these updates before they are committed to the database.

It is therefore necessary to extend the concept of events and how they are handled to the business logic layer. The engineers at Siebel Systems have created the Siebel event framework, which allows them and custom developers to intercept any event before and after the execution of the Siebel C++ code that implements the event handler.

In continuing our example scenario, the standard behavior of Siebel applications is that once a record is updated (and left or saved), the changes are written to the database.

A diagram that depicts this flow would look like the following:

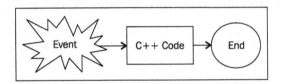

With a fixed flow like the previous one, any additional logic would require editing the C++ code, which is not feasible in Siebel CRM. Instead, Siebel engineers have provided event handlers before and after the internal C++ code is executed, so the diagram in fact looks more like this:

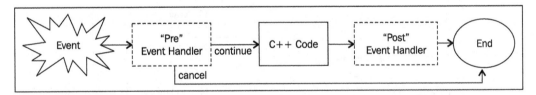

In Siebel terms, the event handlers that are executed before the internal Siebel C++ code are called *Pre* event handlers whereas the ones that are executed after the C++ code are called *Post* event handlers. *Pre* event handlers also provide the ability to cancel the execution flow, for example when the validation result is negative—thus avoiding the execution of the Siebel C++ code.

Event handlers can be implemented at different levels such as the browser, server instance of an applet, and the business component level. Developers can use techniques such as **runtime events**, **scripting**, and **user properties** to implement custom event handlers.

The following table describes the possible implementation technology for each level of event handler:

Technology → Level ↓	Event Handler	Runtime Events	Scripting	User Properties
Browser Applet	*Pre*	No	Yes (Browser Script)	No
Server Applet	*Pre*	Yes	Yes (Server Script)	No
Business Component	*Pre*	Yes	Yes (Server Script)	No
Business Component	*Post*	Yes	Yes (Server Script)	Yes (Named Method)
Server Applet	*Post*	Yes	Yes (Server Script)	Yes (Named Method)
Browser Applet	*Post*	No	Yes (Browser Script)	No

It is important for Siebel developers to understand the sequence of event handler invocation. For example, any runtime event defined for a business component will be executed before any script associated with the business component. With the information from the preceding table we can derive the following flow diagram:

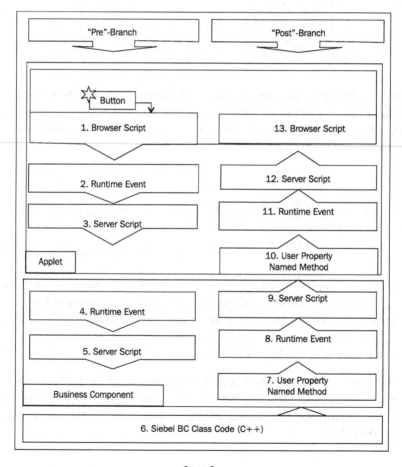

From the preceding diagram we can learn the following:

- *Pre* event handlers are executed before the internal C++ code for the business component

- *Post* event handlers are executed after the business component code

- Browser-side *Pre* event handlers are executed before server-side event handlers

- Applet *Pre* event handlers are executed before business component event handlers

- Runtime events are executed before scripts

- The Named Method user property can be used to handle *Post* events on the server side for business components and applets

- *Post* event handlers are executed in reverse order of *Pre* event handlers with business component event handlers being executed before applet server-side event handlers

We will learn more about event handlers, runtime events, and scripting in upcoming chapters of this book. In the remainder of this chapter, we will focus on user interface elements such as buttons and menu items, which are mostly based on user properties.

Controlling method invocation

There are circumstances when we do not wish that a method can be executed by the user. For example, a record that has not been created by the current user should be prevented from deletion. The respective menu items and buttons should be inactive or **grayed out**.

The Siebel event framework has a special event handler named `CanInvokeMethod` that allows us to control the activation or deactivation of methods and therefore the active or **grayed out** state of menu items and buttons.

The `CanInvokeMethod` event is triggered every time a different record is selected to provide context sensitivity at the record level. The Siebel event framework then determines whether it **can invoke** the method, hence the name "*CanInvoke*Method", for the current record. The event handler is executed once for each method exposed on the current view. This includes methods invoked by application menu items and toolbar buttons as well as all applet menu items and applet buttons.

Developers can use script in the PreCanInvokeMethod event handler or user properties to provide logical instructions when to allow the invocation of a specific method or not.

Custom methods, in particular, which are not pre-registered in the Siebel event framework, must be made known to the Siebel application so that buttons or menu items that refer to these methods become active and clickable.

The case study examples in the following sections describe the techniques for registering custom methods with the Siebel event framework.

Creating applet buttons

At the beginning of this chapter, we discussed how menu items and toolbar buttons use command object definitions to invoke methods that are then handled by the Siebel application's event framework.

Applet buttons are different from menu items and toolbar buttons in a sense that they specify the method to be invoked directly in their own **MethodInvoked** property. They do not use command objects.

Case study example: Creating a custom applet button that invokes a workflow process

As described in *Chapter 3, Case Study Introduction* the AHA business analyst team has put forth the requirement to create orders for business customers directly from the AHA Customer Profile Form Applet by means of a button click. The button should only be clickable when the customer type is *Business*.

The AHA technical architect team has inspected the preconfigured Siebel applications and found that the required behavior is available in the standard applications by means of the **Account - New Order** workflow process. The only additional configuration would be the dynamic activation or deactivation of the button.

The following procedure describes how to create a custom applet button that invokes the Account - New Order workflow process and how to control the state of the button depending on the customer type:

1. Navigate to the **AHA Customer Profile Form Applet**.
2. Check out or lock the applet if necessary.
3. Open the applet in the **web layout editor**.
4. Drag a **MiniButton** control from the **Palettes** window to the first placeholder (marked with an **x**) after the **Query Assistant** button.

5. In the **Properties** window enter the following values for the new button:

   ○ **Name**: AHA Order Button

   ○ **Method Invoked**: AHANewOrder

   ○ **Caption**: New Order

6. Save the changes and close the web layout editor.

7. In the **Object Explorer**, expand the **Applet type** and select the **Applet User Prop** type.

8. In the **Applet User Props** list, create a new record with the following values:

   ○ **Name**: CanInvokeMethod: AHANewOrder

   ○ **Value**: [Type] = LookupValue("ACCOUNT_TYPE", "Business")

> The preceding new applet user property ensures that any user interface element that exposes the AHANewOrder method is grayed out unless the language independent value in the **Type** field of the Account business component is *Business*. The LookupValue() function should be used for any field that is associated with a static pick list in order to ensure language independency of the repository objects.

If we wish to constantly keep the button enabled, we can simply set the Value of the applet user property to **TRUE**.

9. Compile the **AHA Customer Profile Form Applet**.

10. Navigate to the **Account business component**.

11. Check out or lock the business component if necessary.

12. Navigate to the list of business component user properties for the Account business components.

13. Execute a query with *Named Method** as the search string to retrieve all user properties for named methods.

14. Inspect the list and find the active user property with the highest sequence number.

> In Siebel Industry Applications 8.1.1 this is the *Named Method 26* user property.

15. Copy the record for the **Named Method 26** user property and rename the copy to **Named Method 35**.

As discussed in *Chapter 13*, we can leave a gap of nine to avoid conflicts with user properties defined by Oracle engineering in future versions of Siebel CRM.

16. Edit the **Value** column of the new user property to look as follows (changes are highlighted as **bold** text):

```
"AHANewOrder", "INVOKESVC", "Account", "Workflow Process Manager",
"RunProcess", "'ProcessName'", "Account - New Order",  "'RowId'",
"[Id]"
```

This user property value defines that when the *AHANewOrder* method is invoked on the *Account* business component, the *Account - New Order* workflow process is run with the current record's *ROW_ID* value.

17. Set the **Comments** column for the new user property to **Created for AHA prototype**.

18. Compile the **Account business component**.

19. If you are using the Siebel Sample Database to follow the case study examples, the following steps are **not** necessary.

20. Navigate to the **Account - New Order** workflow process in Siebel Tools.

21. Expose the **WF/Task Editor Toolbar** in the Siebel Tools toolbar area if necessary by right-clicking anywhere in the toolbar area and selecting the toolbar.

22. Click the **Publish/Activate** button in the WF/Task Editor Toolbar to publish and activate the **Account - New Order** workflow process.

23. Repeat step 21 for the **Goto_Order** workflow process. This workflow process is a subprocess in the **Account - New Order** workflow process.

24. Launch the Siebel Mobile or Developer Web Client and navigate to the **AHA Process Start View**.

25. Create a test account record without setting the **Type** field.

26. Observe that the **New Order** button is **grayed out**.

27. Set the type of the test account to *Business* and press *Tab* to leave the field.

28. Observe that the **New Order** button is now **clickable**.

29. Click the **New Order** button.

30. Observe that the application creates a new service order and navigates to the **Order Entry - Detail Orders View** as a result of the workflow execution.

Did you know?

It is a recommendable practice to handle the method invocation on the business component level rather than the applet level as shown in the previous example procedure. By obeying this recommendation, we ensure that the business logic resides in the correct application layer and that only a minimum of configuration is necessary to provide the same functionality on other applets.

The file User Properties.txt in this chapter's code file contains the names and values for the user properties created in the preceding example procedure. The reader may find it convenient to copy and paste the text from the file to Siebel Tools.

Configuring command objects

When we wish to create menu items in the application or applet menus or toolbar buttons, we must start with configuring command objects. A command object, as shown earlier in this chapter, is a reusable object definition that is referenced from the aforementioned user interface elements. Command objects can invoke one of the following:

- **Method and arguments**: The method must be handled on the application, applet, or business component layer
- **Business service, method, and arguments**: Business services are reusable programs defined in the Siebel Repository
- **Pop-up applet**: When the command is invoked, an applet is loaded in a popup window

The following table describes the most important properties of the Command object type:

Property	Description
Business Service	When this property is set to the name of a business service, the command invokes the business service's method (defined in the **Method** property) with the list of arguments defined in the **Method Argument** property.
Method	When the Business Service property is empty, this property references the name of a method that is handled by the application, applet, or business component layer objects.
Method Argument	Input arguments for the method. For example, the GotoUrl method requires a method argument like URL=`http://someserver.com`.
Show Popup	When set to **TRUE**, the command invokes the creation of a new pop-up window. Used for special applets such as About View and often with the `GotoApplet` method. The Method Argument property is used to specify the applet mode and name.
HTML Popup Dimension	Specifies the **size** of the popup applet when **Show Popup** is set to true.
Display Name	Used as the label for the invoking object (menu item or toolbar button) when the object itself has no label defined.
HTML Bitmap	References a bitmap that is displayed on the toolbar button that references the command. The bitmap will be displayed when the method can be invoked and the toolbar button is clickable.
HTML Disabled Bitmap	References a bitmap that is displayed in the *grayed out* state. Bitmaps referenced by command object definitions must reside in the **HTML Command Icons** bitmap category.
Target	Specifies which application layer handles the method invocation. Valid values are **Server**, **Browser**, **Service**, and **Active Applet**.

Accelerators

Command objects can be associated with **Accelerator** child object definitions. Accelerators define the keyboard shortcuts that the end user can use to invoke the command without the need to use the mouse.

For easier identification of the respective keyboard shortcuts, menu items always display the keyboard shortcuts implemented by the command's accelerator as shown in the following screenshot:

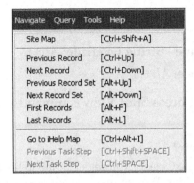

The **Navigate** menu of the Siebel CRM application displays the keyboard shortcuts such as *Ctrl+Shift+A* for the **Site Map** command in the right half of the menu.

Case study example: Creating a command with an accelerator

As defined in *Chapter 3*, AHA end users should be able to navigate quickly to the **AHA Customer Process Start View** by means of a keyboard shortcut or toolbar button. The following example procedure demonstrates how to implement this requirement:

1. Navigate to the **Command** object type in Siebel Tools.

2. In the **Commands** list, create a **new** record with the following property values:

   ○ **Name:** AHA Process Start View

   ○ **Project:** AHA User Interface

   ○ **Display Name - String Override:** Go to Process Start View

   ○ **HTML Bitmap:** Home

   ○ **Method:** GotoView

   ○ **Method Argument:** AHA Customer Process Start View

   ○ **Target:** Server

   ○ **Comments:** Created for AHA prototype

3. In the **Object Explorer**, expand the **Command** type and select the **Accelerator** type.

4. In the **Accelerators** list, create a new record with the following property values:

   ○ **Name**: 1

   ○ **Display Name - String Override**: *Alt+H*

   ○ **Key Sequence**: *Alt+H*

5. Compile the **AHA Process Start View** command.

Did you know?

We can use the Object Explorer's Flat tab to list all Accelerator object definitions. We can then use queries to identify whether the desired keyboard shortcut is still available.

When choosing a keyboard shortcut, we must ensure that it is not yet occupied and that it does not interfere with the browser's keyboard shortcuts.

Case study example: Configuring application menu items

The command we created in the previous section can now be associated with menu items and toolbar buttons. The following example procedure describes how to associate a command with an application menu item:

1. Navigate to the **Generic WEB** menu.

2. Check out or lock the menu if necessary.

3. In the **Object Explorer**, expand the Menu type and select the **Menu Item** type.

4. In the **Menu Items** list, create a new record with the following property values:

   ○ **Name**: AHA Navigate - Process Start View

   ○ **Caption - String Override**: Go to Process Start View

   ○ **Command**: AHA Process Start View

   ○ **Position**: 4.25 (leaving a gap of 10 to the highest position number starting with 4.)

   ○ **Comments**: Created for AHA prototype

5. Compile the **Generic WEB** menu.

6. In the **Developer Web Client**, open the **Navigate** menu and verify that a new menu item labeled **Go to Process Start View [Alt+H]** exists at the bottom of the menu.

7. Click the new menu item.

8. Observe that the **AHA Customer Process Start View** is open.

9. Navigate to the **Home Page View**.

10. Press *Alt+H*.

11. Observe that the **AHA Customer Process Start View** is open.

Case study example: Configuring toolbar buttons

The following procedure describes how to create a new toolbar button that uses the command created previously in this chapter:

1. Navigate to the **HIMain** toolbar.

2. Check out or lock the toolbar if necessary.

3. In the **Object Explorer**, expand the **Toolbar** type and select the **Toolbar Item** type.

4. In the **Toolbar Items** list, create a new record with the following property values:

   ○ **Name**: AHA Process Start View

   ○ **Command**: AHA Process Start View

   ○ **Display Name - String Override**: Go to Process Start View

   ○ **HTML Type**: Link

   ○ **Position**: 17 (leaving a gap of 10 to the highest existing position value)

   ○ **Comments**: Created for AHA prototype

5. Compile the HIMain toolbar.

6. In the **Developer Web Client**, verify that a new toolbar button, with a **house** icon, appears to the right of the **Site Map** button.

7. Click the new toolbar button and verify that the **AHA Customer Process Start View** is open.

A Siebel Tools archive file (Command_Menu_Toolbar.sif) is available with this chapter's code file. The file represents the command, menu, and toolbar definitions created or modified in the previous section.

Case study example: Configuring applet menu items

We can consider adding all available functionality to an applet's menu. By adding this, we ensure that end users can always find a list of available commands by clicking the **Menu** button or right-clicking in the applet.

The following example procedure describes how to add an applet menu item to the AHA Customer Profile Form Applet using the web menu editor. We will use a copy of a preconfigured command object definition to provide the functionality of creating a new order for the selected customer record:

1. Navigate to the **Account-New Order** command.
2. Copy the **Account-New Order** command and rename the copy to **AHA New Order**.
3. Change the **Project** property to **AHA User Interface**.
4. Change the **Method** property to **AHANewOrder**.
5. Compile the **AHA New Order** command.
6. Navigate to the **AHA Customer Profile Form Applet**.
7. Check out or lock the applet if necessary.
8. Right-click the **AHA Customer Profile Form Applet** and select **Edit Web Menus**.
9. In the **web menu editor**, double-click the **New Item** entry.
10. In the **Menu Item Properties** dialog, enter the following values:
    ○ **Menu text**: New Order
    ○ **Invoke Command**: AHA New Order
11. Compare your work with the following screenshot:

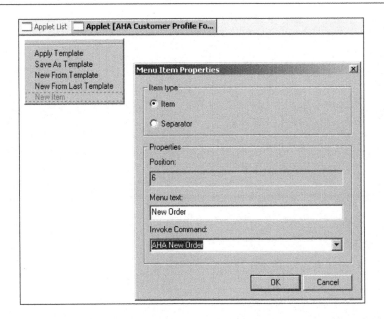

12. Click **OK**.

13. Save and close the web menu editor.

14. Compile the **AHA Customer Profile Form Applet**.

15. Test your changes in the Developer Web Client and verify that the applet menu of the AHA Customer Profile Form Applet now contains a **new menu item** labeled **New Order**. The menu item will only be clickable when the type of the customer is *Business*.

Summary

The Siebel event framework provides various possibilities for developers to create user interface elements such as menu items and buttons. In this chapter, we studied the functionality of the Siebel event framework as well as the configuration of command objects that support menu items and toolbar buttons.

We also learned how to control the activation or deactivation of menu items and buttons via the CanInvokeMethod event handler and how to use the Named Method business component user property to handle method invocations.

In the following chapter, we will discuss the concept of Siebel business services.

17
Business Services

Whether we download data from a Siebel list applet to a file or view the price waterfall for a discounted order item, **Business Services** provide the majority of logic and functionality in Siebel CRM applications. In this chapter, we will discuss the concept of business services and learn how to explore the functionality of preconfigured standard business services.

The chapter is structured as follows:

- Understanding Business Services
- Preconfigured Business Services
- Testing Business Services

Understanding business services

A business service can be understood as a program that provides a predefined set of functions. A function, in general programming terminology, is a part of a program and has defined input and output parameters. Business services are defined in the Siebel Repository and contain **methods**, which themselves have input or output **method arguments**.

The following diagram compares Siebel Business Services with general programming terms:

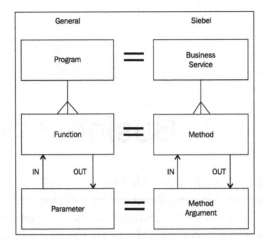

We can use Siebel Tools to inspect the structure of the business services, which could be either delivered with the Siebel out of the box repository or written by custom developers.

To do so, we navigate to the **Business Service** type in the **Object Explorer** and select the desired business service from the list. When we expand the Business Service type, we can inspect the methods and by expanding the **Business Service Method** type, we can inspect the input and output arguments of each method.

Developers who take a first look at the impressive list of hundreds of preconfigured business services often find themselves discouraged in their quest for understanding the logic behind these services.

There are several reasons to feel intimidated. For example, many business services simply have no defined methods, nor arguments. Many of them lack a description and even a search in the Siebel bookshelf does not provide greater insight.

On the other hand, many of the preconfigured business services in the Siebel Repository are well described and the approach to understand them is the opposite of spending hours of fruitless scrolling in Siebel Tools. These preconfigured business services are described in detail across various bookshelf documents. So the ambitious developer may be confronted with a business service only while working in a specific area of Siebel applications. Examples for such areas are:

- Enterprise Application Integration (EAI)
- Siebel Order Management
- Siebel Marketing and Loyalty

- Data Validation
- Siebel Financial Services
- Universal Customer Master (UCM)

We will describe some of the most important preconfigured Siebel business services later in this chapter.

Most preconfigured business services are implemented as C++ classes, so their code is not visible to the Siebel Tools user. Custom developers can use Siebel eScript (a variant of ECMA script and similar to JavaScript) to implement custom business services. We will discuss how to write custom business services in eScript in a later chapter.

Invoking business service methods

When we have decided to use a business service, we must know how to invoke its methods, pass the necessary input arguments, and retrieve the output arguments. To facilitate method invocation and output retrieval, the Siebel framework provides a proprietary data type called **Property Set**.

As the name suggests, a property set is a set of properties—another name for an array of arguments. In addition, a property set can contain an arbitrary number of child property sets, allowing for the creation of hierarchical data structures.

The following diagram describes the structure of a property set:

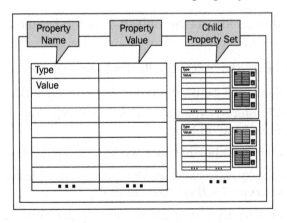

From the preceding diagram, we can learn the following:

- A property set has two properties with fixed names—**Type** and **Value**
- A property set can have an arbitrary number of additional freely named properties

- A property set can have an arbitrary number of child property sets
- Child property sets can have children themselves and the number of generation levels is not limited

When we use Siebel workflow to invoke business service methods, the Siebel framework dynamically generates property sets in memory. Developers who write scripts to work with business services can use methods defined by the Siebel object interfaces API to generate property sets. We will discuss Siebel workflow and scripting later in this book.

Each business service method has a specific set of input and output arguments. To invoke the method, we must prepare a property set, called the input property set, which contains at least the input arguments defined by the method. The business service method will produce a so-called output property set, which contains the output arguments with the computed values as defined by the method.

To illustrate this, we can use the *Eliza* business service, which is a sample preconfigured business service written in eScript.

Did you know?

Eliza is a famous computer program written by Joseph Weizenbaum in the 1960s. Its purpose is to demonstrate natural language processing by passing an answer or question back on each input. (Source: Wikipedia— http://en.wikipedia.org/wiki/ELIZA)

The following procedure guides us through an inspection of the Eliza business service:

1. In the **Object Explorer**, select the **Business Service** type.
2. In the **Business Services** list, query for the business service named **Eliza**.
3. In the **Object Explorer**, expand the Business Service type and select the **Business Service Method** type.
4. Observe that the **Eliza** business service has one method named **Analyze**.
5. In the Object Explorer, expand the Business Service Method type and select the **Business Service Method Argument** type.
6. Observe that the **Analyze** method has one input argument named **InputMessage** and one output argument named **OutputMessage**.

    The following screenshot shows the arguments for the Analyze method of the Eliza business service:

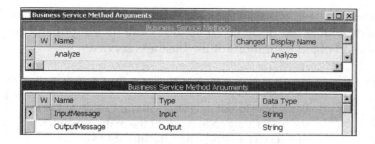

7. In the **Object Explorer**, select the **Business Service** type.

8. Right-click the **Eliza** business service and select **Edit Server Scripts**.

9. Inspect the eScript code in the script editor. The code is shown in the following screenshot:

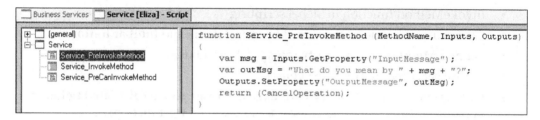

The code of the Eliza business service does the following:

- Reads the `InputMessage` argument from the `Inputs` property set and assigns the value to a variable named `msg`

- Concatenates the string `"What do you mean by"` with the value of the `msg` variable and assigns the result to a variable named `outMsg`

- Sets the value of the `OutputMessage` property in the `Outputs` property set to the value of the `outMsg` variable

- Returns to the calling instance, canceling all subsequent event handling

As indicated previously, not all preconfigured business services are written in plain eScript code. The inspection of the code is put here for learning purposes only.

We now have a better understanding of how business services work. To invoke the **Analyze** method of the **Eliza** business service we would have to create an input property set with a single property named **InputMessage** with a value of, for example, `"Hello"`. After invocation of the Analyze method we will be able to retrieve the value of the **OutputMessage** property from the output property set. Its value would be `"What do you mean by Hello?"`, the result of the text concatenation that took place in the Analyze method.

It is not necessary to have access to the code behind a business service method as long as the developer has declared all methods and their input and output arguments as child object definitions of the business service.

Did you know?
Being able to use a service without having to know the underlying code is one of the main principles of a **service-oriented architecture (SOA)**.

We can invoke business service methods from a large variety of interaction points from within the Siebel application framework and from external applications. The following is a list of the most important invocation techniques:

- Business Service step in a Siebel **workflow process**
- InvokeMethod function in Siebel **scripting**
- **Command** object definition (used by **menu items** and **toolbar buttons**)
- **Named Method user property** (on applets and business components)
- **Action set** (used by **runtime events**)
- Expressions in **Siebel Query Language** (for example, in **calculated fields** or **personalization**, using the `InvokeServiceMethod()` function)
- From **EAI Receivers** and the **EAI Dispatch Service**
- **External programs** (Java, COM, .NET)
- External **SOAP requests** (Inbound Web Services)

In upcoming chapters of this book, we will discuss the concepts of Siebel workflow processes and scripting in greater detail.

Preconfigured business services

The Siebel Repository for **Siebel Industry Applications (SIA)** 8.1.1 contains more than 1,200 preconfigured business services. While most of them are for internal use by Oracle engineering only, there are many business services that are documented explicitly for use by custom developers. Because Oracle describes the business services and their methods in context with their originating functional area, there is no official comprehensive list of business services available. However, information in the Oracle Siebel documentation library is well organized and can be searched online with Google (`http://www.google.com`) or Oracle Search (`http://search.oracle.com`). For example, a list of business services related to **Enterprise Application Integration (EAI)** can be found in the Integration Platform Technologies guide in the Siebel bookshelf (`http://download.oracle.com/docs/cd/E14004_01/books/EAI2/EAI2_PredefinedEAI2.html`).

The list of business services that we can display in Siebel Tools should be seen as the library of out of the box application functionality. It is among our duties as developers to acquaint ourselves with that library. By using existing functionality rather than developing our own code, we can significantly reduce effort, costs, and risks for our project.

The following table describes some of the most important preconfigured business services in alphabetical order. The list only references business services of generic nature, leaving out the hundredfold of application-specific services we find in the Siebel Repository:

Business Service	Functional Area	Description
Asynchronous Server Requests	Server Requests	By using this business service, developers can issue job requests for any batch server component programmatically. The calling code will not wait for the return of the methods.
Data Validation Manager	Data Validation	This business service consumes data validation rule sets (entered in administrative views in the web client), interprets the rule expressions (in Siebel Query Language), and invokes the defined action (for example, message display) when rule validation fails.
EAI Data Transformation Engine	EAI, Data Mapping	Can be used to map between internal and external representations of business data.
EAI File Transport	EAI	The Send method of this and other *Transport* business services writes the content of the Value input property to the destination.
EAI Siebel Adapter	EAI, Data Access	This is the universal adapter service for any EAI-based data access.
EAI XML Converter	EAI	Used to convert a Siebel proprietary hierarchical property set to an XML document and vice versa.
EAI XSLT Service	EAI	Allows developers to utilize **XSLT (XML Stylesheet Transformation)** files for advanced data mapping.

Business Service	Functional Area	Description
Outbound Communications Manager	Communications	Interacts with the Communications Outbound Manager server component to implement multi-channel communication such as e-mail or fax.
PRM ANI Utility Service	Utilities	Contains various methods for property set manipulation and other helper functions.
Read CSV File	EAI	Converts the contents of a **CSV** (**comma separated values**) file to a hierarchical property set.
Row Set Transformation Toolkit	Order Management	A universal service to manipulate data sets in memory. Used mainly in the product selection and pricing workflows.
SIA BC Utility Service	Utilities	Provides methods to invoke methods on business components.
Spell Checker	Utilities	Allows execution of spellcheck functionality on any input text.
Synchronous Server Requests	Server Requests	Similar to the Asynchronous Server Requests business service. The caller will wait for the return.
Unified Messaging Service	Utilities	Interacts with the Unified Messaging Framework to generate messages and process the user response.
Universal Inbox	Utilities	Allows developers to populate and manipulate data in the user's inbox.
Usage Tracking Service	Utilities	Tracks access to Siebel views and writes information to files.
Workflow Process Manager	System	This business service executes workflow process definitions.
Workflow Utilities	Utilities	Contains various methods that are useful for workflow development.
XML Gateway	EAI	Used primarily for virtual business components (VBCs) that allow data access to external systems.

Business Service	Functional Area	Description
All business services with class CSSEAIDataSyncService	EAI	Business services of that class are also known as Application Services Interfaces (ASIs) and serve as encapsulated data synchronization interfaces. They are often exposed as inbound web services.
All business services with class CSSWSOutboundDispatcher	EAI	Business services of that class are known as *proxy* business services and implement outbound web services.

Testing business services

Developers who wish to acquaint themselves can, besides reading the documentation, use the **Business Service Simulator** view in the **Administration - Business Service** screen of the Siebel Web Client.

This view allows creation or upload of an input property set for the chosen business service method, execution of the method, and inspection or download of the output property set.

> It must be noted that we should not be led into false assumptions by the name *Simulator*. Whatever the code behind the business service method is programmed to do, it will be executed without the possibility to roll back the changes made by the code.

The following example procedure describes how to test the **Spell Checker** business service. The process of testing other preconfigured or custom business services is similar:

1. Log in to the **Siebel Mobile Web Client**, connecting to the **sample** database, using **SADMIN** as username and password.

2. Navigate to the **Site Map**.

3. Navigate to the **Administration - Business Service** screen, **Simulator** view.

4. In the upper list applet, create a new record.

5. Enter Spell Checker as the **Service Name** and OpenSession as the **Method Name**.

The Input Arguments list in the middle of the view allows us to create input property sets. The input arguments for the OpenSession method are **Language ID** and **User ID**. We can derive this information from the Business Service Method Arg list in Siebel Tools.

6. In the **Input Arguments** list, create a new record and enter 1 in the **Test Case # field.

   Use the *Tab* key to navigate through the columns of the record and observe that we can enter values for the **Value** and **Type** properties. The **Child Type** column is a multi value field that allows us to enter child property sets. The **Property Name** column is also a multi value field that allows us to create an array of properties.

7. Click the select button in the **Property Name** column.

8. In the **Property Set Properties** applet, create a new record and enter Language ID in the **Property Name** field and ENU in the **Value** field.

9. Create a second record in the **Property Set Properties** applet and enter **User ID** as the property name and SADMIN as the value.

10. Compare your work with the following screenshot:

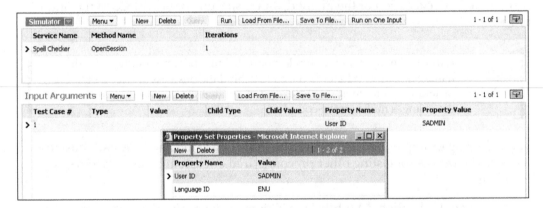

The preceding screenshot shows the Property Set Properties applet with two properties — **User ID** and **Language ID** – and their values. These two properties are now part of an input property set for test purposes.

11. Click the **OK** button to close the **Property Set Properties** window.

12. In the upper list applet, click the **Run on One Input** button to execute the OpenSession method of the **Spell Checker** business service with the currently selected input property set. This establishes a new session for the Spell Checker service. We can now use the session to execute a spellcheck on a sample text.

13. In the upper list applet, create a new record and specify `Spell Checker` as the **Service Name** and `SubmitRequest` as the **Method Name**.

14. In the **Input Arguments** list applet, create a new record and enter 2 as the test case number.

15. Click the select button in the **Property Name** column.

16. In the **Property Set Properties** applet, create a new record and enter `Text` in the **Property Name** field and enter the following text in the **Property Value** field:

    `This text has a prroblem.`

    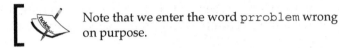
    Note that we enter the word `prroblem` wrong on purpose.

17. Click the **OK** button to close the **Property Set Properties** window.

18. Ensure that the record with test case number **2** is selected.

19. In the upper list applet, click the **Run on One Input** button.

20. Observe the new record in the **Output Arguments** list applet at the bottom of the view. The record represents the output property set of the `SubmitRequest` method of the Spell Checker business service.

The output property set can be viewed by clicking the select buttons in the **Child Type** and the **Property Name** columns to see the child property sets and the property array respectively. It is also possible to click the **Save to File...** button on the Output Arguments list applet to save the entire output property set to an XML file.

The following screenshot shows the XML representation of the output property set created by the SubmitRequest method of the Spell Checker business service:

```
TempFile[1].xml - Notepad
File  Edit  Format  View  Help
<?xml version="1.0" encoding="UTF-8"?>
<?Siebel-Property-Set EscapeNames="true"?>
<PropertySet ErrorWord="prroblem" ErrorPosition="16">
<Suggestions parole="81" problematic="81" problem="97" probe="85" problems="92">
</Suggestions>
</PropertySet>
```

We can observe that the output property set contains two properties (`ErrorWord` with a value of `prroblem` and `ErrorPosition` with a value of `16`) indicating that the first word with spelling errors in the input text occurs after the 16th character.

In addition, the output property set contains a child property set of Type `Suggestions`, which contains five properties with suggested spellings and a number indicating the likelihood of being the best suggestion. The `problem` property has a value of `97`, which is the highest value given.

An end user would now press a button to invoke another method of the Spell Checker service, for example to allow the Spell Checker service to change the wrong word to the correct spelling.

We can investigate how the Spell Checker business service is embedded in Siebel CRM by visiting the **Public Notes** view in the **Accounts** screen. The notes list applet hosts a **Check Spelling** button which invokes the Spell Checker business service and passes the note text. The following screenshot shows the spell checking functionality in the **Public Notes** view of the **Accounts** screen in the Siebel Web Client:

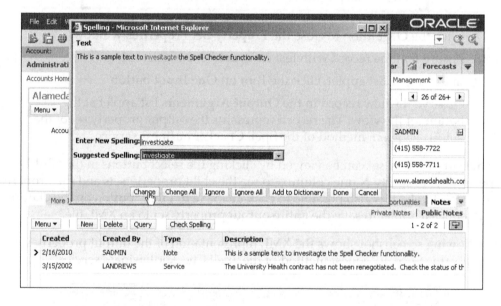

The Spelling dialog allows an end user to identify incorrect spelling and correct it using the **Change** or **Change All** button.

As indicated previously, the Spell Checker business service is just one among hundreds of preconfigured business services. It is a good example of encapsulating reusable functionality that goes beyond simple data manipulation.

Case study example: Invoking a business service method from a runtime event

As indicated in *Chapter 3, Case Study Introduction* AHA has the requirement of tracking all *view hits* to be able to identify frequently used views and to provide data for business process management. The preconfigured **Usage Tracking Service** has been identified as the solution for this requirement.

The solution also includes the use of the runtime event architecture that has been introduced in *Chapter 16, Menus and Buttons*. We will however discuss how runtime events work in more detail in the following section.

Runtime events

As indicated in *Chapter 16*, we can use runtime events to handle events in Siebel applications. We can understand runtime events as a means to registering distinct events such as a method invocation on a business component or applet with an **action set**. An action set, as the name suggests, is a set of discrete actions that can be one of the following:

- Invoke a business service method and pass input arguments
- Set a profile attribute (a variable that is available from server and browser-side code)
- Invoke a method on the object that experienced the event

Action sets and runtime events are registered in the **Administration - Runtime Events** screen in the Siebel Web Client. The following diagram describes the architecture of runtime events:

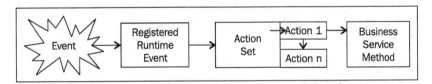

When the event occurs, the Siebel application identifies the registered instances of this event and invokes the actions in the associated action set in the specified sequence.

The following procedure describes how to enable the tracking of view hits by associating the Usage Tracking Service with the **ViewActivated** event of the Siebel application layer. Because the Usage Tracking Service is only available for application object manager server components, we must execute the tasks in the procedure on a Siebel Web Client, connected to the Siebel Server infrastructure:

1. Log on to the **Siebel Web Client** using an administrative user account.
2. Navigate to the **Administration - Runtime Events** screen, **Action Sets** view.
3. Create a new action set named **Usage Collection**.
4. In the second list applet from the top, click the **New** button to create a new action definition.
5. Set the **Name** and **Sequence** fields to **1**.
6. Set the **Type** field to **BusService**.
7. In the form applet at the bottom of the view, enter Usage Tracking Service in the **Business Service Name** field.
8. Enter EventType=Runtime Event in the **Business Service Method** field.
9. Navigate to the **Events** view in the **Administration - Runtime Events** screen.
10. Create a new record and set the **Sequence** field to **2**.
11. Set the **Object Type** field to **Application**.
12. In the **Object Name** field, click the select button and select the technical name of the application you are using, for example *Siebel Sales Enterprise*.

> **Did you know?**
>
> If you are unsure about the technical application name, you can look up the value of the **ApplicationName** parameter in the Siebel Developer Web Client's configuration file (.cfg). The .cfg file is typically referenced in the Windows shortcut by the /c switch.

13. In the **Event** field, enter ViewActivated.
14. Set the **Action Set Name** field to **Usage Collection** (the name of the action set created earlier).
15. Navigate to the **Administration - Application** screen, **System Preferences** view.
16. Set the system preferences for Siebel Usage Collection according to the following table.

Setting system preferences is specific for the Usage Tracking Service.

System Preference	Description	Example Value
UsageTracking Enabled	Controls whether Usage Tracking is enabled.	TRUE
UsageTracking Log Time Period	Defines the interval for how often a new file is created. Possible values are Hourly, Daily, Weekly, and Monthly.	Daily
UsageTracking LogFile Dir	The directory where usage tracking log files will be written to. Should be a shared directory for a multi-server installation.	\\appserver1\usage
UsageTracking LogFile Format	Allows specification of the output format of the log files. Possible values are XML, CSV, and W3C.	XML

Source: Siebel Content Publishing Guide, Version 7.8: `http://download.oracle.com/docs/cd/B31104_02/books/ContentPub/booktitle.html`

17. Restart the application object manager component.

To verify the correct setup of Siebel Usage Collection, we can log in to the Siebel Web Client and navigate to several views. After a few minutes, an XML file should be present in the directory specified by the **UsageTracking LogFile Dir** system preference.

The following screenshot shows a portion of the Siebel Usage Tracking log file in XML format:

```xml
<?xml version="1.0" encoding="ASCII" ?>
- <events>
 + <event>
 + <event>
 - <event>
    <userId>SADMIN</userId>
    <ipaddr>127.0.0.1</ipaddr>
    <sessid>ZNLk02a0qCX7k1UY6ti8yqzX5Jop.J7W8wPtN8ebZ3QyeVizTr04P-
      WJSmLAeoih</sessid>
    <type>ViewActivated</type>
    <viewid />
    <name>Account Screen Homepage View</name>
    <rowid />
    <start>03/02/2010 19:12:45</start>
    <end>03/02/2010 19:12:52</end>
    <status>Success</status>
  </event>
```

The entries in the file indicate the user name, IP address of the client machine, the time of accessing and leaving the view, and the view name.

Summary

Business Services constitute the majority of Siebel CRM functionality. In this chapter, we learned how business services, their methods, and the property set memory structures work.

By using preconfigured business services, we can leverage existing functionality without the need to implement custom code. We can use the business service simulator to acquaint ourselves with the preconfigured functionality.

Business service methods can be invoked in various ways, of which workflow process steps and runtime events are the most common. In this chapter, we learned how to invoke a business service method from a runtime event.

In the next chapter, we will learn how to use integration objects to support integration interfaces.

18
Supporting Integration Interfaces

This chapter introduces the major objects of the **interface layer** of Siebel CRM applications, namely **Integration Objects**. Because they are widely used in reports, standard **Enterprise Application Integration** (**EAI**) connectors, web service interfaces, and custom EAI interfaces, a developer must understand these object types. In this chapter, we will learn how to configure integration objects to be able to support integration interfaces.

The chapter is structured as follows:

- Understanding integration objects
- Creating internal integration objects
- Defining integration component keys
- Testing integration objects
- Advanced settings for integration objects

Understanding integration objects

What we have learned so far in this book is generally aimed at providing an interface for users that allows them to interact with data and functionality provided by the business layer of Siebel CRM applications. While screens, views, and applets provide the human interface, integration objects provide the **EAI interface**.

The following diagram illustrates this:

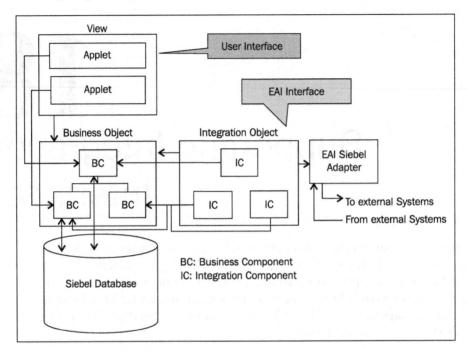

From the preceding diagram, we can learn the following:

- Views and applets constitute the user interface for human interaction with the data and functionality provided by business components.

- The business layer, constructed by business objects and business components, is the single point of access for users and EAI interfaces. The business layer defines the logic for accessing the tables in the Siebel database.

- Integration objects and integration components constitute the integration layer by mapping to business objects and business components respectively.

- The **EAI Siebel Adapter** business service serves as the unique access point for external systems to deliver outgoing data and process incoming data.

- EAI Siebel Adapter uses the information in integration objects to invoke methods on the business components and fields referenced by the integration components and their integration component fields.

The EAI Siebel Adapter business service must always be used in conjunction with integration objects to query or manipulate Siebel data exposed by business components. In the remainder of this chapter, we will explain how integration objects and EAI Siebel Adapter can be used to support integration interfaces.

Structure of integration objects

The following screenshot from the Object Explorer in Siebel Tools describes the structure of the Integration Object type in the Siebel Repository:

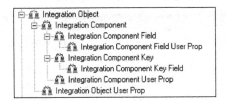

From the preceding screenshot we can learn the following:

- An integration object contains one or more integration components
- An integration component contains one or more integration component fields
- An integration component contains one or more integration component keys, which are made up of integration component key fields
- User properties can be defined on all levels to drive the behavior of the business services, namely EAI Siebel Adapter, that work with the integration object definitions

Internal and external integration objects

Integration objects that reference Siebel business objects are called internal integration objects. They can be used for read and write operations on business components. The EAI Siebel Adapter business service is designed to work with internal integration objects. Data that is passed to the EAI Siebel Adapter's methods must therefore match the structure defined by the internal integration object. Siebel Tools provides a wizard to create internal integration objects by defining the business object and its components that should be exposed by the internal integration object.

The following screenshot shows the **Internal Account Interface** integration object in Siebel Tools as an example for an internal integration object:

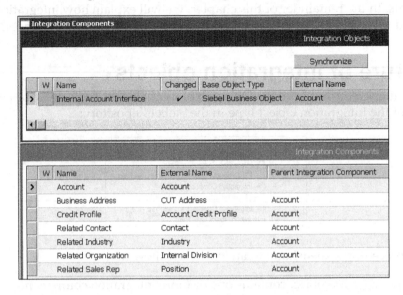

The **Base Object Type** property of **Siebel Business Object** allows us to identify the Internal Account Interface integration object as internal. The **External Name** property contains the name of the business object — *Account* – to which the integration object maps. The list of **integration components** shows seven business components, identified by the External Name property, which are arranged hierarchically by the **Parent Integration Component** property. In the previous example, the Account integration component is the parent of the *Business Address* and the other integration components.

To be able to create integration touch points with external systems, we can also register the data schema of external systems as **external integration objects**. Siebel Tools provides wizards to read the schema information from a variety of sources such as **XML Schema Definition (XSD)** files, **Data Type Definition (DTD)** files, and enterprise applications such as SAP R/3 and Oracle eBusiness applications.

The screenshot shows the *Ariba Order Request* integration object as an example of an external integration object:

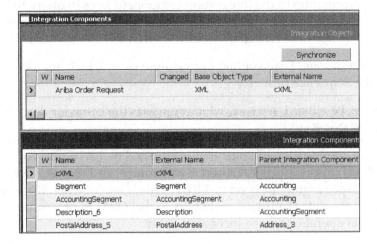

The **Base Object Type** property of *XML* allows us to identify that the Ariba Order Request integration object has been created by importing an external XSD file.

The Siebel EAI toolkit contains the **EAI Data Transformation Engine** business service, also known as **Data Mapper**, which is capable of converting instances of integration objects from a source to a target instance. For example, it can be used to map data represented by an internal integration object instance to an external application's data schema represented by an external integration object. This is useful for situations where no external data mapping facility is available.

Integration component keys

Internal integration objects can be used in two directions — outbound and inbound. The outbound direction is used when EAI Siebel Adapter queries for data and writes it to its output property set. The inbound direction is taken when the input property set for EAI Siebel Adapter contains incoming data that should be written to the Siebel database.

For these write operations — inserting, updating, and deleting records via the EAI Siebel Adapter - we must specify **integration component keys**. These keys enable EAI Siebel Adapter to look up existing records.

An integration component key is composed of one or more **integration component key fields**. When, for example, the `Insert` method of EAI Siebel Adapter is invoked, it will use the information in the integration component keys to query the existing Siebel data for records that have the same key field values as the incoming data. If the data already exists, the Insert method will fail.

An integration component can contain one or more keys, which are used in the order specified by the **Sequence** property.

The key type can be either **User Key**, which supports the behavior described previously, or **Status Key**.

A status key is a combination of fields that is returned by EAI Siebel Adapter's inbound methods (Insert, Update, Upsert, Synchronize, and Execute) when the `StatusObject` input argument is set to **TRUE**. This is useful when the external system that sent the data requires a reply from Siebel CRM to determine whether the inbound data operations were successful or not.

The status key typically contains the operation field that is populated by EAI Siebel Adapter with the name of the operation executed against the Siebel data. In addition, other data and system fields such as the *Id* field can be used in the status key.

Creating internal integration objects

Siebel Tools provides a wizard that assists developers in the task of creating internal and external integration objects. Because the focus of this chapter is on supporting integration interfaces with EAI Siebel Adapter, we will only discuss how to create internal integration objects.

Case study example: Creating an internal integration object

As defined in *Chapter 3*, one of AHA's requirements is to support reporting on data used by sales representatives. AHA intends to use Oracle's BI Publisher, which is the standard reporting tool for Siebel 8.1 and higher. The **Account** business object should be used to create the integration object. The business analyst team has identified the following business components and fields as relevant for reporting (the business component name is followed by its hierarchy level in parentheses and the list of fields):

- **Account** (Parent): Name, CSN, Account Status, Type, Partner Flag, Account Status Date, Price List, Currency Code, Credit Auto Approval Limit, Payment Type, Bill to Address multi value fields, Ship to Address multi value fields

- **Audit Trail Item 2** (Child): Employee Login, Field, Old Value, New Value, Date, Operation

- **AHA Customer Offer** (Child): Offer Date, User Login Name, Product Name, Response Type, Response Text

- **AHA Customer Document** (Child): Document Type, Document Id, Document Status, Responsible User Login Name, Verified Flag

The following procedure describes how we can use the Integration Object wizard in Siebel Tools to create an internal integration object:

1. If necessary, expose the **Integration Object** type in the **Object Explorer**.
2. Create and lock a new Project named **AHA EAI Objects**.
3. Click the **New** button in the **Edit** toolbar.
4. In the **New Object Wizards** dialog, click the **EAI** tab.
5. Double-click the **Integration Object** icon.
6. In the **Integration Object Builder** dialog, enter the following values:
    - Project: AHA EAI Objects
    - Source System: EAI Siebel Wizard
7. Click **Next**.
8. In the **Integration Object Builder** dialog, enter the following values:
    - Source Object: Account
    - Source Root: Account
    - Name: BIP AHA Customer Data

 The prefix *BIP* is necessary to display the integration object in the BIP Administration screen.

9. Click **Next**. It may take a while for the next dialog to load.
10. If a message appears that indicates missing or invalid business components or links, verify that none of the objects mentioned in the message is relevant for the new integration object and click **Next** to continue.

11. In the **Choose Integration Components** dialog, deselect and select the uppermost root object (**Account**) to ensure that only the Account business component is selected.

12. Scroll down in the hierarchy tree and click the checkbox next to the following components to include them in the integration object:
    ◦ Account_Bill To Business Address
    ◦ Account_Ship To Business Address
    ◦ AHA Customer Document
    ◦ AHA Customer Offer
    ◦ Audit Trail Item 2

13. Click **Next**.

14. Acknowledge the message that a large number of (integration component) fields have been deactivated because the respective business component fields are calculated fields. We can later activate these fields to allow the calculated values to be used in outbound messages. However, it is not possible to populate a calculated field from external systems.

15. Click **Finish**.

16. Verify that the new integration object is displayed in the **Integration Objects list**.

17. Set the **Comments** property of the BIP AHA Customer Data integration object to **Created for AHA prototype**.

Deactivating unneeded integration component fields

The Integration Object wizard creates one integration component field for each field in the chosen business components. Because some business components such as Account have a large number of fields, it is important to ensure that only those integration component fields that are needed for the interface are active. Deactivating the unneeded integration component fields is a manual process and the following procedure describes how to accomplish it:

1. Navigate to the **BIP AHA Customer Data** integration object.

2. In the **Object Explorer**, expand the Integration Object type and select the **Integration Component** type.

3. In the **Integration Components** list, select the **Account** integration component.

4. In the **Object Explorer**, expand the **Integration Component** type and select the **Integration Component Field** type.

5. In the **Integration Component Fields** list, create a new query.

6. In the Name column, enter NOT(followed by the list of fields defined for the Account integration component. The field names must be separated by the keyword OR. The field list should also include the EAI Siebel Adapter system fields named **operation** and **searchspec** as well as all fields used as **integration component key fields**. The following search string is an example of retrieving the fields not required for the Account integration component:

```
NOT(Name OR CSN OR Account Status OR Type OR Partner Flag OR
Account Status Date OR Price List OR Currency Code OR Credit Auto
Approval Limit OR Payment Type OR operation OR searchspec)
```

7. Execute the query. The result set now contains only fields that we do not need for the integration interface. We must now deactivate all these fields.

8. Because Siebel Tools does not support the *Ctrl+A* shortcut or a similar command to simply select all records with a single click, we must perform the following steps:

   ◦ In the **Integration Component Fields** list, select the first record

   ◦ Press the *Shift* key and select the **last record of the current page** (do not scroll down)

   ◦ Keep the *Shift* key pressed and drag the scroll bar button to the end of the list

   ◦ Keep the *Shift* key pressed and select the last record

   ◦ Release the *Shift* key

9. In the **Edit** menu, select **Change Records…**

10. In the **Change 1** section of the **Change Selected Records** dialog, select **Inactive** for the **Field** section and set the **Value** to **Y**. The following screenshot shows the dialog after these settings:

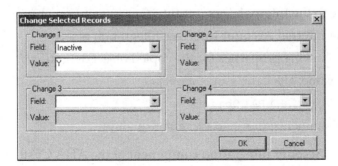

11. Click the **OK** button.

12. Verify that all selected records are inactive by inspecting the **Inactive** flag or by observing the font color (a light rose color indicates the inactive state of a record in Siebel Tools).

13. Repeat steps 3 to 12 for the Audit Trail Item 2, AHA Customer Offer, and AHA Customer Document integration components using the query technique described in step 6 and the list of field names at the beginning of this section.

14. Compile the BIP AHA Customer Data integration object.

Did you know?

The process of deactivating unneeded integration component fields is that important in creating an internal integration object which exactly matches the required schema. We must deactivate the fields rather than delete them in order to keep the **Synchronize** feature enabled.

The Synchronize feature allows the refreshing of an internal integration object when new fields have been added to business components. If unneeded integration component fields are deleted, the Synchronize wizard will recreate them as new active definitions, rendering the integration object dysfunctional.

Defining integration component keys

The following procedure describes how to define user keys and status keys for integration components. In the example, we create a copy of the Internal Account Interface integration object to provide the AHA team with an interface that allows querying and manipulating of account data. The Name and CSN fields will serve as key fields:

1. Navigate to the **Internal Account Interface** integration object.

2. Copy the **Internal Account Interface** integration object.

3. Set the following properties for the copied object definition:
    ○ Name: AHA Customer Interface
    ○ Project: AHA EAI Objects
    ○ Comments: Created for AHA prototype

4. Select the **Account integration component** of the AHA Customer Interface integration object.

5. Navigate to the **Integration Component Fields** list.

6. Query for the **CSN** integration component field and uncheck the **Inactive** flag, making the field active.

7. Navigate to the **Integration Component Keys** list for the **Account** integration component.

8. Deactivate all user key definitions.

9. In the **Integration Component Keys** list, create a new record and enter the following property values:

    ◦ Name: AHA User Key 1

    ◦ Key Sequence Number: 1

    ◦ Key Type: User Key

10. In the **Object Explorer**, expand the **Integration Component Key** type and select the **Integration Component Key Field** type.

11. Create a new record and enter the following values:

    ◦ Name: Name

    ◦ Field Name: Name

    ◦ Sequence: 1

12. Create another record with the following properties:

    ◦ Name: CSN

    ◦ Field Name: CSN

    ◦ Sequence: 2

13. Select the integration component key named **Status Key** and display the list of integration component key fields.

14. Create two new records similar to steps 11 and 12 to include the **Name** and **CSN** fields in the status key.

15. Compile the **AHA Customer Interface** integration object.

A Siebel Tools archive file (Integration Objects.sif) is available with this chapter's code file. The file represents the two integration objects created in this chapter's case study examples.

Testing integration objects

We can use the **Business Service Simulator** view, introduced in the previous chapter, to conveniently test new and customized integration objects. To verify the functionality, we must invoke the methods of the **EAI Siebel Adapter** business service and provide the correct input property sets.

The following table describes the methods and their arguments of the EAI Siebel Adapter business service:

Method	Description	Input Arguments	Output Arguments

Query	Executes a query on the business components referenced by the integration object's integration components.	`OutputIntObjectName:`
		
		 The name of an internal integration object. Defines the structure of the output property set.
		
		 `SearchSpec:`
		
		 Allows providing query criteria in Siebel Query Language.
		
		 `PrimaryRowId:`
		
		 When provided, the query is executed against the primary business component and matches the Id field with the property value.
		
		 `SiebelMessage:`
		
		 The Query method accepts a hierarchical input property set, which must match an internal integration object.
			`SiebelMessage:`
			
			 A hierarchical property set with its structure defined by the internal integration object given by the `OutputIntObjectName` input property.
			
			 `NumOutputObjects:`
			
			 The number of records in the SiebelMessage.

Method	Description	Input Arguments	Output Arguments

QueryPage	Similar to the Query method. In addition, the QueryPage method allows creation of a series of (smaller) output property sets, visibility control, and sorting.	`PageSize:`
		
		The number of records in the output property set (the *page*).
		
		`StartRowNum:`
		
		The number of the first record to include in the output property set.
		
		`ViewMode:`
		
		Allows visibility control as in *My* and *All* views.
		
		`SortSpec:`
		
		A comma separated list of integration component fields that defines the sort order of records the output property set.
			`SiebelMessage:`
			
			A hierarchical property set with its structure defined by the internal integration object given by the OutputIntObjectName input property.
			
			`LastPage:`
			
			When set to false, additional records exist in the query result. When set to true, the last page of the record set is reached. This property is necessary for implementing loops with the QueryPage method.

Insert	Uses the integration component key information to look up matching records. When no matching record exists, a new record is created. When a record with the same key field values already exists, an exception is thrown.	`SiebelMessage:`
		
		A hierarchical property set that must match an internal integration object definition.
		
		`StatusObject:`
		
		When set to **TRUE**, the output property set contains records that match the status key definition of the integration object.
		
		`ObjectLevelTransactions:`
		
		When set to **TRUE**, each record in the input `SiebelMessage` is committed separately to the database.
		
		When set to **FALSE** (the default), the commit operation is only executed when the entire input `SiebelMessage` has been processed without errors.
			`SiebelMessage:`
			
			Contains the status objects when the `StatusObject` input property has been set to **TRUE**.
			
			`PrimaryRowId:`
			
			The ROW_ID value of the new record.

Method	Description	Input Arguments	Output Arguments
Update	Similar to the Insert method. The major difference is that when a record exists in the database with the same key field values, an update is executed. When the record does not exist, an exception is thrown.	Similar to the Insert method.	Similar to the Insert method.
Upsert	Combines the Update and Insert methods. When a record with the same key field values exists in the database, it will be updated. When no matching record is found, a new record will be inserted.	Similar to the Insert and Update method.	Similar to the Insert and Update method.
Delete	Identifies existing records by various mechanisms and deletes them. When no matching record is found, an exception is thrown.	Similar to the Query method.	Similar to the Insert and Update method.
Synchronize	Combines the Insert, Update, and Delete functionality by applying the data in the input `SiebelMessage` to the existing records in the database.	Similar to the Insert and Update method.	Similar to the Insert and Update method.

Method	Description	Input Arguments	Output Arguments
Execute	Allows definition of the desired method (query, insert, update, delete) for each record in the input `SiebelMessage` separately using the operation and searchspec system fields.	Similar to the Insert and Update method.	Similar to the Insert and Update method.

The following example procedure describes how to test an internal integration object for queries using the EAI Siebel Adapter **Query** and **Upsert** methods in the Business Service Simulator view:

1. Log on to the **Siebel Developer Web Client** with administrative privileges.

2. Navigate to the **My Accounts** list view.

3. Create a test account record and press *Ctrl+S* to save it.

4. Retrieve the ROW_ID value of the test record by pressing *Ctrl+Alt+K* and copying the value of the **Row #** field from the **About Record** dialog to the clipboard.

5. Navigate to the **Administration - Business Service** screen, **Simulator** view.

6. In the upper list applet, create a new record and enter the following values:

    ○ **Service Name**: EAI Siebel Adapter

    ○ **Method Name**: Query

7. In the **Input Arguments** list applet, create a new record and set the **Test Case #** column to **1**.

8. Open the multi value group applet for the **Property Name** column by clicking on the select icon in the column.

9. In the **Property Set Properties** list applet, create a new record with the following values:

    ○ **Property Name**: PrimaryRowId

    ○ **Value**: <paste the ROW_ID value from the clipboard>

10. Click **Save**.

11. Create a second record in the **Property Set Properties** list applet and enter the following values:

    ○ **Property Name**: OutputIntObjectName

    ○ **Value**: AHA Customer Interface

12. Click **Save**.

13. Click **OK** to close the **Property Set Properties MVG** applet.

14. In the upper list applet, click the **Run on One Input** button to execute the Query method with the input property set created in steps 7 to 13.

15. Observe that a new output property set is created in the **Output Arguments** list applet at the bottom of the view.

16. Open the **MVG** applet for the **Child Type** column, which should have a value of **SiebelMessage**.

17. Continue to click the **MVG** icon in the **Child Type** field until the **Type** column has a value of **Account**.

18. Open the **MVG** applet for the **Property Key** column.

19. Verify that the list of fields for the account record is displayed and matches the list of active integration component fields of the **Account** integration component in the **AHA Customer Interface** integration object.

20. Click the **X** button to close the **MVG** applet.

Did you know?

Using the **Save to File…** button in the **Output Arguments** list applet, we can export the entire output property set to an XML file, which may be more convenient for inspection.

The following procedure describes how to test an integration object for update and insert operations using the Upsert method of EAI Siebel Adapter:

1. Execute the EAI Siebel Adapter's Query method as shown in the previous procedure.

2. In the **Output Arguments** list applet, click the **Move to Input** button.

3. Observe that a new record is created in the **Input Arguments** list applet.

4. Set the **Test Case #** column of the new record to **2**.

5. Use the **MVG** icon in the **Child Type** column to navigate to the property set with type **Account**.

6. Open the **MVG** list applet of the **Property Key** column.

7. Scroll down to the **Location** field and change its value to **EAI Siebel Adapter Update**.

8. Click **OK**.

9. Click the **X** button to close the **MVG** list applet.

10. Open the **MVG** list applet for the **Property Name** column in the **Input Arguments** list applet.

11. Create a new record with the following values:
    - ° **Property Name**: StatusObject
    - ° **Value**: true

12. Click **Save**.

13. Click **OK**.

14. In the upper list applet, create a new record with the following values:
    - ° **Service Name**: EAI Siebel Adapter
    - ° **Method Name**: Upsert

15. Ensure that test case 2 is selected in the middle applet and click the **Run on One Input** button.

16. Inspect the output property set as shown in the previous procedure.

17. Observe that the Account property set contains fields defined by the status key of the AHA Customer Interface integration object and that the operation field is set to update.

18. Repeat the procedure from step 5 to 16 but this time change the CSN field, which is part of the integration component's user key, to AHA000 and the Location field, which is part of the table user key, to EAI Siebel Adapter Insert.

19. Observe that the operation field of the status object is now set to **insert**.

20. Navigate to the **Accounts** screen and verify by querying with **EAI Siebel Adapter*** in the **Site** field that two records exist.

21. Delete the test records if necessary.

By following test procedures similar to the preceding ones, we ensure that our new integration objects work for queries as well as for update or insert operations.

Advanced settings for integration objects

We can specify user properties on all levels of an integration object—object, component, and field level – to define specialized behavior. The following table describes the most important user properties for **integration objects (IO)**, **integration components (IC)**, and **integration component fields (ICF)**. The table also informs us on the applicability of the user properties for each level:

User Property	Description	IO	IC	ICF
ViewMode	Can be set to the Siebel visibility codes (*Sales Rep, Manager, All, Organization, Catalog*, and so on) to override the current view mode of the business component during queries.	Yes	Yes	No
AdminMode	When set to Y, the business component will be switched to administration mode, which allows all insert, update, and delete operations.	Yes	Yes	No
AllLangIndependentVals	When set to Y, EAI Siebel Adapter uses the **language independent code (LIC)** value for a multilingual list of values.	Yes	No	No
PICKLIST	When set to Y this field level user property causes EAI Siebel Adapter to validate the values to be inserted in pick list fields. When set to N, validation occurs at the object manager level.	No	No	Yes
Ignore Bounded Picklist	This field level user property, when set to Y, advises the EAI Siebel Adapter to ignore errors that arise from providing invalid values for a bounded pick list field.	Yes	Yes	No
NoDelete, NoInsert, NoQuery, NoSynchronize, NoUpdate	These component level user properties allow overriding of the respective properties of the business component.	No	Yes	No
FieldDependency	Allows specification of the name of another field, which EAI Siebel Adapter will process before the field that has the user property defined.	No	No	Yes
PREDEFAULT	Overrides the pre-default value of the business component field.	No	No	Yes

User Property	Description	IO	IC	ICF
sortorder	Can be set to **ASC** for ascending or **DEC** (sic) for descending. When EAI Siebel Adapter executes a query, the sort order will override the business component's SortSpec property.	No	No	Yes
sortsequence	Allows specifying sequential numbering of sorted fields.	No	No	Yes

Source: Oracle Siebel Documentation: Integration Platform Technologies: Siebel Enterprise Application Integration, Version 8.1 (`http://download.oracle.com/docs/cd/E14004_01/books/EAI2/booktitle.html`).

Summary

Integration objects and the EAI Siebel Adapter business service play a vital role in integrating Siebel with external applications including Oracle's BI Publisher (the standard reporting engine for Siebel 8.1 and above).

In this chapter, we learned how internal integration objects work and how we can use the Integration Object wizard in Siebel Tools to create them.

We also discussed the post-wizard configuration steps for integration objects as well as basic testing procedures.

Finally, we described the most important user properties that we can use to fine-tune the behavior of EAI Siebel Adapter during read or write operations.

The next chapter is the first of two chapters on Siebel Workflow. In the following chapter, we will learn how to create, test, and publish workflow processes.

19
Siebel Workflow

The Siebel Workflow framework represents the foundation of business process automation in Siebel CRM applications. This chapter is the first of two in which we will learn basic and advanced configuration techniques for Siebel Workflow. The goal of this chapter is to gain deep understanding of Siebel Workflow and to learn basic techniques which enable us to create, test, publish, and manage workflow processes in Siebel CRM applications.

The chapter is structured as follows:

- Understanding Siebel Workflow
- Designing and creating workflow processes
- Simulating and testing workflow processes
- Publishing, activating, and managing workflow processes
- Invoking workflow processes
- Defining runtime events
- Defining decision steps

Understanding Siebel Workflow

In order to gain a thorough understanding of Siebel Workflow, we can use the Siebel Sample Database as a safe environment for exploration. In the following procedure, we will invoke a preconfigured workflow process with a click on a menu item and use Siebel Tools to investigate the object definitions behind the user interface.

The workflow process that serves as an example creates a new quote for an existing account and navigates to the *Quote Line Items* view to allow the end user to continue the business process by entering line items for the new quote. We must emphasize at this point that this simple workflow process is just one of hundreds of preconfigured workflow processes in Siebel CRM. The majority of Siebel CRM functionality relies on the Siebel Workflow framework in very different ways.

Following the given procedure, we can explore how a Siebel workflow process supports the business process of creating a quote for an existing customer account.

1. Log in to the **Siebel Sales** application, connecting to the **Sample** database as **SADMIN**.

2. Navigate to the **Accounts** screen, **My Accounts** view.

3. Right-click on any account record in the list and select **New Quote** from the menu.

4. Observe that the application automatically navigates to the **Quotes** screen, **Line Items** view and that a new quote record has been created.

5. Observe that the account for the new quote is the one we clicked on in step 3.

The following screenshot shows the **My Accounts** list view. The context menu item for creating a new quote for the selected account is highlighted:

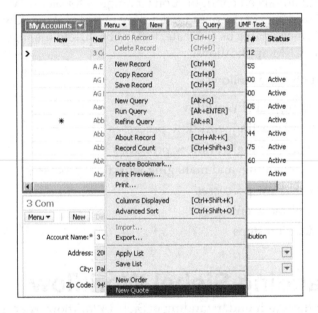

We will now use Siebel Tools to investigate the applet menu item definition and the workflow process invoked by it:

1. Log in to **Siebel Tools**, connecting to the **Sample** database as **SADMIN**.

2. In the **View** menu, select the **Options** command.

3. In the **Options** dialog, select the **Object Explorer** tab.

4. Ensure that all child elements for the **Applet** type are displayed.

5. Close the Options dialog.

6. In the **Object Explorer** window, select **Applet**.

7. Query for the **Account List Applet** in the applet list.

8. Expand the Applet type in the Object Explorer window.

9. Select **Applet User Prop** in the Object Explorer window.

10. In the list of applet user properties, identify the user property named **Named Method: NewQuote**.

11. Inspect the **Value** of the user property.

The following screenshot shows the user properties for the Account List Applet:

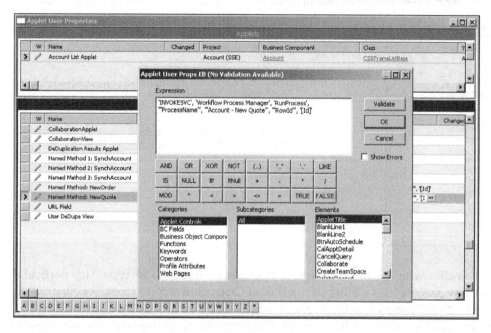

The value of the **Named Method: New Quote** user property is visible in the expression builder, which can be invoked by clicking the ellipsis button (**...**) in the **Value** column.

The value of the user property indicates that when the NewQuote method is invoked, a **business service** named *Workflow Process Manager* is invoked with its RunProcess method. The name of the workflow process to be run is *Account - New Quote*.

Invoking workflow processes by user interface elements such as menu items and buttons is quite common in Siebel CRM applications. Other methods to invoke workflow processes are discussed later in this chapter.

We can now continue the exploration by inspecting the definition of the
Account - New Quote workflow process in Siebel Tools:

1. In the **Object Explorer** window, select the **Workflow Process** type.

2. In the list, query for the **Account - New Quote** workflow process.

3. Right-click the workflow process and select **Edit Workflow Process**.

4. In the editor, use the **Palette** window to identify the different types of steps
   used in this workflow process.

The following screenshot shows the **Account - New Quote** workflow process in the
Workflow Process Editor in Siebel Tools:

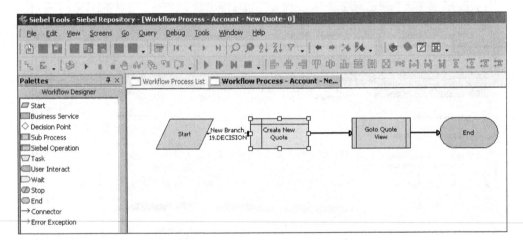

The workflow consists of four steps. A step's shape indicates its type. This particular
workflow process uses a **Start** step, a **Siebel Operation** step to create a new quote
record, a **Sub Process** step to invoke another workflow process, and an **End** step,
which indicates the end of the process. The steps of a workflow process are connected
using Connector branches.

5. Double-click the **Goto Quote View** step in the editor.

6. The **Goto_Quote** workflow process is displayed in a new tab.

7. Verify that the **Goto_Quote** workflow process uses a **User Interact** step to
   navigate to the **Quote Item Detail View**.

Right-click the step and select **View Properties Window**. In the
Properties window, inspect the **User Interact View** property.

In summarizing our findings made during this exploration, we can say that when an end user clicks the **New Quote** menu item on an existing account, the **Account - New Quote** workflow process is executed by the Workflow Process Manager business service. The workflow process uses a Siebel Operation step to create a new quote record for the account and a Sub Process step to invoke a second workflow process, which handles the view navigation. Subsequently the end user is navigated to the **Quote Item Detail View**.

Did you know?

The **Workflow Process Manager** business service is **always** used to execute a workflow process definition. Depending on the invocation technique, the business service can run within a user session or as a separate server process.

Siebel Workflow step types

The following table describes the step types of the Siebel Workflow framework:

Step Type	Symbol (Shape)	Description
Start	Start	Defines the start point of a workflow process. It is possible to define one or more event condition branches to trigger the workflow process using Siebel runtime events.
Business Service	Business Service	Allows the specification of a business service and its method to be invoked as well as passing the values of input and output arguments from and to workflow process properties.
Decision Point	Decision	Defines one or more branch conditions, which are followed when the condition evaluates to *True*. Only one branch at a time can be followed (Siebel Workflow processes are sequential in nature). The branching logic is defined on the branches (connectors) leading from this step type.
Sub Process	Sub Process	Invokes another workflow process. Arguments can be passed between the calling and the nested workflow processes.
Siebel Operation	Siebel Operation	Serves as a mechanism to execute commands similar to those typically invoked by end users or external systems. Commands include inserting, updating, deleting, and querying records as well as navigating through record sets.
Task	Task	Creates an item in an end user's **Universal Inbox** list that points to a task. (Integrates Siebel Workflow with **Siebel Task UI** in Siebel 8 and higher.)

Step Type	Symbol (Shape)	Description
User Interact	User Interact	Implements navigation to a view and waits for user interaction such as the click on a button before the workflow proceeds. Widely used in Siebel standard interactivity applications and Siebel Version 7, in both of which Task UI is not available.
Wait	Wait	Allows developers to specify a time interval that the workflow process spends in a waiting state. Not applicable for workflow processes that run in end user sessions.
Stop	Stop	A defined exit point. Allows specification of a message to be displayed when the step is reached. Typically used in conjunction with exception connectors.
End	End	Indicates the successful completion of a workflow process.
Connector	→	Defines the normal flow of operation between steps.
Error Exception	→	Allows definition of a branch that is chosen when the step from which this connector originates encounters an error condition. Widely used to implement exception handling.

Workflow process properties

Similar to a classic program written in any modern programming language, a workflow process has a set of variables that can be used by developers to hold data and pass them between steps.

The Siebel term for these variables is **Process Properties**. As such they are child objects of the workflow process definition and are distinguished primarily by their name and data type.

Siebel Workflow provides the following data types for process properties:

- **String**: Stores alphanumeric characters.
- **Number**: To store numbers for calculations.
- **Date**: To store date and timestamp values.
- **Hierarchy**: Used to store entire property set hierarchies. Mainly used in integration scenarios.
- **Integration Object**: References an integration object definition to define the hierarchical structure of the data stored within the process property.
- **Binary**: Used to store data that is only used within the workflow process and not passed to or from the workflow process.

In addition to a data type and a name, a workflow process property can be declared as being able to be populated from outside of the workflow process, passed out of the workflow process (or both), or used only within the workflow process.

Designing and creating workflow processes

It is important to understand that a workflow process is a program. The programming language is implemented as the Siebel Tools workflow framework, which allows us to graphically define the flow of steps, the decision logic, and exception handling.

The main difference between Siebel Workflow and classic programming languages is that we do not need to write program code. In the late nineties, many graphical programming interfaces emerged and the term *fourth generation language* (4GL) was coined to commonly describe them.

Did you know?

Siebel Tools does not allow us to write program code in the workflow process editor. When specialized behavior is needed, we must use existing business services or write our own business service methods using the Siebel scripting framework.

We will discuss Siebel scripting for business services later in this book.

As developers, we may find ourselves in the situation of being asked by the business analyst team to assist in translating business requirements into automation logic.

For example, a business analyst could ask for our opinion on the following requirement (as defined in *Chapter 3, Case Study Introduction*):

AHA wishes to use a single entity named "Customer Document" to contain all opportunities, quotes, orders and campaign responses in a single list.

The above requirement implies that for every opportunity, quote, order, and campaign response record, a record in the AHA Customer Document business component must be created and synchronized. When document records are deleted, we must also cater for the deletion of the appropriate record in the AHA Customer Document business component.

The design work for a workflow process can be described with the following list:

- Identify **variables** and map them to **workflow process properties** of the appropriate data type

- Identify **data operations** such as insert, update, and delete and map them to **Siebel Operation** step calls

- Identify complex **application logic** and find supporting **business services** and methods

- Identify **decision logic** and map it to **Decision** steps and branches

- Identify potential for **errors** and cater for **exception handling**

Experienced developers may find it useful to use the workflow process designer in Siebel Tools to draft the new workflow process. This is a recommended practice as it is commonplace in computer technology to iteratively find solutions by going from a rough but working draft to a finer end product.

The workflow process editor

The workbench for creating and testing workflow processes is the workflow process editor in Siebel Tools. It consists of the following windows:

- **Editor canvas**: Here we can outline the flow of steps by using drag and drop techniques

- **Palettes window**: From this docking window, we can drag step types to the canvas

- **Properties window**: The familiar docking window allows us to define the properties for each selected step or branch in the canvas editor

- **Multi Value Property Window (MVPW)**: Allows us to define detailed input and output arguments for each selected step

The following screenshot shows the workflow process editor with the four windows described previously in Siebel Tools:

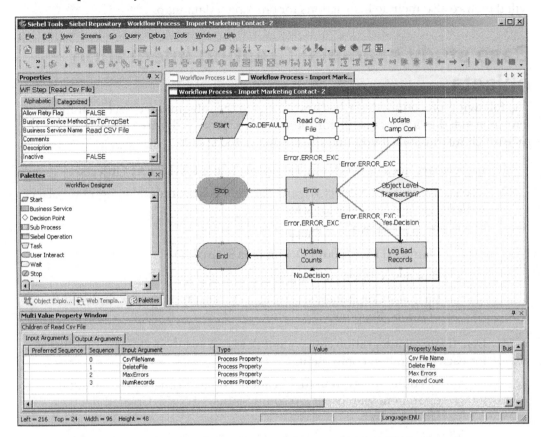

In the following case study scenario, we will create a workflow process that synchronizes the quotes, orders, opportunities, and marketing responses of an account with the list of customer documents represented by the **AHA Customer Documents** business component.

We will use two pre-built business services—EAI Siebel Adapter and EAI Data Transformation Engine – for this purpose. As pointed out in *Chapter 17, Business Services* it is highly recommendable to explore and use pre-built business services.

In *Chapter 18, Supporting Integration Interfaces* we learned that **EAI Siebel Adapter** relies on integration object definitions. Therefore the scenario includes instructions to create two integration objects.

The **EAI Data Transformation Engine** business service can be used to transform one integration object instance to another by means of a **data map**. The scenario will therefore also include instructions for creating a data map.

Case study example: Creating integration objects

The following procedure describes how to create the integration object definitions that are needed as a prerequisite for the workflow process. Please refer to *Chapter 18* for explicit instructions if you find the following too sparse:

1. If necessary, lock or check out the project named **AHA EAI Objects.**

2. Use the **Integration Object** wizard to create a new internal integration object with the following characteristics:
   - Project: AHA EAI Objects
   - Name: AHA Account Documents Source IO
   - Business Object: Account
   - Business Components: Account, Quote, Opportunity, Order Entry - Orders, Response

3. Deactivate all integration component fields except the following ones listed for each integration component:
   - Account: Integration Id, Location, Name, Primary Organization, operation, searchspec, Account Status, CSN, Id, Created By, Updated By
   - Opportunity: Integration Id, Name, Primary Organization, Sales Stage, operation, searchspec, Id, Created By, Updated By
   - Order Entry - Orders: Order Number, Order Type, Primary Organization, Revision, Status, operation, searchspec, Id, Created By, Updated By
   - Quote: Integration Id, Primary Organization, Quote Number, Revision, Status, operation, searchspec, Id, Created By, Updated By
   - Response: Description, Status, operation, searchspec, Id, Created By, Updated By

4. Set the **Type** property of the following fields from **System** to **Data** in all integration components: Id, Created By, Updated By.

5. Repeat step 2 to create a second internal integration object with the following characteristics:

    ◦   Project: AHA EAI Objects
    ◦   Name: AHA Customer Documents Target IO
    ◦   Business Object: Account
    ◦   Business Components: Account, AHA Customer Documents

6. Repeat step 3 to deactivate all integration component fields except the following ones listed:

    ◦   **Account**: Integration Id, Location, Name, Primary Organization, operation, searchspec, Account Status, CSN, Id, Created By, Updated By

    ◦   **AHA Customer Documents**: Document Id, Document Status, Document Type, Responsible User Id, Verified Flag, Account Id, operation, searchspec

    ◦   Create a user key definition named **User Key 1** for the **AHA Customer Documents Target IO** integration component with the **Document Id** field as the sole key field.

    ◦   Create a status key definition named **Status Key 1** for the **AHA Customer Documents Target IO** integration component with **Document Id** and **operation** as key fields.

    ◦   Compile the AHA Account Documents Source IO and AHA Customer Documents Target IO integration objects.

A Siebel Tools archive file (`Integration Objects.sif`) is available with this chapter's code files. The file represents the two integration objects created in the preceding section.

Case study example: Creating a data map

The following procedure describes how to create a data map using the two integration object definitions created in the previous section:

1. Log in to the **Siebel Developer Web Client**. Use SADMIN if you connect to the Sample database.

2. Navigate to the **Administration - Integration** screen, **Data Map Editor** view.

3. In the **Integration Object Map** list, create a new record with the following values:

    ◦   Name: AHA Account Documents Map
    ◦   Source Object Name: AHA Account Documents Source IO

     °   Target Object Name: AHA Customer Documents Target IO

     °   Comments: Created for AHA prototype

4. In the middle list applet (**Integration Component Map**), create five new records as per the following table:

Name	Source Component Name	Target Component Name
Account	Account	Account
Quote	Quote	AHA Customer Documents
Order	Order Entry - Orders	AHA Customer Documents
Opportunity	Opportunity	AHA Customer Documents
Response	Response	AHA Customer Documents

Compare your work with the following screenshot:

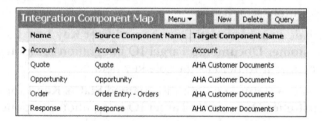

5. Select the **Account** component map in the middle applet.

6. In the bottom applet (**Integration Field Map**) create four new records as per the following table:

Source Expression	Target Field Name
[Integration Id]	Integration Id
[Name]	Name
[Location]	Location
[Primary Organization]	Primary Organization

7. Select the **Quote** component map in the middle applet.

8. In the bottom applet (**Integration Field Map**) create four new records as per the following table:

Source Expression	Target Field Name
"Quote"	Document Type
[Id]	Document Id
[Status]	Document Status
[Updated By]	Responsible User Login Id

9. Select the **Order** component map in the middle applet.

10. In the bottom applet (**Integration Field Map**) create four new records as per the following table:

Source Expression	Target Field Name
[Order Type]	Document Type
[Id]	Document Id
[Status]	Document Status
[Updated By]	Responsible User Login Id

11. Select the **Opportunity** component map in the middle applet.

12. In the bottom applet (**Integration Field Map**) create four new records as per the following table:

Source Expression	Target Field Name
"Opportunity"	Document Type
[Id]	Document Id
[Sales Stage]	Document Status
[Updated By]	Responsible User Login Id

13. Select the **Response** component map in the middle applet.

14. In the bottom applet (**Integration Field Map**) create four new records as per the following table:

Source Expression	Target Field Name
"Response"	Document Type
[Id]	Document Id
[Status]	Document Status
[Updated By]	Responsible User Login Id

Compare your work with the screenshot below. The screenshot shows the integration field map for the **Response** component.

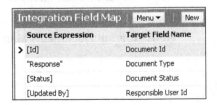

While typically used for integration with external applications, data maps can also be helpful for internal use such as in our scenario. The data map created in the previous section directs the EAI Data Transformation Engine business service to write the results of the Source Expression from fields in four different source components to a single target component.

An ADM import file (AHA Account Documents Map.xml) is available with this chapter's code files. The file represents the EAI data map created in the preceding section.

Case study example: Creating a workflow process with business service steps

The following procedure describes how to create a Siebel Workflow process that invokes business service methods and uses workflow process properties to pass arguments between them:

1. In **Siebel Tools,** create and lock a new project named AHA Workflows.

2. In the **Object Explorer,** select the **Workflow Process** type.

3. In the **Object List Editor,** create a new record with the following properties:

   ○ **Name**: AHA Synchronize Customer Documents

   ○ **Project**: AHA Workflows

   ○ **Business Object**: Account

4. Right-click the new workflow process and select **Edit Workflow Process.**

5. In the **Multi Value Property Window (MVPW),** select the **Process Properties** tab and create new records as per the following table:

Name	Default String	Data Type
AHA Source IO Name	AHA Account Documents Source IO	String
AHA Source Data		Hierarchy
AHA Map Name	AHA Account Documents Map	String
AHA Target Data		Hierarchy
AHA Get Status Object	true	String
AHA Status Object Data		Hierarchy

6. Press *Ctrl+S* to save your changes.

7. Drag the following step types from the **Palettes** window and drop them side by side on the drawing canvas:

    ◦   Start

    ◦   Business Service (**three times**)

    ◦   End

8. Select the first business service step.

9. Right-click the first business service step and select **View Properties Window**.

10. In the **Properties** window, enter the following values:

    ◦   **Name**: Get Account Docs

    ◦   **Business Service Name**: EAI Siebel Adapter

    ◦   **Business Service Method**: Query

11. Press *Ctrl+S* to save your changes.

 You should save your changes frequently in order to avoid locking conflicts, which can occur when changes are made in multiple windows.

12. In the **Input Arguments** tab of the **Multi Value Property Window** create two records as follows:

 Important:
Always use the pick lists when provided to avoid typos:

Input Argument	Type	Property Name
OutputIntObjectName	Process Property	AHA Source IO Name
PrimaryRowId	Process Property	Object Id

Compare your work with the following screenshot:

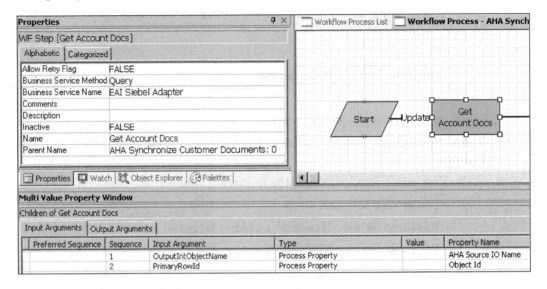

13. In the **Output Arguments** tab of the **Multi Value Property Window** create one record as follows:

Property Name	Type	Property Name
AHA Source Data	Output Argument	SiebelMessage

14. Select the second business service step.

15. In the **Properties** window, enter the following values:

   ○ Name: Map
   ○ Business Service Name: EAI Data Transformation Engine
   ○ Business Service Method: Execute

16. In the **Input Arguments** tab of the **Multi Value Property Window** create two records as follows:

Input Argument	Type	Property Name
MapName	Process Property	AHA Map Name
SiebelMessage	Process Property	AHA Source Data

17. In the **Output Arguments** tab of the **Multi Value Property Window** create one record as follows:

Property Name	Type	Property Name
AHA Target Data	Output Argument	SiebelMessage

18. Select the third business service step.

19. In the **Properties** window, enter the following values:
    ° Name: Synchronize
    ° Business Service Name: EAI Siebel Adapter
    ° Business Service Method: Synchronize

20. In the **Input Arguments** tab of the **Multi Value Property Window** create two records as follows:

Input Argument	Type	Property Name
SiebelMessage	Process Property	AHA Target Data
StatusObject	Process Property	AHA Get Status Object

21. In the **Output Arguments** tab of the **Multi Value Property Window** create one record as follows:

Property Name	Type	Property Name
AHA Status Object Data	Output Argument	SiebelMessage

22. Press *Ctrl+S* to save your changes.

23. Drag the black **Connector** icon from the **Palettes** window to the **Start step** and drop it.

24. Verify that the arrow connects the Start step and the first business service step by inspecting the color of the connector's endpoints. If both endpoints are red, the connection is valid; if one of the endpoints (typically the arrowhead) is white, drag the endpoint to one of the **x** labels of the target shape.

25. Repeat steps 23 and 24 to connect all steps with a connector.

26. Save your changes.

    Compare your work with the screenshot below.

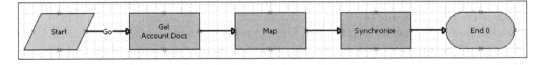

27. Click in the canvas area to select the entire workflow process.

28. Right-click the canvas and select **Validate...**

29. In the **Validate** dialog, click the **Start** button.

30. Monitor the status bar of the **Validate** dialog. When the message indicates that the number of tests failed is zero, the workflow process is valid.

31. In case of errors or warning messages, click the respective message to display the full text in the **Details** area of the **Validate** dialog. Every error (for example, unconnected steps) must be corrected. After the corrective action, repeat the validation until no errors or warnings are reported.

The workflow created in the procedure above accomplishes the following:

- In the **Get Account Docs** step, the **EAI Siebel Adapter's** *Query* method is invoked. EAI Siebel Adapter will use the *AHA Account Documents Source IO* integration object and the value of the *Object Id* process property, which is passed to the workflow process at runtime, to query for an account record and retrieve the account data as well as child business component data of quotes, opportunities, orders, and responses. The resulting hierarchical property set is passed to the *AHA Source Data* process property.

- In the **Map** step, the account data represented by the *AHA Source Data* process property is passed to the *Execute* method of the **EAI Data Transformation Engine (DTE)** business service. The information in the *AHA Account Documents Map* will be used by the DTE to create an output property set that inherits its structure from the *AHA Customer Documents Target IO* integration object. The resulting hierarchical property set is passed to the *AHA Target Data* process property.

- In the **Synchronize** step, **EAI Siebel Adapter's** *Synchronize* method is invoked and the data represented by the *AHA Target Data* process property is passed. The *Synchronize* method will insert new records, update existing records, and delete any record in the *AHA Customer Documents* business component that is not present in the *AHA Target Data* property set. By setting the *StatusObject* input argument to *true*, the *Synchronize* method is instructed to create an output property set that provides information about the operations (insert, update, delete) carried out on each record of the *AHA Customer Documents* business component. This output is passed to the *AHA Status Object Data* process property.

A Siebel Tools archive file (AHA Synchronize Customer Documents(1).sif) is available with this chapter's code files. The file represents the AHA Synchronize Customer Documents workflow process after the changes made in the preceding section.

Simulating and testing workflow processes

Similar to classic programming, developers need a secure test environment to verify that the new workflow process definition works as expected. Siebel Tools provides us with an integrated workflow process simulator to accomplish this task.

The simulation environment uses the Siebel Developer Web Client, so it is mandatory to complete the one-time setup of the Siebel Tools debugging options. These settings are made in the **Debug** tab of the **Tools Development Options** dialog, which we can open by selecting the **Options...** command in the **View** menu of Siebel Tools.

The necessary settings in the **Debug** tab have already been described in *Chapter 2, Developer Tasks*.

The following procedure describes how to use the Siebel workflow simulator:

1. Ensure that all necessary settings have been made in the **Debug** tab of the **Siebel Tools** options dialog.

2. In the Siebel client, find or create one or more **test records**. For our scenario, it is necessary to have one account with at least one associated opportunity, quote, or order.

3. Use the **About Record** menu option to retrieve the **ROW_ID** value of the parent test record. In our scenario, we must retrieve the account's ROW_ID value.

4. In Siebel Tools, navigate to the **AHA Synchronize Customer Documents** workflow process and open it in the editor if necessary.

5. In the **Multi Value Property Window**, modify the **Object Id** process property and enter the value of the account's ROW_ID in the **Default String** column. It is recommendable to remove this default value after testing.

6. Save the workflow process.

7. Log out of all instances of the Siebel Developer or Mobile Web Client. Use the **Windows Task Manager** if necessary to verify that no instance of `siebel.exe` is running.

8. Right-click in the grey toolbar area of Siebel Tools and verify that the **Simulator** toolbar is displayed.

9. Right-click in the workflow editor canvas and select **Simulate...**

10. Click the green arrow button in the **Simulator** toolbar to start the simulation.

11. Wait until the Siebel Mobile Web Client has been started completely. The client automatically navigates to the **Workflow Simulator Wait View** and displays a **progress bar** window. Siebel Tools should come to front automatically when the startup process is complete.

12. Right-click the yellow simulator background in Siebel Tools and select **Watch Window**.

13. In the **Watch** window, click the uppermost plus sign if necessary to expand the display of workflow process properties and their current state. We can use the Watch window to observe how process properties and hierarchical data structures are modified while we step through the workflow process.

14. Click the second button (**Simulate Next**) in the Simulator toolbar to execute the next step in the workflow process. The step to be executed is highlighted with a red solid border.

    The following screenshot shows the AHA Synchronize Customer Documents workflow process in the simulator after execution of the *Get Account Docs* step:

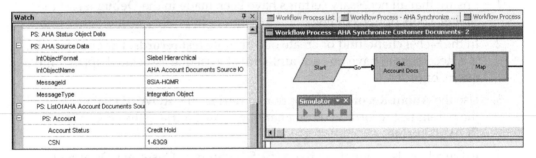

15. Inspect the **PS: AHA Source Data** process property in the **Watch** window by expanding the hierarchy. We can verify that the account and related quotes, orders, and so on are stored in the process property as a result of the EAI Siebel Adapter's Query method.

16. Click the **Simulate Next** button in the **Simulator** toolbar again to execute the **Map** step.

17. In the **Watch** window, inspect the **PS: AHA Target Data** process property and verify that the DTE has successfully produced the desired output.

18. Click the **Simulate Next** button again to execute the **Synchronize** step.

19. In the **Watch** window, inspect the **PS: AHA Status Object Data** property to verify the outcome of EAI Siebel Adapter's Synchronize method.

20. Click the **Simulate Next** button once more to execute the **End** step and complete the simulation.

21. Click **OK** to acknowledge the message that indicates successful completion of the simulation.

22. In the Siebel Developer Web Client navigate to the **AHA UI Test View**. This view has been created in a previous chapter and should allow you to verify that the customer document data has been synchronized successfully.

The following screenshot shows the AHA UI Test View with an account from the Siebel Sample Database:

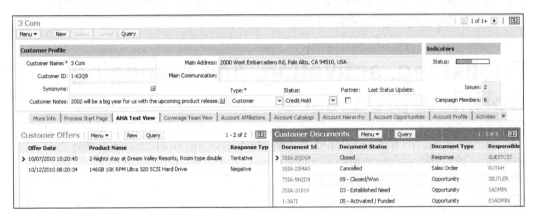

We can observe that the **Customer Documents** list applet shows documents of different types. The data in the applet has been synchronized by the AHA Synchronize Customer Documents workflow.

Did you know?

If we wish to continue testing the workflow, we can keep the Siebel Mobile or Developer Web Client running. However we must return to the **Workflow Simulator Wait View** before we can run the simulation in Siebel Tools again.

To return to the Workflow Simulator Wait View, we can navigate to the **Administration - Business Process** screen in the site map and then click on the **Workflow Simulator** view link.

As an alternative (the site map link is only present in Siebel Industry Applications) we can store a URL similar to the following as a browser favorite.

```
http://localhost/start.swe?SWECmd=GotoView&SWEView=Wor
kflow+Simulator+Wait+View
```

If errors occur during the simulation, we should always use the **Watch** window to read the **Error Message** process property. Typically the error message text includes sufficient information to guide us to a solution.

We must then close the simulation window, correct the error, save the workflow process and start the simulation again. The Siebel Mobile or Developer Web Client can stay open during this time.

Once the workflow process has been tested successfully, we should remove the **Default String** entry in the Object Id process property.

Publishing, activating, and managing workflow processes

Once a workflow process has been successfully simulated and tested, we can publish it by setting its status to **Completed**. Before the Siebel application can access the workflow process, we must also activate it by copying its definition to so-called runtime tables in the Siebel database.

Siebel Tools provides the functionality to accomplish these tasks. In addition, we will discuss the administrative views in the **Administration - Business Process** screen of the Siebel Web Client, which allow us to manage workflow processes.

Did you know?

It is not necessary, or even possible, to compile Siebel Workflow processes. Because they are not part of the SRF file, it is easier and faster to deploy modified or new workflow processes without server downtime.

The following diagram illustrates the steps of publishing, activating, and deploying workflow processes:

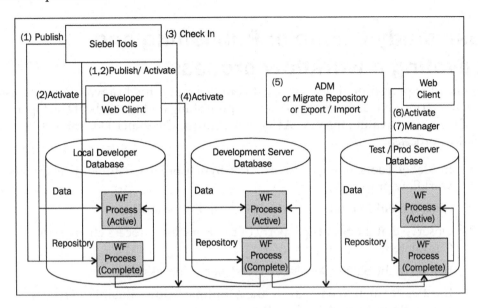

From the preceding diagram we can learn the following:

- **(1)**: Developers use the **Publish** functionality in Siebel Tools to mark workflow processes as Complete.
- **(1,2)**: The **Publish/Activate** functionality allows developers to execute both the publishing and the activation, copying the workflow process definition to the data tables, in one step.
- **(2)**: We can **activate** completed workflow processes from the Siebel Developer Web Client if they have not been activated from Siebel Tools.
- **(3)**: Completed workflow processes must be **checked in** like all other repository object definitions to be copied to the repository tables in the development server database.
- **(4)**: If necessary, we can use Siebel Tools or the Developer Web Client to activate workflow processes in the **development server** database.
- **(5)**: We can use **Application Deployment Manager** (ADM), the Migrate Repository process, or Siebel Tools export and import functionality to **migrate** a workflow process definition from a source repository such as development to a target repository such as test or production. ADM is capable of automatically activating migrated workflow processes.
- **(6)**: If we do not use ADM, we must use the Siebel Web Client to activate migrated workflow processes in test or production environments.

- **(7)**: The **Administration - Business Process** screen provides various views that allow us to manage and administer workflow processes at runtime.

Case study example: Publishing and activating a workflow process

The following procedure describes how to publish and activate a workflow process. In our scenario, we will use Siebel Tools for publishing and the Siebel Developer Web Client for activating the new **AHA Synchronize Customer Documents** workflow process:

1. In **Siebel Tools**, navigate to the **AHA Synchronize Customer Documents** workflow process.

2. Click the **Publish** button in the WF/Task Editor toolbar.

3. Observe that the **Status** property of the workflow process changes to **Completed**.

4. Log on to the Siebel Developer Web Client if necessary.

5. Use the site map to navigate to the **Administration - Business Process** screen, **Repository Workflow Process** view.

6. In the upper list applet, query for the **AHA Synchronize Customer Documents** workflow process and select it.

7. Click the **Activate** button in the upper list applet.

8. In the lower list applet, query for the AHA Synchronize Customer Documents workflow process.

9. Verify that the workflow process is listed in the lower list applet and has a deployment status of **Active**.

Did you know?

You can publish and activate multiple workflow processes at once by selecting more than one record and clicking the respective buttons in Siebel Tools or the Developer Web Client.

A workflow process that has a status of **Completed** in the Siebel Repository is read-only. To make changes to the workflow process definition, we must select it and click the **Revise** button in the WF/Task Editor toolbar. This produces a copy of the workflow process with the **Version** property incremented to 1 higher than the current maximum version number for that workflow process.

The new version's status is now **In Progress** and we can make changes to it. The publish–activate cycle must be repeated for each new version of a workflow process. Once we publish the new version in Siebel Tools, the **Status** property of older versions is set to *Not In Use*.

Managing workflow processes

The **Repository Workflow Process** view allows us to see all workflow processes in the Siebel Repository that have a status of **Completed**.

Once the workflow process is activated, and subsequently copied to the data tables, we can see and modify it in the **Active Workflow Processes** list applet at the bottom of the view.

The following screenshot shows the Active Workflow Processes list applet:

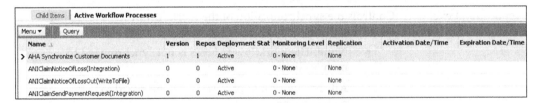

The following table describes some of the columns in the Active Workflow Processes list and the possible settings for workflow processes:

Column	Description
Version	The version of the workflow process in the database tables.
Repository Version	The version of the workflow process in the repository.
Deployment Status	The status of the workflow process. Possible values:
	• **Active**: The workflow process is active
	• **Inactive**: The workflow process has been deactivated by the administrator by selecting **Deactivate Process** from the applet menu
	• **Outdated**: There is a newer active version of the same workflow process
	Note: Only one version of a workflow process can be active at any time.

Column	Description
Monitoring Level	Controls how much information is stored when a workflow process instance is executed. Possible values:
	• **0 - None**: No monitoring is taking place
	• **1 - Status**: Information such as start and end time for each process instance is stored in the database
	• **2 - Progress**: Records level 1 information plus information about each step instance
	• **3 - Detail**: Records level 2 information plus process property information once the workflow process is completed
	• **4 - Debug**: Writes level 3 information after each step
	Information about where to view the monitoring data is provided later in this section.
Replication Level	Controls the synchronization of the workflow process to mobile clients via Siebel Remote. Possible values:
	• **None**: The workflow process is not synchronized to mobile clients
	• **All**: The workflow process is synchronized to mobile clients
	• **Regional**: Only replication servers are synchronized
Activation Date/ Time	These timestamps control when the workflow process becomes available. If not set, the workflow is always available.
Expiration Date/ Time	

Viewing workflow process instance data

When the monitoring level (described in the above table) of an active workflow process is set to **1 - Status** or higher, we can use the **Workflow Instance Monitor** views in the Administration - Business Process screen to review the recorded data.

In the **Process Instances** view, we can review the list of recorded instances for each workflow process.

When the monitoring level is set to **2 - Progress** or higher, we can use the **Step Instances** view to see all steps for a given workflow process instance. This view also provides a list of all process property values for each step when the monitoring level for the workflow process is set to **3 - Detail** or **4 - Debug**.

The following screenshot shows the **Step Instances** view in the Workflow Instance Monitor category of the Administration - Business Process screen in the Siebel Web Client:

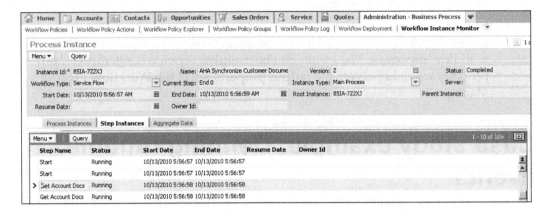

The screenshot does not show the Process Properties list applet at the bottom of the view.

The **Aggregate Data** view provides a chart applet that aggregates the workflow process instances by their status.

Invoking workflow processes

Workflow process definitions are always executed by the Workflow Process Manager business service. So when the question arises as to how to invoke workflow processes, we can rely on our knowledge on how to invoke a business service method. In *Chapter 17*, we already pointed out the invocation techniques for business services. For convenience the following shortened list conveys the most important invocation mechanisms for workflow processes:

- **Workflow policies**: These can be defined by an administrator in the **Workflow Policies** view of the **Administration - Business Process** screen. A workflow policy consists of a set of conditions and a set of actions, which are executed when all conditions are satisfied. Workflow policies require additional server-side configuration steps that are out of the scope of this book.

- **Runtime events**: These and their associated action sets are a real-time mechanism to invoke business service methods, and subsequently workflow processes, when the application engine registers an event on the application, applet, or business component level. In the next section, we will provide an example of how to use runtime events to execute workflow processes.

- **Buttons and menu items**: These are often configured in conjunction with the **Named Method** user property on applets or business components to invoke business service methods, of course including the Workflow Process Manager's *RunProcess* method.

- **Scripts**: In Siebel scripts, to be discussed in upcoming chapters, we can use the Workflow Process Manager business service as a means to invoke workflow processes. The scripts can be useful to provide handcrafted input property sets and process the output property set of the Workflow Process Manager.

Case study example: Defining runtime events

The following procedure describes how to define a runtime event in a workflow process. In our scenario, we will invoke the **AHA Synchronize Customer Documents** workflow process every time an account record is updated:

1. In Siebel Tools, navigate to the **AHA Synchronize Customer Documents** workflow process.

2. Click the **Revise** button in the **WF/Task Editor** toolbar to create a new editable version.

3. Right-click the new version and select **Edit Workflow Process** to open the editor.

4. Select the connector leading from the **Start** step.

5. In the **Properties** window for the connector, set the **Name** property of the connector to **Default**.

6. Press *Ctrl+A* to add a new point to the connector.

7. Drag the new point downwards so that the connector is bent.

8. Drag a second connector from the Palettes window to the **Start** step and ensure that it is correctly connected between the Start step and the first business service step.

 Using multiple connectors from the Start step ensures that we can still invoke the workflow process from other points in the application.

9. Press *Ctrl+A* to add a new point to the new connector and use the new point to bend the connector upwards.

10. In the **Properties** window, set the **Name** of the new connector to **Update**.

11. If necessary use the *Ctrl+B* or *Ctrl+F* keyboard shortcuts to move the text along the connector.

    Compare your work with the following screenshot:

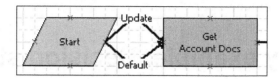

12. Select the **Update** connector.

13. In the **Properties** window enter the following values (in the sequence indicated):

    ○ Type: Condition

    ○ Event Object Type: BusComp

    ○ Event Object: Account

    ○ Event: WriteRecordUpdated

14. Save your changes.

15. Click the **Publish/Activate** button in the **WF/Task Editor** toolbar to mark the workflow process as complete and copy it to the runtime tables.

Activating a workflow process that contains event definitions has the effect of **action** sets and runtime event definitions being created automatically. We can inspect this data by navigating to the **Administration - Runtime Events** screen. In the **Events** view we can start a new query and type the following search string in any text column:

```
[Updated] >= Today()
```

When we execute the query, we will see all event definitions that were recently updated and we should be able to see the event we just defined in the workflow process. The event is also associated with a freshly created action set definition, which we can open by drilling down on the action set name.

The action set contains one action that invokes the Workflow Process Manager's RunProcess method and passes the ID of the active workflow process.

To refresh the application's runtime event cache we can either restart the application or select **Reload Runtime Events** from the **Action Sets** list applet menu.

To test the runtime event configuration, we can navigate to the **Accounts** screen and make changes to an account record in the AHA Test UI View. After stepping off the modified record or by pressing *Ctrl+S* to save the record explicitly, the AHA Synchronize Customer Documents workflow process should execute, which we can verify when the list of Customer Documents is refreshed manually by using the *Alt+Enter* keyboard shortcut.

Case study example: Decision steps and Siebel operations

The following requirement can be used to learn how to use decision steps and Siebel Operation steps in workflow processes: Each workflow process created for AHA should be enabled to create an activity record for verification purposes. The activity must be associated with the parent record and should only be created when the *AHA Create Activity* process property is set to **TRUE**.

The following procedure describes how to extend the AHA Synchronize Customer Documents workflow process with the decision logic described previously:

1. Navigate to the **AHA Synchronize Customer Documents** workflow process.
2. Check out or lock the workflow process if necessary.
3. In the **WF/Task Editor** toolbar, click the **Revise** button.
4. Observe that a copy of the workflow process is created automatically and that the Version property is increased.
5. Open the new workflow process version in the editor.
6. In the **Multi Value Property Window** create a new process property with the following values:
   - Name: AHA Create Activity
   - Default String: TRUE
7. Save your changes.
8. Delete the connector between the **Synchronize** step and the **End** step.
9. Position the End step below the Synchronize step.
10. Drag a **Decision Point** item from the **Palettes** window and drop it to the right of the **Synchronize** step.
11. Position a **Siebel Operation** step below the **Decision Point** step.
12. Set the **Name** property of the **Decision Point** step to **Create Activity?**.

13. Set the following properties of the **Siebel Operation** step:
    - Name: `Create Activity`
    - Business Component: `Action`
    - Operation: `Insert`

14. Drag the **Connector** item from the **Palettes** window to the editor repeatedly to create the following branch connections:
    - From the **Synchronize** business service step to the **Decision Point** step
    - From the **Decision Point** step to the **Siebel Operation** step
    - From the **Decision Point** step to the **End** step
    - From the **Siebel Operation** step to the **End** step

15. Rename the connector from the **Decision Point** step to the **Siebel Operation** step to **YES.CONDITION**.

16. Use the *Ctrl+B* and *Ctrl+F* keyboard shortcuts to position the branch label.

17. Rename the connector from the **Decision Point** to the **End** step to **NO.DEFAULT** and position the label so that it is readable.

18. Compare your work with the following screenshot:

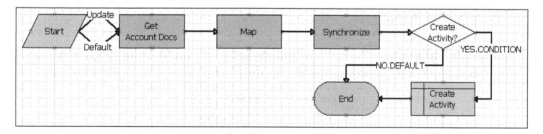

19. Double-click the **YES.CONDITION** connector. The **Compose Condition Criteria** dialog opens.

20. In the **Compose a Condition** section, enter the following values:
    - Compare to: `Process Property`
    - Operation: `All Must Match (Ignore Case)`
    - Object: `AHA Create Activity`

21. Click the **New** button to the right of the **Values** field.

22. In the **Add Values** dialog enter `TRUE`.

23. Click **OK** to close the **Add Values** dialog.

24. Click the **Add** button in the **Compose Condition Criteria** dialog to add the new condition to the Conditions list on top of the dialog.

25. Compare your work with the following screenshot:

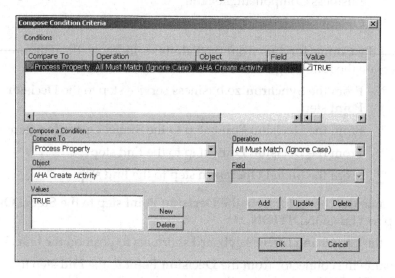

26. Click **OK** to close the **Compose Condition Criteria** dialog.

27. Select the **NO.DEFAULT** connector and set its **Type** property value to **Default**.

28. Save your changes.

29. Select the **Siebel Operation** step.

30. In the **Multi Value Property Window**, select the **Field Input Arguments** tab and create new records according to the instructions in the following table:

Field Name	Type	Value
Type	Literal	Administration (select from pick list)
Description	Literal	Customer documents have been synchronized.
Due	Expression	TimeStamp()

31. Save your changes.

32. Validate the workflow process and correct any errors.

33. Simulate the workflow process with a test account as described in a previous section.

34. Once the simulation proves that a new activity record is created for the account, click the **Publish/Activate** button to mark the workflow process as complete and activate it in your developer database.

A Siebel Tools archive file (`AHA Synchronize Customer Documents (2).sif`) is available with this chapter's code file. The file represents the workflow process after the changes made in the preceding section.

In the above procedure we learned how to use the Decision Point step to evaluate conditions and how to use the Siebel Operation step to interact with business components. In the following sections, we will discuss some important details for each step type.

Understanding decision point steps

We can use a decision point step to evaluate conditions and select one of its originating branches. It is important to understand that the conditions are stored within the branches, or connectors, themselves (not in the Decision Step).

As we have seen in the previous example procedure, we can double-click a connector that originates from a decision point step to open the **Compose Condition Criteria** dialog. Alternatively, we can right-click the connector and select **Edit Conditions...**.

The **Compose Condition Criteria** dialog allows us to specify one or more conditions, which all must evaluate to *true* to allow the Workflow Process Manager to choose the connector and subsequently the next step in the workflow process.

In the **Compare To** drop-down box, we can choose the type of object that provides the values for comparison. The choices are:

- Applet
- Business Component
- Process Property
- Expression

By selecting Applet or Business Component as the object type, we can specify an applet or business component name from the **Object** drop-down list. We must also specify a field of the applet's business component or of the business component itself that provides the value for comparison.

As shown in the previous example procedure, we can also select one of the process properties.

If we choose **Expression** in the **Compare To** dropdown box, we can specify a freeform expression in Siebel Query Language for evaluation.

The **Operation** drop-down list allows selection of one of various operators such as **All Must Match**, **Greater Than**, and **Is Not Null**.

The **Compose Condition Criteria** dialog has two sections—the **Conditions** list on top and the **Compose** section on the bottom. We can edit or delete existing conditions or add new conditions by clicking the appropriate buttons in the **Compose** section.

We can create as many connectors leading from a decision step to other steps as we need. Similar to `case` constructs in programming, one of the connectors can be defined as the `default` connector by setting its **Type** property to **Default**. However, we must be aware that conditions defined in connectors originating from a decision point step must be unambiguous in nature.

Understanding Siebel Operation steps

We can best understand the Siebel Operation step type when we imagine it as an invisible user. This is because we can use Siebel Operation steps to invoke the same methods that are available to end users by means of applet buttons or keyboard shortcuts.

Siebel Operation steps execute against a business component within the context of the business object associated with the parent workflow process. This means that link definitions drive the child record sets in the same way as when we operate with the data in a Siebel view.

The following table compares the available operations, to be set in the **Operation** property of a Siebel Operation step, against end user actions and describes them:

Operation	End User Action	Description
Insert	Create a new record.	Creates a new record for the business component. Default values and other properties of business component and field influence the new record.
		Field values for the new record must be specified in the **Field Input Arguments** tab of the **Multi Value Property Window (MVPW)**.

Operation	End User Action	Description
Update	Update fields and step off the record.	Updates the currently active record set and saves changes. Validation logic and other properties of business component and field influence the update behavior. The **Search Spec Input Arguments** tab of the MVPW can be used to create a search specification to limit the record set influenced by the update. Field values are specified in the MVPW's **Field Input Arguments** tab. This operation has one output argument named **NumAffRows**, which contains the number of rows affected by the update operation.
Upsert ("Update or Insert")	Query for a record using search criteria. When the record exists, update it. When no record exists, create a new record.	Uses the **Search Spec Input Arguments** list in the MVPW to define the search criteria. The **Field Input Arguments** tab defines the field values for the insert or update operation. Besides the **NumAffRows** output argument, the Upsert operation has an **IsInsert** output argument, which has a value of *true* when a new record has been created.
Delete	Delete one or more records.	Uses the **Search Spec Input Arguments** list to identify records to delete.
Query	Query for records.	The **Search Spec Input Arguments** tab of the MVPW must be used to create the search specification. After the step is executed, the business component instance represents the record set.

Operation	End User Action	Description
QueryBiDirectional	Query for records.	The main difference between this operation and the Query operation is that the record set created using the Query operation only allows navigation from the first to the last record (forward) and not backward.
		The QueryBiDirectional operation results in a record set that can be traversed forward and backward.
		This operation should only be used when we intend to use the PrevRecord operation (see below).
NextRecord	Navigate to the next record in the record set.	Typically preceded by a Query or QueryBiDirectional operation, the NextRecord operation activates the next record.
		The value of *true* of the **NoMoreRecords** output argument indicates that the end of the record set has been reached.
PrevRecord	Navigate to the previous record in a record set.	Must be preceded by a QueryBiDirectional operation and navigates backward in the record set.
		Also provides a **NoMoreRecords** output argument to check if the first record of the set has been reached.

 In the next chapter, we will learn how to traverse a record set using the Siebel Operation step.

Case study example: Replacing applets on the AHA Customer Process Start View

Because we have now implemented the logic to synchronize the customer documents list as required by AHA, we can finalize our work on the AHA Customer Process Start View by replacing the applets as follows:

Replace this applet	with this applet
Account Activity List Applet	AHA Data History List Applet
Account Contact List Applet	AHA Customer Documents List Applet

After compiling the view, we can test it by verifying that the AHA Customer Documents List Applet displays a list of customer documents after an update to the parent account record.

It may be beneficial to use the Siebel Sample Database to test the view because this database contains a variety of test data such as accounts with associated opportunities, quotes, orders and responses.

A Siebel Tools archive file (AHA Customer Process Start View.sif) is available with this chapter's code files. The file represents the AHA Customer Process Start View after the changes suggested in the preceding section.

Summary

The Siebel Workflow framework provides a graphical editor and declarative workspace in Siebel Tools to define program flows that can be triggered by a simple business service invocation.

In this chapter, we introduced essential facts about Siebel Workflow processes, their step types, and properties along with real-life examples.

In the course of this chapter, we learned how to use predefined business services, decision steps, and Siebel operation steps to support business process requirements.

In the next chapter, we will explore advanced workflow topics such as exception handling, subprocesses and loops.

20
Advanced Siebel Workflow Topics

While we create program flows with the Siebel Workflow framework, we may find ourselves in the situation where we wish to control the behavior of the workflow process in case of errors. In other situations, it may be useful to reuse existing workflows as subprocesses or to traverse record sets in a loop. For Siebel developers, it is important to master these advanced topics to gain full advantage of Siebel Workflow.

In this chapter, we will learn how to implement the following functionality in Siebel Workflow:

- Exception handling
- Subprocesses
- Loops and iterations
- Advanced workflow techniques

Exception handling in workflow processes

Those among us who are familiar with classic programming know how important it is to handle erroneous situations within the program flow. Most modern programming languages such as Java or C# provide this kind of exception handling. Because Siebel Workflow is in fact a programming language, it is important to understand how we can handle exceptions within a workflow process.

There are two techniques for exception handling in Siebel workflow processes:

- **Error exception connectors**: Allow developers to handle the errors that occur at the execution of a discrete workflow step
- **Error process**: Allows specification of a specialized workflow process to be executed when an error occurs at any step of the original workflow process

In the following section, we will discuss both approaches.

Using error exception connectors

An error exception connector can be used to define the path in case of errors. In the sense of programming, it resembles a `catch` block. Any process steps attached to the exception connector will only be executed when the originating step fails. The **Stop** step is frequently used as a final end point of an exception branch.

The **Account - Get SAP 46C Order List** workflow process, part of the standard Siebel Repository and shown in the following screenshot, demonstrates the practical use of exception connectors as well as the **Stop** and **Wait** step.

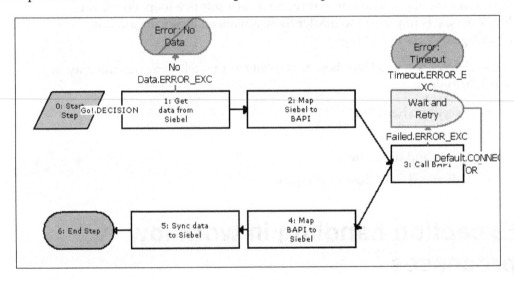

The steps labeled *1: Get data from Siebel* and *3: Call BAPI* are the origin of an exception connector. The first occurrence ends directly in a Stop step (*Error: No Data*). The second exception branch executes a Wait step. When the Wait step fails due to a time out, the second Stop step (*Error: Timeout*) is reached.

Using stop steps

Stop steps are useful when an error message should be displayed (or written to the log file). A Stop step's main property is **Error Code**, which defines the translatable error message. When we define a Stop step, we can choose from a list of predefined error codes. The full list of error codes can be inspected by navigating to the **Screens** menu in Siebel Tools, then choosing **System Administration | Analytic Strings**.

Did you know?

The label *Analytic Strings* is used in **Siebel Industry Applications (SIA)** 8.1. A different label may be used in older versions. It is a reminder of the fact that Siebel *Analytics*, the predecessor of Oracle Business Intelligence Enterprise Edition, used the Siebel message list for storing translatable *strings*.

Any entry in the messages list with an **Error Symbol** can be used in the Stop step. The following screenshot shows a portion of the available error messages:

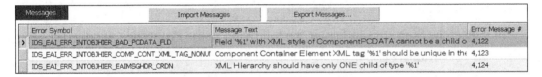

Error Symbol	Message Text	Error Message #
IDS_EAI_ERR_INTOBJHIER_BAD_PCDATA_FLD	Field '%1' with XML style of ComponentPCDATA cannot be a child o	4,122
IDS_EAI_ERR_INTOBJHIER_COMP_CONT_XML_TAG_NONUI	Component Container Element XML tag '%1' should be unique in the	4,123
IDS_EAI_ERR_INTOBJHIER_EAIMSGHDR_CRDN	XML Hierarchy should have only ONE child of type '%1'	4,124

When we inspect the **Message Text** more closely, we find that it contains placeholders in the format %1. At runtime we can replace these placeholders with real text, for example the name of an object or data from the business component.

A special group of messages is provided for customer use. These messages have an Error Symbol starting with WF_ERR_CUSTOM_ followed by a number. Their Message Text consists only of the %1 placeholder, which makes them perfect for creating custom messages with a free choice of text.

Case study example: Creating an error exception with a stop step

The following procedure describes how to add an error exception connector and a Stop step with a custom error message to the **AHA Synchronize Customer Documents** workflow process:

1. Navigate to the **AHA Synchronize Customer Documents** workflow process.
2. Check out or lock the project containing the workflow process if necessary.

3. Create a revised version of the workflow process if necessary.

4. Open the workflow process in the editor.

5. From the **Palettes** window drag a **Stop** step and position it above the decision step.

6. From the **Palettes** window drag the red **Error Exception** connector and drop it on the **Synchronize** step.

7. Connect the beginning of the **Error Exception** connector to the x connection point on top of the **Synchronize** step.

8. Connect the end of the **Error Exception** connector to the **Stop** step.

9. Compare your work with the following screenshot:

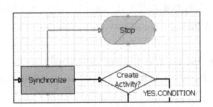

10. Select the **Stop** step and enter the following in the **Properties** window:

    ○ **Name**: Stop

    ○ **Error Code**: WF_ERR_CUSTOM_1

11. Save your changes.

12. In the **Multi Value Property Window**, create a new record with the following values:

    ○ **Name**: %1

    ○ **Type**: Expression

    ○ **Value**: "The following error occurred during synchronization: " + [&Error Message]

13. Save your changes.

14. Validate the workflow process.

When an error occurs during the Synchronize step, the Stop step will be executed and the message displayed will be the result of the expression specified as the replacement text for the %1 placeholder. As shown in step 12 of the example procedure above, we can reference process properties by using square brackets, [and], and an ampersand, &, before the property name. It is worth mentioning that this technique would only work in a monolingual environment because the text in double quotes is not translated.

A Siebel Tools archive file (AHA Synchronize Customer Documents(3).sif) is available with this chapter's code files. The file represents the AHA Synchronize Customer Documents workflow process after the changes in the preceding section.

Using error processes

There are various situations which could require creating exception connectors from **every** step within a workflow process. This would result in a very cluttered and unreadable flow diagram.

To overcome this, we can specify the logic in the case of errors, for example by writing the error message to a file or *cleaning up* in a simple workflow process and associating it as the **Error Process** (the name of the property) to any other workflow process. By doing so, we reach a very high level of reusability.

An error process inherits all values from the calling workflow process if process properties exist with the same names in both process definitions. This also applies of course to the preconfigured process properties such as *Error Message*.

The **ISSErrorHandler** workflow process, serving as the error process for several standard workflow processes in the Siebel Data Quality module, for example, uses the **EAI File Transport** business service to write various process property values to a text file.

The following screenshot shows the ISSErrorHandler workflow process:

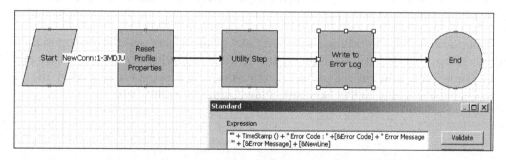

The *Write to Error Log* step, invoking the **Send** method of the **EAI File Transport** business service, is selected and a portion of the expression builder is visible. The expression concatenates the current time stamp, the error code, and the error message of the calling workflow process. Subsequently, the concatenated string is written to a file.

Subprocesses

Reusability of business logic is a key success factor for any software project, including Siebel CRM projects. The **Sub Process** step ensures that we can invoke often needed process flows from within another workflow process easily.

Subprocesses can not only help to increase the level of reusability but are also needed when more than one business object is involved in the process. As we have learned in the previous chapter, a workflow process can only be associated with one business object, which provides the context, and links, to the business component data.

If we need to operate on more than one business object, we must implement a subprocess. The **Account - New Quote** workflow process, associated with the Account business object, is a simple but very explanatory example of this. The following screenshot shows the **Account - New Quote** workflow process:

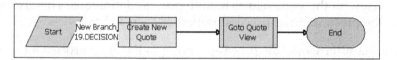

The **Goto Quote View** step is a **Sub Process** step. The main property of a Sub Process step is **Subprocess Name**, which is set to the name of a workflow process that is invoked at this step. Data can be exchanged between the parent and the child workflow process by means of the **Input Arguments** and **Output Arguments** tab in the **Multi Value Property Window**.

We can double-click a Sub Process step in the workflow process editor to open the subworkflow process in a new editor window. The following screenshot shows the **Goto_Quote** workflow process, which is the workflow process referenced by the **Goto Quote View** step in the **Account - New Quote** workflow process:

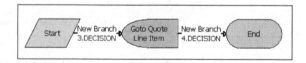

Inspection of the **Business Object** property of the Goto_Quote workflow process shows that it runs in the context of the **Quote** business object. The purpose of this workflow process lies within the **User Interact** step labeled *Goto Quote Line Item*, which opens the Quote Item Detail View. This view is associated with the Quote business object, hence the necessity to implement the view navigation in a separate subprocess.

Did you know?

As indicated previously, the **User Interact** step type can be used to accomplish view navigation. Because this only makes sense in user-facing workflow processes, the **Workflow Mode** property of the workflow process must be set to **Interactive Flow**.

Loops and iterations

A common task for programmers is to create loops or iterations across a record set and operate on each record. The Siebel Workflow Framework supports looping constructs with the **Siebel Operation** step. The following case study example shall serve as an example of a loop in Siebel Workflow.

Case study example: Iterations on a child record set

AHA managers want to be able to see the currently expected revenue for a customer. The implementation should include a button on the **AHA Customer Profile Form Applet** that invokes a workflow process. The workflow process should query all opportunities for the account that have a close date in the **next 30 days** and **sum** up the **expected revenue** of these opportunities. A message dialog should then display the result.

The following procedure describes how to implement this requirement using Siebel Operation and Stop steps:

1. Check out or lock the AHA Workflows project if necessary.

2. Create a new workflow process with the following property values:

    ○ **Name**: AHA Get Projected Revenue

    ○ **Project**: AHA Workflows

    ○ **Business Object**: Account

3. Open the **AHA Get Projected Revenue** workflow process in the editor.

4. In the **Multi Value Property Window (MVPW)** create the following **Process Properties**:

Name	Data Type	Default Number	Default String
AHA Currency Code	String		
AHA Current Revenue	Number	0	
AHA Record Count	Number	0	
AHA Last Record	String		false
AHA Total Expected Revenue	Number	0	
AHA Number Of Days	Number	30	
AHA Minimum Expected Value	Number	0	

5. Save your changes.

6. Using the **Palettes** icons, create a workflow layout similar to the following screenshot. Set the **Name** property for each step and connector according to the screenshot:

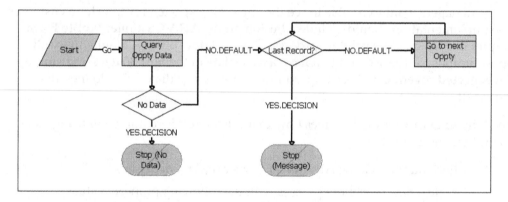

7. Select the **Query Oppty Data** step and set the following values in the **Properties** window:

   ◦ **Business Component**: Opportunity

   ◦ **Operation**: Query

8. In the **MVPW** navigate to the **Search Spec Input Arguments** tab and create a new record with the following values:

   ◦ **Expression Business Component**: Opportunity

   ◦ **Filter Business Component**: Opportunity

   ◦ **Type**: Expression

○ **Search Specification**: " [Primary Revenue Expected Value] >=" +
[&AHA Minimum Expected Value] + " AND [Primary Revenue Close
Date] <= Today()+" + [&AHA Number Of Days] + " AND [Primary
Revenue Close Date] >= Today()"

The preceding search specification expression queries for all opportunity
records that have an expected revenue – represented by the `Primary
Revenue Expected Value` field – equal to or greater than (>=) the value of
the `AHA Minimum Expected Value` process property, which defaults to zero.
The close date, represented by the `Primary Revenue Close Data` field, must
be within the period between the current date, returned by the `Today()`
function, and the number of days specified by the `AHA Number Of Days`
process property.

9. In the **MVPW** select the **Output Arguments** tab and create the following
records:

Property Name	Type	Output Argument	Business Component	Business Component Field
AHA Record Count	Output Argument	NumAffRows		
AHA Total Expected Revenue	Business Component		Opportunity	Primary Revenue Expected Value
AHA Currency Code	Business Component		Opportunity	Currency Code

The previous output arguments define the following:

○ The number of rows in the query result set will be saved to the `AHA
Record Count` process property

○ The value in the `Primary Revenue Expected Value` field of the
first opportunity record will be saved to the `AHA Total Expected
Revenue` process property

○ The value in the `Currency Code` field of the first opportunity record
will be saved to the `AHA Currency Code` process property

10. Save your changes.

11. Double-click the **YES.DECISION** connector leading from the *No Data*
decision step and specify the following condition:

○ **Compare To**: `Process Property`

○ **Object**: `AHA Record Count`

○ **Value**: `0` (zero)

○ **Operation**: `All Must Match` (Ignore Case)

12. Select the **Stop (No Data)** step and specify **WF_ERR_CUSTOM_1** as the value for the **Error Code** property.

13. In the **Input Arguments** tab of the **MVPW**, create a new record with the following values:

    ○ **Name:** %1

    ○ **Type:** Expression

    ○ **Expression:** "No Opportunities found with an expected revenue of more than " + [&AHA Minimum Expected Value] + " and a close date between today and " + (Today() + [&AHA Number Of Days]) + "."

    The above expression concatenates static text with values of process properties and the Today() function to a message text. Because the Stop step is only reached when the AHA Record Count process property is zero, the message is only displayed when there are no opportunity records for the current account that match the search specification in the *Query Oppty Data* step.

14. Select the **NO.DEFAULT** connector leading from the *No Data* decision step and set its **Type** property to **Default**.

15. Save your changes.

16. **Double-click** the YES.DECISION connector leading from the *Last Record?* decision step and specify the following condition:

    ○ **Compare To:** Process Property

    ○ **Object:** AHA Last Record

    ○ **Value:** true

    ○ **Operation:** All Must Match (Ignore Case)

17. Select the **Stop (Message)** step and specify WF_ERR_CUSTOM_2 as the value for the **Error Code** property.

18. In the **Input Arguments** tab of the **MVPW**, create a new record with the following values:

    ○ **Name:** %1

    ○ **Type:** Expression

    ○ **Expression:** "Total expected revenue for the customer account is " + [&AHA Currency Code] + " " + [&AHA Total Expected Revenue] + "."

    The preceding expression concatenates static text with values of process properties to a message text, which is displayed after the loop has reached the last record.

19. Select the **NO.DEFAULT** connector leading from the **Last Record?** decision step and set its **Type** property to **Default**.

20. Save your changes.

21. Select the **Go to next Oppty** step and set the following values in the **Properties** window:

    ○   **Business Component**: Opportunity

    ○   **Operation**: NextRecord

22. In the **Output Arguments** tab of the **MVPW**, create the following records:

Property Name	Type	Value	Output Argument	Business Component	Business Component Field
AHA Current Revenue	Business Component		NumAffRows	Opportunity	Primary Revenue Expected Value
AHA Total Expected Revenue	Expression	(see the following)			
AHA Last Record	Output Argument		NoMoreRecords		

The **Value** for the expression to populate the AHA Total Expected Revenue process property must be set to:

```
[&AHA Total Expected Revenue] + [&AHA Current Revenue]
```

This adds the expected revenue of the current opportunity record to the AHA Total Expected Revenue process property value. While the loop executes, the AHA Total Expected Revenue process property will aggregate the sum of the expected revenue values for all records.

1. **Save** your changes.

2. **Validate** the workflow process.

3. Log on to the **Siebel Developer Web Client** and create a test account record with at least two opportunities. Ensure that the opportunity records have the **revenue** and **probability** fields populated with meaningful values. Also set the **close date** field to a date between the current date and 30 days in the future.

4. Record the **ROW_ID** value of the test account record.

5. Log out of the **Developer Web Client**.

6. Set the recorded **ROW_ID** as the **Default String** value for the **Object Id** process property and save the workflow process.

7. Simulate the workflow process and observe its behavior in the **Watch** window.

The workflow process created in the previous example procedure implements the following:

1. The **Query Oppty Data** step executes a query among the opportunity records associated with the active account record.

2. When the result set is empty, a message is displayed and the workflow process stops.

3. When the query returns data, the workflow process iterates through the record set and uses the AHA Total Expected Revenue process property to store the sum of the expected revenue values.

4. After the last record has been processed, a message displays the total expected revenue and the workflow process stops.

A Siebel Tools archive file (AHA Get Projected Revenue.sif) is available with this chapter's code files. The file represents the AHA Get Projected Revenue workflow process created in the previous section.

To finalize the requirement, we should create a button control on the **AHA Customer Profile Form Applet**. The method invoked by the button should be handled at the business component level by means of a new instance of the **Named Method** business component user property. Please refer to *Chapter 16, Menus and Buttons* for instructions on how to create an applet button that invokes a workflow process.

Advanced workflow techniques

On several occasions, the ambitious workflow developer will reach a point where the functionality of standard workflow steps such as Siebel Operation is not sufficient to implement the requirements.

Engineers at Siebel Systems and Oracle have developed more than 1,300 workflow processes and created the following business services to assist during the workflow development cycle:

- Workflow Utilities
- SIA BC Utility Service
- PRM ANI Utility Service

In addition, we can use one of the following **EAI transport** business services to easily write data to files for debugging purposes.

- EAI XML Write to File
- EAI File Transport

In the following section, we will briefly introduce the methods of these business services and provide examples for their usage.

Workflow Utilities

The Workflow Utilities business service has one public and four hidden methods. Because the public **Echo** method is the only one that is used in the preconfigured workflow processes, it is the only method to be discussed in this section.

The Echo method is designed to serve as a step in a workflow process at which developers can use the Input and Output Arguments list to operate on the current set of process properties.

We can find a typical example of such operations in the **eMail Response - Identify Language** workflow process. The **Set Language Code CHS** business service step uses the Echo method to set the **MsgLanguageCode** process property to **CHS** as an output argument. The following screenshot shows the **Properties** window and MVPW for this step:

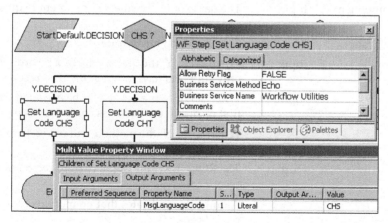

Even if the manipulation of process properties could be accomplished in other workflow process steps, it is recommendable to utilize the Echo method of the Workflow Utilities business service because of the optimized transparency and readability of the workflow process itself.

Later in this section, we will implement a workflow step with the Workflow Utilities business service.

SIA BC Utility Service

As the name suggests, the SIA BC Utility Service is only available in **Siebel Industry Applications (SIA)** and supports developers who want to interact with **business components (BC)**.

The business service has found wide adoption in the Siebel developer community and has two methods:

- BCInvokeMethod
- BCNextRecord

The BCInvokeMethod method allows us to specify the name of a business component and a method to be invoked. A typical usage scenario for this method is to invoke the RefreshBuscomp method on a business component after the data of the business component has been modified.

The BCNextRecord method can be used to iterate through a record set and has the following arguments:

Name	Type	Description
Business Component Name	Input	The name of the business component to query.
Search Specification	Input	Search criteria for the query.
Forward Only	Input	When set to Y, the query returns a record set that only supports navigation to the next record.
From First	Input	When set to Y, the query will be executed from the first record in the business component's record set.
		When set to N, the method will navigate to the next record in the record set.
Row Id	Output	The ROW_ID value of the current record of the record set.
		A null value indicates that no more records are in the record set.
		This output argument is typically used to implement the loop by checking it for null in a decision step branch.

A working example of the `BCNextRecord` method can be found in the **HTIM SPA Enhanced Approval Workflow** in the SIA Repository. The relevant portion of the workflow process is shown in the following screenshot:

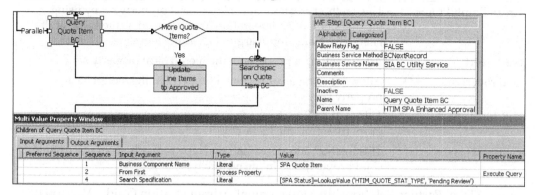

The **Query Quote Item BC** step implements the **BCNextRecord** method of the SIA BC Utility Service. The *Yes* branch of the **More Quote Items?** decision step checks the **Siebel Operation Object Id** process property, used to take the Row Id output argument, to verify if there are more records in the query result set.

The SIA BC Utility Service can be useful for working with business components. However, we should also consider the functionality of the Siebel Operation step when the requirement includes iterations over a record set.

PRM ANI Utility Service

The PRM ANI Utility Service originates in the **Siebel Partner Relationship Management (PRM)** application. This business service has specialized methods for creating and manipulating hierarchical process properties that are typically used in EAI scenarios.

The methods of the PRM ANI Utility Service are described in the following table:

Method	Description
CreateEmptyPropSet	This method creates a new hierarchical property set by using the definition of an integration object, passed as the value of the Hierarchy Name input argument, as the template.
SetProperty	Allows setting a property in the hierarchical property set.
GetProperty	Allows reading a value from a property in the hierarchical property set.
SetChildType	This method can change the Type property of one or more child property sets in the hierarchy.
GetChildType	This method allows reading the Type property from one or more child property sets in the hierarchy.

Source: Siebel Partner Relationship Management Administration Guide, Version 8.1:

http://download.oracle.com/docs/cd/E14004_01/books/PRMAdm/booktitle.html

Various prebuilt workflow processes such as the **Transfer Cart Outbound Create Header Process** use the PRM ANI Utility Service.

EAI XML Write to File

When working with hierarchical process properties we may find it beneficial to be able to inspect the property sets as a whole instead of trying to locate the property value in the Watch window during debugging.

The prebuilt EAI XML Write to File business service can serve as a vehicle to quickly write an entire hierarchical property set to an XML file for inspection.

The following methods are available in the business service:

- **WritePropSet**: Can be used to write any property set to a file.
- **WriteXMLHier**: Accepts only property sets with a **Type** of **XMLHierarchy**.
- **WriteEAIMsg**: Accepts only property sets with a **Type** of **SiebelMessage**. Property sets of this type are created by the **EAI Siebel Adapter** business service methods and by the EAI Data Transformation Engine as well as various other business services in the EAI sector.

The following example procedure describes how to use the EAI XML Write to File business service to write data to an XML file. The example uses the **AHA Synchronize Customer Documents** workflow process:

1. Ensure that the AHA Workflows project is checked out or locked.

2. Navigate to the **AHA Synchronize Customer Documents** workflow process.

3. Create a revised version of the workflow process.

4. Open the new version in the workflow process editor.

5. Delete the connector between the **Map** and the **Synchronize** step.

6. Align the workflow process steps so that there is enough space to place a new business service step between the **Map** and the **Synchronize** step.

7. From the **Palettes** window drag-and-drop a business service step between the **Map** and the **Synchronize** step.

8. In the **Properties** window, set the following values:

   ○ **Name**: Write File

   ○ **Business Service**: EAI XML Write to File

   ○ **Business Service Method**: WriteEAIMsg

9. **Save** your changes.

10. In the **Input Arguments** tab of the MVPW create two records as follows:

Input Argument	Type	Value	Property Name
FileName	Literal	C:\TEMP\Target_Data.xml	
SiebelMessage	Process Property		AHA Target Data

11. **Save** your changes.

12. **Connect** the workflow process steps using the **Connector** icon from the **Palettes** window.

13. **Save and validate** the workflow process. Correct any reported errors or warnings.

14. Simulate the workflow process. An XML file should be created in the path specified by the `FileName` input argument. The file contains the XML representation of the customer data after the mapping to the AHA Customer Documents Source IO integration object.

It is important to mention that writing data to files like in the preceding scenario is intended for the development cycle and for debugging purposes only. Before the workflow process is published the production environment we must remove these steps to avoid performance issues.

A Siebel Tools archive file (AHA Synchronize Customer Documents(4).sif) is available with this chapter's code files. The file represents the AHA Synchronize Customer Documents workflow process after the changes in the preceding section.

EAI File Transport

The EAI File Transport business service's **Send** method can be used to write simple text messages to a file. The Send method has the following input arguments:

- **FileName**: Specifies the path to write the file to.
- <Value>: The text to write to the file. The method writes everything in the Value property to the file.
- **AppendToFile**: When set to **true**, the text in the Value property will be appended at the end of the file. When set to **false**, any file with the same path will be overwritten.

Case study example: Using dot notation to access hierarchical data

Working with hierarchical process properties can be challenging. In some situations it might be necessary to fetch the value of a specific property that is deep inside the hierarchy.

In the following example procedure, we explain how to use the **dot notation**, which is named after the technique of using dots to separate element names, to access data in a hierarchical process property. The example extends the AHA Synchronize Customer Documents workflow process to read the value of the **customer service number (CSN)** field for later use:

1. Ensure that the **AHA Workflows** project is checked out or locked.
2. Navigate to the **AHA Synchronize Customer Documents** workflow process.
3. Create a revised version of the workflow process.
4. Open the new version in the workflow process editor.
5. Create a new process property named AHA CSN.

6. Insert a **Business Service** step between the **Get Account Docs** and the **Map** step.

7. In the **Properties** window, enter the following values for the new business service step:
    ○ **Name**: Read CSN
    ○ **Business Service**: Workflow Utilities
    ○ **Business Service Method**: Echo

8. Save your changes.

9. In the **Input Arguments** tab of the **MVPW** create a record with the following values:
    ○ **Input Argument**: EchoData
    ○ **Type**: Process Property
    ○ **Property Name**: AHA Source Data

10. In the **Output Arguments** tab of the **MVPW** create a record with the following values:
    ○ **Property Name**: AHA CSN
    ○ **Type**: Output Argument
    ○ **Output Argument**: EchoData.ListOfAHA Account Documents Source IO.Account.CSN

The preceding string uses **dot notation** to access the *CSN* field in the *Account* integration component. The elements between the dots are the Type of the property sets. To correctly reference a property within a hierarchy of property sets we must use the Type property's value of each element in the hierarchy and separate them by dots. The last element is the name of the property to read. We can investigate the correct path by using the file export technique described in the previous section or by using the Watch window.

11. Save your changes.

12. Connect all steps.

13. Save and validate the workflow process. Correct any errors or warnings.

14. Run the workflow process in the simulator and use the **Watch** window to verify that the AHA CSN process property is populated with the CSN of the current customer account.

A Siebel Tools archive file (AHA Synchronize Customer Documents(5).sif) is available with this chapter's code files. The file represents the AHA Synchronize Customer Documents workflow process after the changes in the previous section.

Summary

Siebel developers face several challenges while implementing workflow processes in Siebel Tools. In this chapter, we provided information about popular advanced techniques for configuring workflow processes.

Efficient exception handling is a key issue in programming and workflow development. We learned how to use the error exception connector and error processes to implement exception handling in Siebel Workflow.

Subprocesses, also shown in this chapter, allow implementation of reusable processes.

Furthermore we discovered the Siebel Operation step's ability to iterate through record sets and learned how to use preconfigured utility business services and dot notation to work with hierarchical property sets.

In the next chapter, we will learn how to implement Tasks to guide end users through business processes.

21
Siebel Task User Interface

End users in large corporations often find themselves challenged by complex and lengthy business processes, many of which have to be carried out in Siebel CRM applications. To provide guidance through these business processes, Siebel CRM features the **Task User Interface (UI)**. Siebel developers must thoroughly understand how to create and publish tasks, to mention two of the main topics in this chapter.

The chapter is structured as follows:

- Understanding the Siebel Task UI
- Creating task applets and task views
- Creating tasks
- Publishing, activating, and administering tasks
- Using applet messages

Understanding the Siebel Task UI

The Siebel Task UI is available in Siebel versions 8.0 and higher and is intended to guide end users through business processes while maintaining the highest level of data quality and process consistency. Task UI is available for the **High-Interactivity (HI)** client only and consists of the following components:

- **Task Editor**: A flowchart editor in Siebel Tools serves as the developer's workbench to create and modify task flows.
- **Tools Wizards**: Developers can use wizards in Siebel Tools to create tasks, task views, task applets, and transient business components.
- **Administrative views**: Administrators can activate and associate tasks with responsibilities in several administrative views in the Siebel Web Client.

- **Task Pane**: Situated on the left-hand side of the Siebel UI, the task pane allows end users to see tasks to which they have access to and invoke them by clicking on the task name. When a task executes, the task pane shows the current step of the task.

- **Task Player**: Replaces the standard UI with the task views when a task is executed.

The following screenshot shows one of the preconfigured tasks of Siebel SIA 8.1.1, **Email Treatments**, executed in Siebel Marketing:

The task pane shows the current step (**Create Email Treatment**). The task view in the player allows the end user to enter data for a new e-mail treatment.

- **Integration with Siebel Universal Inbox**: Tasks can be automatically or manually paused and then resumed by clicking on an item in the user's Inbox list.

The preceding list shows that Siebel Task UI involves end user, administrator, and developer roles. To gain a better understanding of the Task UI and its related objects, we will discuss them in greater detail in the next section.

Tasks and related repository objects

The Object Explorer in Siebel Tools provides access to the **Task** object type. A Task object definition consists of the following main elements:

- **Task Property**: Similar to workflow process properties; serve as local variables during task execution. They can be used to hold and pass values between task steps.

- **Task Step**: This includes types we are already familiar with such as *Siebel Operation*, *Decision Point*, and *Business Service*. The most important step type however is **Task View**, which is bound to a specialized view definition.

- **Task Chapter**: Each task step is associated with a **task chapter** to provide consistent end user guidance.

Tasks are created and modified in Siebel Tools by means of the task editor. The task editor uses the same technology as the workflow process editor, which is a benefit for developers who are familiar with the latter.

The following screenshot shows the **Email Treatment** task opened in the Siebel Tools task editor:

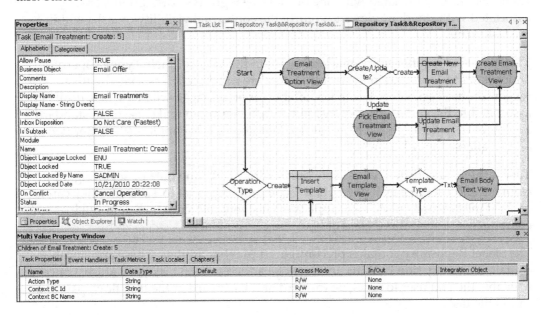

The screenshot shows a portion of the task flow in the editor canvas as well as the **Properties** window and the **Multi Value Property Window**. We can see familiar step types such as Siebel Operation and the task-specific Task View types (rounded shapes).

In addition to the Task object type, we find the following object types, or variants thereof, in the Siebel Repository:

- Task Group
- View Task Group (child element of the View type)
- Task View (special type of view)
- Task Applet (special type of applet)
- Playbar Applet (special type of applet)
- Transient Business Component (special type of business component)

Each task can be associated with one or more **task groups**. Task groups are associated with standard views to control the contextual visibility of tasks within the **task pane**.

Task views only differ from standard views in the value of their **Type** property, which is set to Task, and in the fact that they are not directly associated with a responsibility. Task views become available for an end user when the task itself is associated to the end user's responsibility. Task views can make use of all standard applets and applet types such as task applets, and playbar applets (the latter two are only available for task views).

Task applets are created for the sole purpose of displaying data or soliciting input from the end user in a task flow. Their **Type** property is set to **Task** and they cannot be used in standard views. Task applets exclusively reference **transient business components**, a specialized class of business components.

The Siebel Repository contains preconfigured **playbar applets**. These applets only contain the **navigation buttons** and must be added to each task view at least once to enable the end user to navigate forward and backward in the task flow, pause, or cancel the task.

Transient business components serve as the data provider for **task applets** and can be distinguished from standard business components by their **Type** property, which is set to **Transient**, their **base table (S_TU_LOG)** and their **class** (**CSSBCTaskTransient**).

The following diagram illustrates the objects discussed in the preceding section and their relationship to each other:

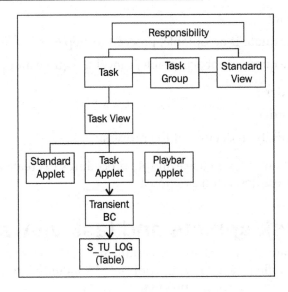

From the diagram, we can summarize the following information:

- A task contains one or more task views
- A task view can utilize standard applets, task applets, and playbar applets
- Task applets reference transient business components that use the S_TU_LOG table to store data
- Task groups are associated with standard views to provide UI context
- Responsibilities control end user access to tasks

Case study example: Supporting a business process with Task UI

As indicated in *Chapter 3*, the Sales – Retail Order business process should be supported with Siebel Task UI. The following list describes the steps of the process. Please refer to *Chapter 3, Case Study Introduction* for a full description of the business process:

1. Query for the retail partner account.
2. If the query returns no results, create a new account.
3. If the Always Generate Quote flag is set to *Y* or is undefined, create a new quote for the account.
4. If the flag is set to *N*, proceed to step 6.

5. Verify the quote:
    ◦ If the quote is acceptable, proceed to step 6
    ◦ If the quote is not acceptable, cancel the quote and proceed to the end

6. Create an order.
7. Submit the order.
8. Create an activity to document the process.

In the following sections we will use example procedures to create a prototype task for the business process described previously.

Creating task applets and task views

The AHA technical architecture team has conducted workshops with the end user community and identified the following applets to be included in the task view layouts for the steps of the business process:

Step	Applet(s)	Comments
1	AHA Partner Query Task Applet	Create a new task applet (and transient business component) that allows end users to enter query criteria for the following fields: • Name • CSN • City
2	AHA Customer Profile Form Applet	Use the existing custom form applet.
3,5	Copy of Quote Form Applet	Copy the Quote Form Applet and modify the copy.
6,7	Copy of Order Entry - Order Form Applet (Sales)	Copy the applet and modify the copy.

Preparation steps

The following activities must be completed to prepare the new Task UI. As the developer tasks of creating fields and applets have already been discussed in previous chapters of this book, please refer to these chapters for details. For the sake of brevity, instructions are kept to a minimum.

New business component field: AHA always generate quote flag

The following shortened procedure describes how to create a new field for the Account business component. The field will define whether a quote should always be generated for a given account or not:

1. Create a new field for the **Account** business component with the following characteristics:

    ○ Name: AHA Always Generate Quote Flag

    ○ Join: S_ORG_EXT_X

    ○ Column: ATTRIB_11

    ○ Predefault Value: Y

2. Expose the new field in the **AHA Customer Profile Form Applet** using a checkbox control. Label the control **Always Quote**.

3. **Compile** the Account business component and the AHA Customer Profile Form Applet.

New applet: AHA simple quote form applet

The following procedure guides us through the task of creating the AHA Simple Quote Form Applet:

1. Copy the **Quote Form Applet** and rename the copy **AHA Simple Quote Form Applet**.

2. Set the **Project** property of the AHA Simple Quote Form Applet to **AHA User Interface**.

3. Delete the following items from the **Edit** web template: Revision, **Sales Rep**, Service Account, Billing Account, Organization, Billing Profile, Created, Due, Campaign, Agreement, Entitlement, Network, MRC Total, NRC Total.

4. Rearrange the remaining items.

5. Remove the **More** flag from all items.

6. Delete the following buttons: Revise, Select Favorites, Submit, Auto Order, ToggleLayout.

7. Save your work and compare it with the following screenshot in **Preview** mode:

8. Compile the AHA Simple Quote Form Applet.

New applet: AHA simple order form applet

The following procedure guides us through the task of creating the AHA Simple Order Form Applet:

1. Copy the applet named **Order Entry - Order Form Applet (Sales)** and rename the copy **AHA Simple Order Form Applet**.

2. Set the **Project** property of the AHA Simple Order Form Applet to **AHA User Interface**.

3. Delete the **Search Specification**.

4. Delete the following items from the **Edit** web template: all items in *More mode* except the Comments control, Revision, Opportunity.

5. Rearrange the remaining items.

6. Remove the **More** flag from the **Comments** control.

7. Delete the **Revise** and **ToggleLayout** buttons.

8. Change the caption of the Submit button to **Submit Order**.

9. Save your work and compare it with the following screenshot in **Preview** mode:

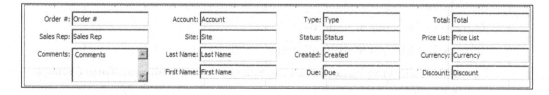

10. Compile the AHA Simple Order Form Applet.

New transient business component: AHA partner query TBC

The following procedure describes how to create a new transient business component to support a new task applet:

1. Create a new project named **AHA Task UI** and lock it.

2. Click the **New** button in the toolbar.

3. Double-click the **Transient BusComp** icon in the **Task** tab of the **New Object Wizards** dialog.

4. Set the following values in the **New Business Component** page:

    ○ Project: AHA Task UI

    ○ Name: AHA Partner Query TBC

5. Click **Finish**.

6. Ensure that the new **AHA Partner Query TBC** business component is selected in the **Object List Editor**.

7. Navigate to the **Field** list for the new business component.

8. In the **Fields** list, create three new records as follows:

Name	Type	Length
Partner Name	DTYPE_TEXT	100
Partner CSN	DTYPE_TEXT	30
Partner City	DTYPE_TEXT	50

9. Observe that Siebel Tools populates the **Column** property automatically.

10. Compile the AHA Partner Query TBC business component.

New task applet: AHA partner query task applet

The following procedure describes how to create a new task applet using the Task Applet wizard:

1. Click the **New** button in the toolbar.

2. In the **Task** tab of the **New Object Wizards** dialog, double-click the **Task Form Applet** icon.

3. In the **General** page, set the following values:

    ○ **Project**: AHA Task UI

    ○ **Name**: AHA Partner Query Task Applet

- ○ **Display title**: Partner Query
- ○ **Task**: (leave empty)
- ○ **Upgrade behavior**: Preserve
- ○ **Transient business component**: AHA Partner Query TBC

4. Click **Next**.

5. In the **Web Layout - Fields** page, select the following fields:

  - ○ **Partner Name**
  - ○ **Partner CSN**
  - ○ **Partner City**

6. Click **Next**.

7. Click **Finish**.

8. The applet web layout editor opens automatically.

9. Arrange the controls as per the order of step 5.

10. Set the **HTML Type** property of all controls to **Text**.

11. Double the width of the **Partner Name** text box.

12. Save your changes and compare your work with the following screenshot:

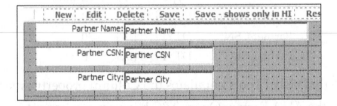

13. Close the web layout editor.

14. Compile the AHA Partner Query Task Applet.

Two Siebel Tools archive files (Applets.sif and AHA Partner Query TBC.sif) are available with this chapter's code files. The files represent the applets and the transient business component created in the preceding sections.

New task view: AHA partner query task view

The following procedure describes how to create a new task view using the Task View wizard:

1. Click the **New** button in the toolbar.

2. In the **Task** tab of the **New Object Wizards** dialog, double-click the **Task View** icon.

3. In the **New View** page, enter the following values:
   ○ **Project**: AHA Task UI
   ○ **Name**: AHA Partner Query Task View
   ○ **Title**: Partner Query
   ○ **Business Object**: Account
   ○ **Upgrade behavior**: Preserve

4. Click **Next**.

5. In the **View Web Layout - Select Template** page, select the **View Basic** template.

6. Click **Next**.

7. In the **Web Layout - Applets** page make no selection.

 We do not select any standard applet for this task view.

8. Click **Next**.

9. Click **OK** to acknowledge the message that there are no tasks for the business object.

10. In the **Task View - Select Task** page, click **Next**.

11. In the **Task View - Task Applets** page, select the **AHA Partner Query Task Applet** in the **Available Applets** list.

12. Click the upper arrow button to add the AHA Partner Query Task Applet to the **Selected Applets** list.

13. Click **Next**.

14. In the **Task View - Select Playbar Applets** page, select the **Task Playbar Applet - Top** applet as the bottom playbar applet.

15. Click **Next**.

16. Click **Finish**.

17. The view web layout editor opens automatically.
18. Right-click in the layout editor and select **Preview**.
19. Compare your work with the following screenshot:

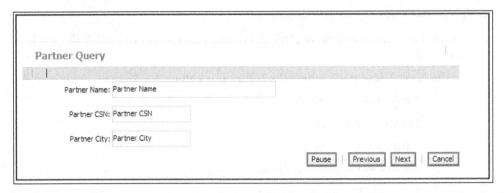

20. Close the editor.
21. Compile the AHA Partner Query Task View.

New task view: AHA create account task view

To create the task view for step 2 of the task described earlier in this chapter, we can use the New Task View wizard again.

Follow the steps in the previous section to create a new task view named **AHA Create Account Task View** but this time add the standard applet named **AHA Customer Profile Form Applet** and the playbar applet. Compare your work with the following screenshot:

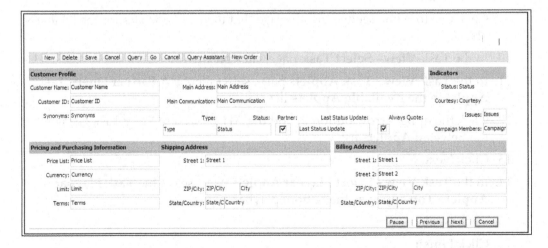

New task view: AHA create quote task view

In a similar manner as for the AHA Create Account Task View, create a new task view named **AHA Create Quote Task View**. Use the **AHA Simple Quote Form Applet** above the playbar applet.

New task view: AHA create order task view

In a similar manner as for the AHA Create Account task view, create a new task view named **AHA Create Order Task View**. Use the **AHA Simple Order Form Applet** above the playbar applet.

> **Did you know?**
>
> If you wish to speed up the process of creating task views, you can use the **Copy Record** command to copy an existing task view. Then use the **Object Explorer** to navigate to the list of **View Web Template Items** and replace the applets using the pick list in the **Applet** property. When you do so, ensure that the appropriate **Applet Mode** is selected and verify your work using the web layout editor.

A Siebel Tools archive file (`Views.sif`) is available with this chapter's code files. The file represents the task views created in the previous sections.

Creating tasks

As we have seen in the previous sections, the decision to provide end users with a task-based user interface has far-ranging consequences. For example, the UI itself in terms of form and list applets has to be carefully designed, typically with much more consideration than is taken in our brief example. In addition, the business logic has to be designed as task steps which are called between the task views.

The following procedure describes how to create the task flow itself. We will use the task views created in the previous sections:

1. Click the **New** button in the toolbar.
2. In the **Task** tab of the **New Object Wizards** dialog, double-click the **Task** icon.
3. In the **New Task** page, enter the following values:
    - **Project**: AHA Task UI
    - **Name**: AHA Sales Process
    - **Display Name**: Sales Process
    - **Business Object**: Account

4. Click **Finish**.

5. The new task is opened in the editor automatically. A start and end step are provided as a starting point.

6. Delete the connector between the start and end step.

7. Click the canvas to select the task definition.

8. In the **Multi Value Property Window (MVPW)** select the **Task Properties** tab and create the following property records (setting **String** as the **Data Type**):

   ○ **AHA Partner Name**

   ○ **AHA Partner CSN**

   ○ **AHA Partner City**

   ○ **AHA Create Quote Flag**

   ○ **AHA Name Search**

   ○ **AHA CSN Search**

   ○ **AHA City Search**

   ○ **AHA Query Operator** (set the **Default** property to **AND**)

9. In the **Chapters** tab of the **MVPW**, create the following records:

Name	Display Name - String Override	Color (select from color picker)
Query	Partner Lookup	Red
Partner	Create Partner	Orange
Quote	Create Quote	Yellow
Order	Create Order	Green

Creating the task flow layout

In order to simplify the instructions for creating a task, we do not discuss each and every single detail such as drag and drop operations with which the reader should already be familiar with. We can use the same techniques as in the workflow process editor to arrange the steps on the task editor canvas as shown in the following screenshot:

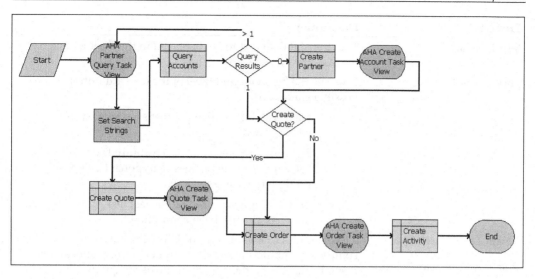

Because task view steps are empty after arranging them on the canvas, we must right-click them and select **Bind Task View**. We can then select the appropriate task view for the step. Please use the preceding screenshot as a guide for creating the task flow and binding the correct task view to each task view shape.

The business service, decision point, and Siebel operation steps can be renamed using the **Name** property. Connectors originating from decision steps can be labeled using the **Label** property. The *Ctrl+B* and *Ctrl+F* keyboard shortcuts allow us to align the branch labels as shown in the preceding screenshot.

In the following procedures we describe the configuration activities for each task step and explain the technical details.

Configuring task view steps

After assigning a task view to a task view step shape using the **Bind Task View** command, we must specify additional properties for each task view. The most important properties for the task view step type are described in the following table:

Property	Description
Chapter	The name of one of the task's chapters. Each task step must be assigned to a chapter.
Disable Cancel	These properties allow controlling the state of the Cancel, Pause, and Previous buttons of the playbar applets. When set to **TRUE**, the respective button is disabled.
Disable Pause	
Disable Previous	

Property	Description
Display Name	The (translatable) text to be displayed in the Task UI when the task view is active.
Forward Button Type	Controls the behavior and label of the forward button. Possible values are:
	• **Next**: The button that proceeds to the next step is labeled **Next**.
	• **Submit**: The button label is **Submit**. Data will be committed to the business components. Typically used on the last task view.
	• **Finish**: Typically used on the last task view when all data has already been committed.
Retain Task Search Spec	**TRUE** and **FALSE** values control how the business component should handle the current search specifications from the task itself, the applet, or the user's query. When set to **TRUE** the current query is kept. When set to **FALSE**, the record set is retrieved with a new query execution.
Retain Applet Search Spec	
Retain User Search Spec	

The following procedure describes how to configure the first task view step, **AHA Partner Query Task View**, in our example task:

1. Select the **AHA Partner Query Task View** step in the task editor.

2. In the **Properties** window, enter the following values:

    ○ **Chapter**: Query

    ○ **Disable Previous**: TRUE

    ○ **Forward Button Type**: Next

    ○ **Display Name - String Override**: Enter query criteria

3. In the **Multi Value Property Window**, select the **Output Arguments** tab and create the following records:

Property Name	Type	Business Component	Business Component Field
AHA Partner Name	Business Component	AHA Partner Query TBC	Partner Name
AHA Partner CSN	Business Component	AHA Partner Query TBC	Partner CSN
AHA Partner City	Business Component	AHA Partner Query TBC	Partner City

4. Save your changes.

The previous configuration ensures that the **Previous** button in playbar applets displayed in the task view will be disabled (which makes sense because it is the first task view). The settings in the MVPW will assign the input from the end user from the transient business component's fields to task properties so we can use them later.

The remaining task views should be configured as follows using the **Properties** window:

- AHA Create Account Task View
    - Chapter: Partner
    - Forward Button Type: Next
    - Display Name - String Override: Create Partner Account

- AHA Create Quote Task View
    - Chapter: Quote
    - Forward Button Type: Next
    - Display Name - String Override: Create New Quote

- AHA Create Order Task View
    - Chapter: Order
    - Forward Button Type: Submit
    - Display Name - String Override: Create New Order

Setting the **Forward Button Type** property to **Submit** ensures that all open transactions are committed and the task proceeds to the end.

Configuring business service steps

Working with business services in tasks is similar to workflow processes. The following procedure describes how to configure the **Set Search Strings** business service step in our example flow and explains the details of the configuration:

1. Select the **Set Search Strings** step in the editor.
2. In the **Properties** window, enter the following values:
    - **Business Service: Workflow Utilities**
    - **Business Service Method: Echo**
    - **Chapter: Query**

3. In the **Output Arguments** tab of the **MVPW** enter the following records (set the **Type** property to **Expression** for all records):

Property Name	Value
AHA Name Search	IIf ([&AHA Partner Name] IS NULL,"[Name] LIKE '*'","[Name] ~LIKE '" + [&AHA Partner Name] + "'")
AHA CSN Search	IIf ([&AHA Partner CSN] IS NULL,""," " + [&AHA Query Operator] + " [CSN] ~LIKE '" + [&AHA Partner CSN] + "'")
AHA City Search	IIf ([&AHA Partner City] IS NULL,""," " + [&AHA Query Operator] + " EXISTS([City] ~LIKE '" + [&AHA Partner City] + "')")

4. Save your changes.

The purpose of the expressions is to prepare a set of valid search specifications for the Siebel Operation step. The IIf() function is used to determine whether the task property, referenced using square brackets, [and], and preceded by an ampersand (&) sign, is empty using the IS NULL operator.

The second argument of the IIf() function is returned when the task property is empty. In the cases of the **AHA CSN Search** and the **AHA City Search** properties, an empty string ("") will be returned. For the **AHA Name Search** property, the return value will be the [Name] LIKE '*'.

In case the task properties have values, the third argument of the IIf() function will be returned and the return values will be query strings, which are the results of concatenating the constant and variable values to a search string.

The search strings use the ~LIKE operator, which allows case insensitive search. Because the **City** field is a multi value field in the Account business component, we must use the EXISTS() function to search within the entire set of address records associated with the account.

Configuring Siebel Operation steps

Siebel Operation steps are widely used in tasks to invoke the **business component methods** needed to query or manipulate the record set. The following procedure describes how to configure the **Query Accounts** step of our example task. The step uses the search strings created by the previous invocation of the Workflow Utilities Echo method:

1. Select the **Query Accounts** step in the editor.
2. In the **Properties** window enter the following values:
   - ° **Business Component**: Account
   - ° **Chapter**: Query
   - ° **Operation**: Query
3. In the **Task Step Context** tab of the **MVPW**, create a new record with the following values:
   - ° **Name**: Query
   - ° **Type**: Expression
   - ° **Expression Business Component**: Account
   - ° **Filter Business Component**: Account
   - ° **Search Specification**: [&AHA Name Search] + [&AHA CSN Search] + [&AHA City Search]
4. Save your changes.

The previous expression concatenates the values of the task properties populated by the previous business service step to a single search specification, which is then used to query the Account business component.

The following is an example of what a generated search specification could look like:

```
[Name] ~LIKE 'ABC Corp.' AND EXISTS([City] ~LIKE 'Chicago')
```

A search spec like the previous would retrieve all account records that have a name of *ABC Corp.* (regardless of case, so records could also be named *abc Corp.*) and that have at least one address in *Chicago*.

The remaining Siebel Operation steps in the example task should be configured as follows:

- Create Partner:
  - ° Business Component: Account
  - ° Chapter: Partner
  - ° Defer Write Record: TRUE
  - ° Display Name - String Override: Create Partner Account
  - ° Operation: Insert

- In the **Fields** tab of the **MVPW**, create the following record:
  - **Field Name**: Partner Flag
  - **Type**: Literal
  - **Value**: Y

- Create Quote:
  - Business Component: Quote
  - Chapter: Quote
  - Defer Write Record: TRUE
  - Display Name - String Override: Create Quote
  - Operation: Insert
  - In the **Fields** tab of the **MVPW**, create the following record:
    - **Field Name**: Price List
    - **Type**: Literal
    - **Value**: Master Price List

> If you do not use the Siebel Sample Database, enter the name of a valid price list instead of *Master Price List*. This price list will be used as the default when there is no price list associated with the account. The Price List field in the Quote business component has been configured as a required field in a previous chapter.

- Create Order:
  - Business Component: Order Entry - Orders
  - Chapter: Order
  - Defer Write Record: TRUE
  - Display Name - String Override: Create Order
  - Operation: Insert
  - In the **Fields** tab of the **MVPW**, create the following record:
    - **Field Name**: Order Type
    - **Type**: Literal
    - **Value**: Sales Order

- Create Activity:
  - Business Component: Action
  - Chapter: Order

- ○ Defer Write Record: FALSE
- ○ Display Name - String Override: Create Activity
- ○ Operation: Insert
- ○ In the **Fields** tab of the **MVPW**, create the following records:

Field Name	Type	Value
Description	Literal	New customer documents have been created via Task UI
Type	Literal	Administration

Use the *Ctrl+S* keyboard shortcut or the **Save** button in the toolbar to save your changes frequently.

The **Defer Write Record** property for Siebel Operation steps controls whether the business component should write each record to the database when the step is executed or wait until a **Commit** step or the end of the task is reached. The business component will wait, deferring the write operation, when the **Defer Write Record** property is set to **TRUE**.

Configuring decision steps and branches

Another similarity to workflow processes lies within the configuration of conditional branches. We use decision points and define the conditions in the connectors leading from the point.

The following procedure describes how to configure the branching logic for the **Query Results** decision point in our example task flow:

1. Double-click the connector labeled **>1**, which connects the **Query Results** decision point to the **AHA Partner Query Task View** step.

2. In the **Compose Condition Criteria** dialog's lower section enter the following values:
   - ○ **Compare to**: Task Property
   - ○ **Object**: Siebel Operation Object Id
   - ○ **Operation**: All Must Match (Ignore Case)

3. Click the **New** button to the right of the **Values** list box.

4. Enter * as the value.

5. Click **OK**.

6. Click the **Add** button to add the new condition to the **Conditions** list in the upper part of the **Compose Condition Criteria** dialog.

7. Click **OK** to close the dialog.

8. Save your changes.

   In this connector, we check the **Siebel Operation Object Id** task property for a value of *, which is assigned automatically when the query result set contains more than one record. In this case, the task returns to the AHA Partner Query Task View so that the end user can enter more precise query criteria.

9. Double-click the connector labeled **0**, ending at the **Create Partner** step, and add the following condition:
   - ° **Compare to: Task Property**
   - ° **Object: Siebel Operation Object Id**
   - ° **Operation: Is Null**

10. Save your changes.

    The **0** connector is followed when the **Siebel Operation Object Id** task property is empty, which indicates that the query result contains no records. In this case, a new record must be created, which is facilitated by the Create Partner step and the AHA Create Account Task View.

11. Double-click the connector labeled **1** and enter the following two conditions:

Compare to	Object	Operation	Value
Task Property	Siebel Operation Object Id	Is Not Null	
Expression		All Must Match (Ignore Case)	`[&Siebel Operation Object Id] <> '*'`

12. Save your changes.

The two conditions in the **1** connector must both be satisfied in order for this connector to be selected. A non-empty (`Is Not Null`) Siebel Operation Object Id task property that does not have a value of * (`<> '*'`) is an indicator that only one record has been retrieved by the query (in that case, the Siebel Operation Object Id contains the ROW_ID of the record). The **1** connector leads to the **Create Quote?** decision point.

The remaining decision connectors, leading from the **Create Quote?** step, should be configured as follows:

- Create the following condition for the **Yes** connector:
  - ° **Compare To: Business Component**
  - ° **Object: Account**

- ◦ **Operation:** All Must Match (Ignore Case)
- ◦ **Field:** AHA Always Generate Quote Flag
- ◦ **Value:** Y

- Set the **Type** property for the **No** connector to **Default**.

The **Yes** connector will only be followed when the **AHA Always Generate Quote Flag** has a value of **Y** for the current account record. Subsequently, the **Create Quote** step is reached. Otherwise the **No** connector is followed and the **Create Order** step is reached.

Now that we have reached a point where we can test the task, we should validate it using the **Validate** command in the context menu. We must correct any errors that may be displayed.

A Siebel Tools archive file (AHA Sales Process Task.sif) is available with this chapter's code files. The file represents the AHA Sales Process task created in the preceding section.

Creating and using task groups

As indicated earlier in this chapter, a task must be listed in at least one task group. The task group itself must be associated with a standard view in order to make the task accessible to end users, including the developer who wants to test the task.

The following procedure describes how to create a new task group and associate it with the **Task Pane View**, the view definition that supports the task pane in which the list of tasks is displayed. By associating the task with the Task Pane View, the task will be accessible from any location in the Siebel Web Client, which is convenient for testing purposes:

1. If necessary, expose the **Task Group** type and the **View Task Group** subtype (of the View type) in the **Object Explorer**.
2. In the **Object Explorer**, select the **Task Group** type.
3. In the **Object List Editor**, create a new record with the following values:
    - ◦ **Name:** AHA Task Group
    - ◦ **Project:** AHA Task UI
    - ◦ **Display Name - String Override:** AHA Business Processes
4. In the **Object Explorer**, expand the **Task Group** type and select the **Task Group Item** type.

5. In the **Task Group Items** list, create a new record with the following values:
    - º **Action Invoked**: AHA Sales Process
    - º **Type**: Task
    - º **Sequence**: 10

6. Compile the AHA Task Group.
7. Navigate to the **Task Pane View**.
8. Check out or lock the view.
9. Expand the **View** type in the **Object Explorer** and select the **View Task Group** type.
10. In the **View Task Groups** list, create a new record with the following value:

    Task Group: AHA Task Group

11. Compile the Task Pane View.

A Siebel Tools archive file (Task Group.sif) is available with this chapter's code files. The file represents the new task group and the modified Task Pane View created in the preceding section.

Publishing, activating, and administering tasks

From our experience with the workflow process editor we are already familiar with the procedures related to publishing, activating, and administering workflow processes. The same functionality applies to tasks.

To publish and activate a task we click the **Publish/Activate** button in the **WF/Task Editor** toolbar, which is the same procedure as for workflow processes. This sets the task's **Status** property to **Completed** and copies the task definition to the runtime tables. The task definition is now read-only. We must click the **Revise** button to create a new editable version, another similarity to workflow processes.

The following procedure describes the steps necessary in the Siebel Web Client to administer an activated task and associate it with a responsibility:

1. Log in to the Siebel Mobile or Developer Web Client using an administrative user account.
2. Navigate to the **Administration - Application** screen, **Tasks** view.
3. In the **Registered Tasks** list applet, create a new record.

4. In the **Task Name** column, use the pick list to select the **AHA Sales Process** task. Only activated tasks appear in this list.

5. In the **Responsibilities** list at the bottom of the view, click the **New** button.

6. Select the **AHA Prototype** responsibility, or any other responsibility that you have, from the list.

7. Click **OK**.

8. Click the **Clear Cache** button on the **Registered Tasks** list applet.

9. Click the **Tasks** button in the toolbar to open the Task Pane.

10. Verify that the task is listed in the task pane.

Did you know?

In case the task has not been activated from Siebel Tools, we must use the **Task Deployment** view in the **Administration - Business Process** screen to locate and activate completed task definitions.

Testing and debugging tasks

The task UI framework, unlike the workflow process framework, does not provide a simulator. Task developers must therefore use their **Mobile or Developer Web Client** to test the task flow.

Under most circumstances it proves very useful to be able to inspect the state of the task properties and business components at each step of the task. To facilitate this, we can add the following entry in the [InfraUIFramework] section of the client's configuration file:

```
EnableRestrictedMenu = TRUE
```

This entry enables the **Debug Mode** item in the **Tools** menu of the Siebel client. We can use this menu item to set the application into task debug mode. In this mode, a pop-up window opens automatically between the task steps and allows us to inspect the task properties and business component instances.

The following screenshot shows the **AHA Sales Process** task in debug mode after clicking the **Next** button in the first task view:

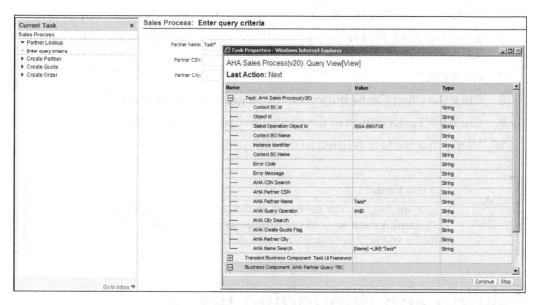

The **Task Properties** window displays the current values of all task properties. By clicking the **Continue** button in the **Task Properties** window we can proceed to the next step in the task.

To test a task it is beneficial to discuss test cases with the business analyst team in order to ensure that the task is tested under real-life conditions.

When errors or undesired behavior occur, we must cancel the task by clicking the **Cancel** button in the playbar applet and log off the Siebel client. In Siebel Tools we must then use the **Revise** functionality to create a new task version, correct the problem, and publish and activate the task again before we can log in to the client to continue testing.

Using applet messages

Applet messages have been introduced along with the Task UI to accommodate the increased need for displaying contextual information to the end user.

The **Applet Message** type is a subtype of the **Applet** type. It supports the use of symbolic strings for easy translation. Furthermore, we can add placeholders to the text, which can be replaced with the content of business component fields at runtime.

The following procedure describes how to create an applet message for the **AHA Sales Process** task. The purpose of the message is to confirm the billing address when the end user enters the order header details in the **AHA Simple Order Form Applet**:

1. Check out or lock the **AHA Symbolic Strings** project if necessary.

2. Create a new Symbolic String with the following values:
   - **Name**: X_AHA_TASKMSG_ORDER_1
   - **Project**: AHA Symbolic Strings

3. Create a new **Symbolic String Locale** record for the new symbolic string with the following values:
   - **Language**: ENU
   - **String value**: A new order will be created for %1 at %2 (this is the billing address).

    The placeholder text %1 and %2 will be replaced with field values at runtime.

4. Compile the **X_AHA_TASKMSG_ORDER_1** symbolic string.

5. Expose the **Applet Message** subtype in the **Object Explorer** if necessary.

6. Navigate to the **AHA Simple Order Form Applet**.

7. Check out or lock the applet if necessary.

8. In the **Object Explorer**, expand the Applet type and select the **Applet Message** type.

9. In the Applet Messages list, create a new record with the following values:
   - **Name**: Message 1
   - **Text Message - String Reference**: X_AHA_TASKMSG_ORDER_1

10. In the **Object Explorer**, expand the **Applet Message** type and select the **Applet Message Variable** type.

11. In the **Applet Message Variables** list, create the following records:

Field	Value
Account	1
Calculated Primary Bill To Address	2

This maps the *Account* field to the %1 placeholder and the *Calculated Primary Bill To Address* field to the %2 placeholder.

12. Navigate back to the AHA Simple Order Form Applet.

13. Open the web layout editor for the AHA Simple Order Form Applet.

14. In the **Controls/Columns** window, select the **Edit** mode.

15. Select all controls by drawing a rectangular shape across them in the editor canvas.

16. Use the arrow buttons on the keyboard to move all controls down in order to create free space on top of the applet.

17. From the **Palettes** window, drag a **Field** control to the free space on top of the form.

18. In the **Properties** window, enter the following values:

    ○ **Name:** AHA Message 1

    ○ **Field:** Message 1

    ○ **HTML Display Mode:** DontEncodeData

    ○ **HTML Type:** PlainText

19. Resize the new control so that it spans across the applet.

20. Save your changes and close the editor.

21. Compile the AHA Simple Order Form Applet.

We can now log on to the Mobile or Developer Web Client and test the AHA Sales Process task.

 Search for a non-existent account in the first view, then create a new account with a billing address, and uncheck the Always Quote flag. The next view should display similarly to the following screenshot.

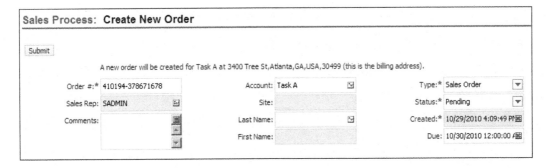

Sales Process: **Create New Order**

| Submit |

A new order will be created for Task A at 3400 Tree St,Atlanta,GA,USA,30499 (this is the billing address).

Order #:*	410194-378671678		Account:	Task A		Type:*	Sales Order
Sales Rep:	SADMIN		Site:			Status:*	Pending
Comments:			Last Name:			Created:*	10/29/2010 4:09:49 PM
			First Name:			Due:	10/30/2010 12:00:00 /

As we can see in the screenshot, the account name and billing address information appears at the placeholder location in the message text.

Did you know?

In the previous example, we specified **DontEncodeData** for the HTML Display Mode property. This allows us to apply HTML formatting such as CSS styles, colors, and line breaks within the message text more easily.

Summary

The Siebel Task UI can be efficiently used to guide end users through complex business processes. Because of its similarity to Siebel Workflow, developers only have to master a slight learning curve.

In this chapter, we discussed the repository object types that are used in the Task UI.

A case study example was provided to discuss all aspects of working with the Task UI such as creating transient business components, task applets, task views, and the like.

The chapter also explained how to publish, activate, administer, and debug tasks.

In the final section, we learned how to use translatable applet messages for more precise end user guidance.

In the next chapter, we will learn how to use Siebel eScript to extend the Siebel CRM functionality.

22

Extending Siebel CRM Functionality with eScript

In the previous chapters of this book, we explored many aspects of configuring Siebel CRM applications in order to adapt the system to our customer's requirements. All the different techniques discussed so far have one thing in common: they are **declarative**. This means that the developer creates and modifies records in the Siebel Repository and defines objects by editing their properties via the Siebel Tools user interface. At no time is it necessary to modify existing code or write code such as SQL scripts or C++ programs.

In the late nineties, when Siebel CRM was in its early versions and declarative options were limited, for example Siebel Workflow did not exist until *Siebel 2000*, developers often relied upon the possibility of extending the existing functionality with custom written program code.

Becoming more mature in versions 7 and 8, the preconfigured functionality of Siebel CRM is often sufficient to implement complex requirements such as in integration scenarios or additional program logic.

However, under certain circumstances it may still be necessary to write custom code. Because Siebel CRM is a complex framework, proper understanding of its functionality and intricacies is a key prerequisite to writing code that fits into this framework flawlessly.

In this and the following chapter, we will learn how the Siebel scripting environment allows us to extend Siebel CRM functionality.

This chapter is structured as follows:

- Introduction to Siebel Scripting
- When to use Siebel Scripting
- Creating a custom business service
- Declaring business service methods and arguments
- Testing and debugging scripts

Introduction to Siebel scripting

The Siebel scripting framework, internally named *extension language* or *EL*, allows custom developers to add code to application, applet, business component, and business service definitions. The following programming languages are supported:

- **eScript**: By far the most popular scripting language for Siebel CRM. Siebel eScript is an implementation of the **ECMA-262** standard, which is also the base of the popular JavaScript language. Siebel eScript is supported on all operating systems on which Siebel CRM can be installed.

- **SiebelVB**: A derivative of Visual Basic is supported as a Siebel scripting language as well, albeit its importance and adoption by developers have declined over the last decade. VBScript is only supported on Microsoft Windows operating systems.

- **Browser JavaScript**: Interpreted by the browser, code implemented in *pure* JavaScript allows developers to manipulate the objects in the browser's **document object model (DOM)**. The Siebel scripting framework provides a set of JavaScript functions to interact with the Siebel objects such as applets and controls.

- **Java**: So-called Java business services allow developers to execute Java code within the Siebel framework.

- **C++ and C#**: A custom **dynamic link library (DLL)** developed for Windows operating systems or a shared object (.so) developed for UNIX-based operating systems can be invoked from within the scripting framework.

In this and the following chapter, we will focus solely on eScript and Browser JavaScript.

Server and browser scripts

Siebel scripts can be executed by the **Siebel Object Manager**, which supports the user session on the Siebel Server, the `siebel.exe` program (also known as the Mobile Web Client), or the browser executable. We refer to scripts that are executed by a Siebel executable as server scripts and to scripts that are executed by the browser as browser scripts.

It must be noted here that the available functionality for browser scripts is limited and that the option of executing JavaScript code in the browser should be regarded only as the last resort.

The following diagram illustrates the architectural differences between server and browser scripts by comparing the Siebel Object Manager against the browser:

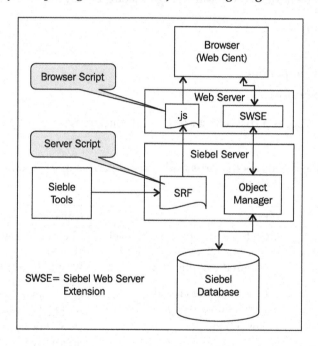

From the previous diagram, we can learn the following:

- All scripts, browser and server script alike, are developed in Siebel Tools and compiled in the SRF file

- Server scripts are read from the SRF file and interpreted by the Object Manager (or `siebel.exe` on mobile clients) at runtime

- Browser scripts must be extracted from the SRF file, using the `genbscript.exe` utility discussed later in this chapter, and placed as JavaScript (`.js`) files on the web server that hosts the **Siebel Web Server Extension (SWSE)**
- The browser downloads the JavaScript files from the web server and interprets the browser scripts at runtime

In this chapter, we will only discuss server scripts. All of the following information applies to server scripts only. Browser scripts will be discussed in the next chapter.

Server scripts are usually deployed for data operations in absence of the user. This means that developers can write script code that invokes business component methods in order to work with the record sets behind the scenes.

Server scripts can be added to the following object types in the Siebel Repository:

- Application
- Applet
- Business Component
- Business Service

Each object type exposes a discrete set of event handlers where developers can place their code.

The following table discusses the pros and cons of scripting to be taken into consideration for each object type:

Object Type	Pros	Cons
Application	Code on the application level is accessible from all objects within the application. Event handlers for view navigation are exposed by this object type.	The fact that the code is accessible only from objects within the application can cause problems. Business service methods can be invoked from everywhere and should be considered as an alternative.

Object Type	Pros	Cons
Applet	Developers can implement highly specialized functionality for an individual applet. Button and menu item activation can be controlled with great flexibility.	Placing too much code on the applet (user interface) level compromises the concept of implementing business logic on the business component layer. In addition, the possibility of creating duplicate code is very high. Business services or business component user properties or applet user properties should be considered as an alternative.
Business Component	The natural place for business logic. It is possible to handle all events regardless of whether they originate from end users or external systems.	Scripts on the business component level are object-specific and not reusable on other business components. This could lead to code duplication and therefore code maintenance problems.
Business Service	Writing business service code is considered the best way to stay *close* to the Siebel CRM standard. Business services have the highest level of reusability. When implemented professionally, custom business services extend Siebel CRM functionality without negatively affecting a potential upgrade.	Writing business services requires a high degree of programming skills. There is a risk of *reinventing the wheel* when developers ignore the rich library of standard business services delivered by Oracle.

Application event handlers

The following table describes the most important event handlers for server scripts on the **Application** object type. For details on the Siebel event framework, please refer to *Chapter 16, Menus and Buttons*:

Event Handler	Description
Application_Start	Code in this event handler is executed when the Siebel application starts. The command line that invoked the application is passed as the `CommandLine` input argument.
Application_PreNavigate	This event handler is executed before ("pre") a new view is loaded. The name of the destination view and its associated business objects are passed as input arguments.
Application_Navigate	Being a "post" event handler (no "pre" in the name), this one is executed after a new view has been loaded.

Applet event handlers

The following table describes the most important event handlers for server scripts on applets:

Event Handler	Description
WebApplet_PreCanInvokeMethod	This event handler is called every time and for every method that can be invoked from the applet (from buttons or applet menu items) at applet load time and when the end user navigates to a different record. This event handler can be useful to complex access control logic to prevent that certain users clicking buttons or menu items.
	Simple access control mechanisms however should be implemented declaratively using the `Named Method` or `CanInvokeMethod` user properties as a declarative alternative.
WebApplet_PreInvokeMethod	Commonly used to *trap* custom method invocations on the applet level. For a more centralized approach, the `PreInvokeMethod` event handler on the business component should be used.

Business component event handlers

The following table describes the most important event handlers for business component server scripts:

Event Handler	Description
BusComp_PreInvokeMethod	This event handler is invoked every time a *specialized* method (a method other than `NewRecord` or other standard methods) is invoked. Developers typically use this event handler to *trap* custom methods on the business component level.
BusComp_PreWriteRecord	Invoked before the Siebel core code commits data changes (insert, update, delete) to the database. By using the `CancelOperation` return value, developers can prevent the Siebel core code executing, which makes this event handler very popular for validation purposes. (See later section for more information on the `CancelOperation` return value.)
BusComp_PreQuery	Invoked before a query is executed on the business component. Mainly used to validate the query criteria entered by the user. As with any *pre*-event handler, developers can verify the current situation and decide to cancel the operation or continue to execute the event flow.
BusComp_SetFieldValue	Invoked when a field value has been changed by an end user, a script, a workflow process or an EAI interface. The current field name is passed as an input argument.
BusComp_PreNewRecord BusComp_NewRecord BusComp_PreDeleteRecord BusComp_DeleteRecord	Among other event handlers, these pairs (the *pre* and *post* part) of event handlers can be used to write code that is executed before and after a certain data operation (new, delete) takes place.

It can be noted here that the business component object type supports the highest number of event handlers compared with other object types.

Business service event handlers

The following table describes all available event handlers for business service server scripts:

Event Handler	Description
Service_PreInvokeMethod	The typical entry point for custom business service methods. Developers use this event handler to *trap* the invoked method and invoke custom functions to process the input property set and create the output property set.
Service_PreCanInvokeMethod	When the business service is invoked from a user interface element such as a menu item or toolbar button, we can use this event handler to programmatically enable or disable the UI elements depending on business logic.
Service_InvokeMethod	Can be used for post-processing a method invocation. Typically not used for custom business services.

The script editor

As indicated previously, all scripts — eScript, SiebelVB, or browser JavaScript – are written and maintained in Siebel Tools. The script editor for eScript provides **syntax highlighting** and inline **script assistance**. The following screenshot shows the eScript editor in Siebel Tools:

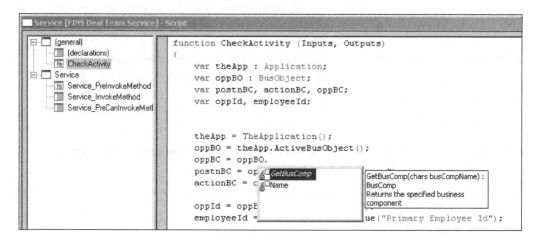

The screenshot shows a portion of the eScript code for the `CheckActivity` method of the preconfigured **FINS Deal Team Service** business service. The original code has been slightly modified to support the **ScriptAssist** feature, which is visible in the screenshot, as well as a pop-up window displaying the available methods for the object type.

The ScriptAssist feature is part of the **ST eScript engine** (ST is short for *strongly typed*), which has become the default eScript engine in Siebel 8. The ST eScript engine supports **strongly defined data types** for variables. Once a variable is strongly typed, by adding a colon and the data type after the variable declaration, the ScriptAssist pop-up dialog can display the available methods for this data type. In the preceding screenshot, the Script Assist popup displays the methods for the BusObject data type. In addition, a tool tip text displays details about the selected method.

Did you know?

The system preference `Enable ST Script Engine` must be set to **TRUE** to enable the ST eScript engine.

Apart from the ScriptAssist feature, the ST eScript engine also allows for faster script performance and less memory consumption compared with older Siebel versions. To realize the performance gain and memory savings, variables must be strongly typed.

The ST eScript engine is backwards compatible with eScript written for its predecessor version.

To open the script editor we can right-click any application, applet, business component, or business service object definition and select **Edit Server Scripts** from the context menu. The explorer panel in the script editor allows us to select the preconfigured event handlers. The (general) section in the explorer pane is used to create, inspect, and modify custom functions or global variable declarations.

We can configure the behavior and font (name and size) used by the script editor in the **Scripting** tab of the development tools options dialog, which we can open by navigating to the **View | Options** menu item.

The following screenshot shows the Scripting tab with example options:

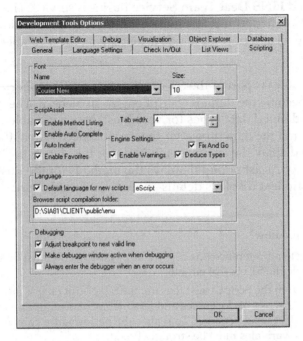

The settings in the **ScriptAssist** section are available only when the ST eScript engine is active and drive the behavior of the ScriptAssist popup as well as other functionalities of the script editor.

The following table explains the settings in the ScriptAssist section:

Setting	Description
Enable Method Listing	When checked, the ScriptAssist popup is active. Otherwise, it is turned off.
Enable Auto Complete	When checked, developers can use the *Ctrl*+SPACE keyboard shortcut to automatically complete keywords such as method names. Otherwise, the feature is turned off.
Auto Indent	When checked, any new line in the script code starts below the first character of the previous line. This assists in writing readable code.
Enable Favorites	When checked, the ScriptAssist popup will display recently used elements on top of the list in *italic* formatting.
Fix And Go	When checked, the Fix And Go feature allows developers to make changes to the code during the debug cycle without the need to compile again.

Setting	Description
Enable Warnings	When checked, the compiler will display warnings in addition to error messages.
Deduce Types	When checked, the compiler will try to deduce the data type of a non-typed variable by using the data type of functions or objects assigned to the variable.

The script debugger

The Siebel Tools scripting environment includes a debugging toolkit, which provides functionalities such as setting breakpoints and stepping through the code while inspecting variable values in the Watch window.

In order for the debugger to work we must correctly set the **Debug options** in the Siebel Tools options dialog. Setting these options has already been described in Chapter 2, *Developer Tasks*.

The script performance profiler

Available since version 8.1, Siebel Tools includes a script performance profiler, which allows the developer to identify slow performing code lines during the development and debugging cycle. We will discuss the script performance profiler in the next chapter.

The Siebel eScript language

The idea of this book is to teach and demonstrate aspects of application configuration and customization for Siebel CRM. The book is neither intended to replace Oracle's Siebel documentation or training offerings nor can this and the next chapter on scripting serve to teach all aspects of the Siebel eScript language.

Before you start to use Siebel scripting, you should verify whether you fulfill the following prerequisite requirements:

- Working knowledge of at least one major programming language such as Java or C++
- Familiarity with programming concepts such as exception handling and encapsulation
- Good command of Siebel Tools
- Exposure to professional training in Siebel CRM development and scripting

In the following section, we will discuss the most important aspects of the Siebel eScript language and provide details on where to find more information.

As indicated previously, Siebel eScript is based on ECMA-262, a standard established by the European association for standardizing information and communication systems (formerly known as ECMA — European Computer Manufacturer's Association). ECMA-262 is also the base for JavaScript, which became popular for its wide adoption in web development. The Siebel ST eScript engine supports ECMA Script version 4.

The language specification for ECMA-262 can be downloaded from the ECMA website at `http://www.ecma-international.org/publications/standards/Ecma-262.htm`.

Because it has the same base as JavaScript, developers who are familiar with the latter will find it easy to use Siebel eScript.

Oracle makes the documentation on Siebel eScript available in the **Siebel eScript Language Reference,** which is part of the Siebel documentation library (also known as Siebel Bookshelf). The Siebel eScript Language Reference can be viewed online or downloaded at `http://download.oracle.com/docs/cd/E14004_01/books/eScript/booktitle.html`.

It is important to understand that the majority of eScript code will be written in order to access and manipulate objects in the **Siebel Object Model**. This includes applets, business components, business objects, and other object types, which constitute the user interface and business logic layer in the Siebel Repository. Standard ECMA Script has no methods to access these object types.

For this reason, the Siebel scripting framework provides an **application programming interface** (**API**) to access the objects in the Siebel Object Model. This API is documented in the **Siebel Object Interfaces Reference** guide, which is part of the Siebel Bookshelf as well. The guide can be viewed online or downloaded at `http://download.oracle.com/docs/cd/E14004_01/books/OIRef/booktitle.html`.

In the following section, we will discuss some basic concepts of Siebel eScript.

Variable declaration and initialization

Variables are declared with the keyword `var`. A simple but valid variable declaration looks as follows:

```
var s;
```

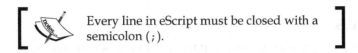

Every line in eScript must be closed with a semicolon (`;`).

The preceding code declares a variable named `s`.

We can initialize the variable along with the declaration such as in the following code snippet:

```
var s = "Test";
```

The preceding code declares a variable named `s` and initializes it with the string `Test`.

In order to gain full advantage of the ST eScript engine, we should also declare the data type of the variable. To do so, we enter a colon (`:`) after the variable name and press *Ctrl*+SPACE to open the **ScriptAssist** popup which helps us in selecting an appropriate data type.

The following screenshot shows the ScriptAssist pop-up with the example code:

After pressing *Ctrl*+SPACE we can continue to type the first characters of the desired data type name. The highlight in the ScriptAssist window will navigate to the appropriate entry and we can press *Enter* to continue with the highlighted text. Alternatively we can type the first characters of the data type name — such as `st` — directly after the colon and press *Ctrl*+SPACE to use the auto complete feature to complete the text to `String`.

The resulting code snippet should look like this:

```
var s : String = "Test";
```

The previous code is a valid declaration of the variable s of the data type String with an initial value of Test.

Comments

We should make ample use of commentary text in our script code to facilitate the understanding of the code when others read it. Comments can be enclosed between /* and */ or preceded with //.

The Siebel script editor highlights comments in green.

The following code snippet demonstrates the use of comments:

```
/* Variable Declaration */
var s : String = "Test"; //used 'String' because
//of more functionality
//than chars
```

The text Variable Declaration is treated as a comment similar to the text after the two forward slashes (//) in the second line.

Blocks and functions

Like many other programming languages, eScript supports conditional blocks (if, switch), loops (while, for), exception handling (try, catch, finally), and custom functions.

All code lines within a block or function must be enclosed between curly brackets — { and }.

The following code snippets demonstrate the correct implementation of code blocks:

```
if (s == "Test")
{
  msg = "Test value found.";
}
```

The first line of the preceding code declares an `if` block. The condition to enter the `if` block is that the `s` variable has a value of `Test`. The code between the curly brackets will only be executed when the condition evaluates to true:

```
for (i = 0; i < 10; i++)
{
   msg = "Value is " + ToString(i);
}
```

The preceding implementation of a `for` loop shows that the syntax requires the specification of a counter initialization (`i = 0`), a condition (`i < 10`), and an increment (`i++`). When the condition is no longer satisfied (the value of the counter `i` is 10 or greater) the loop will end. The code statement within the block will be executed multiple times as long as the condition is satisfied.

The ST eScript engine requires explicit type conversion as demonstrated in the previous code snippet using the `ToString()` function, which converts a numeric value (held by the `i` variable) to a string so that the `msg` variable value is the result of the concatenation of two strings. String concatenation is accomplished using the plus (+) sign.

To declare custom functions we must navigate to the `(general)` node in the script editor's explorer pane. We expand the `(general)` node and select the `(declarations)` sub-node. In the script editor, we then enter the `function` keyword followed by the function name and the input parameter list in parentheses. The following code snippet serves as an example:

```
function myTest(x,y)
```

After this line, we press the *Enter* key. We can then observe that a new entry for our function is added to the `(general)` node.

The following screenshot illustrates this behavior:

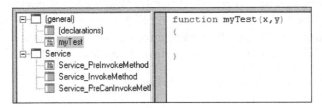

As we can see in the previous screenshot, the script editor automatically adds an empty block for the new function.

In addition, we can add data type declarations for the input arguments and the output argument by modifying the function body as follows:

```
function myTest(x:float,y:float) : float
```

In the previous example, the x and y input arguments must be of the float data type and the return value of the function will be float as well.

The following code example completes the function declaration with a simple return statement that multiplies x and y:

```
function myTest(x : float ,y : float) : float
{
   return x*y;
}
```

The return statement must be used in order to pass back the value of the expression or variable that follows the return keyword. Any code after a return statement is not executed.

Exception handling

As Siebel script developers we must be aware of the fact that our script, as short or long as it may be, will always be part of a much bigger and more complex framework. Therefore, we must ensure that our script handles exceptions professionally.

The Siebel eScript language provides try and catch blocks, which should be part of any script however short it may be. When the code within a try block executes with an error, the script will jump to the catch block where we can place statements to handle the error condition.

For example we could *try* to set a field value on a business component in our main code block. When the set operation fails because of the value not being part of a pick list, an exception condition is reached. When our main code is part of a try block, the script interpreter will jump to the catch block where we can use the Exception object passed to the catch block to extract information about the error and take action such as notifying the end user or writing to a file.

The following example code illustrates this concept:

```
try
{
  var f : String = "New Value";
  var oBC : BusComp;
  //skipping code for readability
  oBC.SetFieldValue("Status",f);
```

```
      //more code here...
   }
   catch(e)
   {
      TheApplication().RaiseErrorText(e.toString());
   }
```

The preceding code spans a `try` block across the code, which instantiates a string and a business component. For the sake of readability, some code is omitted. The `SetFieldValue()` function of the business component object sets the Status field to the value of the `f` variable.

In the case of an error, the `catch` block is reached. The input parameter `e` – we can use an arbitrary name, but `e` is commonly used – contains the `Exception` object that is used in the `catch` block's only code line to extract the verbose error message using the `toString()` function of the `Exception` object `e`.

The `RaiseErrorText()` function of the object returned by the `TheApplication()` function can be used to return from the code with an error message, which is displayed to the end user.

The previous code snippet introduces concepts of Siebel-specific object access methods — the Siebel API – which we will discuss in the next section.

Cleaning up

In order to avoid problems caused by memory being reserved for script objects, a situation which is commonly known as **memory leak**, we must destroy all objects that were instantiated in the script once they are no longer used. This is typically accomplished by using a `finally` block as shown in the following code snippet:

```
   try
   {
      var f : String = "New Value";
      var oBC : BusComp;
      //more code here...
   }
   catch(e)
   {
      TheApplication().RaiseErrorText(e.toString());
   }
   finally
   {
      oBC = null;
      f = null;
   }
```

The previous code example shows the typical location of the `finally` block after the `catch` block. Setting all objects to `null` in the reverse order of their initialization as shown in the previous example code is a recommended practice for ensuring that the garbage collector, part of the script interpreter, clears the allocated memory.

Siebel object interfaces

As indicated previously, Siebel objects such as application, applet, and business component expose a predefined set of methods to interact with them. The following object types support eScript methods and are documented in the **Siebel Object Interfaces** reference guide:

- Application
- Applet
- Business Component
- Business Object
- Business Service
- Property Set

In the following section we will describe the most commonly used methods for the object types mentioned previously.

Application object methods

The following table describes the most important eScript methods for the Application object type:

Method	Description and Example
TheApplication()	Returns an object reference to the application object: `var theApp = TheApplication();`

ActiveBusObject()	Returns an object reference to the currently active business object:
	 `var oBO : BusObject;`
	 `oBO = theApp.ActiveBusObject();`

ActiveViewName()	Returns the name of the active view:
	 `var currView : String;`
	 `currView = theApp.ActiveViewName();`

GetBusObject("Name")	Returns an object reference to the business object named as the input parameter:
	 `var oBO : BusObject;`
	 `oBO = theApp.GetBusObject("Account");`

Method	Description and Example
GetService("Name")	Returns an object reference to the business service named as the input parameter: ```\nvar oSvc : Service;\noSvc = theApp.GetService("EAI File\n Transport");\n```
LookupMessage("Category","Name",arguments)	Returns the translated message text of a message object definition in the category specified by the first input parameter. An arbitrary number of additional arguments can be passed and will be used to replace placeholders in the text. Placeholders are defined for example as %1: ```\ntheApp.LookupMessage("AHA\n Messages","Dialog1",this.Name());\n```
NewPropertySet()	Returns an object reference to a new empty property set instance: ```\nvar oPS : PropertySet;\noPS = theApp.NewPropertySet();\n```
GetProfileAttr("Name") SetProfileAttr("Name","Value")	These two methods support reading and writing profile attributes that serve as globally available variables throughout a user session: ```\ntheApp.SetProfileAttr("AHA1","Test");\nvar t : String;\nt = theApp.GetProfileAttr("AHA1");\n```
RaiseError("Name","Value") RaiseErrorText("Text")	The RaiseError() method retrieves a translatable error message from the **User Defined Errors** message category and replaces placeholders in the text with the values passed as input arguments (see next section for an example). The RaiseErrorText() method uses a value passed as the input argument. Both methods raise an error, as their names suggest, and any code afterwards is not executed. Widely used to display (error) messages to end users as a dialog is displayed automatically.
TraceOn("File","Type","Selection") Trace("Text") TraceOff()	The trace methods allow developers to control the content and amount of *trace files*, which are useful for troubleshooting and debugging. Tracing will be discussed in the next chapter.

Applet object methods

The following table describes the most important eScript methods for the Applet object type:

Method	Description and Example

BusComp()	Returns an object reference to the business component of the applet:
	
	 ```var oBC : BusComp;```
	 ```oBC = this.BusComp();```
	
	 The previous code example uses the this keyword to reference the current object. The code will only work in an applet server script.

BusObject()	Returns an object reference to the business object of the applet's business component.
	
	 ```var oBO : BusObject;```
	 ```oBO = this.BusObject();```

InvokeMethod("Method",Arguments)	Allows invoking of documented methods. The first input parameter is the name of the method. The second is the name of an Array object that contains the input arguments for the method.

Business component methods

The Business Component object type offers the richest set of methods among all objects exposed by the Siebel scripting framework. Script developers use the business component methods to access, modify, and query the data represented by the business component and its fields. The following table describes the most important eScript methods for the Business Component object type:

Method	Description and Example

ActivateField("Field")
 	
ActivateMultipleFields("PropertySet")
	Activates the field named in the input argument or in the input property set (for multiple fields at once when using the `ActivateMultipleFields()` method). Must be used to prepare the business component for queries in order to activate fields that are not active at runtime. Fields are considered active if they fall into at least one of the following categories:
	
	• Mapped to a visible control or list column of the active applet
	
	• Used in a calculated field mapped by the active applet
	
	• **Force Active** property is set to **TRUE**
	
	• **Link Specification** property is set to **TRUE**
	
	• System fields (always active)
	
	`var oBC : BusComp = oBO.`
	`GetBusComp("Account");`
	`oBC.ActivateField("Description");`

ClearToQuery()	This method brings the business component in query mode and prepares it for defining search and sort specifications: `oBC.ClearToQuery();`

SetSearchSpec("Field","Value")
 	
SetSearchExpr("Expression")
	Used to prepare a query. `SetSearchSpec()` must be used in conjunction with a field name and a value. `SetSearchExpr()` takes a **Siebel Query Language** search expression as the input parameter, which makes it useful for more complex query criteria.
	
	`oBC.SetSearchSpec("Name","AHA");`
	`var s = "[Name] LIKE '" + name +`
	`"'";`
	`oBC.SetSearchExpr(s);`

SetSortSpec("SortSpec")	Sets the sort specification. Also used to prepare a query:
	
	`oBC.SetSortSpec("Name`
	`(ASCENDING)");`

Method	Description and Example
SetViewMode(Mode)	Sets the view mode of the business component. The following are valid values for the input argument: • SalesRepView (similar to a "My" view) • ManagerView (similar to a "My Team's view) • OrganizationView (similar to an "All" view) • AllView (similar to an "across Organizations" view) `oBC.SetViewMode(AllView);` Note: The input arguments for the SetViewMode() method are constants and must be used without quotes.
ExecuteQuery(Mode) ExecuteQuery2(Mode,Flag)	Executes the query with the current set of search and sort specifications. The two possible Mode input arguments control how the resulting record set can be accessed. The `ExecuteQuery2()` method also accepts a flag (**"TRUE"** or **"FALSE"**) to ignore the current maximum cursor size. When the flag is set to **"TRUE"** the query retrieves all records regardless of the maximum defined. The **Mode** input argument can be set as follows: • **ForwardOnly**: The record set can only be parsed forward from the first to the last record. • **ForwardBackward**: The record set can be parsed forward and backward. This is the default value if the Mode input argument is not provided and results in slower performance. `oBC.ExecuteQuery(ForwardOnly);`

Method	Description and Example

FirstRecord()
 	
NextRecord()
 	
PreviousRecord()
 	
LastRecord()
	These navigation methods allow script developers to set the cursor in the record set of the business component. All methods return a Boolean value of TRUE or FALSE indicating success or failure of the operation.
	
	``
	if (oBC.FirstRecord())
	{
	   //process data
	}
	``
	
	The previous code example uses an if block to check if there is at least one, the first, record in the business component's record set. As a result of the method invocation, the cursor will be set on the first record of the record set.

GetFieldValue("Field")
 	
SetFieldValue("Field","Value")
 	
GetFormattedFieldValue("Field")
 	
SetFormattedFieldValue("Field","Value")
	Used to get or set values from the field specified in the first input argument. The methods with *Formatted* in the name return and accept field values in the current locale formatting. For example, a script executed on a German object manager will return the date value of 1st of May 2011 as *1.5.2011*.
	
	``
	oBC.GetFieldValue("Name");
	oBC.SetFieldValue("Description","Test");
	``

Method	Description and Example
NewRecord(Indicator) DeleteRecord() WriteRecord()	These methods are also typically invoked by end users via applet buttons. In eScript we can use the `NewRecord()` method to create new records or copy the current record depending on the `Indicator` input argument, which can have one of the following values: • **NewBefore**: Creates a new record as the new first record of the record set • **NewAfter**: Creates a new record as the new last record of the record set • **NewBeforeCopy**: Copies the current record and places the copy at the beginning of the record set • **NewAfterCopy**: Copies the current record and places the copy at the end of the record set The `DeleteRecord()` method is used to delete the current record. The `WriteRecord()` method must be invoked to *commit* record modifications and save the current record.
GetPickListBusComp("Field") GetMVGBusComp("Field")	These two methods allow quick and easy instantiation of the business components referenced by a pick list field or a multi value field. Script developers must use these methods to access and modify these types of fields.

Business object methods

The following table describes the most important eScript method for the Business Object type:

Method	Description and Example
GetBusComp("Name")	Returns an object reference to the business component specified by the input argument. ```\nvar theApp = TheApplication();\nvar oBO : BusObject;\nvar oBC : BusComp;\noBO = theApp.GetBusObject("Account");\noBC = oBO.GetBusComp("Account");\n```

Business service object methods

The following table describes the most important eScript method for the Business Service object type:

Method	Description and Example
InvokeMethod("Method", InputPS, OutputPS)	This method must be used to invoke a method of the business service. The first input argument is the name of the method. The `Input PS` argument is a **Property Set** variable that contains the input argument for the method. The `Output PS` argument is a reference to a second property set that contains the output arguments of the method after its execution. An example for invoking a business service method via eScript will be given in the next chapter.

Property set object methods

The following table describes the most important eScript methods for property sets:

Method	Description and Example

SetProperty("Name","Value")	Used to set a property, referenced by the first input argument, to a value that is passed as the second argument. If the property does not exist, it is created. If it exists, the value gets overwritten:
	
	```var oPS = theApp.NewPropertySet();```
	```oPS.SetProperty("Arg1","Value 1");```

GetProperty("Name")	Reads the value of the property referenced by the input argument:
	
	```var s : String;```
	```s = oPS.GetProperty("Arg1");```

GetType()
 	
 SetType("TypeValue")
 	
 GetValue()
 	
 SetValue("Value")
	These methods can be used to get or set the reserved **Type** and **Value** properties of a property set.
	
	```var t : String = "Test";```
	```oPS.SetType(t);```

AddChild(PropertySet)
 	
 InsertChildAt(PropertySet, index)
	Adds the property set referenced by the first input argument as a child property set. The `InsertChildAt()` method allows specification of an index number to position the child property set:
	
	```var childPS = theApp.NewPropertySet();```
	```oPS.AddChild(childPS);```

Method	Description and Example
GetChild(index)	Returns a reference to the child property set at the index location:
	`var readPS = theApp.NewPropertySet();` `readPS = oPS.GetChild(0);`
Copy()	Creates a copy of the current property set:
	`var copyPS = theApp.NewPropertySet();` `copyPS = oPS.Copy();`

When to use Siebel scripting

Before we continue to learn how to implement scripts, it is necessary to mention that whenever we write script code in Siebel, there is a high risk that one or more of the following situations might occur:

- Similar functionality already exists in the standard Siebel CRM application
- Runtime errors or memory leaks negatively affect the application
- The performance of the application degenerates
- Maintenance and upgrade tasks become more difficult

To avoid any of the preceding things, we should try to fulfill customer requirements with administrative or declarative solutions, which the Siebel application framework provides in abundance, before we resort to scripting.

For example, we can use Siebel Audit Trail to track data changes instead of writing business component scripts, which do the same thing.

The Siebel Workflow framework, discussed in previous chapters, is used intensively by Oracle engineering to implement even the most complex requirements. Whenever additional functionality is needed, Oracle engineers write business services to implement the new logic. By trying to favor administrative solutions and following the path drawn by Oracle engineering, we can dramatically reduce the amount of custom code, which has an overall positive effect on our project.

The following diagram may prove helpful when we have to decide how to resolve any given requirement:

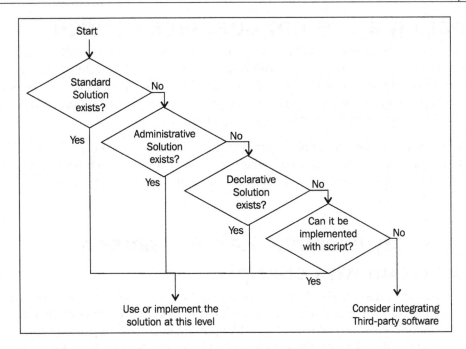

The previous diagram shows that we should start with evaluating the standard Siebel CRM functionality first. If the requirement can be met by using the standard functionality, we should use it.

When the standard functionality does not meet the requirement this is considered a **gap**. We should now investigate whether an **administrative** solution, represented by the features implemented in the administrative screens and views of the web client, can fill this gap.

When no administrative solution can be found, we should try to meet the requirement by using Siebel Tools declaratively, which is by defining objects and their properties.

Only when the declarative possibilities of Siebel Tools do not suffice for us to implement the requirement should we resort to scripting.

Creating a custom business service

As discussed in the previous section, scripting is the last resort for developers. Because of the high risk, we should consider every move very carefully. The decision of where to place our code influences its manageability. We have learned in previous sections of this chapter that we can write script code at the Application, Applet, Business Component, or Business Service object level.

We can reach the highest level of reusability and availability, two important paradigms in modern programming, when we place our code in a business service method. This section will teach us how to implement a business service method with eScript.

Case study example: Retrieve person information with eScript

AHA employees often need to know more about the users who are associated with a record. Activities for example can be associated with one or more persons who can be internal employees or contacts. The AHA team must provide a proof of concept that information stored about these persons can be retrieved and displayed from anywhere in the application. As discussed previously, a business service method is the ideal location for the code that implements this requirement.

Creating a business service definition

The following procedure describes how to create a new business service definition:

1. Create a new project named AHA Business Services and lock it.

2. In the **Object Explorer**, select the **Business Service** type.

3. In the **Object List Editor**, create a new record with the following property values:

    ◦ **Name**: AHA Info Service

    ◦ **Project**: AHA Business Services

    ◦ **Display Name - String Override**: AHA Info Service

    ◦ **External Use**: checked

    ◦ **Comments**: Created for AHA prototype

4. Right-click the new business service definition and select **Edit Server Scripts** to launch the script editor.

5. When prompted, select **eScript** as the scripting language.

Creating custom functions

The following procedure describes how to create a new custom function body for a business service and how to direct method invocations to that function.

1. In the tree pane of the script editor, expand the (general) node and select the (declarations) node.

2. In the editor, type the following code:

   ```
   function getPersonInfo(Inputs, Outputs)
   ```

   Explanation: The function getPersonInfo() takes two property set references (Inputs and Outputs) as input arguments.

3. Press the *Enter* key. Note that a new node for the getPersonInfo() function is created below the (general) node.

4. In the tree pane of the script editor, select the Service_PreInvokeMethod event handler.

5. Enter the following code in the function body (replacing the existing return(ContinueOperation) statement):

   ```
   switch (MethodName)
   {
     case "getPersonInfo": getPersonInfo(Inputs, Outputs);
     break;
     default: break;
   }
   return (CancelOperation);
   ```

   Explanation: The MethodName input argument is passed to the switch block. In case the value of the MethodName argument is **getPersonInfo**, the getPersonInfo() function is invoked and the current input and output property sets are passed to the function. The break statement is used to leave the switch block. The default switch is reached in any other case. We must use CancelOperation as the return code of the event handler in order to avoid errors caused by the invocation of custom functions, which will be handled entirely by our custom business service.

6. Save the changes.

7. If any syntax errors are reported, rectify the code and save it again.

8. In the editor's tree pane, select the getPersonInfo() function.

The following code has to be entered in the getPersonInfo() function block in order to implement the requirement. The explanation of the code lines starts after the code block. Comments have been removed for better readability.

The file `getPersonInfo.txt` in this chapter's code file contains the full code with comments:

```
function getPersonInfo(Inputs, Outputs)
{
  try
  {
    var PersonId : String = Inputs.GetProperty("Person Id");
    var FieldList : PropertySet = Inputs.GetChild(0);
    var ContactBO : BusObject =
                    TheApplication().GetBusObject("Contact");
    var PersonBC : BusComp = ContactBO.GetBusComp("Person");
    var PersonData : PropertySet = TheApplication().NewPropertySet();
    var f : String;
    with (PersonBC)
    {
      SetViewMode(AllView);
      ActivateMultipleFields(FieldList);
      ClearToQuery();
      SetSearchSpec("Id",PersonId);
      ExecuteQuery(ForwardOnly);
    }
    if (PersonBC.FirstRecord())
    {
      f = FieldList.GetFirstProperty();
      while (f != "")
      {
        PersonData.SetProperty(f,PersonBC.GetFieldValue(f));
        f = FieldList.GetNextProperty();
      }
      PersonData.SetType("PersonData");
      Outputs.AddChild(PersonData);
    }
    else
    {
      throw("No record found in Person BC with [Id]='" + PersonId +
          "'.");
    }
  }
  catch(e)
  {
    TheApplication().RaiseErrorText(e.toString());
  }
  finally
  {
```

```
        f = null;
        PersonData = null;
        PersonBC = null;
        ContactBO = null;
        FieldList = null;
        PersonId = null;
    }
}
```

The preceding code demonstrates the following concepts:

- **Exception handling**: The code defines `try` and `catch` blocks to safely handle any exceptions.

- **Memory management**: The `finally` block sets all object instances to **null**, allowing the garbage collector to clean up the memory allocations.

- **Property set operations**: Input arguments for the function are read from the `Inputs` property set. A child property set is created and written to the `Outputs` property set.

- **Business component operations**: The code instantiates the **Person** business component in the **Contact** business object and executes a query.

- **Loops and conditions**: `while` blocks and `if` blocks are used to implement loops and conditional sections.

Detailed discussion of the example code

In the following section, we will discuss the previous code example line by line:

Variable declarations

The code instantiates the following variables:

- **PersonId**: A String, initialized with the value of the **PersonId** property of the `Inputs` property set.

- **FieldList**: A property set that contains the list of fields to be returned by the function as properties (property name = field name). The `FieldList` variable is initialized with the content of the first child of the `Inputs` property set.

- **ContactBO**: A business object that is initialized with a reference to the Contact business object by using the `GetBusObject()` function of the application object returned by the `TheApplication()` function.

- **PersonBC**: A business component reference that is initialized with the Person business component of the Contact business object represented by the `ContactBO` variable.

- **PersonData**: A property set variable to hold the output data.

- **f**: A String variable to hold different values during code execution.

Executing a query

The `with(PersonBC)` block uses the following functions to prepare and execute a query on the **Person** business component in order to retrieve the information for the person with the **Id** value held in the `PersonId` variable:

- `SetViewMode(AllView)`: This function sets the business component to the **All** view mode, which allows data visibility across organizations.

- `ActivateMultipleFields(FieldList)`: Because the field list is passed as a property set, we can use the `ActivateMultipleFields()` function, which will activate all fields in the Person business component that are specified as properties in the `FieldList` property set. It is necessary to activate all non-system fields before querying in order to include the respective columns in the SQL query.

- `ClearToQuery()`: This function clears all current search specifications on the business component.

- `SetSearchSpec("Id", PersonId)`: The search specification for the business component is set to match the `Id` field with the value of the `PersonId` variable.

- `ExecuteQuery(ForwardOnly)`: This executes the query and returns a record set that can only be navigated from the first to the last record. Because we query on the **Id** field, we expect only a **single** record to be returned.

Verifying the query result

It is a recommended practice to use the return value (**TRUE** or **FALSE**) of the `FirstRecord()` function to verify that at least one record is returned by the query. As shown in the previous example code, an `if` block can be used to evaluate the return value.

Reading values from business component fields

Because the names of fields are stored in the `FieldList` property set, we can implement a loop to read the values for these fields from the Person business component represented by the `PersonBC` variable.

The first line in the if block (`f = FieldList.GetFirstProperty();`) populates the `f` variable with the name of the first property in the `FieldList` property set.

The code in the `while (f != "")` block will execute as long as the `f` variable is not empty, which is the case after the last property of the `FieldList` property set has been reached.

The line `PersonData.SetProperty(f, PersonBC.GetFieldValue(f));` creates a new property in the `PersonData` property set. The property will be named after the current value of the `f` variable (the current field name) and the value of the property will be the value of that field in the current record of the Person business component. For example, if `f` has a value of **First Name** and the first name of the person identified by the query is **John**, then a new property named *First Name* with a value of *John* will exist in the `PersonData` property set after execution of the line.

The `f = FieldList.GetNextProperty();` line sets the value of `f` to the name of the next property in the `FieldList` property set. When there is no further property, `f` will be set to an empty string.

Once the `while` block is completed, the `SetType()` function is used to set the Type property of the `PersonData` property set. The `Outputs.AddChild(PersonData);` statement writes the `PersonData` property set in the first child position of the `Outputs` property set.

Handling exceptions

The `else` block in the example code will be reached when **no record** has been returned by the query. In that case, we should notify the end user or external system with a message indicating that no record has been found. This is accomplished by using the `throw` function, which *throws* an exception, which is then *caught* by the `catch` block. The input argument for the throw function will be passed to the catch block's exception object from which it can then be retrieved.

The text passed to the `throw` function is `"No record found in Contact BC with [Id]='" + PersonId + "'."`, which results in a concatenation of the static text portions enclosed in double quotes and the value of the `PersonId` variable.

The `catch(e)` block is reached whenever an exception occurs in the `try` block, including any `throw` statement.

The `RaiseErrorText` application function can be used to invoke the display (or logging) of an error message. The input argument named `e` (the name is irrelevant) represents the Exception object. We can use the `toString()` function to get the full message text and pass it as an input argument to the `RaiseErrorText` function.

Cleaning up

The `finally` block in the example code demonstrates the importance of *"destroying"* the objects and freeing the allocated memory. It is a recommended practice to set all object variables to `null` using a statement similar to the following:

```
oBC = null;
```

Code in the `finally` block is executed after the `try` or `catch` block (if executed). Setting object variables to `null` marks the allocated memory as free and the eScript engine's garbage collector will clear the memory that was used for the variables as soon as possible.

By obeying this practice, we ensure that our code, irrespective of how often it executes or how much memory is allocated, does not produce any memory leaks.

Declaring business service methods and arguments

If we plan to make our business service available to other developers, we should **declare** the methods it implements and their input and output arguments. This is not a technical necessity but it facilitates the work of developers because they can select method and argument names from pick lists in the workflow process or script editors.

The following procedure describes how to declare the `getPersonInfo` method and its arguments:

1. Navigate to the **AHA Info Service** business service.
2. In the **Object Explorer**, expand the **Business Service** type and select the **Business Service Method** type.
3. In the **Business Service Methods** list, create a new record with the following properties:
    - **Name:** `getPersonInfo`
    - **Display Name - String Override:** `Get Person Info`
    - **Comments:** `Retrieves a person by Id and returns field values`
4. In the **Object Explorer**, expand the **Business Service Method** type and select the **Business Service Method Arg** type.

5. In the **Business Service Method Args** list, create the following records:

Name	Type	Data Type	Storage Type	Optional	Display Name - String Override	Comments
Person Id	Input	String	Property		Person Id	ROW_ID of a person record.
FieldList	Input	Hierarchy	Hierarchy		Field List	Child property set. Must contain field names of Person BC as separate properties.
PersonData	Output	Hierarchy	Hierarchy	(checked)	Person Data	Child property set. Contains requested fields and their values.

6. Compile the AHA Info Service business service.

Testing and debugging scripts

The typical task flow for testing and debugging scripts can be described with the following list:

1. Compile the object definition.
2. Set breakpoints.
3. Run the Siebel application in debug mode.
4. Invoke the script code from the application.
5. Use the **Watch** window to verify script operations.
6. In the case of errors, correct the code and save the script.
7. Continue from step 4 and repeat until script executes without errors.
8. Compile the object definition.

Compiling the object definition

Once we have finished the code implementation in the script editor, we must save our work and compile the parent object definition. In the case of our code example, we must compile the new business service named AHA Info Service.

Setting breakpoints

Assuming that we have already defined the Debug settings in the Siebel Tools options dialog (as described in *Chapter 2*), we can now set breakpoints in our code in order to prepare it for debugging. To accomplish this we set the cursor in the script code and press the *F9* key. Alternatively, we can use the **Toggle Breakpoint** command from the **Debug** menu or the hand icon in the Debug toolbar. A red bar indicates a line with a breakpoint.

The following screenshot shows a breakpoint set on the first variable initialization of the example code:

```
        //variable initialization
        var PersonId : String = Inputs.GetProperty("Person Id");
        var FieldList : PropertySet = Inputs.GetChild(0);
        var ContactBO : BusObject = TheApplication().GetBusObject("Contact");
        var PersonBC : BusComp = ContactBO.GetBusComp("Person");
        var i : Number;
        var f : String;
```

Running the Siebel application in debug mode

To run the Siebel application in debug mode, we press the *F5* key. Alternatively, we can use the **Start F5** command in the **Debug** menu or click the arrow button in the Debug toolbar.

The Siebel Developer Web Client is then invoked with the settings defined in the Debug options, which include the /h command line switch. This switch establishes a connection between the siebel.exe program, representing the Siebel application, and Siebel Tools. This is necessary for stepping through the code line by line.

Invoking the script code from the application

Once the Siebel application has started, we must trigger the event handler, which contains our code. In the case of a business component script in the PreWriteRecord event handler this could, for example, include saving a record represented by the respective business component. This will then trigger the PreWriteRecord event handler. If breakpoints are defined in the script code, Siebel Tools will jump to the first breakpoint in the code and code execution will stop.

In our case study example, we wrote a business service script. To test and debug business service methods, we can use the **Simulator** view in the **Administration - Business Service** screen. The following procedure describes how to invoke the getPersonInfo method of the **AHA Info Service** in the business service simulator:

1. Navigate to the **Site Map**.

2. Click the **Administration - Business Service** screen link.

3. Click the **Simulator** view link.

4. In the **Simulator** list applet on top of the view, create a new record with the following properties:

    °   **Service Name**: AHA Info Service

    °   **Method Name**: getPersonInfo

5. In the following **Input Arguments** list applet after the Simulator list applet, create a new record with the following values:

    °   **Test Case #**: 1

6. Click the icon in the **Property Name** column to open the **Property Set Properties** MVG applet.

7. In the MVG applet, create a new record with the following values:

    °   **Property Name**: Person Id

    °   **Value**: 1-2CLU

 1-2CLU is the ROW_ID value of a contact record in the Siebel Sample Database. If you do not use the Siebel Sample Database, you must obtain a valid ROW_ID value for a contact record and use it instead of the sample value provided previously.

8. Click **OK** to close the **Property Set Properties** MVG applet.

9. Click the icon in the **Child Type** column to open the **Property Set MVG** applet. This applet allows us to create child property sets.

10. Click the **New** button in the MVG applet.

11. In the **Type** field, enter FieldList.

12. Click the icon in the **Property Key** field to open the **Property Set Properties** MVG applet.

13. Create three new properties with the following names:

- ○ **First Name**
- ○ **Last Name**
- ○ **Employee Flag**

The following screenshot shows the Business Service Simulator view at this step:

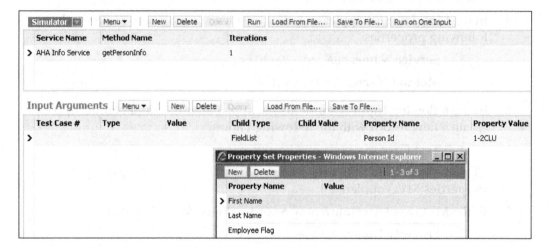

14. Click **OK**.

15. Click **Save**.

16. Click **OK** to close the **Property Set Properties MVG** applet.

17. Optionally, click the **Save To File...** button in the **Input Arguments** list applet and save the downloaded XML file to your disk. We can use the **Load From File...** button to upload saved input argument files instead of typing all values again in order to increase the efficiency of our testing routines.

18. Click the **Run on One Input** button in the upper list applet.

19. Observe that the Siebel Tools task bar icon is flashing.

20. Switch to **Siebel Tools**.

21. The script editor highlights the first breakpoint with a **dark blue bar** indicating that this is the next line to be executed.

22. Press *Shift+F9* to display the **Watch** window.

23. Expand the **Local Variables** section in the **Watch** window if necessary.

24. Use the buttons on the Debug toolbar or keyboard shortcuts to step through the code and inspect the values of the variables in the Watch window:

  ° **Continue** (*F5*): Finishes code execution without reaching any other breakpoint

  ° **Step Into** (*F8*): Steps to the next line and steps into function calls

  ° **Step Over** (*Shift+F8*): Steps to the next line but does not step into function calls

  ° **Step to Cursor** (*Ctrl+F8*): Steps to the next breakpoint or to the cursor position

The following screenshot shows the script editor and the **Watch** window during the debug cycle:

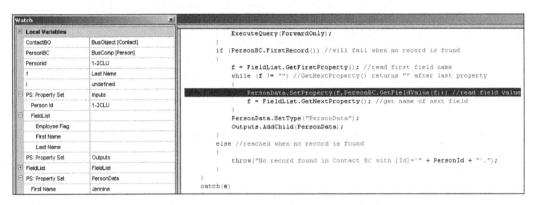

25. After completion of the code, switch back to the Siebel application and verify the data in the **Output Arguments** list applet of the Business Service Simulator. A child property set with a Type of PersonData should exist, which contains three properties representing the first name, last name, and the employee flag of the test record.

Correcting code errors during debugging

In the case of runtime errors, we can correct the script code, save the changes, and continue debugging without the need to recompile the object definition holding the script. This is only applicable when the **Fix And Go** feature (described in an earlier section) has been enabled.

Once the unit test is finished, the object definition must be compiled again.

Summary

The Siebel eScript language allows developers to extend the Siebel CRM application logic with custom scripts. Siebel Tools provides a scripting environment for the Application, Applet, Business Component, and Business Service object types.

In this chapter, we learned how to initialize the scripting environment in Siebel Tools and what event handlers and methods are available for scripting.

A short case study scenario demonstrated how to create a custom business service and how to debug it.

In the next chapter, we will discuss advanced aspects of Siebel scripting such as browser scripting, tracing, and performance considerations.

23

Advanced Scripting Techniques

As outlined in the previous chapter, there are many aspects of Siebel scripting. Server script, for example, is limited to execution on the machine where the Siebel executable resides, so we cannot use it to interact with the browser or the end user. By adding script code to the Siebel Repository we also inherit a high responsibility for the quality and performance of our code, so we should consider preparing our code for tracing and performance.

In this chapter we will discuss browser scripting, tracing, and performance measurement techniques that allow developers to implement complex requirements.

This chapter is structured as follows:

- Browser scripting
- Using translatable messages
- Tracing
- Performance profiling

Browser scripting

The Siebel CRM web architecture supports the use of browser JavaScript. The following object types in the Siebel Repository support browser script:

- Application
- Applet
- Business Component
- Business Service (including property sets)
- Control

The set of available event handlers and methods for these object types is very limited compared with server scripts. In addition, it is important to understand browser scripting as the **last resort**, which we should use only when the given requirement cannot be implemented declaratively or with server script.

The following requirements represent reasons to use browser scripting:

- **Manipulation of applet controls**: The visual appearance of applet controls such as text fields and buttons can be manipulated only via specialized browser script methods provided by the Object Interface API of Siebel CRM.

- **User dialogs**: Complex dialogs and bidirectional communication with the end user often require the use of browser script. For example, we can use JavaScript to open a text entry dialog with an OK and Cancel button.

- **Avoiding server roundtrips**: For performance reasons, it might be necessary to run field validation logic on the browser side without invoking server-side methods.

- **Interaction with desktop applications**: Because the Siebel High-Interactivity client runs in Microsoft Internet Explorer, we can use ActiveX methods to communicate with Windows applications such as Microsoft Excel or Microsoft Word.

Preparing Siebel Tools for browser scripting

Browser scripts are written in Siebel Tools. During compilation of the Siebel Repository File (SRF), Siebel Tools extracts the browser scripts as JavaScript (.js) files to the folder specified in the **Scripting** tab of the Siebel Tools options dialog. For testing and debugging purposes, it is necessary to extract the browser scripts to the language-specific subfolder of the Siebel client's PUBLIC folder.

To change this setting, we navigate to the **Options…** command in the **View** menu. In the **Scripting** tab of the **Development Tools Options** dialog, we enter the full path to the PUBLIC\enu folder (or any other language-specific subfolder) of the Siebel Developer Web Client installation directory and confirm the setting by clicking the **OK** button.

The following screenshot shows an example setting:

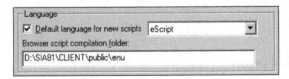

Writing browser script

The process of writing browser script is similar to writing server scripts. We can invoke the **browser script editor**, by right-clicking the object definition that supports browser scripting and selecting **Edit Browser Scripts**.

The browser script editor offers only basic syntax highlighting. Features such as ScriptAssist are available only for Siebel eScript and not for browser script. It is therefore necessary to work very diligently to avoid typing errors and to pay special attention to case.

Browser script example

The following example script demonstrates some of the scenarios mentioned previously. The browser script is implemented in the `PreSetFieldValue` event handler of the **Opportunity** business component. The purpose of the script is to **notify** the end user that the close date of the opportunity has been set to a date in the past without performing a network roundtrip. If the close date is in the past, the control's **background color** will change to red and the end user can choose whether to continue or undo the change by clicking buttons in a dialog:

The following procedure describes how to add browser script to an object definition.

1. Navigate to the **Opportunity** business component.
2. **Check out or lock** the business component if necessary.
3. Right-click the business component and select **Edit Browser Scripts**.
4. Open the script editor for the `BusComp_PreSetFieldValue` event handler.
5. Enter the **script code** in the function body (see code sample that follows this list).
6. Save your changes.
7. Compile the Opportunity business component.
8. Test the browser script using the Siebel Mobile or Developer Web Client by creating a test opportunity record. Set the close date to a date in the past and save the record. The control's background color should change to red and a confirmation dialog should appear.

The following code implements the logic described earlier. Comments and the `finally` block have been removed for the sake of readability. The `Opportunity_BrowserScript.txt` file in this chapter's code files contains the full script code including comments and the `finally` block.

```
function BusComp_PreSetFieldValue (fieldName, value)
{
    if (fieldName == "Primary Revenue Close Date")
    {
        try
        {
            var dInputDate = new Date(value);
            var dCurrentDate = new Date();
            var response;
            var oApplet = theApplication().ActiveApplet();
            var returncode = "ContinueOperation";
            var message = "";
            var oControl;

    if (eval(dInputDate - dCurrentDate) < 0)
            {
                if (oApplet.Name() == "Opportunity Form Applet - Child")
                {
                    oControl = oApplet.FindControl("CloseDate2");
                    oControl.SetProperty("BgColor", "#E8624C");
                }
                message = "You have entered a date in the past.\n" +
                        "Click OK to continue or click Cancel to abort."
                response = confirm(message);
            }
            switch (response)
            {
                case true: returncode = "ContinueOperation";
                        break;
                case false: returncode = "CancelOperation";
                        break;
                default: returncode = "CancelOperation";
                        break;
            }
        }
        catch (e)
        {
            returncode = "CancelOperation";
            theApplication().SWEAlert("Error: " + e.toString());
        }
        return (returncode);
    }
    return ("ContinueOperation");
}
```

In the following sections we will explain the code line by line.

Monitoring changes on a specific field

The `if (fieldName == "Primary Revenue Close Date")` statement verifies the name of the field. The `PreSetFieldValue` event handler is invoked every time a field value has been changed. Because we want to monitor changes only on the **Primary Revenue Close Date** field, we use the `if` block to ensure that our code executes only when this field's value has been modified.

Exception handling

Similar to eScript, browser JavaScript—also based on the ECMA script—uses the same syntax for exception handling. It is a recommended practice to include a `try` and a `catch` block in browser script code to avoid problems when an exceptional situation occurs during code execution.

Variable declaration

The following variables are declared in the example code we have seen in an earlier section:

- `dInputDate`: This variable holds the value entered into the Primary Revenue Close Date field . The variable is a *Date* object created using the `new Date(value);` statement. The value input argument is passed automatically to the `PreSetFieldValue` event handler.

- `dCurrentDate`: This variable is a *Date* object representing the current date. This is achieved by initializing it with the `new Date();` statement.

- `response`: This variable will hold the response from the end user. It will be populated when the end user clicks one of the buttons in the confirm dialog.

- `oApplet`: An object reference to the currently active applet. The function `theApplication().ActiveApplet();` returns this object reference. These functions are part of the Siebel browser scripting API for high-interactivity web clients.

- `returncode`: This variable is used to hold the string that will be returned by the `PreSetFieldValue` event handler. As with any "pre"-event handler, we can decide to return `ContinueOperation` or `CancelOperation` to continue with normal code execution or to abort the operation respectively. It is noteworthy which browser script uses strings for the return value as opposed to server script which uses constants.

- `message`: This variable will hold the message to be displayed to the end user.

- oControl: This variable will represent the applet control and allow manipulation of properties of the control, such as its background color, at runtime.

Did you know?

Some important differences exist between eScript and browser script regarding the syntax. For example the theApplication() function in browser script must be written with an initial lowercase **t** while in eScript it is written with an initial uppercase **T**.

Another difference is that the return value of pre-event handlers — ContinueOperation or CancelOperation — must be enclosed in double quotes (") and therefore handled as a text string in browser script. In eScript, the return value is a constant and not enclosed in double quotes.

Performing date calculations

The main purpose of the example script is to determine whether the date entered by the end user is in the past. The eval(dInputDate - dCurrentDate) < 0 statement accomplishes this by subtracting the current date value from the field value. When the result is less than zero, the current date has a higher value than the date entered, which means that the input date is in the past. The eval() function can be used in JavaScript to carry out calculations on arbitrary object types such as date.

Changing control properties

In case the input date is in the past, the script should change the background color of the **Close Date** control to red. The Siebel browser script API provides specialized methods for **Control** objects that allow manipulation of applet controls. We must use these methods instead of resorting to JavaScript methods that locate the control in the browser's **Document Object Model (DOM)**. The control's identifier, which is used in such methods, can easily change over time, rendering our script defunct.

The script uses the Name() function of the applet object to determine whether the Opportunity Form Applet - Child applet is currently active. The line oControl = oApplet.FindControl("CloseDate2"); retrieves an object reference to the applet control named CloseDate2 (which is the value of the Name property of the control labeled Close Date).

By invoking the SetProperty("BgColor", "#E8624C") function on the control object, we set the background color (BgColor) to a discreet shade of red. The SetProperty() function's first input argument is the short name of a control property. In the case of the BgColor property, the second argument is the **HTML** code representation of the color (#E8624C), which uses hexadecimal notation for the red, green, and blue color channels.

Displaying a confirmation dialog to the end user

The native JavaScript method named confirm() can be used to display a message to the end user. The dialog box will also provide an **OK** and a **Cancel** button. The return value of the confirm() method depends on which button the end user has clicked. When the user clicks the **OK** button, the return value is true. When the end user clicks the **Cancel** button, the return value is false.

The following screenshot shows the confirm dialog displayed to the end user during the execution of the browser script:

Interpreting the end user response

By using the switch(response) block we can evaluate which button the end user has clicked and set the returncode variable accordingly. The value of the returncode variable will be "CancelOperation" when the end user has clicked the **Cancel** button and it will be "ContinueOperation" when the end user has clicked the **OK** button.

Displaying error messages

In case of errors encountered during execution of the code in the try block, the browser's script interpreter jumps to the catch block. In Siebel browser script, we can use the theApplication().SWEAlert(); function—part of the Siebel browser script API—to display a **modal** alert dialog on top of the application. The end user must acknowledge the message before she or he can continue.

Continuing or canceling the flow of operation

Depending on the value returned by a "pre"-event handler function, the application either continues or cancels the normal flow of operation. The return() function must be reached at the right time because any lines of code after it will never be executed. In Siebel browser script, the return() function takes a string parameter that can have either a value of "ContinueOperation", indicating to continue with the normal flow of operation, or "CancelOperation", causing the application framework to bypass the built-in event handler and subsequently abort the operation.

Testing and debugging browser scripts

During compilation of an object definition, such as a business component or applet, which has browser scripts attached, Siebel Tools automatically extracts the script into a set of subfolders of the browser compilation folder specified in the **Scripting** tab of the Siebel Tools options dialog.

As mentioned earlier in this chapter, it is worthwhile to specify the PUBLIC/enu (or another language subfolder depending on our implementation) directory of the client installation folder.

It is a recommended practice to check if Siebel Tools has generated the files after compilation. When inspecting the target directory, we find a subdirectory with a name similar to srf1290179221_444. This folder contains another hierarchy of two folders named bscripts\all.

Did you know?

The name of the browser script root folder is the result of concatenating "srf", the **UNIX timestamp** (the number of seconds elapsed since January 01, 1970) representing the SRF file's compilation time, and a random number preceded by an underscore character (_444 in the above example).

In the all folder, we find the browser script files with an extension of .js. The file names are generated automatically and must not be altered.

To test browser scripts, we must launch the Siebel Mobile or Developer Web Client as usual and take the necessary actions to invoke the script. As opposed to server script, Siebel Tools does not support debugging of browser scripts.

If we wish to debug Siebel browser scripts, we must either use the browser's script debugging capabilities or install a third-party tool such as Microsoft Script Debugger for Internet Explorer.

Extracting browser scripts using the genbscript utility

There are circumstances when we have only an SRF file without access to the Siebel Repository data and need to extract the browser scripts. This could be very likely to occur during the deployment of configuration changes between server environments. To accomplish the task of extracting browser scripts from an SRF file, Oracle provides the **genbscript** (generate browser script) utility, which can be located in the BIN directory of any Siebel Client or Siebel Server installation folder.

The genbscript utility is used at the Windows command line similarly to the following example:

```
genbscript D:\SIA81\CLIENT\BIN\ENU\siebel.cfg D:\SIA81\CLIENT\public\enu
ENU
```

The first parameter is the full path to a valid Siebel Client **configuration file** (.cfg). The second parameter is the path to the **target directory** where the browser script root folder and browser scripts should be generated. The third parameter is the three letter **language code**.

If the target directory already contains a browser script root folder with the same timestamp as the SRF file, the user is prompted to delete that directory and execute genbscript again.

When no current browser script root directory exists, the utility generates it and places the complete set of browser scripts, for all objects in the SRF file that have browser script attached, into the bscripts\all folder.

The following screenshot shows the output of the genbscript utility in the Windows command shell. Depending on the version of Siebel CRM, warning messages can appear referring to standard applets. We can ignore these messages.

```
C:\WINDOWS\system32\cmd.exe

D:\>cd sia81

D:\SIA81>cd client

D:\SIA81\CLIENT>cd bin

D:\SIA81\CLIENT\BIN>genbscript D:\SIA81\CLIENT\BIN\ENU\siebel.cfg D:\SIA81\CLIENT\public\enu ENU
.............................................................................
ne Adapter Applet" had an unexpected browser group:
    "IE5" instead of "all".
.............................................................................
........
Successfully created 10 files in "D:\SIA81\CLIENT\public\enu\srf1290179221_444\bscripts\all".
(Please wait a few seconds for this utility to finish)
```

After running the `genbscript` utility we can continue to use the Siebel CRM application. Because the browser script root folder is **renamed** for every version of the SRF file, the browser automatically gets the latest version of .js files. This eliminates the need to refresh the browser's cache.

Using translatable messages

In the script examples in this and the previous chapter we used several techniques of displaying messages to the end user. In all of the examples, the text that should be displayed to the end user is stored as a **static** string within the script code for the sake of readability.

Using static strings is **not** a recommended practice, so it is time to discuss the options for storing message texts in a central location outside of the script code. This technique also enables us to use the same code for all user interface languages in multilingual environments.

As we have learned in previous chapters, the **Symbolic String** definitions serve this purpose. We can create new Symbolic String object definitions to store the language-specific versions of our message texts.

The `LookupMessage()` and `RaiseError()` server script methods of the **application** object allow developers to retrieve translated text and fill placeholders in the text (defined using the percent sign (%) followed by a number). While the `RaiseError()` method retrieves only messages that belong to the preconfigured *User Defined Errors* message category, the `LookupMessage()` method accepts the name of any message category.

The following procedure describes how to create a new message category.

1. If necessary, expose the **Message Category** object type in the **Object Explorer**.
2. Create a **new project** named **AHA Messages** and lock it.
3. In the **Object Explorer**, select the **Message Category** type.
4. Create a **new** record and enter **AHA Messages** in the **Name** property.

In *Chapter 4, Symbolic Strings*, we have already discussed how to create Symbolic Strings and use them for messages. For this reason, the following instructions are less explicit.

To be able to replace the static text in our script code with a translatable message, we must create a **new Symbolic String** definition. The Symbolic String should have the following characteristics:

- **Name**: X_AHA_NO_RECORD
- **Project**: AHA Symbolic Strings

The **Symbolic String Locale** record for the **ENU** language code could be created as follows:

- **String Value**: No record found in %1 BC with [Id]='%2'.

Note: %1 and %2 will be replaced with the name of a business component and a ROW_ID value respectively at runtime.

We can now add a **new Message** to the AHA Messages category with the following properties:

- **Name**: AHA_NO_RECORD_ID
- **Text - String Reference**: X_AHA_NO_RECORD

To finalize this configuration, we must **compile** the X_AHA_NO_RECORD symbolic string and the AHA Messages category.

The following procedure describes how to use the new message in the getPersonInfo() method of the **AHA Info Service** business service, which we created in the previous chapter:

1. Navigate to the **AHA Info Service** business service.
2. **Check out or lock** the business service if necessary.
3. Open the **server script editor** and select the getPersonInfo function in the **(general)** node.
4. Add a **new String variable** declaration at the end of the variable declaration section as follows:

```
var message : String;
```

5. In the else block, type two forward slashes (//) before the throw statement to comment out the entire line.
6. Type the following code below the commented line:

```
message = TheApplication().LookupMessage("AHA Messages","AHA_NO_
RECORD_ID",PersonBC.Name(),PersonId);


throw(message);
```

The first line populates the `message` variable with the return value of the `LookupMessage()` application method. The message text will be retrieved from the `AHA_NO_RECORD_ID` message in the `AHA Messages` category in the current language of the Object Manager. The name of the business component referenced by the `PersonBC` variable and the value of the `PersonId` variable will be passed as the first and second arguments. These values will fill the `%1` and `%2` placeholders in the message text.

The `throw(message);` statement will cause the script engine to navigate to the `catch` block and populate the `Exception` object (e) with the value of the `message` variable.

7. **Compile** the AHA Info Service business service.

8. **Test** the AHA Info Service's `getPersonInfo` method in the **Business Service Simulator** view as described in the previous chapter. Provide an **invalid** `ROW_ID` such as `AHA000` as the value of the `Person Id` input property to invoke the `else` block. Verify that the message is displayed correctly.

The following screenshot shows the error message that is displayed after execution of the `getPersonInfo` method with an invalid Person Id value.

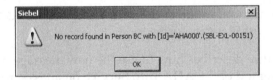

Note that the Siebel error code (`SBL-EXL-00151`) is automatically appended. This specific error code indicates that the `RaiseErrorText()` function has been called within a server script (`EXL` is short for **EX**tension Language).

The `LookupMessage()` and `RaiseError()` methods are available only for server scripts. To use them from browser scripts, we must implement a custom eScript business service with a helper function that invokes these methods and passes the output back to the browser script.

Invoking business service methods from server and browser script

Business services, especially the preconfigured definitions shipped with the standard Siebel Repository, constitute a rich library of functionality ready for use by the developer community. As outlined in *Chapter 16, Menus and Buttons,* every developer should acquaint herself/himself with the standard business services and their methods.

The following code snippet demonstrates how to invoke the `RunProcess` method of the **Workflow Process Manager** business service in Siebel eScript. The technique shown in the code example can be applied to any business service be it preconfigured by Oracle or custom developed.

```
var inputPS : PropertySet = TheApplication().NewPropertySet();
var outputPS : PropertySet = TheApplication().NewPropertySet();
var oService : Service = TheApplication().GetService("Workflow
Process Manager");
var oBC : BusComp; //initialization not shown
inputPS.SetProperty("ProcessName","AHA Test Workflow");
inputPS.SetProperty("RowId",oBC.GetFieldValue("Id"));
oService.InvokeMethod("RunProcess",inputPS,outputPS);
```

In the code example we have just seen, two property sets — `inputPS` and `outputPS` — are instantiated using the `NewPropertySet()` method of the application object returned by the `theApplication()` function. `inputPS` will be used to pass arguments to the business service method and `outputPS` will hold arguments returned by the business service method.

The `GetService()` application method must be used to instantiate a `Service` typed variable representing the business service.

Typically, the `SetProperty()` method will be used several times on the `inputPS` variable to produce the necessary input property set. In the example, the `ProcessName` and `RowId` input properties are populated.

Finally, we invoke the desired method with the `InvokeMethod()` method of the business service variable. In Siebel eScript, the `InvokeMethod()` method takes three input arguments — the name of the method and two references to the input and the output property set.

Invoking business services from browser scripts is accomplished in a similar manner. The following code snippet shows a Siebel browser script that invokes the `RunProcess` method of the Workflow Process Manager business service.

```
var inputPS = theApplication().NewPropertySet();
var outputPS = theApplication().NewPropertySet();
var oService = theApplication().GetService("Workflow Process
Manager");
var oBC; //initialization not shown
inputPS.SetProperty("ProcessName","AHA Test Workflow");
inputPS.SetProperty("RowId", oBC.GetFieldValue("Id"));
outputPS = oService.InvokeMethod("RunProcess",inputPS);
```

We can note the following differences between server and browser script:

- The `theApplication()` method in browser script starts with a lowercase "t" whereas the same method in server script starts with an uppercase "T".

- Browser script does not support strong typed variables.

- The syntax for the `InvokeMethod()` method in browser script requires the output property set variable to hold its return value. In server script, the output property set variable is passed as the third input argument.

In order to avoid security issues, invocation of business service methods from external sources, which includes browser scripts, is restricted. When we intend to invoke a business service from browser scripts, we must register this business service using the `ClientBusinessServiceN` application user property.

For the above code snippet to work, we must for example register the **Workflow Process Manager** business service with the application object definition used in our implementation. This is already preconfigured for most application object definitions but we might have to add other business services—preconfigured or custom built—with our applications.

The following screenshot shows the **Siebel Automotive** application's user properties:

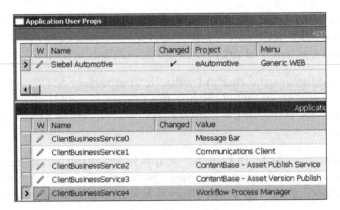

The `ClientBusinessService4` user property registers the **Workflow Process Manager** business service. To register a custom business service we must add a new instance of the `ClientBusinessServiceN` user property to the application object definition (increasing the number suffix by 1) and enter the name of the business service as the user property's value. After compiling the application object definition, external systems and browser scripts can invoke methods of the registered business services.

Tracing

Custom script often has a strong impact on the behavior of a Siebel CRM application in terms of functionality and performance. Developers and administrators who wish to maintain certain standards for monitoring script execution and performance can rely upon the **tracing** functionality, which is available for Siebel **server script** languages such as eScript.

Tracing allows us to write explicit information about the script execution, including timings and the SQL code produced by the script, to files. Script tracing is available on a global scale on the object manager level (not discussed in this book) and on the script level (discussed in the following section).

To implement tracing on the script level, we must use the `TraceOn()`, `Trace()`, and `TraceOff()` methods provided by the application object returned by the `theApplication()` function.

The following code snippet demonstrates the use of the tracing functionality.

```
TheApplication().TraceOn("C:\\SEBL_TRACE_$p_$t.txt","Allocation","All
");
//arbitrary code
TheApplication().Trace("Reached important point in code");
//arbitrary code
TheApplication().TraceOff();
```

This code will produce a file on the `C:\` drive. The file name will contain the current process ID replacing the $p placeholder, along with the current thread ID replacing the $t placeholder, in order to guarantee a unique file name even when the code executes in the context of an object manager process serving hundreds of users.

The input arguments `"Allocation"` and `"All"` to the `TraceOn()` method specify that **all** object allocations and de-allocations will be written to the file. A second option is to specify `"SQL"` as the second and `""` (an empty string) as the third argument to write the SQL produced implicitly by the script code to the file.

The `Trace()` method can be optionally used by the developer to write information to the file while the code reaches important stages.

The `TraceOff()` method ends the tracing cycle.

Considerations for script tracing

The following has to be taken into consideration when we use the tracing methods in Siebel scripts:

- Browser scripts do not support tracing methods. To accomplish tracing of browser scripts we can write a custom eScript business service that allows invocation of the tracing methods via a business service method invocation in browser script.

- Because of the potentially negative performance impact, we should consider allowing the turning off of tracing in production environments. This can be accomplished by conditionally invoking the `TraceOn()` method in the `ApplicationStart` event handler. As an alternative, we can remove all tracing code before moving the code to production environments.

- The trace file will be written on the machine where the code executes. If we have to deal with heterogeneous server environments (a mix of Microsoft Windows and Unix-based operating systems) we must ensure that the file path is reachable from all machines (Unix does not support drive letters and backslashes).

- If our company uses Siebel Remote to support Mobile Web Clients we must be aware of the fact that trace files might get written to laptop drives where they might be unavailable for immediate access.

Performance profiling

As responsible and thoughtful developers we should strive to use configuration techniques with the least negative performance impact. Many performance problems in Siebel CRM projects arise from custom script code.

The following are exemplary reasons for slow application performance during script execution (the list is not complete):

- The script interpreter is generally slower than the execution of precompiled C++ code

- The script induces complex and long-running SQL statements against the database

- Loop constructs can cause the same code to be invoked many times

To overcome these problems we can either resort to **administrative or declarative solutions** or design our script code to avoid these issues.

To support developers with the latter task, Siebel Tools provides the **Script Performance Profiler** (available with the ST eScript engine in Siebel 8.1 or higher). The performance profiler allows developers to inspect the performance figures for each line of code early during the debugging cycle. Developers can therefore identify potential performance bottlenecks in their code and react accordingly.

The profiler can be enabled or disabled by checking or unchecking the **Enable Profiler** flag in the **Scripting** tab of the Siebel Tools options dialog. The following screenshot shows the flag in checked mode:

The following procedure describes how to use the Script Performance Profiler during debugging:

1. Ensure that the profiler is **enabled** as described above.

2. Invoke the **Debugger** for any eScript code as usual.

3. From the **View** menu select **Profiler | Call Tree**.

4. A new tab labeled **Script Performance Profiler** is opened in the editor pane.

5. In the **Script Performance Profiler** tab, expand the **Root** node and the node representing your script object.

6. **Execute** the code several times to collect performance statistics.

7. Inspect the statistics in the **Script Performance Profiler** tab.

The next screenshot shows a section of the **Script Performance Profiler** tab after several executions of the getPersonInfo method of the **AHA Info Service** business service:

Function / Source Line	Call Count	Total Time (ms)	Max Time (ms)	Min Time (ms)
⊟ Root	1	1532	0	0
⊞ Service[LogViewInfo]::Service_PreInvokeMethod	1	1030	1030	1030
Service[LS PCD Service]::Service_PreCanInvokeMe...	46	0	0	0
⊟ Service[AHA Info Service]::Service_PreInvokeMeth...	26	502	157	0
⊟ Service[AHA Info Service]::getPersonInfo	26	345	110	0
Application::TheApplication	57	0	0	0
Application::TraceOn	5	16	16	0
Application::RaiseErrorText	4	0	0	0
Application::GetBusObject	24	15	15	0
BusObject::GetBusComp	24	47	47	0
Application::NewPropertySet	24	0	0	0
BusComp::SetViewMode	21	0	0	0
BusComp::ActivateMultipleFields	21	0	0	0
BusComp::ClearToQuery	21	0	0	0
BusComp::SetSearchSpec	21	0	0	0
BusComp::ExecuteQuery	21	172	78	0

Among other information, the profiler displays the **call count** for each method invocation as well as the maximum, minimum, and total **time** (in milliseconds) spent for the method invocation. In the preceding screenshot, the `ExecuteQuery()` method was executed **21** times. The maximum execution time was **78** milliseconds and the total execution time for all **21** iterations was **172** milliseconds. Compared with other's methods, the `ExecuteQuery()` method consumed the majority of the method's total execution time of **345** milliseconds.

Using the information provided by the Script Performance Profiler, developers can make informed decisions over whether to alter the code or resort to declarative or administrative solutions such as Siebel Workflow.

Summary

The Siebel scripting environment includes the possibility of attaching browser scripts to object definitions such as applications, applets, business components, and business services. In this chapter, we discussed how to write and extract browser scripts.

In addition we explored the concepts of using translatable messages instead of using hardcoded strings. Another concept introduced in previous chapter was tracing, which allows us to produce detailed trace files from within our script code.

Finally, we introduced the Script Performance Profiler, a helpful utility that allows developers to identify slow-running function calls in their code.

In the next chapter we will discuss the deployment options for migrating configuration changes between environments.

24

Deploying Configuration Changes between Environments

After the development cycle and first unit tests, it is necessary to deploy the configuration changes made in the Siebel CRM development environment to other environments such as test and production. Configuration changes may affect object definitions created or modified in the Siebel Repository, files such as web template files, and administrative data such as List of Values. In this chapter, we will discuss the functionality of Siebel CRM to successfully manage the deployment of configuration from one environment to another.

The chapter is structured as follows:

- Repository migration
- Exporting and importing repository data
- Exporting and importing administrative data
- Application Deployment Manager (ADM) overview

Repository migration

At certain release stages in a Siebel CRM project, after developers have modified or created hundreds or thousands of object definitions in the Siebel Repository, it is necessary to deploy the entire Siebel Repository from the development database to the target environment, be it one of various test environments or the final production environment. This task, commonly referred to as **dev2prod** (**dev**elopment **to prod**uction), is supported by the *Migrate Repository* procedure, which is provided by the **Siebel Database Configuration Assistant**.

The configuration assistant provides a graphical user interface to capture relevant parameter information and then invokes the **Siebel Upgrade Wizard**, which executes the necessary tasks to complete the migration. The *Migrate Repository* procedure includes the following tasks:

- **Export** the entire Siebel Repository from the source database to a file
- **Import** the data from the flat file to the target database
- **Rename** the old Siebel Repository in the target database
- **Synchronize** the tables and indexes of the target database with the data layer object definitions of the new repository
- **Update** the schema version information in the target database

Despite the fact that the majority of the tasks in the preceding list can be carried out manually (using shell commands and scripts), it is highly recommendable to use the tools provided by the Siebel application framework to ensure accuracy and allow monitoring of the process.

We can invoke the *Migrate Repository* procedure from any machine where the **Siebel Database Server Utilities (dbsrvr)** are installed. This is necessarily a **Siebel Server** machine because the Database Server Utilities can only be installed on a machine hosting a Siebel Server installation.

On Microsoft Windows operating systems, we can use the Windows start menu entries to launch the Database Server Configuration Wizard. On Linux and other UNIX-based operating systems, we have to run preconfigured scripts on the command shell. Details about the Configuration Wizard can be found in the book *Siebel CRM 8 Installation and Management*, by the same author.

The following table describes the process of invoking the Siebel Database Configuration Wizard and executing the Migrate Repository procedure. The example is for Microsoft Windows operating systems:

Step	Description	Tasks and Example Values
1	Start the Configuration Wizard	Click the **Database Server Configuration** shortcut in the Windows start menu.
2	Siebel Server directory	Keep the default path. Click **Next**.
3	Siebel **Database Server Utilities** directory	Keep the default path. Click **Next**.

Step	Description	Tasks and Example Values
4	Database Platform	Select **Oracle Database Enterprise Edition**.
		Click **Next**.
5	Task selection	Select **Migrate Repository**.
		Click **Next**.
6	Action selection	Select **Read source repository directly from the database**.
		Click **Next**.
7	Target environment	Select **The target environment will be offline when migration starts**.
		Click **Next**.
8	Schema changes	Select **There are new schema changes to be applied**.
		Click **Next**.
9	Select base language	Select **English (American)**.
		Click **Next**.
10	ODBC Data Source Name (source)	Enter `Siebel_DSN`.
		Note: This is the name of the System DSN for the source enterprise.
		Click **Next**.
11	Siebel Database User Name and Password (source)	**User Name**: `SADMIN`
		Password: `7xvfert8`
		Click **Next**.
12	Siebel Database Table Owner and Password (source)	**Table Owner**: `SIEBEL`
		Password: `34ujnpq9`
		Click **Next**.
13	Source and target repository name	Keep the defaults ("Siebel Repository").
		Click Next.
14	Target Database Platform	Select **Oracle Database Enterprise Edition**.
		Click **Next**.

Step	Description	Tasks and Example Values
15	Unicode selection	Select **UNICODE Database.**
		Click **Next.**
16	ODBC Data Source Name (target)	Enter the name of the System DSN for the target enterprise.
		Note: We may have to create system DSN entries for the source and target databases on the machine where this process executes.
		Click **Next.**
17	Siebel Database User Name and Password (target)	**User Name:** SADMIN
		Password: 99trfmn5
		Click **Next.**
18	Siebel Database Table Owner and Password (target)	**Table Owner:** SIEBEL
		Password: plm4qcf6
		Click **Next.**
19	Index and data table space names (target)	Index Table Space Name: SIEBELDB_IDX
		(Data) Table Space Name: SIEBELDB_DATA
		Click **Next.**
20	Oracle parallel indexing	Keep the default (**Does not use...**)
		Click **Next.**
21	Security group and log output directory	Keep the defaults.
		Click **Next.**
22	Apply configuration changes	Select **Yes apply configuration changes now.**
		Click **Next.**
23	Summary	Review the summary information.
		Click **Next.**
24	**Target Enterprise Shutdown** (not part of the wizard)	At this point, we must ensure that all Siebel Servers in the target environment are shut down.
25	Do you want to execute configuration?	Click **Yes.**

Step	Description	Tasks and Example Values
26	The Siebel Upgrade Wizard is displayed	Click **OK** in the Siebel Upgrade Wizard dialog.
27	During the installation process, several command windows are opened	Ensure that you do not close or make selections in any of the command windows.
		Wait for the Siebel Upgrade Wizard to complete.
28	The configuration wizard displays the message **Execution successful**	Click **OK** to confirm successful execution of the configuration wizard.
29	The configuration wizard jumps to the Siebel Server directory selection	Click **Cancel** in the Siebel Configuration Wizard dialog.
30	Confirm exiting the configuration wizard	Click **Yes**.
31	Siebel Upgrade Wizard displays **Complete**	Click **OK** in the Siebel Upgrade Wizard dialog.

To verify the successful execution of the Migrate Repository procedure, we should use Siebel Tools to connect to the target database and verify that the Siebel Repository has been imported.

Additional verification steps include querying the target database with SQL tools of our choice to check for the existence of new tables, columns, or indexes — in case they have been created during the development project.

After successful migration of a Siebel Repository to a target database we must copy the accompanying SRF file to the target server and (if applicable) to Mobile Web Client machines. When browser scripts have been developed, the `genbscript` utility (described in the previous chapter) must be used to extract browser scripts from the SRF file. The resulting browser script folder must be copied to the language-specific subfolder of the public directory (for example `PUBLIC\enu`) on the web server machine that hosts the **Siebel Web Server Extension (SWSE)**.

Exporting and importing repository data

When a full repository migration is not needed, which is very likely the case in test situations, we can use the **Export Repository** and **Import Repository** procedures provided by the Database Server Utilities. The invocation of these procedures is similar to the process described in the previous section.

Both procedures simply invoke the `repimexp` command line utility and pass the parameters entered using the Configuration Wizard. The `repimexp` utility can also be used manually, for example to export and import repositories from and to local developer databases.

The result of the export procedure is a flat file with a `.dat` suffix. This file contains all repository data. We can then use the import procedure to load the file's content into a target Siebel database. The import result is a new repository in the target database.

The following procedure describes how to use the `repimexp` command line utility to export a repository into a flat file:

1. Open a command shell on a machine where Siebel Tools or the Siebel Database Server Utilities are installed.

2. At the command prompt, navigate to the `BIN` directory of the Siebel software installation folder. For example, we can navigate to the `D:\SIA81\TOOLS\BIN` path when Siebel Tools is installed on `D:\SIA81\TOOLS`.

3. At the command prompt enter a command similar to the following:

    ```
    repimexp /A E /C "SEAW Local Db default instance" /U AHANSAL /P
    tzU87tr /D SIEBEL /R "Siebel Repository" /F D:\TEMP\siebrep.dat /L
    D:\TEMP\siebrep_exp.log
    ```

The preceding command line example invokes the `repimexp` utility with the following minimum set of required parameters:

Parameter	Description
/A	Action to be executed. Possible values are **E** (export), **I** (import), **X** (import language-specific data only), and **D** (write information about a flat repository file to the command window).
/C	The name of an **ODBC data source** (DSN) to be used to connect to the database. Double quotes must be used to enclose the name if it contains spaces.
/U	The **username** to be used to connect to the database.
/P	The **password** for the user account.
/D	The name of the **table owner**.
/R	The name of the **repository** to export or import.
/F	The full path to the **data file**.
/L	Full path to a **log file**, which will contain the information written to the command window.

A full list of required and optional parameters can be obtained by entering `repimexp` without further parameters at the command line.

4. Wait for the process to finish. The export process can be monitored at the command prompt, which displays the progress table by table.

The following screenshot shows the output of the `repimexp` utility during an export process:

```
Connecting to the database...
Connected.
Making 2nd connection to exported datasource: SEAW Samp Db default instance...
Connected.
Starting common api.
Process Name: Repository Import/Export Utility, Status: Started, Parameter: , Message

Exporting Tables
    Exporting table            S_ACCELERATOR ... exported        236 rows
    Exporting table          S_ACCELRTR_INTL ... exported         57 rows
    Exporting table          S_APLT_BRSSCRPT ... exported         19 rows
    Exporting table           S_APLT_MMI_INTL ... exported        669 rows
    Exporting table           S_APLT_TMV_INTL ... exported          0 rows
    Exporting table            S_APLT_TM_INTL ... exported          2 rows
    Exporting table            S_APLT_TM_VAR ... exported        100 rows
    Exporting table           S_APLT_TXT_MSG ... exported         57 rows
    Exporting table           S_APLT_WTI_INTL ... exported        566 rows
    Exporting table                 S_APPLET ... exported      17577 rows
```

A command similar to the following can be used to import an existing flat file into a target database:

```
repimexp /A I /C "SEAW Local Db default instance" /U AHANSAL /P tzU87tr
/D SIEBEL /R "Test Repository" /F D:\TEMP\siebrep.dat /L D:\TEMP\siebrep_
imp.log /G ALL
```

The preceding command line example will invoke the `repimexp` utility for an import action. The majority of parameters are similar to the export action. The /A (action) switch must be followed by I to execute an import process. The /G switch is specific to the import action and must be followed by a comma separated list of three-letter language codes or ALL (for all languages) in order to specify the languages that should be imported from the .dat file.

As described in the previous section, we must also cater for the correct deployment of the SRF file and, if applicable, the generation of browser scripts.

Exporting and importing selected repository objects

When the process of exporting or importing the entire repository is not applicable, we can use the Siebel Tools **archive files** (`.sif`) to export and deploy selected object definitions from a source database to a target database.

The process of working with archive files has been described in the sections *Archiving object definitions* and *Importing archived object definitions* of *Chapter 2, Developer Tasks*.

In a deployment scenario, we would use the Siebel Tools archive feature to export one or more object definitions from the development database. Then we could use Siebel Tools to connect to a target database — for example, a test environment — and import the archive file's content. Scenarios like the preceding are only supported when both environments are on the same Siebel base version such as 8.1.

It must be noted here that we can also use the **Application Deployment Manager (ADM)** functionality of Siebel 8 or higher to export and deploy selected repository objects. An overview of ADM will be given later in this chapter.

Exporting and importing administrative data

Under certain circumstances, developers not only modify object definitions in the Siebel Repository but also create or modify administrative data such as List of Values or EAI Data Maps. This type of data resides outside of the repository tables and is therefore not within the scope of the tools and utilities discussed so far in this chapter.

With the ADM, introduced with Siebel Version 7.7, the Siebel application framework provides a simple and extensible technique to export and import administrative data. ADM uses basic Siebel EAI technology such as integration objects, EAI Siebel Adapter, and workflow processes. It must be noted here that, for some prominent object types, it is also possible to use native export and import features. For example, EAI Data Maps or iHelp items can be exported and imported as XML files by using the respective menu commands on the administrative views for these objects.

The following procedure uses List of Values data to describe how to export administrative data using ADM:

1. Log on to the Siebel client using an administrative user account.

2. Navigate to the **Application Deployment Manager** screen via the site map.

3. Navigate to the **Deployment Projects** view.

4. Create a new deployment project record or copy an existing project.

5. Enter the following values:

    ° Name: AHA LOV

    ° Export to File: checked

    ° Session Configurable: checked

6. In the lower list applet, create a new record with the following values:

    ° Data Type Name: LOV

    ° Deployment Method: Upsert

    ° Deployment Filter: [Value]='TODO_TYPE'

 This filter ensures that only records for the List of Values type TODO_TYPE are exported.

As an alternative to typing the filter manually, we can click the select button in the **Deployment Filter** field and pick one of the predefined queries for the data type. Because of the fact that business component field names, referenced by predefined queries, and integration object component field names, used by ADM, may differ, we may receive errors when we use the predefined query option.

7. Click the **Validate Filter** button in the lower list applet. If no message is displayed, the filter is valid. If an error message appears, correct the syntax of the deployment filter and validate again until no error is displayed.

8. Click the **Enable** button in the upper list applet. Once a deployment project is enabled, it can no longer be modified. We must copy the deployment project record to be able to modify the project.

9. Navigate to the **Deployment Sessions** view.

10. Create a new session record.

11. Select the deployment project created before from the drop-down list in the **Project Name** field.

12. Press *Ctrl+S* to save the record. This populates the lower list applet with the data objects.

13. Click the **Deploy** button in the upper list applet.

14. In the **Export** dialog box, enter the name of a folder where the export files should be written to.

15. Click the **Export** button.

16. Verify that the **Status** field changes to **Export Completed**. This indicates successful export of the data. The most likely cause for an error during export is that the target folder was not reachable.

The target folder now contains three new files. The .ini file should be removed from the folder as it exists only for logging purposes. The XML file with _des in the name is the so-called **descriptor file**,which must accompany the other XML file, the data file, when we intend to use the **Siebel Management Server** to deploy the data file as part of an ADM package.

If we only intend to import the data in the target environment via the Application Deployment Manager screen, the only file we need to keep is the **XML data file**.

The following procedure describes how a file containing administrative data can be imported in a target environment:

1. Log on to the Siebel client at the target enterprise using an administrative user account.

2. Navigate to the **Application Deployment Manager** screen, **Deployment Sessions** view.

3. Right-click in the upper list applet to open the context menu and select **Deploy from Local File**.

4. Click the **Browse** button.

5. In the **Choose File** dialog, navigate to the folder that contains the **XML data file** and select the file.

6. Click the **Open** button.

7. Click the **Import** button.

We can verify the success of the import in the following ways:

- When the **Message Broadcast bar** on the bottom of the application window is enabled, a success message will appear within the update interval time frame, which is set to two minutes by default.

- Navigate to a view that allows verification of the data import. For example, to verify a List of Values import, we can navigate to the List of Values view in the **Administration - Data** screen.

- Navigate to the **Administration - Integration** screen, **EAI Queue** view. Query for a queue using the name of the import file as part of the queue name. In the lower list applet, verify that the **Status** field for the import file has a value of **Confirmed**.

Application Deployment Manager (ADM) overview

Siebel Application Deployment Manager (ADM) can be used to migrate configuration changes from a source Siebel enterprise to one or more target Siebel enterprises.

In Siebel 8, ADM supports the following data types:

- **Administrative data**: It is created or modified by administrators using the administrative screens in the Siebel Web Client. As discussed in the previous section, we can simply export and import administrative data using the Application Deployment Manager screen or deploy administrative data using an ADM package. ADM supports the registration of new data types by developers. This requires the creation of integration objects and content objects in the Siebel Repository and is not within the scope of this book.

- **Repository data**: **Repository** objects can be exported to Siebel Tools Archive (.sif) files. When using ADM functionality embedded in Siebel Tools, a descriptor file is created along with the .sif file so that repository data can be part of an ADM package.

- Files on Siebel servers.

- Files on web servers with the **Siebel Web Server Extension** (**SWSE**) installed.

The following file types can be deployed using ADM:

- Siebel Repository File (.srf)

- Siebel Web Template (.swt)

- BI Publisher Report Templates and related files (.rtf and others)

- Cascading style sheets (.css), graphic files, and browser scripts

The deployment functionality of ADM relies upon the **Siebel Management Server** framework. The following diagram describes the Siebel Management Server framework:

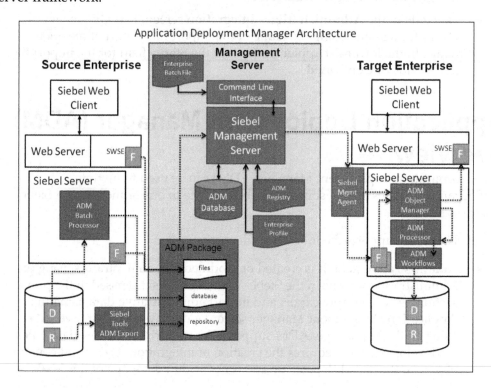

From the preceding diagram, we can learn the following:

- Configuration changes in the source enterprise can be made at the repository level, administrative data level, or to files that reside on the Siebel Server or the web server.

- An **ADM package** is a directory structure that is created using the admpkgr command line utility.

- **Repository data (R)** is exported to the package directory using **Siebel Tools**. This can be done manually or via command line scripts.

- **Administrative data (D)** such as **List of Values (LOV)** can be exported manually using the Application Deployment Manager screen or automatically using the **ADM Batch Processor** server component.

- New and modified **files (F)** must be copied to the package directory using common file copy mechanisms.

- The **Siebel Management Server** must be installed and configured to support the deployment of ADM packages to target enterprises. Java programs on the Siebel Management Server forward the package content to **Siebel Management Agents**, which serve as an entry point on each Siebel Server in the target environment.

- The **Siebel Management Agent** communicates with the **ADM Object Manager** and invokes **ADM workflow processes**, which process the incoming repository and administrative data and subsequently write it to the Siebel database.

- The **Siebel Management Agent** also forwards the files to the Siebel Server's WEBMASTER directory, which is then synchronized with the web server.

More information about the installation of the Siebel Management Server infrastructure, the configuration of ADM, and the deployment process can be found in the book *Siebel CRM 8 Installation and Management* by the same author.

Summary

The Siebel CRM framework provides various mechanisms to migrate configuration changes between environments. In this chapter we discussed the most important of these mechanisms.

The Migrate Repository procedure, supported by the Siebel Upgrade Wizard, allows the automated export and import of the entire Siebel Repository from one Siebel environment to another Siebel environment.

Deployment Projects and sessions in the Application Deployment Manager screen are a useful mechanism to quickly migrate administrative data such as List of Values from a source environment to a target environment.

If the Siebel Management Server infrastructure is installed, ADM can be used to deploy packages, which can contain repository objects, administrative data, and files.

A
Installing a Siebel CRM Self-Study Environment

If you wish to follow this book's case study examples or wish to have a safe self-study environment for Siebel CRM, you need at minimum the following Siebel software and documentation:

- Siebel Mobile Web Client
- Siebel Sample Database
- Siebel Tools
- Siebel Bookshelf

In this appendix, we will briefly outline the necessary steps to download, install, and configure Oracle Siebel CRM software.

Hardware requirements

The following minimum hardware configuration is recommended to completing the installation successfully and allow flawless operation of the self-study environment:

- 2 GB RAM
- 1.5 GHz CPU
- 10 GB free disk space for installation files and software

The **System Requirements and Supported Platforms** document, part of the Siebel CRM documentation by Oracle, provides detailed information about hardware and software requirements for each Siebel version. The document for version 8.1 can be found at http://download.oracle.com/docs/cd/E11886_01/V8/CORE/SRSP_81/booktitle.html.

It is also possible, and recommendable, to install a self-study environment on a virtual machine. Oracle's VirtualBox product is freely available as Open Source Software at http://www.virtualbox.org.

Third-party software requirements

The following third-party software should be installed as a prerequisite:

- 32-bit Microsoft Windows operating system (XP or later)
- Microsoft Internet Explorer browser (version 6 or 7)
- **Java Runtime Environment (JRE)** 1.5 or later
- Download Management Software (for example **Free Download Manager** available at http://freedownloadmanager.org)
- Archive software (for example **7-Zip** available at http://www.7-zip.org)

Downloading and extracting Siebel CRM software installers

The following is the process of downloading and extracting Siebel CRM software installers:

- Register at Oracle E-Delivery
- Understand the license agreement
- Download the installation archives
- Download Oracle Siebel Documentation
- Extract the installation archives
- Extract the Siebel installers
- Adjust browser security settings

In the following section, we will discuss these steps in detail.

Registering at Oracle E-Delivery

Oracle makes Siebel CRM software available for download on its E-Delivery website at http://edelivery.oracle.com. Before we can download software from this site, we have to register with our name, company, and e-mail address and accept the trial license terms and export restrictions outlined on the website. Oracle will send a notification e-mail after approximately one business day.

Understanding the license agreement

Oracle grants an unlimited developer license for its software. The license agreement grants "a nonexclusive, nontransferable limited license to use the programs only for the purpose of developing, testing, prototyping, and demonstrating your application, and not for any other purpose."

It is important that we read and understand the license agreement.

Downloading the installation archives

Because of the size of the .zip archives that contain the Siebel CRM installation files, it is highly recommendable to use a download management tool such as Free Download Manager.

After logging in to Oracle's E-Delivery website, we choose **Siebel CRM** in the **Select a Product Pack** drop-down list and choose **Microsoft Windows (32-bit)** in the **Platform** drop-down list. The following screenshot shows this selection:

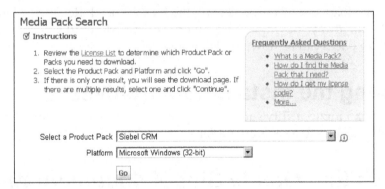

After clicking the **Go** button a list of media packs is displayed. To obtain the installers for **Siebel Industry Applications 8.1.1**, used throughout this book for the case study examples, we must click the media pack named **Siebel Business Applications (with Translations) Media Pack 8.1.1.0 Release for Microsoft Windows (32-bit)** (Part Number B52660-07).

From the resulting list, the following .zip archives must be downloaded and stored in a single folder:

- **Siebel Business Applications Version 8.1.1.0 Siebel Client (Part 1 of 2)**
  Part Number: V14869-01 Part 1 of 2 (Full size: 1.9 GB)
  This archive contains the base installer for the Siebel Mobile/Developer Web Client and some language packs (including the American English (enu) language pack).

- **Siebel Business Applications Version 8.1.1.0 Siebel Client (Part 2 of 2)**
  Part Number: V14869-01 Part 2 of 2 (Full size: 624 MB)
  This archive contains the remaining language packs for the Siebel Mobile/
  Developer Web Client.

- **Siebel Business Applications Version 8.1.1.0 Siebel Client Part 2 (Part 2 of 2)**
  Part Number: V15040-01 Part 2 of 2 (Full size: 953 MB)
  This archive contains the base installer for the Siebel Sample Database as well
  as language packs for Handheld applications and the sample database.

- **Siebel Business Applications Version 8.1.1.0 Siebel Tools**
  Part Number: V15391-01 (Full size: 1.9 GB)
  This archive contains the Siebel Tools installer.

- **Siebel Business Applications Version 8.1.1.0 ImageCreator Files**
  Part Number: V14502-01 (Full size: 213 MB)
  This archive contains the Image Creator files for all supported
  operating systems.

The ZIP Preview feature of Free Download Manager can be used to dramatically
reduce the download size by only selecting the files we need. Regarding language
packs, we should always download the **American English (enu)** language pack.
Other language packs can be downloaded as needed.

Extracting the installation archives

We should use an **unzip utility** such as 7-Zip to extract the entire content of the
downloaded .zip files to a separate folder.

Downloading Oracle Siebel documentation

The Oracle Siebel Documentation (also known as Siebel Bookshelf) can be accessed
online and downloaded in various versions from the following Oracle Technology
Network website:

```
http://www.oracle.com/technetwork/documentation/siebel-087898.html
```

To support the examples in this book, it is recommendable to download the **Siebel
Business Applications 8.1 Documentation Library**.

Extracting the Siebel installers

The **Siebel Image Creator**, extracted along with the installation archives, must be
used to create the Siebel installation images.

The following procedure describes how to create a Siebel installation image for Siebel Tools, the Siebel Mobile or Developer Web Client, and the Siebel Sample Database using the Siebel Image Creator:

Step	Description	Tasks and Example Values
1	Start the Siebel Image Creator	Double-click the `Windows_ImageCreator.exe` file.
2	The Welcome dialog is displayed	Click **Next**.
3	Display of options	Choose **Create a new image**.... Click **Next**.
4	Specify the directory to which the installer images should be copied	Example: C:\Siebel_Install_Image. Click Next.
5	Application type selection	Select "**Siebel Industry Applications**". Click Next.
6	Select operating system platform	Select **Windows**. Click **Next**.
7	Select products	Select the following: <ul><li>Siebel Tools</li><li>Siebel Web Client</li><li>Siebel Sample Database</li></ul> Click **Next**.
8	Specify languages	Select **ENU – English (American)**. Click **Next**.
9	Progress of the file extraction process is displayed	Wait for completion.
10	Success message is displayed	Click **Finish**.

As a result, the folder specified in step 4 of the previous procedure now contains several subfolders with the installers for the Siebel Mobile or Developer Web Client, Sample Database, and Siebel Tools.

Adjusting the browser security settings

In order to allow the browser to download and install the ActiveX controls for the Siebel High-Interactivity Framework, we must adjust the security settings of Microsoft Internet Explorer as follows:

1. Open **Internet Explorer**.
2. Navigate to the **Tools** menu and select **Options**.

3. In the **Options** dialog, click the **Security** tab.

4. Click the **Trusted Sites** icon.

5. Click the **Sites** button.

6. Uncheck the flag **Require server verification (https:) for all sites in this zone**.

7. In the **Add this website to the zone** field enter `http://localhost`.

8. Click the **Add** button.

9. Repeat steps 7 and 8 and create an entry for your machine's hostname.

 You can obtain the hostname of your machine by entering hostname in a command shell window.

10. Click the **Close** button.

11. Click the **Custom Level** button in the **Security Level** area.

12. From the **Reset to** drop-down list on the bottom of the dialog, select **Low**.

13. Click **Reset....**

14. Click **Yes**.

15. Click **OK**.

16. Click **Apply**.

17. Click **OK**.

Installing Siebel CRM client software

The installation process for a self-study environment is as follows:

- Install the Siebel Mobile Web Client
- Install the Siebel Sample Database
- Install Siebel Tools
- Configure Siebel Tools to connect to the sample database
- Download the Demo Users Reference

Installing the Siebel Mobile Web Client

The following procedure describes how to install the Siebel Mobile Web Client. The Windows user account used during this installation must have administrative rights:

Step	Description	Tasks and Example Values
1	Start the Oracle Universal Installer	Double-click the `oui.exe` file in the `Siebel_Web_Client/Disk1/ install` folder.
2	The Welcome dialog is displayed	Click **Next**.
3	Specify the home directory	Example: `C:\Siebel\8.1\Client_1` (default value).
		Click **Next**.
4	Prerequisite checks	The installer performs checks for prerequisite checks. Verify that all checks are passed successfully.
		Click **Next**.
5	Select Languages	Select **English**.
		Click **Next**.
6	Welcome to Siebel Business Applications Client Setup	Click **Next**.
7	Type of Client	Select "**Mobile Web Client**".
		Click **Next**.
8	Siebel Remote Server hostname	Keep the default value.
		Click **Next**.
9	Search Server Information	Keep the default values.
		Click **Next**.
10	Summary	Review the summary information.
		Click **Install**.
11	The installation progress is displayed	
12	Microsoft Internet Explorer is launched	The browser loads the predeploy.htm file in the client's bin directory to load the preconfigured ActiveX controls.
		When the page displays **The download is complete...** the browser window must be closed to continue with the installation.
13	The installation process continues	
14	Success Message	Click **Exit** and **Yes** to leave the installer.

Installing the Siebel sample database

The following procedure describes how to install the Siebel Sample Database. The installation path must be set to the folder where the Siebel Mobile Web Client has been installed previously:

Step	Description	Tasks and Example Values
1	Start the InstallShield Wizard.	Double-click the `install.exe` file in the `Siebel_Sample_Database` folder.
2	Choose Setup Language	Example: English. Click **OK**.
3	The Welcome dialog is displayed	Click **Next**.
4	Setup Type	Select **Custom**. In the **Destination Folder** section, click **Browse...** and navigate to the Siebel client installation directory. Click **Next**.
5	Select Components	Keep **Sample Files** selected. Unselect **Sample Search Index**. Click **Next**.
6	Choose Languages	Select **English (American)**. Click **Next**.
7	Select Program Folder	Keep the default. Click **Next**.
8	Installation progress is displayed	Leave the installer window open and wait for the process to finish.
9	Event Log	Summary information is displayed. Click **Next**.
10	The wizard displays successful completion	Click **Finish**.

Installing Siebel Tools

The following procedure describes how to install Siebel Tools.

Step	Description	Tasks and Example Values
1	Start the Oracle Universal Installer.	Double-click the `oui.exe` file in the `Siebel_Tools/Disk1/install` folder.
2	The Welcome dialog is displayed.	Click **Next**.
3	Select a Product to install	Select **Siebel Business Application Tools**. Click **Next**.
4	Specify the home directory	Example: `C:\Siebel\8.1\Tools_1` (default value). Click **Next**.
5	Prerequisite checks	The installer performs checks for prerequisite checks. Verify that all checks are passed successfully. Click **Next**.
6	Select Languages	Select **English**. Click **Next**.
7	Siebel Database Server	Select **Oracle Database Server**. Click Next.
8	Database Identification	Database Alias: orcl Table Owner: SIEBEL Click **Next**.
9	File System	Directory Path Example: `C:\Siebel\8.1\Client_1\SAMPLE\FILES` Click **Next**.
10	Siebel Remote Server hostname	Keep the default Click **Next**.
11	Enterprise Server Information	Gateway Name Server address: localhost. Enterprise Server: Siebel Click **Next**.
12	Summary	Review the summary information. Click **Install**.
13	The installation progress is displayed	
14	Success Message	Click **Exit** and **Yes** to leave the installer.

Configuring Siebel Tools to connect to the sample database

The following procedure must be followed to allow Siebel Tools to connect to the Siebel Sample Database:

1. Use **Windows Explorer** to navigate to the Siebel Mobile Web Client installation directory.

2. Open the uagent.cfg file in the client's BIN\ENU directory with **Notepad**.

3. Copy the value of the ConnectString parameter in the [Sample] section of the uagent.cfg file to the clipboard.

4. Navigate to the **Siebel Tools installation** directory.

5. Open the tools.cfg file in the Siebel Tools BIN\ENU directory with **Notepad**.

6. Overwrite the value of the ConnectString parameter in the [Sample] section of the tools.cfg file with the value you copied in step 3.

7. Save and close all files.

Using the Demo Users Reference

The **Demo Users Reference** document in the Siebel Bookshelf (http://download. oracle.com/docs/cd/E14004_01/books/DemoUser/DemoUserTOC.html) can be used to find demo user accounts with different roles, which may be useful during exploration of standard Siebel CRM functionality.

B Importing Code Files

This book contains case study examples that are complemented by code files. In this appendix, we will briefly discuss the techniques to import the code files. The following will be covered:

- Importing Siebel Tools archive files (SIF)
- Importing administrative data files

Importing Siebel Tools archive files (SIF)

The following procedure describes how to import a Siebel Tools archive file:

1. Log in to **Siebel Tools** if necessary.
2. In the **Tools** menu, select **Import from Archive...**
3. In the **Select Archive to Import** dialog, browse to a `.sif` file.
4. Click the **Open** button.
5. Keep the default settings for conflict resolution (merge) and click **Next**.

6. In the **Review Conflicts and Actions** page, we can optionally change the merge settings by right-clicking elements which are present in both the repository and the file. The following screenshot shows this page:

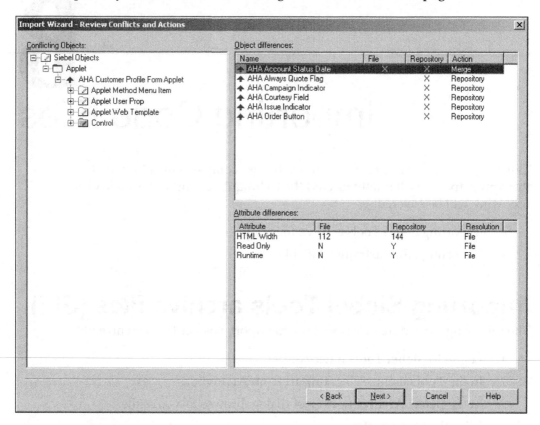

7. Click **Next**.

8. Click **Yes** to confirm the summary message.

9. Wait for the import process to finish.

10. In the **Summary** page, click **Finish** to close the Import Wizard.

By following the procedure described previously, you can import the `.sif` archives provided with the code files in order to follow the book's case study examples. Please note that the archive files may only be imported in a self-study environment and must not be applied to production environments.

Importing administrative data files

The following procedure describes how to import administrative data files:

1. Log in to the **Siebel Web Client**.

2. Navigate to the **Application Deployment Manager** screen, **Deployment Sessions** view.

3. Right-click in the upper list applet to open the context menu and select **Deploy from Local File**.

4. Click the **Browse** button.

5. In the **Choose File** dialog, navigate to the folder that contains the XML data file and select the file.

6. Click the **Open** button.

   The screenshot below shows the **Deployment Sessions** view with the **Deploy from Local File** dialog:

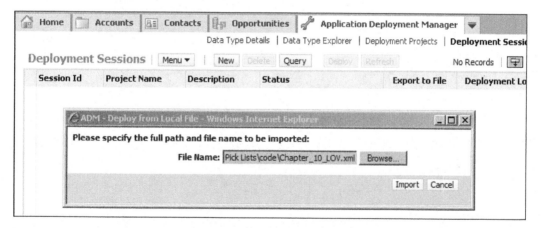

7. In the **Deploy from Local File** dialog, click the **Import** button.

8. A message broadcast will indicate the successful import. The time for the message to appear depends on the update interval of the Message Broadcast bar on the bottom of the Siebel application window and is two minutes by default.

9. In case of errors, ensure that you are using the correct version of Siebel CRM applications. All code files have been produced for Siebel Industry Applications (SIA) 8.1.1.

By following the procedure described above, you can import administrative data files into your self-study environment in order to follow this book's case study examples. Please note that the administrative data files may only be imported in self-study environments and must not be imported in productive environments.

C
More Information

You are at the end of the book. Congratulations! However, you may have just begun with a steep learning path. In order to ease the mission of finding additional information about Siebel CRM, this appendix provides the following information:

- Getting trained
- Finding information

Please note that the internet addresses in this chapter have been thoroughly revised at the time of writing this book. Given the nature of the internet, they could have changed in the meantime.

Getting trained

The success of a Siebel CRM project, or any standard software implementation project in general, is linked to the education of the professionals who undertake it. Complex systems like Siebel CRM will not reveal their intricate patterns to naive consultants (or their managers) who believe in self-study or **fast-track** trainings.

The money saved on training (or no training) will be spent equally fast on project delay. It is paramount for the Siebel professional to expose him or herself to high quality instructor-led training, which is provided for example by Oracle University and its training partners throughout the world.

The following website addresses shall serve as an entry point for your personal training plan.

- Oracle University: `http://education.oracle.com`
- Oracle Partner Network: `http://opn.oracle.com`
- Oracle Technology Network: `http://otn.oracle.com`

Finding information

Siebel CRM has been developed under the assumption that customers will employ their own technicians or hire external consultants to install, configure, and manage the software. Documenting the necessary steps to do so and also providing information about the features of Siebel CRM has evolved into what is known today as the Siebel Bookshelf.

The Siebel Bookshelf

Oracle has made the entire Siebel documentation available on its web servers. We can access the documentation library for each version from Siebel 6 and above online or download it from the following internet address: `http://www.oracle.com/technetwork/documentation/siebel-087898.html`.

Before we start downloading and installing Siebel CRM, we should ensure that we have read and digested the information given to us by the technical writers at Oracle. The following is a list of recommended Bookshelf guides for the ambitious newbie:

- Deployment Planning Guide
- Developing and Deploying Siebel Business Applications
- Fundamentals
- Going Live with Siebel Business Applications
- Installation Guide (for your operating system)
- Overview: Siebel Enterprise Application Integration
- System Administration Guide

Oracle forums

Not every trick, bug, or workaround can be found in the official Siebel documentation. While you are reading these lines, somebody encounters a problem or explores some functionality within Siebel CRM. Many Siebel professionals use the Oracle Forums to post questions and findings. Experienced consultants pick up the posts and answer them, so the community has a great place to search for information outside the official documentation.

We can access the Oracle Forums at `http://forums.oracle.com`.

My Oracle Support

Customers, partners, and employees of Oracle have access to the Oracle support system, which not only allows creation of service requests, but also searching of the knowledge base of resolved service requests, bulletins, and other documents.

My Oracle Support is a centralized portal for all Oracle products and can be accessed via the URL `http://support.oracle.com`.

The Internet community

Various channels exist to share findings and knowledge on the internet. Over the past few years, many IT professionals decided to create their own websites, weblogs, or Twitter channels to distribute information on Siebel CRM.

A good starting point for our research in this vast amount of information may be Google's blog search: `http://blogsearch.google.com`.

The author's blog on Siebel CRM and Oracle Business Intelligence can be found at `http://siebel-essentials.blogspot.com`.

Index

C

GetService("Name") 451
GetService() application method 485
GetType() method 457
GetValue() method 457

H

Help | Contents, menu item 11
hierarchical pick lists 211
hierarchical static pick lists
  exploring 213, 214
hierarchy, process properties 350
High-Interactivity (HI) 403
history toolbar 11
HTML bitmap property 302
HTML disabled bitmap property 302
HTML popup dimension property 302
Hyperlink Field property 262
Hypertext Markup Language (HTML) 273

I

icon map
  about 33, 288
  using 288, 289
if block 463, 464, 477
IfNull(expression1,expression2) function
  143
Ignore Bounded Picklist, user property 342
IIf() function 420
IIf(expression,return1,return2) function 142
importing
  administrative data files 517
  Siebel Tools archive files (SIF) 515, 516
import repository 495
indexes 156, 157
InputPS argument 457
InsertChildAt() method 457
InsertChildAt(PropertySet, index) method
  457
Insert method 330, 337
insert operation 378
installing
  Siebel CRM client software 510
  Siebel Mobile Web Client 511
  Siebel sample database 512
  Siebel tools 513
integration component (IC) 342

integration component fields (ICF) 342
integration component keys 329
  about 329
  defining 334, 336
  inbound direction 329
  outbound direction 329
integration layer, Siebel Repository
    metadata
  automation layer 29
  business services 29, 30
  commands 31
  external integration objects 29
  internal integration objects 27, 28
  tasks 31
  workflow processes 30, 31
Integration Manager (EIM) module 18
integration object, process properties 350
integration objects
  about 325-327
  advanced settings 342, 343
  component keys 329
  creating 354, 355
  external integration objects 327-329
  internal integration objects 327-329
  structure 327
  testing 336-341
integration objects (IO) 342
inter child column property 183
interface, table type 153
Internal Account Interface integration
    object 328
internal integration objects
  about 327
  creating 330-332
  unneeded integration component fields,
    deactivating 332-334
Internet Community 521
inter parent column property 183
intersection table
  creating 222, 223
inter table property 183
INVOKE 251
INVOKEALL 251
InvokeMethod("Method",Arguments) 452
InvokeMethod("Method", InputPS,
    OutputPS) 457
InvokeMethod() method 485, 486

Thank you for buying
Oracle Siebel CRM 8 Developer's Handbook

About Packt Publishing

Packt, pronounced 'packed', published its first book "Mastering phpMyAdmin for Effective MySQL Management" in April 2004 and subsequently continued to specialize in publishing highly focused books on specific technologies and solutions.

Our books and publications share the experiences of your fellow IT professionals in adapting and customizing today's systems, applications, and frameworks. Our solution based books give you the knowledge and power to customize the software and technologies you're using to get the job done. Packt books are more specific and less general than the IT books you have seen in the past. Our unique business model allows us to bring you more focused information, giving you more of what you need to know, and less of what you don't.

Packt is a modern, yet unique publishing company, which focuses on producing quality, cutting-edge books for communities of developers, administrators, and newbies alike. For more information, please visit our website: www.packtpub.com.

About Packt Enterprise

In 2010, Packt launched two new brands, Packt Enterprise and Packt Open Source, in order to continue its focus on specialization. This book is part of the Packt Enterprise brand, home to books published on enterprise software – software created by major vendors, including (but not limited to) IBM, Microsoft and Oracle, often for use in other corporations. Its titles will offer information relevant to a range of users of this software, including administrators, developers, architects, and end users.

Writing for Packt

We welcome all inquiries from people who are interested in authoring. Book proposals should be sent to author@packtpub.com. If your book idea is still at an early stage and you would like to discuss it first before writing a formal book proposal, contact us; one of our commissioning editors will get in touch with you.

We're not just looking for published authors; if you have strong technical skills but no writing experience, our experienced editors can help you develop a writing career, or simply get some additional reward for your expertise.

**Oracle GoldenGate 11g
Implementer's guide**

Design, install, and configure high-performance data replication
solutions using Oracle GoldenGate

Foreword by Dr. Volker Kuhr, Oracle Advanced Customer Support,
Team Leader for Distributed Databases

John P. Jeffries   [PACKT] enterprise 88

Oracle GoldenGate 11g
Implementer's guide

ISBN: 978-1-849682-00-8   Paperback: 280 pages

Design, install, and configure high-performance data
replication solutions using Oracle GoldenGate

1. The very first book on GoldenGate, focused on
   design and performance tuning in enterprise-
   wide environments

2. Exhaustive coverage and analysis of all aspects
   of the GoldenGate software implementation,
   including design, installation, and advanced
   configuration

3. Migrate your data replication solution from
   Oracle Streams to GoldenGate

**Web 2.0 Solutions with Oracle
WebCenter 11g**

Learn WebCenter 11g fundamentals and develop real-world
enterprise applications in an online work environment

Plinio Arbizu   with Amit Gupta   [PACKT] enterprise 88
Ashok Aggarwal   Sukanta Hazra

Web 2.0 Solutions with Oracle
WebCenter 11g

ISBN: 978-1-847195-80-7   Paperback: 276 pages

Learn WebCenter 11g fundamentals and develop
real-world enterprise applications in an online work
environment

1. Create task-oriented, rich, interactive online
   work environments with the help of this Oracle
   WebCenter training tutorial

2. Accelerate the development of Enterprise 2.0
   solutions by leveraging the Oracle tools

3. Apply the basic concepts of Enterprise 2.0 for
   your business solutions by understanding them
   completely

Please check **www.PacktPub.com** for information on our titles

The Oracle Universal Content Management Handbook

ISBN: 978-1-849680-38-7   Paperback: 356 pages

Build, administer, and manage Oracle Stellent UCM Solutions

1. Build a complete Oracle UCM system from scratch and quickly learn to configure, administer, and operate it efficiently

2. Match and exceed savings and efficiency expectations, and avoid devastating data losses with important tips and tricks

3. Migrate content like a pro—bring mountains of new content in faster than you ever dreamed possible

WS-BPEL 2.0 for SOA Composite Applications with Oracle SOA Suite 11g

ISBN: 978-1-847197-94-8   Paperback: 616 pages

Define, model, implement, and monitor real-world BPEL business processes with SOA powered BPM

1. Develop BPEL and SOA composite solutions with Oracle SOA Suite 11g

2. Efficiently automate business processes with WS-BPEL 2.0 and develop SOA composite applications

3. Get familiar with basic and advanced BPEL 2.0

Please check **www.PacktPub.com** for information on our titles

CPSIA information can be obtained
at www.ICGtesting.com
Printed in the USA
LVOW03s1810150416

483809LV00009B/223/P